Federated Learning in Finance

Federated Learning in Finance: Unlocking Privacy-Preserving and Cyber Resilience using AI is an edited volume designed to explore how Federated Intelligence can help the finance industry defend against cyber threats, detect fraud, and comply with regulations, all while keeping sensitive financial data secure and distributed.

This book provides a comprehensive roadmap for integrating federated learning (FL) and artificial intelligence (AI)-driven cyber security into financial ecosystems. Unlike conventional AI systems that require data centralization, Federated Intelligence enables financial institutions to collaborate securely, train powerful AI models, and combat cyber threats.

Swati Sah is currently serving as Professor at Sharda University, India. Prior to this, she held an academic position at Amity University, Uzbekistan. In May 2018, she was appointed as Head of the Department of Computer Science at Patan College for Professional Studies (PCPS), Nepal, an institution affiliated with the University of Bedfordshire, UK. Dr. Sah holds a Master of Computer Applications (MCA) degree from Uttar Pradesh Technical University, Lucknow, India, and an M.Sc. from Birmingham City University, United Kingdom.

Rejwan Bin Sulaiman is currently serving as Lecturer in Cyber Security at the University of Law, United Kingdom. He earned his Ph.D. in Artificial Intelligence and Cybersecurity from the University of Bedfordshire, where his doctoral research focused on federated learning-based approaches for secure and privacy-preserving financial AI systems. He has held academic positions at several institutions, including Northumbria University and Arden University.

Aditya Dayal Tyagi is currently serving as Assistant Professor at Sharda University, Greater Noida, India. With over 20 years of professional experience in academia and research, he has developed expertise in diverse domains including federated learning, deep learning, influence maximization, wireless networks, information security and sentiment analysis. His work focuses on leveraging data-driven intelligence and privacy-preserving AI to enhance cyber and information resilience, optimize decision-making, and improve the efficiency of large-scale social networks. His research extends to applying deep learning models for sentiment analysis, uncovering patterns in user-generated data to drive smarter, AI-powered insights.

Federated Learning in Finance

Unlocking Privacy-Preserving and Cyber Resilience using AI

Edited by Swati Sah, Rejwan Bin Sulaiman,
and Aditya Dayal Tyagi

CRC Press
Taylor & Francis Group
Boca Raton London New York

CRC Press is an imprint of the
Taylor & Francis Group, an **informa** business

Designed cover image: Shutterstock ID: 2505223117

First edition published 2026
by CRC Press
2385 NW Executive Center Drive, Suite 320, Boca Raton FL 33431

and by CRC Press
4 Park Square, Milton Park, Abingdon, Oxon, OX14 4RN

CRC Press is an imprint of Taylor & Francis Group, LLC

ISBN: 9781041115106 (hbk)
ISBN: 9781041115113 (pbk)
ISBN: 9781003660330 (ebk)

DOI: 10.1201/9781003660330

Typeset in Sabon
by Newgen Publishing UK

Contents

Preface

The past decade has witnessed a remarkable convergence of three powerful forces in financial services: ubiquitous data, accelerated machine-learning innovation, and an ever-expanding cyber-threat landscape. Banks, insurers, fintech start-ups, and market regulators now sit atop petabytes of sensitive information—customer transactions, credit histories, behavioral telemetry, and real-time trading feeds—while simultaneously facing stricter privacy mandates (GDPR, CCPA, India's DPDP Act), mounting geopolitical risk, and unprecedented expectations for resilient digital infrastructure.

Traditional centralized learning pipelines are ill-equipped for this moment. They demand data aggregation in a single location, creating attractive "honeypots" for adversaries, compounding compliance burdens, and amplifying the reputational cost of any breach. Federated learning (FL) offers a paradigm shift: models travel to the data rather than the reverse, clients exchange only encrypted gradients or parameters, and a privacy-preserving global model emerges from iterative, decentralized collaboration. In parallel, advances in homomorphic encryption, secure multi-party computation, and trusted execution environments are rendering once-theoretical privacy guarantees commercially viable.

Yet federated learning in finance is still in its nascency. Practitioners wrestle with uneven data distributions across institutions, domain-specific adversarial threats such as model inversion or data-poisoning attacks, and new regulatory questions around algorithmic accountability when training occurs beyond a firm's perimeter. Academic researchers call for benchmarks, threat models, and reproducible case studies that reflect the idiosyncrasies of financial time series, imbalanced fraud data, real-time payments, and quantum-era cryptographic risks. Policymakers and standards bodies seek guidance on harmonizing AI governance with Basel III, PCI-DSS, PSD2, and sector-specific cyber-resilience frameworks.

This book—*Federated Learning in Finance: Unlocking Privacy-Preserving and Cyber Resilience using AI*—was conceived to address these intersecting needs. It assembles a multi-disciplinary cohort of scholars, developers, compliance professionals, and security engineers to chart the emerging terrain where decentralized machine learning meets financial risk management. While plenty has been written on FL's mathematical foundations and on AI's transformative role in banking, few volumes treat *privacy, security, regulatory compliance, and financial utility as co-equal design objectives*. Our contributors do precisely that, offering viewpoints that move fluidly between cryptography labs, data-science pods, SOC war rooms, and board-room audit committees.

SCOPE AND STRUCTURE

The chapters are organized around four thematic pillars:

1. **Foundations and Governance**
   We open with regulatory challenges, the mechanics of FL, and a survey of standards—including Zero-Trust AI principles—that underpin secure, trustworthy deployment. Readers will gain a common vocabulary for threat modeling decentralized training pipelines, assessing privacy budgets, and mapping algorithmic lifecycles to compliance obligations.
2. **Security Threats and Defenses**
   Subsequent chapters dissect adversarial vectors unique to finance: coordinated data-poisoning campaigns against anti-money-laundering models, gradient leakage risks in credit-scoring consortiums, and man-in-the-middle compromises of aggregation servers. Countermeasures span differentially-private optimization, Byzantine-robust aggregation, blockchain-anchored audit trails, and quantum-resistant federated protocols.
3. **Applications and Case Studies**
   Practitioners from global banks, payment networks, and insurtech firms present real-world implementations—fraud-detection consortia, cross-border sanctions screening, decentralized credit risk assessment for under-banked populations, and stress-testing of digital-asset custody. Emphasis is placed on measurable ROI, model-explainability dashboards for regulators, and lessons learned from pilots that failed.
4. **Frontiers and Adoption Road-Maps**
   We close with forward-looking analyses of autonomous federated systems, adaptive learning for cyber-resilience, and quantum threats. The final roadmap chapter synthesizes technical, organizational, and policy recommendations for scaling FL from proof-of-concept to critical production workloads.

Throughout, contributors weave together *AI engineering rigor, cyber-security diligence, and domain-specific financial insight*—a triad we deem essential for responsible progress.

INTENDED AUDIENCE

- **Data scientists and ML engineers** seeking design patterns that balance model performance with strict privacy guarantees.
- **Cyber-security and risk officers** tasked with protecting distributed AI pipelines against novel attack surfaces.
- **Regulators and policy analysts** exploring governance frameworks for cross-institutional model training.
- **Academics and students** in computer science, finance, and information assurance who require a coherent reference bridging theory and practice.
- **C-suite decision-makers** evaluating investment in privacy-enhancing technologies and collaborative analytics consortia.

No single stakeholder can alone resolve the intricate trade-offs between accuracy, confidentiality, interpretability, and resilience. We hope this volume fosters the multi-party dialogue that federated learning itself exemplifies.

Acknowledgements

This endeavor would not have been possible without the dedication of our contributing authors, who navigated aggressive timelines while maintaining scholarly depth; the anonymous reviewers, whose incisive feedback sharpened each chapter; and the production team at *CRC Press, Taylor & Francis Group*, whose commitment to open, high-quality scholarship is reflected in the absence of publication charges and the book's inclusion in leading abstracting services.

We are indebted to the pioneering institutions—commercial banks, cooperative credit unions, fintech accelerators, and regulatory sandboxes—that granted permission to share implementation details, sometimes redacted but always instructive. Finally, we thank our research groups and students at Sharda University and the Northumbria University, London, whose curiosity continually pushes the frontier of federated, secure, and ethical AI.

As global finance digitizes at unprecedented pace, *privacy-preserving collaborative intelligence* will become not a niche experiment but a strategic necessity. We invite readers to engage critically with the ideas herein, adapt them to their own contexts, and contribute to a future in which innovation and stewardship co-exist—where the power of machine learning serves not only profits, but also the collective trust on which every financial system depends.

Swati Sah, Rejwan Bin Sulaiman, and Aditya Dayal Tyagi
Editors

Editor Biography

Swati Sah is currently serving as a professor at Sharda University, India. Prior to this, she held an academic position at Amity University, Uzbekistan. In May 2018, she was appointed as Head of the Department of Computer Science at Patan College for Professional Studies (PCPS), Nepal, an institution affiliated with the University of Bedfordshire, UK. Dr. Sah holds a Master of Computer Applications (MCA) degree from Uttar Pradesh Technical University, Lucknow, India, and an MSc from Birmingham City University, United Kingdom.

With over 12 years of experience in teaching and research, she has been actively engaged with various professional associations and academic bodies. Her research interests lie in the areas of cyber security, artificial intelligence (AI), and machine learning (ML). She has contributed to several scholarly publications and has presented her work at international conferences. Her current work focuses on leveraging AI and ML techniques to enhance cyber threat detection and prevention frameworks. She is also passionate about interdisciplinary applications of emerging technologies and continues to explore innovative solutions addressing real-world challenges in digital security and intelligent systems.

Rejwan Bin Sulaiman is currently serving as Lecturer in Cyber Security at the University of Law, United Kingdom. He earned his PhD in Artificial Intelligence and Cybersecurity from the University of Bedfordshire, where his doctoral research focused on federated learning-based approaches for secure and privacy-preserving financial AI systems. He has held academic positions at several institutions, including Northumbria University and Arden University.

Dr. Sulaiman's research spans cybersecurity, AI, computer vision, and ML, with particular interest in developing decentralized AI models that enhance data security and user privacy. His work has been published in leading venues such as IEEE, Springer, and CRC Press, contributing to the advancement of secure machine learning frameworks in distributed environments.

He is a certified ethical hacker (CEH) and the founder of STEMResearch.Ai, an initiative that supports and mentors early-career researchers in STEM fields. He is also a fellow of the Higher Education Academy (FHEA) and has received multiple awards recognizing his innovative teaching practices and dedication to academic excellence

Aditya Dayal Tyagi is currently serving as Assistant Professor at Sharda University, Greater Noida, India. With over 20 years of professional experience in academia and research, he has developed expertise in diverse domains including federated learning, deep learning, influence maximization, wireless networks, information security, and sentiment analysis. His work focuses on leveraging data-driven intelligence and privacy-preserving AI to enhance cyber and information resilience, optimize decision-making, and improve the efficiency of large-scale social networks. His research extends to applying deep learning models for sentiment analysis, uncovering patterns in user-generated data to drive smarter, AI-powered insights.

He is the author of a book titled *AI-Powered Pricing: Transforming Business with Intelligent Pricing Models*. His one patent is published and many are under processing. He has actively published in reputed international journals and conferences, showcasing his commitment to advancing the frontiers of federated learning and decentralized AI models. His work aims to bridge the gap between cutting-edge AI research and real-world applications, particularly in secure and scalable machine learning for the finance industry and sustainable decision-making. Beyond research, he engages in academic collaborations, workshops, and professional forums, contributing to innovation and translational research. His dedication to interdisciplinary innovation continues to shape emerging trends in intelligent systems and federated learning.

Contributors

Sangeeta Arora
Department of Computer Science, Noida Institute of Engineering and Technology, Greater Noida, India

Ayasha
Christ College of Science and Management, Bengaluru, India

Ravi Prakash Chaturvedi
Sharda School of Computing Science and Engineering, Greater Noida, India

Poornima D.
St. Claret College Autonomous Bengaluru, India

Sonjoy Ranjon Das
Global Banking School, Leeds, UK

Jagjit Singh Dhatterwal
SR University, Warangal, Telangana, India

Bijesh Dhyani
Graphic Era Deemed To Be University, Dehradun, India

Shaik Valli Haseena
Presidency College, Bengaluru, India

Himanshu
Dronacharya Group of Institutions, Greater Noida, India

Md Aminul Islam
University of Oxford, Oxford, UK

A. S. Jayasurya
Department of Electrical and electronics, University Teknoloi Petronas, Petronas, Malaysia

Jesupriya J.
Presidency College, Bangalore, India

Peer Mohammed Jeelan
Presidency College, Bangalore, India

Soumya K.
Department of CS and IT, Jain Deemed To Be University, Kerala, India

Kuldeep Singh Kaswan
Galgotia University, Greater Noida, India

Divya K. S.
Department of CS, Kristu Jayanti Deemed To Be University, Bangalore, India

Nasrulla Khan K
Presidency College, Bangalore, India

Harish Kumar
Presidency University, Bengaluru, India

Mohit Kumar
Sharda University, Greater Noida, India

K. R. Prasanna Kumar
Department of Computer Science and Design, Kongu Engineering College, Tamil Nadu, India

A. P. Ponselva Kumar
Department of Information Technology, Kongu Engineering College, Tamil Nadu, India

K. Logeswaran
Department of AI and Data Science Engineering, School of Engineering and Technology, CHRIST University, Bangalore, India

Yashasvi Makin
Meta Platforms, Inc., USA

Sunil Kumar Makkar
Galgotia University, Greater Noida, India

Kiran Malik
GL Bajaj Institute of Technology and Management, Greater Noida, India

Kavita Mathad
Indira University, Pune, India

Aimee E. Mirto
Regent College London, London, UK

Annu Mishra
Sharda School of Computing Science and Engineering, Greater Noida, India

Mahi Monjina
RNB Lab, London, UK

Brundha N.
M S Ramaiah College of Arts Science and Commerce, Bangalore, India

Sushil Kumar Narang
Chitkara University Institute of Engineering and Technology, Chitkara University, Punjab, India

Amitava Pal
ICFAI University, Jharkhand and International Institute of Sports and Management, Mumbai, India

Chandra Prakash
Amity School of Engineering and Technology, Amity University, Punjab, India

Shyam R.
Presidency College, Bangalore, India

Md Mizanur Rahman
Regent College, London, UK

Deepa S.
Department of Computer Science, Christ University, Bangalore, India

Neetha S. S.
Department of Computer Science, Christ University, Bangalore, India

Muhammad Fahad Saleem
Arden University, Manchester, UK

Divya Saleela
University of Southampton, Southampton, UK

S. Savitha
Department of Computer Science and Engineering, K.S.R. College of Engineering, Tamil Nadu, India

Shashank Semwal
Graphic Era Deemed To Be University, Dehradun, India

Simna Shanavas
Presidency College, Bengaluru, India

Swati Sharma
Department of Computer Science and Engineering, KIET group of Institutions, Delhi NCR, India

Rajneesh Kumar Singh
Sharda School of Computing Science and Engineering, Greater Noida, India

Shivangi Singh
Department of Computer Science, Christ University, Bangalore, India

Vikram Singh
TCS, North America, Pennsylvania, USA

P. Suresh
Department of Database System, School of CSE, Vellore Institute of Technology, Vellore, India

Vivek Tomar
Graphic Era Deemed To Be University, Dehradun, India

Himani Tyagi
Sharda University, Greater Noida, India

Swetha C. V.
Presidency College, Bangalore, India

Dhanashri Vaishali
Bangalore University, Bangalore, India

Srikanth Yerra
Campbellsville University, Tennessee, USA

Chapter 1

Regulatory challenges and compliance in federated learning (FL) for financial applications

K. Logeswaran, S. Savitha, P. Suresh, K. R. Prasanna Kumar, A. P. Ponselva Kumar, and A. S. Jayasurya

1.1 INTRODUCTION

1.1.1 The data-driven dilemma in modern finance

Data is now a big term in modern-day finance. From here, it becomes this new oil that stimulates innovation, personalization, and competitive advantage in an industry where even the slight disruption makes the profits thin. It aids in the day-to-day operations of finance, ranging from the subtle coordination of high-frequency trading algorithms to risk assessments for loans at a global scale. Data exists to enable institutions to develop a thorough understanding of their customers and predict market changes accurately so that they can deliver offerings that find easy acceptance into the lives of their customers. This promises immense possibilities: envision the future alive with effortless financial transactions, equal opportunity for capital access, and financial advice tailored snugly to the needs of the customer [1]. Today, for any organization, collecting, processing, and analyzing large datasets is no longer a strategic advantage but an absolute necessity to progress in this industry.

As beneficial is the information-rich environment, its growth presents a serious, and ever-growing challenge. The very commodity that provides enormous opportunity also presents the industry's greatest risk. Every data point collected, every transaction recorded, every credit check reported, every personal data collected has the propensity to threaten. Enter the data-driven dilemma: a double-edged sword in which one side offers remarkable innovation and the other brings serious risk. Those centralized, "data lakes" that are useful for machine learning (ML) modelers have become prime targets for criminals. A single breach can cause considerable financial destruction and can tarnish decades of goodwill and reputation with a customer-base, which is more valuable than any dataset. The effect of a significant data breach can cripple an organization, cause headlines to persist well into the future and can elicit regulatory scrutiny that is equally devastating [2]. This dynamic continues to put burdens on financial firms to pursue data-driven value, while also protecting (nurturing) their digital asset. This is not only a theoretical challenge; it's a real challenge that every Chief Information Officer and Chief Risk Officer faces.

1.1.2 The rise of artificial intelligence (AI)/ML and the regulatory imperative

This strain has increased considerably with the advent of AI and ML. The true strength of financial information comes out when sophisticated algorithms work on it. Such algorithms can detect patterns that may be invisible to us. These technologies have come to play a

DOI: 10.1201/9781003660330-1

crucial role in a lot of aspects. AI systems spearhead the battle against money laundering (AML) by thoroughly analyzing millions of transactions to look for suspicious behavior. They also assist in the determination of creditworthiness by developing models that estimate risk more comprehensively than older scorecards [3]. They also power the algorithmic trading platforms that process most trades on worldwide markets. The concept is straightforward: greater amounts of data result in improved, more accurate models. This constant demand for data has prompted a centralized system, whereby the concept is to bring all data from across an entire global organization into a single accessible hub for training.

As AI became more data-driven, an equally important reaction emerged based on societal values and law [4]. There is now a worldwide consensus that personal data is not merely a property of the company, but is a human right: a protest movement has turned into important regulations. The European Union (EU)'s Global Data Protection Regulation (GDPR) represented a seminal moment, creating a globally influential statute that set strict rules based on data minimization, purpose limitation, and—of great importance—recognition of the right to data sovereignty. It made clear that individuals own their data and imposed strict limits on a company's ability to transfer employees' or consumers' data to other nations. In the knowledge of GDPR, governments around the world have detailed regulations in place to add further protection. The California Consumer Privacy Act (CCPA) in the United States and, more significantly, the Digital Personal Data Protection Act (DPDPA) of India have further enhanced this new marketplace. These protections are not mere guidance; they have created laws that are subject to mandatory compliances that have enormous financial consequences, which are often based on a percentage of global revenues [5].

1.1.3 Thesis: The inevitable shift toward privacy-preserving AI

This chapter argues that the clash between traditional AI architectures and the modern regulatory landscape is not a temporary hurdle to be overcome with clever legal workarounds or incremental policy adjustments. It represents a fundamental, architectural incompatibility that renders the centralized model of AI development obsolete from a compliance perspective. The prevailing paradigm, which assumes that data must travel to the algorithm, is broken. Continuing to pursue this path is not just a technical challenge; it is an untenable business risk, exposing financial institutions to severe legal, financial, and reputational damage [6]. The industry is at a crossroads, and the path forward does not involve finding ways around the wall of regulation, but rather adopting a new architecture that is inherently designed to respect it.

It's clear that making a strategic and technological shift toward Privacy-Preserving AI (PPAI) isn't just a theoretical idea anymore; it's become an urgent necessity. In this chapter, we argue that Federated Learning (FL) is leading the way in this transformation, providing a "compliance-by-design" framework that tackles the fundamental issues head-on [7]. By flipping the traditional model on its head, FL allows the algorithm to come to the data instead of transporting large, sensitive datasets across borders. This means AI models can be trained locally, safely within the digital boundaries of an organization or a country. Only the aggregated, anonymized insights—the lessons learned by the model, rather than the raw data—are shared and combined to create a stronger, collective intelligence. This isn't just a temporary fix for a flawed system; it's a fresh blueprint for AI development that naturally aligns with the principles of data sovereignty, minimization, and purpose limitation. Throughout this chapter, we'll show that adopting FL isn't just about reducing risk; it's about paving the way for powerful and legal collaborative AI innovation across borders.

1.1.4 Chapter roadmap

To build this argument, we'll take a closer look at several key areas. We will begin by venturing into the intricate realm of worldwide regulations. We will go beyond headlines to dissect the key concepts underlying significant legislations such as GDPR and DPDPA and how they affect financial information [8]. To make these conceptual legal notions more tangible, we will utilize visual aids, such as a regulation timeline and a map of banned data transfers.

Then we'll proceed to discuss the shortcomings of the conventional centralized AI design. We'll illustrate with a neat diagram of this non-compliant system. We will supplement it with an artificially induced compliance violation simulation to demonstrate how and why this method falls short in practice.

After we've identified the problem, we'll shift to discussing the solution. We'll introduce the compliant architecture of FL, visually contrasting it with the centralized model. To strengthen this comparison, we'll provide a "Compliance Scorecard" that evaluates both models against key regulatory principles.

Finally, to ensure a well-rounded perspective, we'll address ongoing questions and future challenges surrounding FL. These challenges range from legal liability issues to the need for industry-wide technical standards [9]. Through this structured exploration, the chapter aims to give a clear understanding of why FL is an important step for any financial institution looking to innovate responsibly in the AI era.

1.2 THE GLOBAL REGULATORY GAUNTLET FOR FINANCIAL DATA

1.2.1 The accelerating trend of data sovereignty

For many years, the central concept of the digital era was that information could circulate freely and effortlessly across borders. The internet was viewed as a communal area where information could flow as freely as concepts, without the restrictions imposed by nations. This concept was vital for multinational firms, particularly in the finance sector. It enabled a New York-based bank to execute transactions in London, perform analytics in Bangalore, and keep backups in Singapore. Everything was a component of a seamless and effective worldwide system. The data's location pertained solely to operational logistics and expenses. Nonetheless, that period has evidently come to a close. We have entered a new era centered on data sovereignty, indicating that data must adhere to the laws and regulations of the nation where it is gathered.

This shift represents more than just a new layer of regulation; it is a fundamental reassertion of the nation-state in the digital realm. Governments worldwide now view the vast repositories of their citizens' data not as abstract bits and bytes, but as strategic national assets, critical to both economic competitiveness and national security. The logic is clear: a nation that does not control its data cannot fully protect its citizens, its economy, or its critical infrastructure. This has triggered a global domino effect, leading to the construction of what can only be described as digital ramparts around national borders [8]. As illustrated in Figure 1.1, timeline of key regulations is not an isolated or passing trend. What began with pioneering legislation has become a global standard, with dozens of countries implementing laws that dictate where data can be stored, how it can be processed, and under what strict conditions, if any, it can leave. For the financial sector, which operates on a global scale by definition, this accelerating trend has turned the once-flat digital world into a complex and treacherous landscape of overlapping legal jurisdictions. The simple act of moving a

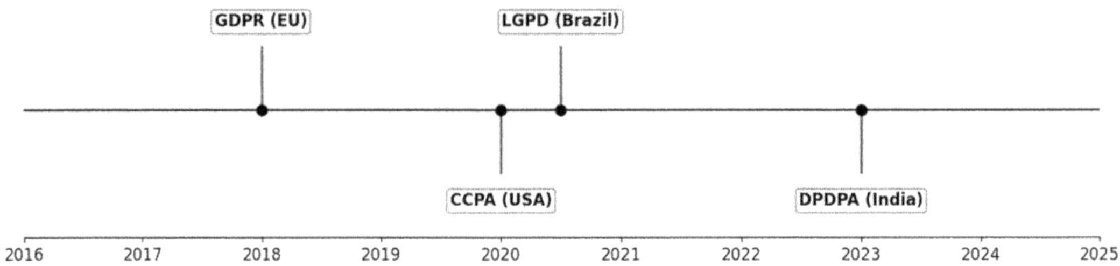

Figure 1.1 Timeline of major Global Data Protection Regulations.

customer's file from one server to another across a border is no longer a technical operation but a significant legal event, fraught with compliance risk [9].

1.2.2 Foundational principles of data protection

To navigate this new landscape, one must understand the philosophical bedrock upon which these regulations are built. While the specific articles and clauses may differ from one country to another, a set of core, foundational principles is shared among nearly all modern data protection frameworks. These principles represent a global consensus on what constitutes the responsible and ethical handling of personal information, and they stand in direct opposition to the "collect everything" ethos that has often characterized the development of data-intensive AI systems.

First and foremost is the principle of data minimization. This tenet dictates that an organization should only collect and process the data that is absolutely necessary to fulfill a specific, declared purpose [10]. It is a direct challenge to the concept of the sprawling "data lake," where vast quantities of raw data are amassed on the speculative premise that they might one day be useful for training a future algorithm. For an AI model developer, this raises difficult questions: is every data field in a customer's profile truly necessary to assess their credit risk, or are some merely correlational conveniences? The burden of proof has shifted; organizations must now justify every piece of data they hold, rather than collecting it by default.

Closely related is the principle of purpose limitation. This principle asserts that data collected for one explicit purpose cannot be repurposed for another without a separate, legitimate basis, which often means securing fresh consent. A customer may provide their transaction history to a bank for the purpose of account management, but does that consent extend to using that same history to train a new, experimental marketing AI? Most modern laws would argue it does not. This creates significant friction for the iterative nature of AI development, where new use cases for existing datasets are constantly being discovered [11].

The most operationally disruptive principle, however, is that of Data Residency and Sovereignty. As discussed, data residency mandates that certain types of data, particularly sensitive personal and financial information, must be stored on servers physically located within the country's borders. Data sovereignty takes this a step further, asserting full legal authority over that data regardless of where it is processed. This principle is the primary driver behind the fragmentation of the global digital space [12]. It effectively shatters the model of a single, centralized data warehouse for a global enterprise, forcing a move toward a federated, geographically distributed data architecture. For financial institutions, this means that the data of their German customers must stay in Germany, their Indian customers' data in India, and their Brazilian customers' data in Brazil, fundamentally breaking the cross-border data flows required to train a single, unified AI model.

1.2.3 Visualizing a breach of data residency

These principles can seem abstract, so let us consider a concrete, realistic scenario. Imagine a large, multinational bank with significant operations in both the European Union and India. The bank's data science team is tasked with building a next-generation fraud detection model. Their current models, trained on data from single regions, are effective but limited; they struggle to identify novel, cross-border fraud patterns. The team hypothesizes, correctly, that a model trained on a combined, global dataset incorporating the diverse transaction behaviors of both European and Indian customers would be far more powerful and accurate [13].

From a purely technical standpoint, the solution is straightforward: extract the relevant customer transaction data from the German and Indian data centers and transfer it to a central, high-performance computing cluster, perhaps located in the United States, for model training. This is the traditional, and until recently, standard approach. However, in the current regulatory environment, this logical action constitutes a clear and direct compliance violation.

As Figure 1.2 visually demonstrates, the moment the bank initiates this transfer, it triggers a regulatory tripwire. The red line connecting Germany and India on the map represents

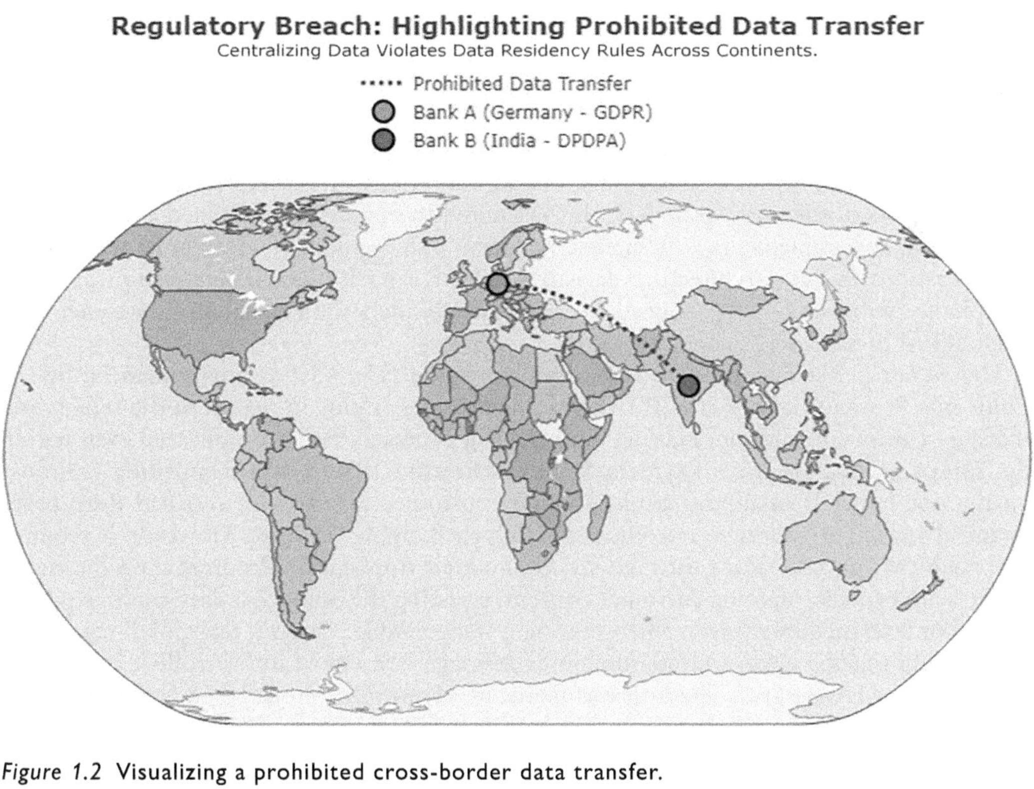

Figure 1.2 Visualizing a prohibited cross-border data transfer.

not a flow of data, but a prohibited act. By moving the data of its German customers out of the EU, the bank violates the stringent cross-border transfer restrictions of GDPR. Simultaneously, by moving the data of its Indian customers, it runs afoul of the data localization and transfer rules stipulated by the DPDPA. The bank is caught in a compliance trap: the very action required to improve its security model is forbidden by the laws designed to protect its customers. This is not a niche edge case; it is the central, defining challenge for any global financial institution seeking to leverage AI. The map does not just show geography; it illustrates the new, invisible legal borders that have been drawn across the digital world, making the old ways of working impossible.

1.2.4 Analysis of landmark regulations

The challenge visualized above is not born from a single law but from a tapestry of interconnected global regulations. While a comprehensive legal survey is beyond the scope of this chapter, an analysis of a few landmark acts reveals the depth and uniformity of the compliance challenge.

The EU's General Data Protection Regulation (GDPR) is the unambiguous push factor in this global wave. Its effectiveness comes from two features. Its wide extraterritorial application is the first factor; the GDPR protects the data of EU citizens regardless of where the company processing it is based. An American bank in New York serving a customer in Paris is fully under the jurisdiction of GDPR rules. Second, it carries a strict requirement for consent and a rigorous enforcement regime, with up to 4% of a company's global annual turnover at stake as a penalty [14]. Article 22 is particularly significant for AI usage because it grants individuals the right to opt out of decisions based on autonomous processing, such as profiling, which has significant legal ramifications for AI-driven credit scoring and lending.

In accordance with this trend, India's DPDPA of 2023 codified these principles in one of the world's fastest-growing and largest digital economies. The DPDPA set the concept of a "Data Fiduciary"—the entity that determines the purpose and manner of data processing, placing significant responsibility and accountability on businesses. Even as it allows for some cross-border data transfers, this is limited to countries sanctioned by the central government and implements a "whitelist" solution that includes an element of geopolitical considerations in data architecture decisions [15]. For each financial institution in India, compliance with the DPDPA is needed and greatly hinders the inclusion of customer data in global AI processes.

This is not just a European or Indian phenomenon. The CCPA, now enhanced by the California Privacy Rights Act (CPRA), grants customers rights in regard to the selling and sharing of their information, making data-sharing contracts more complicated even within the United States. The EU's Payment Services Directive (PSD2) is a compelling paradox, on the one hand. It mandates banks to share customer details with certified third-party financial service providers to encourage an "Open Banking" culture. However, it requires that such sharing take place through secure, audited Application Programming Interfaces (APIs) with explicit, ongoing customer consent, stressing the point that data can't be passed around or leveraged freely even when sharing is unavoidable. Overall, this global regulatory architecture sends a clear and unambiguous message: the era of uncontrolled, centralized data gathering is over [16]. The future of financial AI must be founded on a new foundation that respects the digital borders of the modern world.

1.3 THE COLLISION COURSE: TRADITIONAL AI VS. REGULATORY COMPLIANCE

1.3.1 The flawed architecture of centralized data pooling

For the better part of two decades, the blueprint for enterprise-level data science has been guided by a simple, powerful idea: centralization. The prevailing wisdom, born from the technical demands of ML, was that algorithms perform best when they have access to the largest, most diverse dataset possible. This logic gave rise to the era of the "data lake" or the central "data warehouse": a massive, unified repository where data from every corner of a global organization could be aggregated, cleaned, and made available for analysis. From a purely computational standpoint, the architecture is elegant and efficient. It provides a single source of truth, simplifies data access for analytics teams, and allows for the efficient allocation of high-performance computing resources [17]. For a data scientist, this centralized model is the ideal workshop, a place where all the necessary raw materials are neatly organized and readily available for building and testing sophisticated models.

This architectural paradigm, however, was conceived in a world where the legal landscape was vastly different. It was designed to solve a technical problem on how to train the best possible model without consideration for the legal and ethical complexities that have since come to define the digital age. As a result, the very design that is so technically optimal is, from a regulatory perspective, fundamentally and irrevocably flawed. Figure 1.3 provides a stark, schematic representation of this problem. It illustrates a flow that was once considered best practice: data from disparate, geographically isolated silos of a bank in the EU, another in India being extracted from its local context and funneled into a single, central server [18]. The arrows in this diagram represent the act of data transfer, the lifeblood of the centralized model. But in the context of modern regulation, these arrows now represent lines of transgression, each one crossing a legal and jurisdictional boundary that cannot be ignored.

The core of the issue is that this architecture directly contradicts the foundational principles of data protection we have discussed. It is the physical embodiment of a model that violates data residency by design, as it requires moving data out of its country of origin. It inherently clashes with the principle of data minimization, as the default approach is to pool entire raw datasets rather than just the necessary information. Furthermore, this centralization creates a single point of failure that is as much a security risk as it is a compliance one [19]. By concentrating the most sensitive customer data from across the globe into one

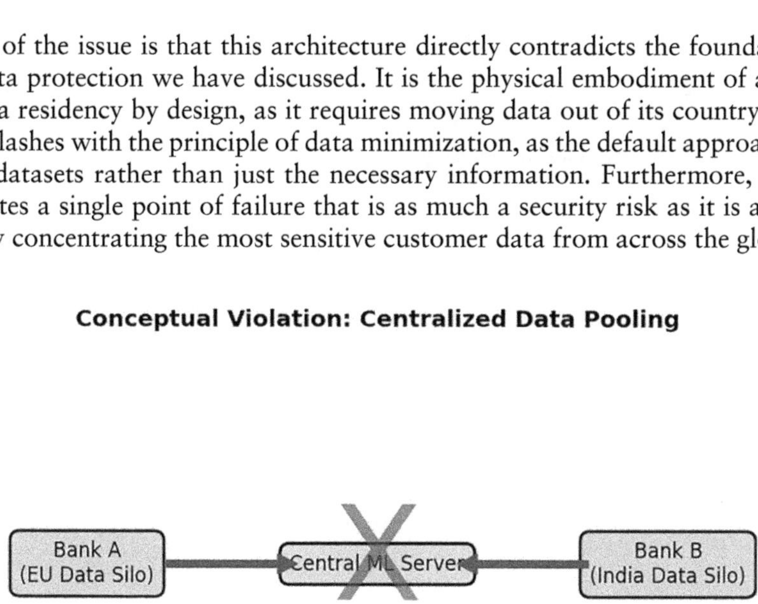

Figure 1.3 Schematic of a non-compliant centralised ML architecture.

location, an organization creates an irresistible "honeypot" for malicious actors. A successful cyberattack on such a server is no longer a localized incident; it is a global catastrophe, a breach that instantly triggers reporting obligations and legal liabilities in dozens of jurisdictions simultaneously. The architecture that was built for technical efficiency has, in the new regulatory climate, become a blueprint for disaster.

1.3.2 A practical demonstration of a compliance breach

To move from the architectural diagram to a tangible, operational reality, let us consider the first step a data science team would take to implement the centralized model. After identifying the necessary datasets in the German and Indian data centers, a data engineer would be tasked with writing a script to consolidate them. The goal is simple: merge the two datasets into a single, unified table that can be fed into an ML training pipeline. In a programming language like Python, using the popular pandas library, this operation can be accomplished with a single line of codea command to concatenate the two data frames. It is a routine, almost trivial, technical task [20].

Yet, it is in the execution of this simple command that the entire system breaks down, not due to a technical bug, but due to a fundamental legal prohibition. Figure 1.4 illustrates what this failure looks like in practice. It is not a cryptic programming error but a clear, unambiguous "FATAL ERROR: COMPLIANCE BREACH" message. This output serves as a powerful, practical demonstration of the collision course. The simulated terminal window

```
--- Data Silos ---
🏦 Bank A (EU) Data:
  customer_id  transaction_value  country  is_fraud
0      EU_001               1200  Germany         0
1      EU_002                340  Germany         0
2      EU_003               5000  Germany         1
3      EU_004                150  Germany         0
🏦 Bank B (India) Data:
  customer_id  transaction_value country  is_fraud
0      IN_001              95000   India         0
1      IN_002              12000   India         0
2      IN_003              75000   India         0
3      IN_004             250000   India         1
--- Centralized ML Approach (Attempting to Pool Data) ---
✅ Data successfully pooled into a central server.
  customer_id  transaction_value  country  is_fraud
0      EU_001               1200  Germany         0
1      EU_002                340  Germany         0
2      EU_003               5000  Germany         1
3      EU_004                150  Germany         0
4      IN_001              95000    India         0
5      IN_002              12000    India         0
6      IN_003              75000    India         0
7      IN_004             250000    India         1
┌──────────────────── 🚨 FATAL ERROR: COMPLIANCE BREACH 🚨 ────────────────────┐
│                                                                              │
│ ACTION: Pooling data from 'Germany' and 'India'.                             │
│                                                                              │
│ VIOLATIONS DETECTED:                                                         │
│   -> GDPR (EU): Transferring personal data outside the EU without a          │
│      valid adequacy decision or appropriate safeguards.                      │
│   -> DPDPA (India): Processing personal data outside India may violate       │
│      data localization and cross-border transfer rules.                      │
│                                                                              │
│ CONCLUSION: This centralized approach is NOT COMPLIANT.                      │
│ A different paradigm like Federated Learning is required.                    │
│                                                                              │
└──────────────────────────────────────────────────────────────────────────────┘
```

Figure 1.4 Simulated regulatory breach in code.

shows the action being attempted "Pooling data from 'Germany' and 'India'" and immediately flags the resulting violations. It explicitly names the regulations being broken, citing GDPR for the illegal cross-border transfer of EU data and DPDPA for the violation of India's data localization rules [21].

This simulated breach is the crucial link between legal theory and operational practice. It shows that the regulatory constraints are not abstract legal concepts that can be navigated by policy teams alone; they are hard stops that physically prevent the execution of the traditional AI development workflow. The error message is, in effect, the system's way of enforcing the law

At a technical level, it makes it clear that the problem is not with the code itself, but with the underlying assumption that the code is legally permitted to run. For any financial institution, the implication is profound. The established, time-tested methods for building powerful, global AI models are no longer viable. The old blueprint is obsolete. Attempting to build the future of financial AI on this flawed foundation is not just a risky strategy; as the terminal window shows, it is a guaranteed failure. A new approach is not just desirable, it is the only way forward [22].

1.4 FL AS A COMPLIANCE-BY-DESIGN FRAMEWORK

1.4.1 Introducing the FL paradigm

The preceding sections have established a clear and seemingly intractable deadlock. On one hand, the technological imperative of AI demands access to vast, diverse datasets to achieve optimal performance. On the other, a formidable legal framework, built on principles of data sovereignty and privacy, expressly forbids the very data aggregation that these systems require. The centralized model, for all its computational elegance, has led us to a compliance dead end. To break this impasse, a simple evolution is insufficient; what is required is a revolution in architectural thinking [23]. This is the role of FL, a paradigm that offers not a workaround for existing regulations, but a fundamental redesign of the ML process that aligns with them by its very nature.

At its core, FL is a simple but profound inversion of the traditional data flow. For decades, the unquestioned assumption has been that to learn from data, the data must travel to a central algorithm. FL challenges and reverses this premise. The new paradigm is this: the algorithm travels to the data. Instead of forcing countless patients from different countries to travel to a single, central hospital, the FL model is akin to a team of specialist doctors traveling to visit each patient in their local clinic, learning from them in their own environment, and then collaborating to synthesize their findings into a more advanced medical understanding. The patients or the raw data never have to leave the safety and security of their local, regulated environment.

Figure 1.5 provides a clear architectural schematic of this compliant new model. In stark contrast to the flawed diagram of centralization, there are no arrows indicating the movement of raw data from the silos. The local data of Bank A in the EU and Bank B in India remains securely within its respective jurisdictional perimeter [24]. The only information that travels is the intelligence itself. The process is cyclical: first, the central server dispatches a copy of the base AI model (the "traveling doctor") to each local institution. The model then trains exclusively on the local data, learning the unique patterns contained within it. Crucially, in the second phase, it is not the data that is sent back to the central server, but only a set of anonymized, mathematical "model updates" or "gradients": a compact,

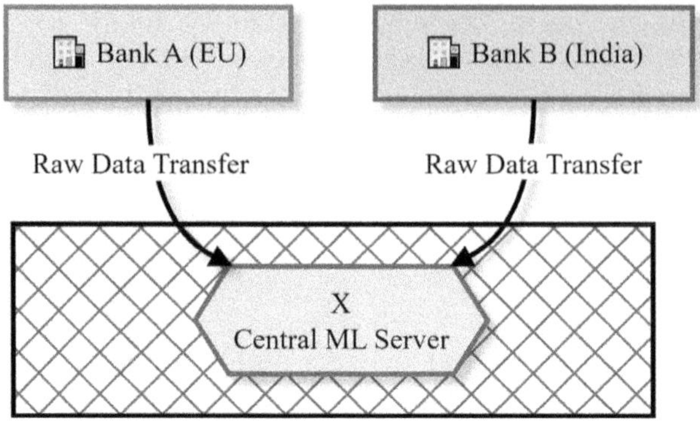

Figure 1.5 Compliant architecture of a federated learning system.

abstract summary of what the model has learned. The central server then performs a process of secure aggregation, averaging these updates to create an improved, more intelligent "global model," which can then be sent back to the local institutions for the next round of training. This cyclical, decentralized process allows for collaborative learning without collaborative data exposure [25].

1.4.2 Mapping FL mechanisms to regulatory requirements

The true elegance of the FL paradigm lies not just in its technical ingenuity, but in how seamlessly its core mechanisms map onto the foundational principles of modern data protection law. It is not a system that has been retrofitted for compliance; it is a system that achieves compliance by its intrinsic design.

The most immediate and obvious alignment is with the principles of Data Residency and Cross-Border Transfers. As established, this is the primary hurdle for centralized AI. FL resolves this issue completely and elegantly. Because the raw financial data never leaves the local server within its country of origin, the principle of data residency is never violated. The German bank's data stays in Germany; the Indian bank's data stays in India. The information that crosses borders—the model updates—is not considered raw personal data under most legal interpretations [26]. It is an abstract mathematical representation, not a customer's transaction history. This single feature dismantles the primary roadblock that has stalled global AI collaboration in finance.

Next, consider the principle of data minimization. Centralized systems operate on a principle of data maximization, demanding access to entire raw datasets. FL, by contrast, is the ultimate expression of data minimization from the perspective of the central server. The central aggregator never sees, accesses, or processes any individual customer data. Its view is restricted entirely to the aggregated parameter updates provided by the participating nodes. This dramatically reduces the data exposure and attack surface, as the most sensitive information is never concentrated in one place. The system is designed to function with the minimum possible information exchange required to improve the model's performance, a direct reflection of the spirit and letter of the law.

This inherent minimization also reinforces the principle of purpose limitation. The model updates sent from a local node are highly specific to the task for which the model was trained. The mathematical gradients generated for a fraud detection model are a function of

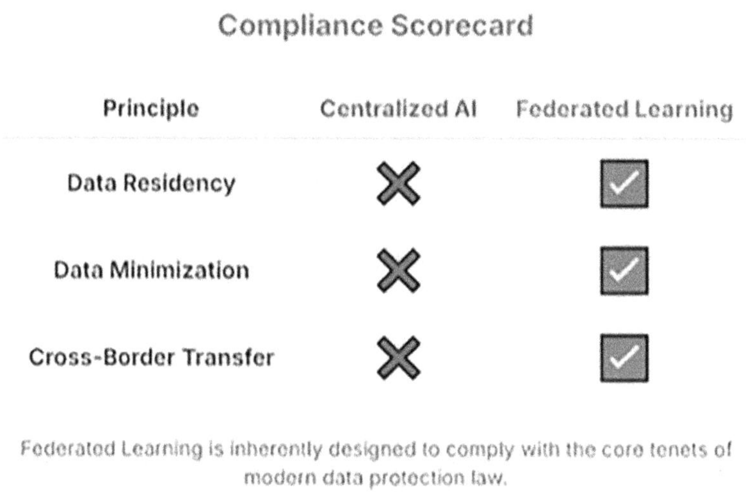

Figure 1.6 Compliance Scorecard: Centralized AI vs. federated learning.

that specific objective. They are not a general-purpose dataset that can be easily re-analyzed or repurposed to, for instance, create a new marketing campaign or assess credit risk for a different product. While not an absolute guarantee against misuse, it creates a strong technical barrier that aligns with the legal requirement that data be used only for the explicit purpose for which it was collected.

To summarize this direct comparison, Figure 1.6 presents a clear Compliance Scorecard. The table provides an at-a-glance validation of these points, evaluating the traditional centralized approach against FL on the key regulatory principles. The sea of red marks against the centralized model, contrasted with the green marks for FL, offers a powerful visual conclusion: one architecture is a relic of a past regulatory era, while the other is a blueprint for the future.

1.4.3 Use case: Compliant fraud detection and credit scoring

To move from principle to practice, let us revisit the scenario of the multinational bank attempting to build a global fraud detection model. Figure 1.7 illustrates that under the centralized model, this was impossible. With FL, it becomes not only possible but also more effective. The bank can establish a federated network connecting its operations in the EU, the United States, and India. A global fraud model is dispatched to each region. The model trains on the local transaction data within each country, learning the specific patterns of European fraud, the nuances of American financial crime, and the unique typologies of Indian fraudulent activity.

Each local model then sends its learnings, not its data, back to a central aggregator. The aggregated global model now possesses a far more sophisticated and holistic understanding of fraud than any single regional model could achieve on its own. It can identify complex, cross-border money laundering schemes that would be invisible to a model trained only on German data. The bank achieves a superior security outcome while maintaining perfect compliance with GDPR, DPDPA, and other relevant regulations. The data never moved, but the intelligence did. This paradigm extends powerfully to other core financial

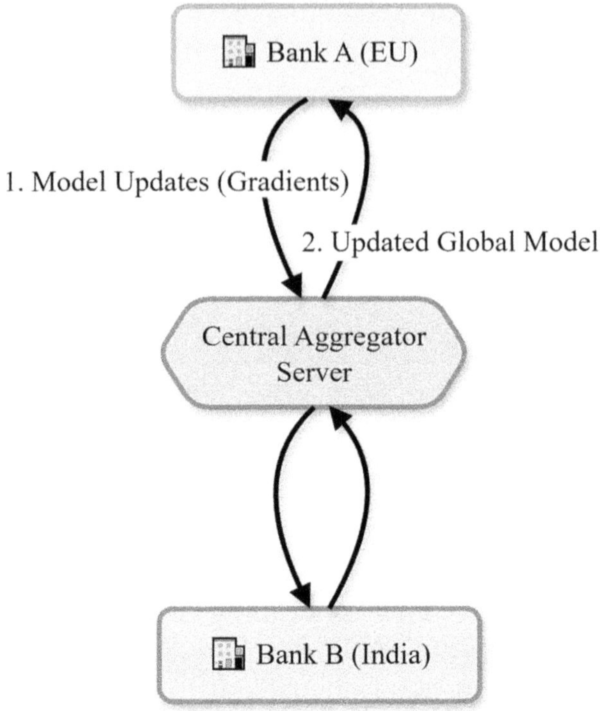

Figure 1.7 Compliant architecture with central aggregator server.

applications, such as credit scoring. A persistent challenge in lending is the potential for AI models to inherit and amplify historical biases present in the training data, leading to unfair outcomes for certain demographic groups. FL offers a compelling solution. A lender could partner with various community banks or financial institutions serving diverse populations. By using FL, they could train a more equitable credit scoring model that learns from the financial data of a much broader and more representative cross-section of society [27]. This can be achieved without any of the partner institutions having to share their sensitive, local customer information. The resulting model would not only be more accurate but also demonstrably fairer, helping the institution meet both its regulatory obligations and its ethical commitments to fair lending. In both fraud detection and credit scoring, FL proves to be more than just a compliance tool; it is a catalyst for more effective, equitable, and collaborative financial intelligence.

1.5 LINGERING REGULATORY QUESTIONS AND FUTURE CHALLENGES

While FL presents a powerful and elegant solution to the compliance deadlock created by traditional AI architectures, it would be a mistake to view it as a panacea. The paradigm, for all its innovation, is not a magic wand that resolves every legal and ethical complexity associated with data processing. Instead, by shifting the architectural model, it moves the legal and ethical questions into new, more nuanced territory. The introduction of any new technology into a highly regulated space like finance inevitably creates a "pacing problem," where the capabilities of the technology outstrip the evolution of the law. FL is currently operating within this legal grey area. While it solves the clear-cut problem of cross-border data transfer, it raises a host of second-order questions that are complex, challenging, and as yet, largely unanswered by regulators. A responsible and forward-looking analysis requires us to engage directly with these lingering questions, as they will undoubtedly shape the future adoption and governance of this transformative technology.

1.5.1 The controller–processor dilemma in federated networks

At the heart of modern data protection law, particularly the GDPR, lies a critical distinction between the roles of the "Data Controller" and the "Data Processor." The Controller is the entity that determines the "purposes and means" of the processing of personal data; it is the primary decision-maker and bears the ultimate responsibility for compliance. The Processor, in contrast, is an entity that processes data on behalf of the Controller, acting only on its instructions. In a simple, centralized model, these roles are often clear: a bank (the Controller) might hire a cloud computing provider (the Processor) to store its data. But how do these definitions apply to the decentralized, collaborative ecosystem of an FL network? The answer is far from clear, and the ambiguity has significant legal consequences. Consider a consortium of several European and Asian banks that collaborate to train a federated AML model. Who is the Data Controller in this scenario? One could argue that each individual bank remains the sole Controller of its own customer data. After all, the data never leaves their servers, and they are the ones who ultimately decide to participate in the federated training process [28]. In this interpretation, the entity that operates the central aggregation server might be seen as a simple Data Processor, merely carrying out the technical instructions of the participating banks to combine the model updates. This seems like a clean and straightforward interpretation, but it may oversimplify the reality of the network.

An alternative, and perhaps more accurate, view is that of joint controllership. In many federated setups, the central entity that organizes the consortium and designs the global model's architecture is not a passive actor. It often defines the overarching purpose of the processing (e.g., "to build a global AML model"), specifies the data types required for local training, and designs the very algorithm that will be sent to the participants. In such a case, both the central aggregator and the individual participating banks could be seen as jointly determining the purposes and means of the processing. This designation of joint controllership is legally significant. It implies shared responsibility and liability. If a compliance breach occurs, all participants could be held accountable, and a complex legal agreement would be required to delineate the specific responsibilities of each party. The question is pivotal: does a bank that simply agrees to participate in a federated network take on a new level of legal responsibility for the actions of the entire consortium? The lack of clear regulatory guidance on this point remains a significant hurdle for the establishment of large-scale, multi-institution federated ecosystems.

The legal ambiguity at the heart of FL can be best understood by visually contrasting the relationship models, as shown in Figure 1.8. Scenario A depicts the traditional, straightforward model. Here, the roles are clearly defined: the bank acts as the sole "Data Controller," making all key decisions and bearing ultimate responsibility. It gives direct instructions to a "Data Processor," such as a cloud provider, which simply executes tasks on its behalf. The hierarchy is clear, and liability is easy to assign.

Scenario B, however, illustrates the complex, interconnected web created by an FL network. The clear hierarchy dissolves. The participating banks are no longer just individual controllers but become "Joint Controllers," sharing responsibility for the collective

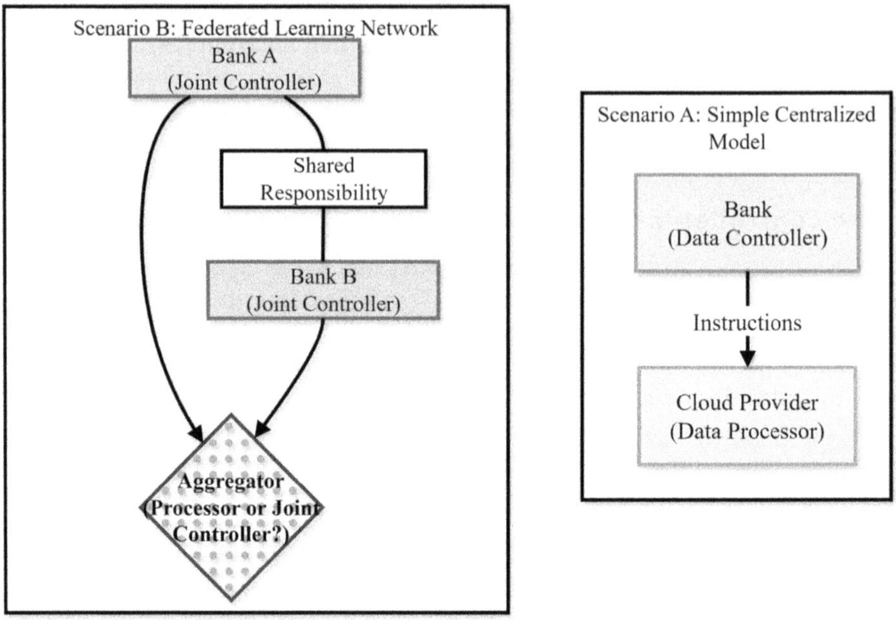

Figure 1.8 Controller–processor relationship models.

processing activity. The role of the central aggregator becomes ambiguous—is it merely a processor acting on instructions, or does its role in designing and managing the global model make it a joint controller as well? This shared responsibility, represented by the link between the banks, introduces a new layer of legal complexity and is the central dilemma that current regulations struggle to address.

1.5.2 Accountability, liability, and model explainability

The ambiguity surrounding the controller–processor relationship leads directly to an even more challenging set of questions regarding accountability and liability. If a federated model produces a harmful outcome, who is to blame? Imagine the federated credit scoring model we discussed earlier denies an individual a loan. The applicant, exercising their rights under GDPR, requests an explanation for the decision. The local bank that deployed the model cannot provide a complete answer on its own, because the model's logic is a composite of learnings from a dozen other institutions. The final decision was not based solely on that bank's data, but on the aggregated intelligence of the entire network. This creates a serious challenge for the "right to an explanation," a cornerstone of algorithmic fairness. How can a meaningful explanation be provided when no single party has a complete view of the data that influenced the outcome? The distributed nature of the system, which is its greatest strength from a privacy perspective, becomes its greatest weakness from an explainability standpoint.

This accountability gap becomes even more pronounced when considering malicious actions. What if one of the participating banks, either intentionally or through a security lapse, contributes "poisoned" data to the training process? This poisoned data could be designed to subtly bias the global model, perhaps to discriminate against a certain demographic or to create a hidden vulnerability. When the flawed global model is deployed and causes financial harm, the question of liability becomes a legal labyrinth. The victim has suffered damages, but is the responsible party the malicious actor who poisoned the data, the central aggregator who failed to detect the anomaly, or all the other "good faith" participants whose models were unknowingly corrupted? Proving causation and assigning liability in such a decentralized system is an incredibly complex task that current legal frameworks are ill-equipped to handle.

Moreover, the intrinsic nature of the model updates, albeit not raw data, does involve some risk. It has been demonstrated by researchers that under certain conditions, it is possible to perform "inference attacks" on model gradients to obtain information about training data. While difficult to enact, theoretical capability exists. This raises another complex legal question: is the effective extraction of personal data from anonymized model updates a data breach? And if so, who is accountable for it? These are not merely matters of technicalities; they raise fundamental legal and ethical questions that fundamentally affect our method of attributing responsibility in the age of decentralized, collaborative AI.

1.5.3 The need for evolving legal standards and regulatory sandboxes

The difficulties surrounding role definition, accountability, and explainability lead to one main conclusion: the law has not yet aligned with the technology. FL and various Privacy-Enhancing Technologies (PETs) function in an area where legal precedents are limited and clear regulatory directions are nearly absent. This generates uncertainty and risk, which can subsequently hinder innovation. The legal and compliance departments of a financial institution, encountering these uncertainties, will understandably recommend prudence, which could delay the embrace of a technology that provides significant advantages for both the sector and its clients. To realize the complete potential of FL, the legal and regulatory structures need to develop in tandem with the technology.

A solely reactive strategy, in which regulators take action only after a significant incident happens, is inadequate. A proactive and cooperative approach is essential among technologists, legal specialists, financial institutions, and the regulatory agencies. A highly promising approach to encourage this collaboration is the regulatory sandbox. A sandbox is a managed, real-world testing space in which businesses can introduce new products and services while being closely monitored by the regulator. It enables practical experimentation within a specific and restricted framework, creating a secure environment to recognize and reduce possible risks before launching a product to the broader market. A highly effective method for promoting this cooperation is the regulatory sandbox, a procedure illustrated in Figure 1.9.

1.6 CONCLUSION

1.6.1 Summary of key arguments

This chapter began by establishing a fundamental and growing conflict at the heart of modern finance: the collision between the insatiable data requirements of AI and the unyielding legal mandates of a new global data privacy regime. We have charted the rise of a formidable regulatory framework, led by landmark legislation like GDPR and DPDPA, which has firmly established the principles of data sovereignty, minimization, and purpose limitation. This has created an environment where the traditional, centralized approach to

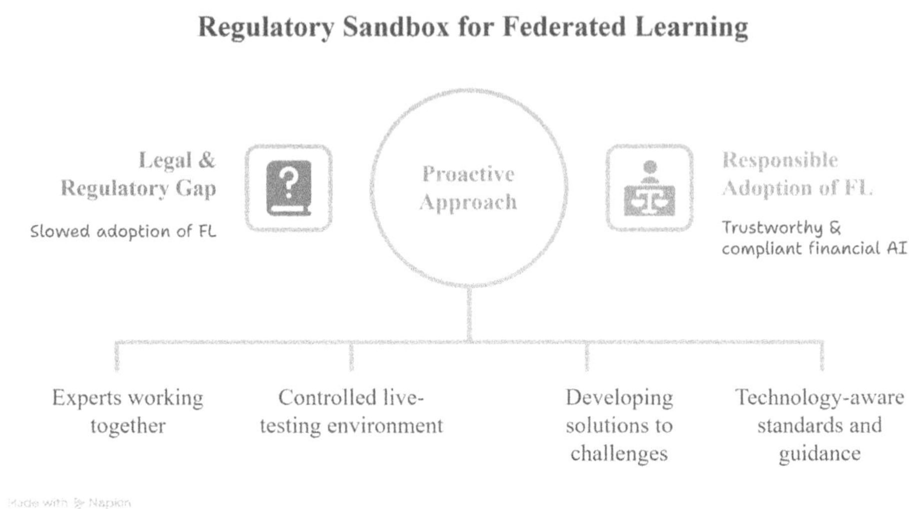

Figure 1.9 Regulatory sandbox for federated learning.

AI—an architecture predicated on pooling vast quantities of raw data across jurisdictional borders—is no longer merely risky, but fundamentally non-compliant. Through architectural diagrams and practical demonstrations, we have shown that this old paradigm is architecturally incompatible with the new legal reality, leading to an operational and compliance deadlock.

In response to this challenge, we have presented FL not as an incremental improvement, but as a necessary architectural evolution. By inverting the conventional data flow and sending the algorithm to the data, FL offers a "compliance-by-design" framework that inherently respects the digital borders of the modern world. Its mechanisms directly align with the core tenets of data protection law, ensuring that sensitive financial information remains secure within its local, regulated environment. The comparative scorecard presented made this conclusion explicit: where centralized AI fails the compliance test, FL provides a viable, powerful, and elegant path forward.

1.6.2 The co-evolution of financial technology and regulation

However, to conclude that FL is a final solution would be to oversimplify the dynamic landscape in which it operates. As we have explored, the technology itself introduces new and nuanced legal questions surrounding liability, accountability, and explainability that current laws are not yet equipped to answer. This does not diminish its value but instead highlights a crucial truth: the future of financial innovation will be defined by the co-evolution of technology and regulation. The path forward is not one where technologists work in isolation, later handing off their creations for legal review. It must be a continuous, collaborative dialogue.

Ultimately, the shift toward FL is about more than just navigating a complex web of regulations. It is about rebuilding trust in a digital financial ecosystem. For institutions to harness the full potential of AI, they must first demonstrate that they can be responsible stewards of their customers' most sensitive information. Adopting privacy-preserving technologies is the most powerful way to make that demonstration. It is, therefore, not simply a defensive compliance strategy, but a proactive and essential step toward building the next generation of financial servicesone that is not only more intelligent but also fundamentally more trustworthy.

REFERENCES

[1] Titilope Tosin Adewale, Titilayo Deborah Olorunyomi, and Theodore Narku Odonkor, "Big data-driven financial analysis: A new paradigm for strategic insights and decision-making," *Int. J. Front. Sci. Technol. Res.*, vol. 4, no. 2, pp. 033–054, 2023, doi: 10.53294/ijfstr.2023.4.2.0060.

[2] Foluke Ekundayo, "Economic implications of AI-driven financial markets: Challenges and opportunities in big data integration," *Int. J. Sci. Res. Arch.*, vol. 13, no. 2, pp. 1500–1515, 2024, doi: 10.30574/ijsra.2024.13.2.2311.

[3] A. Athira and V. K. Ramesh, "Economic policy uncertainty and tax avoidance: International evidence," *Emerg. Mark. Rev.*, vol. 60, no. 4, pp. 4836–4856, Oct. 2024, doi: 10.1016/j.ememar.2024.101135.

[4] Y. Wang et al., "Data-driven green development efficiency of regional sci-tech finance: A case study of the Yangtze River Delta," *Math. Probl. Eng.*, vol. 2022, no. 1, pp. 3408342, Jan. 2022, doi: 10.1155/2022/3408342.

[5] G. Chi, S. Ding, and X. Peng, "Data-driven robust credit portfolio optimization for investment decisions in P2P lending," *Math. Probl. Eng.*, vol. 2019, no. 1, pp. 1902970, Jan. 2019, doi: 10.1155/2019/1902970.

[6] T. Magoč, X. Wang, and F. Modave, "Application of fuzzy measures and interval computation to financial portfolio selection," *Int. J. Intell. Syst.*, vol. 25, no. 7, pp. 621–635, Jul. 2010, doi: 10.1002/int.20415.

[7] J. Barredo-Zuriarrain, F. Ülgen, and O. Radonjić, "Fallacies of market-friendly financial regulation conducted by the Federal Reserve in the 1990s and 2000s," *J. Post Keynes. Econ.*, vol. 43, no. 4, pp. 540–575, Oct. 01, 2020. doi: 10.1080/01603477.2020.1734465.

[8] R. Phillips, "The global export of risk: Finance and the film business," *Compet. Chang.*, vol. 8, no. 2, pp. 105–136, Jun. 2004, doi: 10.1080/1024529042000271425.

[9] A. Smellie, "The work of the Caribbean regional division of the financial action task force," *Commonw. Law Bull.*, vol. 19, no. 4, pp. 1830–1851, Oct. 1993, doi: 10.1080/03050718.1993.9986331.

[10] A. M. Khademian, "A public administration moment: Forging an agenda for financial regulatory reform," *Public Adm. Rev.*, vol. 69, no. 4, pp. 595–602, Jul. 2009, doi: 10.1111/j.1540-6210.2009.02008.x.

[11] S. Caschili and F. Medda, "The Global Trade System and Its Evolution," in *Global Dynamics*, A. Wilson, Ed., Wiley, 2016, pp. 9–25. doi: 10.1002/9781118937464.ch2.

[12] S. Macfeely and P. van de Ven, "GDP and the SNA: Future Challenges," in *Advances in Business Statistics, Methods and Data Collection*, A. van D. Ger Snijkers, Mojca Bavdaž, Stefan Bender, Jacqui Jones, Steve MacFeely, Joseph W. Sakshaug, Katherine J. Thompson, Ed., Wiley, 2023, pp. 43–62. doi: 10.1002/9781119672333.ch3.

[13] B. Guembe, S. Misra, and A. Azeta, "Privacy issues, attacks, countermeasures and open problems in federated learning: A survey," *Applied Artificial Intelligence*, vol. 38, no. 1, Dec. 31, 2024. doi: 10.1080/08839514.2024.2410504.

[14] T. K. Vashishth, V. Sharma, B. Kumar, K. K. Sharma, S. Chaudhary, and R. Panwar, "Blockchain for securing Federated Learning Systems: Enhancing Privacy and Trust," in *Model Optimization Methods for Efficient and Edge AI*, Wiley, 2025, pp. 299–320. doi: 10.1002/9781394219230.ch15.

[15] V. A. Rajasekaran, J. Periyasamy, M. G. Brahmam, and B. Baluswamy, "Architectural patterns for the Design of Federated Learning Systems," in *Model Optimization Methods for Efficient and Edge AI*, Wiley, 2025, pp. 223–239. doi: 10.1002/9781394219230.ch12.

[16] R. M. Pujahari, R. Khan, and S. P. Yadav, "Federated Autonomous Deep Learning for Distributed Healthcare System," in *Federated Intelligent System for Healthcare*, Wiley, 2025, pp. 25–59. doi: 10.1002/9781394271382.ch2.

[17] R. Behl, I. Kashyap, and N. Garg, "Foundations of Federated Intelligent Systems in Healthcare," in *Federated Intelligent System for Healthcare*, Wiley, 2025, pp. 81–99. doi: 10.1002/9781394271382.ch4.

[18] P. P. Ray, "Federated learning for Intelligent IoT Systems: Background, frameworks, and optimization techniques," in *Model Optimization Methods for Efficient and Edge AI: Federated Learning Architectures, Frameworks and Applications*, Wiley, 2024, pp. 241–280. doi: 10.1002/9781394219230.ch13.

[19] K. Hu et al., "Federated learning: A distributed shared machine learning method," *Complexity*, vol. 2021, no. 1, pp. 8261663, Jan. 2021, doi: 10.1155/2021/8261663.

[20] S. Chakraborty, A. K. Turuk, and B. Sahoo, "Federated learning enabled software-defined optical network with intelligent control plane architecture," *Comput. Electr. Eng.*, vol. 118, p. 109329, Aug. 2024, doi: 10.1016/j.compeleceng.2024.109329.

[21] F. Deng, C. Fu, Y. Qian, J. Yang, S. He, and H. Xu, "Federated learning based multi-task feature fusion framework for code expressive semantic extraction," *Softw. Pract. Exp.*, vol. 52, no. 8, pp. 1849–1866, Aug. 2022, doi: 10.1002/spe.3094.

[22] M. Abdel-Basset, N. Moustafa, and H. Hawash, "Privacy-Preserved Federated Learning," in *Deep Learning Approaches for Security Threats in IoT Environments*, Wiley, 2022, pp. 337–355. doi: 10.1002/9781119884170.ch16.

[23] S. K.M., V. P., R. R. K.A., and M. Conti, "LFGurad: A defense against label flipping attack in federated learning for vehicular network," *Comput. Networks*, vol. 254, p. 110768, Dec. 2024, doi: 10.1016/j.comnet.2024.110768.

[24] P. Dubey and M. Kumar, "Integrating explainable AI with federated learning for next-generation IoT: A comprehensive review and prospective insights," *Comput. Sci. Rev.*, vol. 56, p. 100697, May 2025, doi: 10.1016/j.cosrev.2024.100697.

[25] G. Liu, W. Shen, L. Gao, and A. Kusiak, "Active federated transfer algorithm based on broad learning for fault diagnosis," *Measurement*, vol. 208, p. 112452, Feb. 2023, doi: 10.1016/j.measurement.2023.112452.

[26] X. Ma, L. Liao, Z. Li, R. X. Lai, and M. Zhang, "Applying federated learning in software-defined networks: A survey," *Symmetry (Basel).*, vol. 14, no. 2, p. 195, Jan. 2022, doi: 10.3390/sym14020195.

[27] Y. Peng, Z. Chen, Z. Chen, W. Ou, W. Han, and J. Ma, "BFLP: An adaptive federated learning framework for internet of vehicles," *Mob. Inf. Syst.*, vol. 2021, no. 1, p. 6633332, Jan. 2021, doi: 10.1155/2021/6633332.

[28] A. Raheem, Z. Yang, H. Yu, M. A. Manan, F. Sabah, and S. Ahmed, "FUSION: Uncertainty-Guided federated semi-supervised learning for medical image segmentation," *IET Image Process.*, vol. 19, no. 1, p. e70147, Jan. 2025, doi: 10.1049/ipr2.70147.

Chapter 2

The mechanism of federated learning

Dhanashri Vaishali, Harish Kumar, and Poornima D.

2.1 INTRODUCTION TO FEDERATED LEARNING

As the limitations of centralized artificial intelligence (AI) system becomes more apparent, particularly in area concerning data privacy communication bottleneck and compliances with regulations, an alternative approach has gained significant attention in the market. Federated learning (FL), introduced by Google in 2016, this frameworks marked a major turning point in how machine learning (ML) models are trained in distributed environment. Unlike the traditional model they require all data to be collected and stored in a central server, FL takes a radically different route. Instead of transferring the raw data, the learning process happens directly on the device or local server referring to as flights, where the data is originally generated. In a typical FL setting each client's independently trains a copy of the model using its local data set. After this local training phase, only the model parameters—such as weight updates or gradients—are sent to a central server. The server then aggregates these updates to produce an improved version of the global model. This process is repeated over several iterations until the model reaches an acceptable level of accuracy. Crucially, at no point is the raw data itself transmitted or exposed, which significantly reduces the risk of privacy breaches and supports strong data protection practices.

What makes FL especially relevant today is that it aligns naturally with modern data privacy regulations, such as the General Data Protection Regulation (GDPR) in Europe and the Health Insurance Portability and Accountability Act (HIPAA) in the United States. By keeping sensitive information on the user's device or within an organization's secure system, FL minimizes the potential for unauthorized data access or misuse.

Moreover, FL brings practical benefits beyond privacy. Because only small updates are exchanged, it dramatically reduces network load, making it ideal for deployment in bandwidth-constrained environments such as mobile devices, remote healthcare monitors, or rural IoT networks. Its scalability and resilience to low-connectivity conditions mean that large-scale, collaborative learning can happen without the heavy infrastructure burden of centralized systems. Additionally, FL supports personalization, allowing the user to organize and fine tune the shared global model based on their unique data leading to the more context aware and user specific outcomes. In essence of FL it offers a compelling part forward in the era of distributed privacy sensitive and ever growing data environment. It is not merely a work around to data sharing concerns it represents a rethinking of how intelligent systems can learn in harmony with the ethical legal and particular practical realities

DOI: 10.1201/9781003660330-2

2.1.1 Ethical AI principles

As AIcontinues to evolve, ethical concerns surrounding its development and deployment have grown significantly, FL as a decentralized form of ML, brings with it a unique ethical responsibilities and opportunities. Unlike the traditional ML approach that rely on centralized data aggregation, FL operates by training the modules locally on individual devices or servers, sharing only the model updates with the centralized aggregator. The Decentralization introduced a distinct advantage when it came to protecting user privacy, arguably one of the most critical and ethical concerns in AI. Privacy as a foundational principle, is deeply embedded into the FL framework. By keeping raw data on local devices, FL minimizes the risk of personal information being exposed hacked or misused. This inheritance privacy preservation design reflects a commitment to respecting user's autonomy and data privacy. Alongside privacy, Transparency plays a crucial role it is essential that the process involved in FL, how data contributes to the model, what is being updated, and how security is maintained are clearly communicated to the users and stakeholders. This ensures trust and fosters inform Participated in Federated ecosystem. Another ethical concern is fairness. Since FL draws data from a diverse set of users there is a real risk of underrepresenting minority groups or favoring devices with richer or more frequent data if not managed carefully, it can lead to bias model and unequal outcome. Ethical FL must address these imbalances through algorithm designs and inclusive data strategies. Similarly accountability must be established despite the distributed nature of FL. With many contributors involved in training, it becomes important to trace how decisions are made and to provide mechanisms for auditing and addressing issues when outcomes are concerns or harmful. Moreover the principle of safety and reliability is vital in FL settings the model must be tested rigorously across different environments and the devices to ensure consistent and trustworthy performance. Whether dealing with medical diagnostics or financial predictions, users must be able to rely on the model outputs. Finally human, however, science must remain central. Even though FL brings automation closer to the user, decision essentially high impact ones should never be fully seized two machines. Human judgment must guide supervised and when necessary override the algorithm outputs

2.1.2 Federated compliance with regional data laws

In the Indian context, the increasing focus on personal data protection has led to the formulation of comprehensive regulatory frameworks aimed at ensuring responsible data governance. The Digital Personal Data Protection Act (DPDPA), 2023 represents a significant legal shift in how organizations are required to collect, process, and store personal data. The Act emphasizes core principles such as data minimization, purpose limitation, consent-based processing, and data localization—all of which align well with the architecture of FL. Unlike traditional centralized ML, FL ensures that raw user data remains on local devices, and only model updates are shared with a central server for aggregation. This decentralized structure supports privacy-preserving computation and helps reduce the legal risks associated with centralized data storage and cross-border data transfers [1]. Under the DPDPA, it is mandatory for data fiduciaries to obtain explicit and informed consent before processing any personal data. FL systems can integrate consent management at the device level, allowing users to either opt in or opt out of participation. This aligns with the law's intent to give control back to data principals.

In addition, the data localization requirements, especially for sensitive personal data, are naturally addressed through FL since user data never leaves the local storage environment [2].

However, architectural design alone is not sufficient for legal compliance. FL systems must ensure transparency, accountability, and auditability. This includes informing users about how data is used, what updates are sent, and what protective measures are applied. In India, where digital awareness varies significantly across regions and demographics, ensuring user-friendly privacy disclosures and accessible language is essential for ethical deployment. Moreover, even though raw data is not shared, model updates may still pose a risk of inference attacks, and hence FL must incorporate differential privacy (DP) [3], secure aggregation [4], and homomorphic encryption (HE) to enhance data security [5]. The DPDPA also mandates robust mechanisms for grievance redressed, allowing individuals to seek accountability and file complaint in case of misuse. Saturated learning system must be audited and capable of maintaining the activity logs without compromising individual privacy. These logs may have address disputes and support regularities oversights by authorities like the Data Protection Board of India [6]. FL offers an architecture that supports Indian evolving legal landscape around data protection. Decentralized structure inherently supports data minimization, consent, and localized mandates, but fully compliance requires thoughtful integration of legal and ethical safeguards. When implementation responsibility, FL becomes not only a tool for privacy preservation computation but also a model for lawful and trustworthy AI Deployment in India.

2.1.3 Deploying FL in Indian industry

Deploying FL in Indian industries requires a strategic balance of technical design, regulatory awareness, and organizational readiness. The first step is to identify suitable use cases where privacy is paramount and data is distributed, such as healthcare diagnostics, financial forecasting, or industrial IoT analytics [7]. Once use cases are established, organizations must ensure that edge devices or local servers are equipped with adequate computing resources and secure connectivity to support local training tasks without compromising performance [8]. In accordance with India's DPDPA, 2023, companies must obtain clear and informed consent from users, ensure that data processing is purpose-specific, and implement opt-in/opt-out options at the user level [9]. Additionally, privacy risks during model update exchanges must be addressed using techniques likeDP, secure aggregation, or HEto prevent data leakage and inference attacks [10]. The FL server must be capable of managing asynchronous updates, handling data heterogeneity, and adapting to real-world constraints such as device dropouts or low bandwidth. Compliance with Indian data localization laws mandates that all storage and computation take place within national boundaries, either on physical infrastructure or compliant cloud platforms [11]. Companies should also maintain transparent policies, periodic audits, and training logs to ensure traceability and regulatory compliance. Successful deployment also depends on educating internal stakeholders—engineers, managers, legal teams—and investing in change management practices to integrate FL seamlessly into existing operations. With proper governance, monitoring, and technical safeguards, FL offers Indian industries a legally sound and privacy-aware framework to scale AI adoption without compromising on ethical or statutory obligations [12].

2.2 LITERATURE REVIEW

Since its introduction by Google in 2016, FL has undergone significant development, beginning with the foundational Federated Averaging (FedAvg) algorithm proposed by McMahan et al. [13], which initiated the shift from centralized to decentralized ML. This shift was largely motivated by concerns surrounding the data privacy regulatory compliances, and distributed data sources to address the limitations of Fed average in the real world settings. Particularly the challenges of heterogeneous data distribution, researchers proposed algorithms such as FedProx, which incorporates approximately terms in a local optimization functions to stabilize the training across non identical distributed data [14].

Future achievements includes Scholastic Controlled Averaging for Federated Learning (SCAFFOLD) and Fed Nova, have tackled the issues of client drift in non-IID environment by using control variance and normalized strategies, respectively [15, 16]. Alongside these algorithmic improvements privacy preservation mechanisms have been embedded into FL system. Techniques like DP, secure multiparty computation (SMC), and HE have been employed to ensure that local data remains confidential, even during model update and sharing process [3]. Equally importance is reduction of communication overhead, a major bottleneck in FL deployment. Solution for such problem is gradient specification, model compression and selective client participation have led to more efficient communication and reduced bandwidth requirement, Making FL viable even in constrained environment [17]. These advancement have improved the way for FL to be deployed across various sectors. Real world applications now span mobile services such as Google's Gboard Predictive typing [18].

As well as healthcare diagnostics, autonomous driving, fraud detection, and smart city infrastructure. To facilitate research and development, several FL frameworks have been introduced. TensorFlow Federated (TFF) offers a flexible simulation platform with broad community support, though it remains limited in supporting real-device deployment [19]. PySyft provides robust integrations for privacy technologies like DP, SMC, and HE but can be complex to implement in production environments [20]. Flower offers framework-agnostic flexibility and edge-to-cloud compatibility, but its base version lacks advanced security features [21]. FedML, designed for scalability and benchmarking, provides cross-device support but still needs stronger tools for vertical FL modeling [22]. Despite the availability of these frameworks, significant challenges remain, especially in managing non-independent identically distributed (non-IID) data, intermittent client participation, and network instability—factors commonly observed in large-scale deployments.

This chapter addresses these gaps by proposing several key contributions. First, it introduces aggregation and optimization strategies specifically designed for data heterogeneity. Second, it explores adaptive scheduling and fault-tolerance mechanisms to enhance scalability in environments where clients may drop out or participate asynchronously. Third, it evaluates the balance between privacy and utility, proposing lightweight privacy-preserving techniques that maintain competitive accuracy. Fourth, unlike much of the existing literature which remains simulation-based, this chapter presents real-world case studies in mobile healthcare and agriculture, emphasizing FL's utility in low-resource environments. Finally, to standardize evaluation and improve comparability across studies, the chapter proposes a benchmarking framework based on common performance metrics, including model accuracy, convergence rate, communication cost, and privacy leakage. Together, these contributions aim to advance the reliability and scalability of FL in both research and applied contexts.

2.3 FL ARCHITECTURE AND MECHANISM

2.3.1 FL architecture

With the exponential growth of data generated by mobile devices, industrial sensors, and personal technologies, traditional centralized ML approaches face increasing challenges related to data privacy, bandwidth usage, and legal compliance. FL offers a fundamentally different approach by enabling model training at the edge—on the very devices where data is generated. The core architectural framework of FL, outlining its components, operational flow, and the privacy-enhancing mechanisms that make it a compelling solution for decentralized learning is shown in Figure 2.1. The overall workflow of the FL system is depicted in Figure 2.1, where local model updates from distributed devices are aggregated at a central server to produce a global model [23, 24].

FL is built on a collaborative paradigm where multiple clients—such as smartphones, IoT devices, hospitals, or financial systems—train a shared ML model using their local data. The innovation lies in the fact that data never leaves the client device. Instead, only model updates (like weight changes or gradients) are shared with a central server, which aggregates the updates to refine the global model [25].

The Core Components of FL Architecture Are

1. **Clients (Edge Participants):**
   Clients are the individual data holders participating in the FL process. These include mobile phones, hospital databases, smart meters, and other devices or institutions that generate and retain data locally. Each client contributes to model training while preserving the confidentiality of its data [23].
2. **Local Training Module:**
   On each client, the local training module performs computations using the client's own dataset. A copy of the global model is trained locally for one or more epochs,

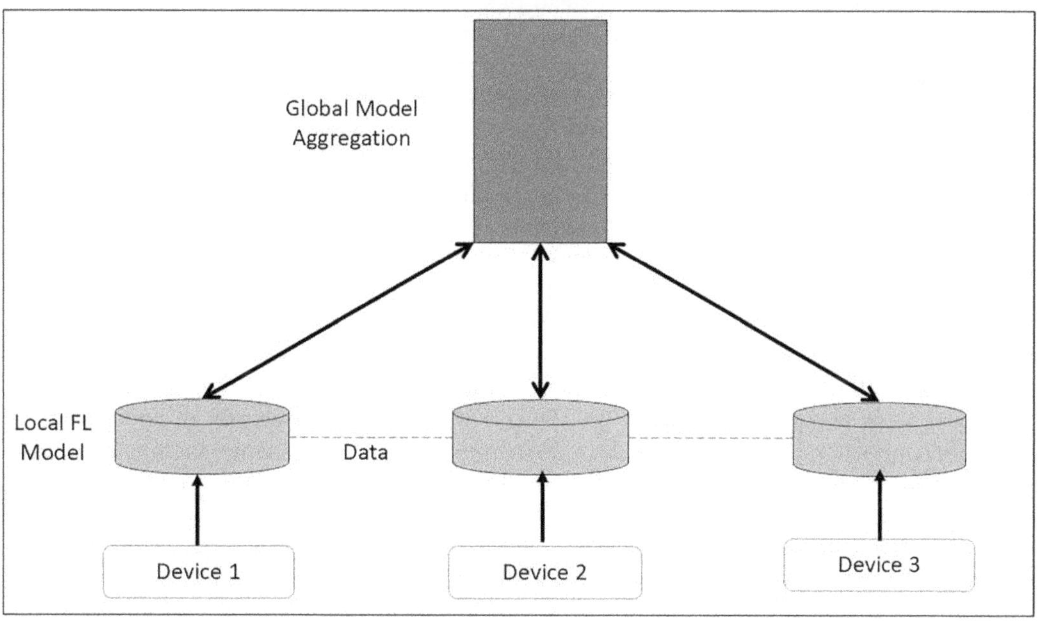

Figure 2.1 Federated learning architecture.

and only the results (e.g., model weight updates) are prepared for transmission back to the server [24].

3. **Communication Module:**
   After local training, the communication module is responsible for securely sending the model updates to the server. Importantly, no raw data is transferred—only trained parameters. This reduces bandwidth use and enhances data privacy [25].
4. **Aggregation Server (Central Coordinator):**
   The server collects all updates from participating clients and aggregates them to update the global model. A common aggregation technique is Federated Averaging (FedAvg), where updates are weighted and averaged. This updated model is then redistributed to all clients [26].
5. **Privacy Enhancement Layer:**
   To reinforce data protection, F L systems often include optional privacy-preserving mechanisms. These may include:

   DP—Adds noise to updates to prevent reverse-engineering of original data [27].
   HE—Allows computation on encrypted data [28].
   SMC—Enables joint computations without revealing private inputs [29].

2.3.2 FL mechanism

FL is an innovative decentralized MLtechnique that allows multiple devices or institutions to collaboratively train a shared model while keeping all data localized at the source [13]. Unlike traditional approaches that rely on centralized data collection, FL enables the training process to occur directly on the client devices—such as smartphones, IoT sensors, or hospital servers—thereby minimizing the risk of data breaches and enhancing user privacy. The process begins when a central server sends a global model to each participating client. These clients perform local training on their private datasets and compute model updates, such as gradients or weight changes, instead of sharing raw data [4].

Once the local training is complete, each client transmits its model update back to the central server. These updates are then aggregated most commonly using the Federated averaging process or (FedAvg) algorithm to produce and improved global model. This averaging model is sent back to all client, and the cycle repeats over multiple iterations until the model converges to a satisfactory level of accuracy [30]. This iterative mechanism allows the system to learn from a vast, diverse range of data while maintaining data locality, which is especially beneficial in sectors like healthcare, finance, and mobile personalization where data sensitivity is paramount [31].

Moreover, FL enhances compliances with privacy regulations such as GDPR in Europe and the same compliances represented as HITAA in the United States because the devices perform local model training, ensuring enhanced privacy protection. FL also reduces network bandwidth usage since only model parameters are exchanged. However, implementing FL at scale poses several challenges. Device may differ significantly in computational capability, network reliability, and data distributions, leading to issues such as communication delay, system heterogeneity, and degraded model performance due to non-IID data. Additionally the system must be fortified against security threats like adverse updates and model poisoning to address this concerns, techniques such as secure aggregation DPanomaly detections have been introduced to reinforce the robustness of FL systems.

In essence, FL provides a scalable, privacy preserving, and efficient method of distribution in AI training, enabling collaborative intelligence without compromising individual data ownership. It stands as a promising solution to the growing global demand for ethical and secure ML systems.

2.4 TYPES OF FL

FL is this tidy solution to the problem of developing ML models when various groups need to collaborate but can be prevented (due to regulatory reasons, company policies, etc.) to share data directly. The central point is regarding maintaining the data confidential and, at the same time, learn something from it, yet the distribution of data across the client actually influences the implementation of FL. You should learn about three major kinds of FL: Horizontal Federated Learning (HFL), Vertical Federated Learning (VFL), and Federated Transfer Learning (FTL). It can be very useful to know these distinctions, especially when selecting the training techniques, composing models and ensuring the safety of data.

It is time to jump into HFL. It is all about organizations having the same type of data (such as features) but they have the data of different users. Considering hospitals in other cities—they will all gather the similar data about the patients such as their age, blood pressure, and each hospital will have various types of patients.

Using the system of HFL, they can collaborate to create a prediction model of some disease without never exchanging any patient information. Some cool uses for this could be healthcare research between hospitals, fraud detection across banks, or even creating recommendation systems for different online shops. Plus, it's pretty easy to set up since everyone's using the same model format, and it scales well since the data structures are similar, which makes it less complicated than other types ofFL.

Then there's VFL. This type happens when different organizations are looking at the same group of users but have totally different data about them. They can team up, combining their unique data to build better models while keeping everything private. For instance, a bank and an online store could work together. The bank has financial info and the store has shopping habits, and together, they can predict credit risk without swapping raw data. But it does come with challenges, like making sure they match users correctly and securely without leaking any sensitive info. They've to use things like HE to keep everyone's data safe.

Lastly, FTL this is a bit different because it's used when clients have completely different data samples and feature sets. It's great for when two parties don't have any overlapping data.

For example, a hospital could team up with an ed-tech company. The hospital knows a lot about patients, while the ed-tech company knows how students learn. Even though they're looking at different people and data types, they could find useful links—like figuring out mental health issues linked to school stress. FTL allows this rather teamwork without any data privacy issues. Some possible applications here could include partnerships where the data types don't line up, boosting AI models in areas with fewer data, or international collaborations where strict data laws are in place. But again, there are hurdles, like designing models that can handle totally different datasets and ensuring they work well in each specific situation.

Table 2.1 Comparison of federated learning types

Feature	*HFL*	*VFL*	*FTL*
Shared Feature Space	Yes	No	No
Shared Sample Space	No	Yes	No
Data Alignment Needed	No	Yes (Sample alignment)	Yes (Advanced mapping)
Complexity	Low	Medium	High
Main Use Case	Same domain, different users	Same users, different features	Cross-domain collaboration

2.4.1 Comparison of FL types

The structural and operational differences among HFL, VFL, and FTL are summarized in Table 2.1.

2.4.2 Choosing the right FL type

Training Workflow and Mechanism FL works through a well-structured and cyclical process that enables decentralized devices to join forces in training a shared model—all while keeping their local data private [18]. This iterative workflow strikes a balance between privacy, efficiency, and scalability, and its key to how FL operates in real-world applications.

Initialization: It all starts at the central server, where a global model is established. This model can either be randomly initialized or pre-trained on publicly accessible data to provide a useful starting point. Once everything is set, the server picks a subset of clients—usually based on their availability, performance, or diversity—to take part in the current round of training. These chosen clients will receive the initial global model, which they'll utilize as a foundation for their local learning tasks.

2.5 OPTIMIZATION IN FL

Since distributed systems pose unique challenges, optimization in FL, is more than usual ML techniques. Unlike central training, FL must contend with low communication bandwidth, device heterogeneity, and data heterogeneity [21]. Due to these reasons, applications of classical optimization techniques directly are futile or inefficient. Researchers have created tailored optimization techniques designed to particularly fit federated settings in an attempt to circumvent these issues. These optimization techniques are designed to ensure:

- Convergence: Finding a world-optimal or near-optimal model irrespective of decentralized updates.
- Equity: Making sure that all the clients, particularly the low-performance or low-data ones, are equally contributing to the model.
- Communication Efficiency: Reducing the quantity and speed of data exchanged among servers and clients.

Techniques such as FedAvg, FedProx, SCAFFOLD, FedNova, and so forth use concepts of optimization to handle imbalanced data, unavailability of devices at certain points, and system-level heterogeneity. Some techniques balance client contributions, whereas some modify local objectives or aggregation techniques to enhance global model performance.

2.5.1 Federated averaging (FedAvg)

FedAvg is one of the most widely adopted optimization algorithms in the FLparadigm. It was proposed to address the need for collaborative model training across decentralized data sources without sharing sensitive raw data. The core idea behind FedAvg is to allow each client to train a model locally using its own dataset and then send the updated model parameters—not the data itself—to a central server. The server aggregates these parameters from all participating clients and updates the global model accordingly. This process is repeated over multiple rounds until the model converges.

Mathematically, FedAvg aims to minimize a global objective function that is a weighted sum of each client's local loss function. If K is the total number of clients and $F_k(w)$ is the loss function for client k, then the overall goal is to minimize $f(w)=\sum_{k=1}^{k} p_k F_k(\omega)$, where p_k is the proportion of data samples held by client k. Each client performs local updates using stochastic gradient descent on its data for a defined number of local epochs. After completing local training, each client sends its updated model weights to the server. The server computes a weighted average of these updates, where the weight corresponds to the client's data size. This average becomes the new global model, which is then shared again with the clients in the next round.

From an algorithmic standpoint, FedAvg can be summarized as a cycle of model broadcasting, local training, and centralized aggregation. The central server begins by initializing the model and selecting a subset of clients for training in each round. Selected clients receive the model, conduct local updates, and send the resulting parameters back to the server. The server performs aggregation and updates the global model. This iterative process continues for a predefined number of communication rounds or until performance goals are met.

FedAvg is especially advantageous in scenarios where communication cost is a bottleneck. By allowing multiple local training steps before communication, the algorithm reduces the frequency of data exchange between clients and server, making it suitable for bandwidth-constrained environments. However, this advantage also introduces challenges. For instance, when clients possess non-IID data or when the number of local updates is too high, the global model can drift and fail to converge. This issue, often referred to as "client drift," becomes particularly problematic when the data across clients is significantly unbalanced or dissimilar.

In terms of complexity, each communication round involves the transmission of model parameters, which is proportional to the size of the model. If the model contains d parameters, then each client sends and receives O(d) values per round. The total communication cost depends on the number of rounds, clients per round, and model size. Computation-wise, each client performs E epochs of training over its local dataset, which contributes to the overall training time. The trade-off between local computation and global communication is a key aspect of FedAvg's efficiency. Convergence analysis shows that under certain assumption such as smooth and convex loss functions in feta average can achieve convergence rate comparable to centralized training. However in real world settings with heterogeneous data and system compatibilities convergence may be slower and less stable. To mitigate these, researchers have provided enhanced process such as FedProx and SCAFFOLD, which introduces corrections terms or modified objects to control the effect of local updates. Despite its limitation fed average remains a foundational algorithms in the FL ecosystem due to its simplicity, scalability, and privacy preservation nature.

2.5.2 FedProx

FedProx introduces a proximal term to the local loss function to limit how much a local model can diverge from the global model:

$$\min F_k(w) + \frac{\mu}{2}\|\omega - \omega_t{}^2\|$$

This regularization is especially helpful when clients are highly diverse, both in data and computational capabilities.

2.5.3 SCAFFOLD (Stochastic controlled averaging for federated learning)

Client drift is probably the most important issue in FL, in which models learned across devices become highly divergent due to non-IID data. SCAFFOLD remedies this by incorporating control variates—auxiliary variables whose only function is that they steer each client's updates towards optimization of the global model.

How it Works:
Both the server and client have control variables.

- These parameters control the training process, minimizing the effects of local biases.
- Thereafter, SCAFFOLD enhances convergence rate and stability, particularly in diverse data settings.

2.5.4 FedNova (federated normalized averaging)

In typical FL settings, clients may perform unequal amounts of local computation depending on multiple resources or data size [20]. This creates bias at model update aggregation. FedNova neutralizes this by normalizing updates by work of each client prior to averaging.

Chief Benefits:

- Guarantees fair effort by each client, regardless of the level of local training they do.
- Eliminates aggregation bias and leads to more stable and consistent learning with heterogeneous client populations.

2.5.5 Other advanced optimization techniques

In addition to the complex Optimization Methods

q-FedAvg (q-Federated Averaging): Through the assessment of their contributions in terms of local loss values, q-FedAvg prioritizes updates from subpar clients. This encourages fairness and stability by compelling the framework to learn from harder or underrepresented instances.

Model-Contrastive FL, or MOON: In FL, MOON adds contrastive learning. Unlike previous neighborhood models, it encourages each client's model to stay close to a global

Table 2.2 Optimization technique in federated learning summary

Technique	*Core Idea*	*Key Advantages*
SCAFFOLD	Uses control variates to reduce client drift	Improves convergence on non-IID data
Fed Nova	Normalizes updates based on local work	Ensures fair and unbiased aggregation
q-FedAvg	Weighs clients based on loss	Helps underperforming clients catch up
MOON	Applies contrastive learning	Maintains cross-client model consistency
Fed Dyn	Adds dynamic regularization	Boosts generalization and avoids overfitting

model. When proximal data is highly imbalanced, this strategy improves consistency across clients.

Federated Dynamic Regularization, or FedDyn: Client-side work in FedDyn incorporates a dynamic regularization term. This makes each client behave in accordance with the global model to prevent overfitting on individual data. FedDyn is best suited to enhance system-wide generalization (Table 2.2).

2.6 PRIVACY AND SECURITY TECHNIQUES IN FL

Honestly, it's not all sunshine and roses just because your data stays on your own device. Sure, FL skips the creepy "send all your info to some big server" move, but don't kid yourself: There's still room for leaks and shenanigans. Attackers? Oh, they absolutely exist. Some folks will try to poke at those model updates and squeeze out private info, or just plain mess with the learning process. That's why nerds everywhere have been cooking up cryptographic tricks and algorithms to keep things tight. This stuff matters big time, especially if you're dealing with, say, hospital records, bank accounts, or anything you'd rather not see on Reddit.

2.6.1 Differential privacy (DP)

So, DP is rather like hiding in a crowd—nobody can say for sure if *your* data is in the mix or not. In FL, the trick is to sprinkle some statistical noise (think: Digital confetti) onto the model updates before they head off to the main server.

Working:

- You toss some random noise (Gaussian, Laplacian, whatever math flavor you like) onto gradients or weights.
- There's this slider called epsilon (ε)—lower means more privacy, but also maybe your model gets dumber. You have to find a sweet spot.

Benefits:

- Makes it way harder for creepers to figure out who's in the dataset or reverse-engineer your info.

- You can tweak it—privacy or accuracy, pick your poison.

2.6.2 Secure multiparty computation (SMPC)

Now, SMPC is like a bunch of people doing math together without showing each other their numbers. In FL, it's used to mush everyone's updates together without peeking at anyone's homework.

Mechanism:

- Everyone encrypts their updates with some shared protocol.
- The server does its thing *without* decrypting.
- To actually see the result, everyone's have to chip in. Teamwork makes the dream work, I guess.

Pros and Cons:

- Killer privacy—math says so.
- But, wow, it's slow and chews through your CPU.
- Not exactly ideal when you want stuff done yesterday.

2.6.3 Homomorphic encryption (HE)

HE is wild—imagine doing math on locked boxes without ever opening them. The server never sees the raw data, just the encrypted mess, but still gets the right answer.

Upsides:

- Data stays secret from start to finish.

Real talk:

- It's heavy. Like, don't try this at home if you want quick results or are running on hold.

2.6.4 Secure aggregation protocols

Google's all about this with Gboard. The idea: The server only gets the group's combined update, not the details from each user.

How it works?

- Each person slaps a random mask on their update.
- When the server adds them up, the masks cancel, so only the group total pops out.

Benefits:

- Even if the server gets hacked, individual secrets stay secret.

2.6.5 Adversarial threats in FL

- Model Inversion: Hackers try to recreate your data from the model.
- Membership Inference: Attempt to identify whether a particular sample was used in training.
- Poisoning: Some joker sends in garbage data to ruin the whole thing.
- Free-Riders: Slackers who fake their updates to get the benefits without lifting a finger.

2.6.6 Robustness and defense

- Keeping the Monsters at Bay, A few tricks:
- Smart Client Selection: If a user acts sketchy or sends weird data, drop or down-rank them.
- Anomaly Detection: Use ML or stat tricks to spot the weirdos.
- Robust Aggregation: Algorithms like Krum, Trimmed Mean, or Federated Median help ignore the baddies and focus on the real stuff.

Bottom line: FL is way more private than the old-school way, but it isn't bulletproof. You need all these extra layers and a healthy dose of paranoia to keep things truly secure. Welcome to the future—bring your own tinfoil hat.

2.7 APPLICATIONS OF FL

FL is really changing the game for how we build and use ML models, especially where keeping data private and secure is super important. Unlike the old-school ways that gather data in one place, FL lets different devices, organizations, or areas work together to train models—without ever sending out raw data. This setup not only helps protect everyone's information but also makes it easier to follow the new rules about data handling.

Because of this, FL is breaking new ground in lots of areas, from healthcare and finance to smart cities and tech designed just for you. We're going to dive into some real-world examples of FL in action, showing how this cool technique boosts intelligence, keeps privacy in check, and encourages teamwork—while making sure sensitive info stays safe and spread out.

2.7.1 In healthcare

We're talking about some of the most delicate and personal info out there—things like medical histories, scans, and genetics. While sharing this data can really help improve diagnosis and research, it's also heavily watched over by laws like HIPAA in the United States, GDPR in Europe, and India's DPDPA that control how and where patient info is stored and used.

This is where FL shines: It lets hospitals, clinics, and research centers team up on training AI models without ever sending out patient info. Each place keeps their data on-site, training their models locally and just sharing encrypted updates. This way, they can work together while still keeping patient privacy intact. For example, think about spotting brain tumors through MRI scans. Hospitals can use FL to create a joint diagnostic model by training on their own scan data. While the model can learn from a wide range of data, the actual scans stay on the hospital's secure servers, which keeps them compliant with privacy standards.

The perks here are pretty great. First off, the accuracy of diagnoses goes up because FL models learn from all sorts of patient backgrounds and imaging types, making them stronger at picking out rare or tricky cases. Plus, with patient data staying put, healthcare providers can meet their legal and ethical duties while still jumping into advanced research. And it also opens the door for bigger collaborations across hospitals or even countries, letting us push medical science forward without setting up giant data banks that could risk privacy breaches.

2.7.2 Moving over to finance

This is an industry where things get really sensitive. We're talking customer transactions, account info, and credit history—all heavily regulated data. Because of strict privacy laws and the competitive nature of the field, banks often can't share data even when working together could help combat fraud, understand risks, or improve customer service.

Federated Learning comes through again, giving financial institutions a safe way to work together without risking any confidentiality. It allows AI models to be trained on data from different places without ever moving that raw data around. This creates chances for smarter, more reliable financial systems while staying within the regulations.

One good example is in credit risk modeling. Several banks can use FL to train models together that assess how risky a borrower might be by learning from a variety of data—like transaction habits and payment history—from different places. Since no raw info is shared, each bank keeps full control of its own customer data while gaining a more accurate and diverse view of risk.

The benefits here are solid, too. For one, improved fraud detection is a big deal. By pooling their intelligence without sharing data, FL helps create models that can spot unusual patterns and suspicious activities, even if they're not obvious when looking at just one bank's info. Plus, training on a broader set of data improves how well the model can assess risk, making it fairer, especially for customers with thinner credit records. And last but not least, FL lines up with all those financial privacy regulations, so institutions can still innovate while playing by the rules.

2.7.3 Mobile devices and edge computing

As our gadgets like smartphones, wearables, and IoT devices get better, there's a big chance to make them not just smart but also able to adapt in real-time. These devices are always collecting sensitive info, like where we go, how we type, what we say, and our health stats. But sending all that data up to the cloud to train AI models raises some serious red flags about privacy and speed.

That's where FL comes in. It lets devices learn right on the spot, so they can pick up on user behavior without ever sharing raw data with a central server. The outcome? Super personalized user experiences that keep your info private and still work fast. A great example is Google's Gboard keyboard, which uses FL to get better at predicting what you'll type next. It learns from how you input text—like your typing style and preferences—but your actual words never leave your phone. So, the keyboard gets smarter as you use it, without risking your privacy.

Some key benefits:

You get a Personalized User Experience: FL lets devices learn from how you use them, so features like recommendations and voice assistants become more tailored to you.

There's less Cloud Dependency: Since training happens right on the device, you don't need constant internet access or cloud storage all the time, which saves bandwidth and speeds things up.

Data Privacy is Stronger: Stuff like your messages or health info stays safely on your device, helping companies stick to privacy laws and keeping your details confidential.

2.7.4 Switching gears to manufacturing and industrial IoT

We're in the era of Industry 4.0. Data-driven decisions are key in modern manufacturing. Factories produce tons of data—from how machines run to how production flows—that can be used to boost efficiency, cut downtime, and keep maintenance on track. But sharing this sensitive operational data can really raise eyebrows about confidentiality and security.

Federated Learning offers a solid solutions here it allows different factories and productions line to work together to train smart models without putting their secret data out. This way, companies can take into valuable insights while keeping their sensitive information safe. One standout example in predictive maintenance using FL. Different factories can team up to create models that sports early signs of equipment's wear and potential failures by looking and more. These models keep getting better as they learn together helping each facilities dodging costly breakdowns without sharing raw information.

Key benefits include:

Reducing downtime and maintenance cost by catching the problem before they happen. FL powered models helped keeping these equipment's running smoothly, which boosts the productivity.

Protecting proprietary data: Every factory keeps its control over its own data and trade secrets ensuring that valuable information will stay hidden.

Scalable industrial integration: FL can be easily applied across many manufacturing sites enabling organization to scale their insights while adjusting the local setup and condition.

2.7.5 Smart cities and intelligent transportation

As cities evolved into smart and more interconnected spaces, they increasingly tap into data forms various sources like traffic cameras environmental sensors, public transport system and connected Vehicles. While these data can transfer urban planning and mobility for the better, it also brings up importance to important issues surrounding centralized surveillance and data privacy.

Federated learning is an exciting solution, these approaches allow various city department, municipalities, and private transport providers to collaborate and develop ML models without needing to share the raw data. In doing so, FL empowers cities to become more intelligent and efficient while safeguarding the privacy of their cities. One of the most important and impactful applications of FL in smart cities is real time traffic flow prediction rather than funneling all data to the central server, district zone within a city can utilize FL to jointly train models with their local sensor data. These models can aid in anticipating conjunctions, optimizing traffic signals, and planning alternative routes, thereby enhancing overall traffic flow throughout the city without compromising the privacy of a specific location.

Key benefits:

- Smarter Traffic Management: FL enables cities to develop systems that alleviate congestion, reduce commute times, and lessen emissions, fostering a smoother and greener urban environment.
- Enhanced Public Safety: By utilizing distributed data from emergency services, smart streetlights, or connected vehicles, FL facilitates quicker response times and proactive safety measures without needing to centralize sensitive data.
- Privacy-First Urban Intelligence: Since data remains at its original source, citizen privacy is well-protected. FL effectively balances the pursuit of data-driven innovation with the ethical use of data.

2.7.6 Education and e-learning

As online and digital learning continues to play a vital role in education, various platforms are collecting wealth of data on how students engage with content from quiz attempts to video interactions and the amount of time spent on a single lesson. This data offers valuable insights for enforcing learning outcomes, but it also brings forth significant privacy concerns, particularly regarding sensitive information such as student performance, behavior, and progress.

FL presents a promising solution. It allows multiple school, universities, or E learning platform to collaboratively create intelligent models without having to share raw data. This means that we can develop smart, more personalized educational tools while ensuring the student data remains private and secure.

A great example for FL in education sector is the development of personalized recommendation system that suggest customized learning paths. These systems are trained using interactions data from student at various institution, ensuring that no personal data ever leaves a student's device or the school network. The outcome is a model that comprehends a wide array of learning behavior and adapt accordingly, ultimately benefiting all learners.

Key benefits:

- Personalized Learning Experiences: FL enables adaptive learning platforms to recommend content, courses, or exercises tailored to individual learning styles and progress, fostering a more engaging and effective educational journey.
- Student Privacy Protection: As all training occurs locally and only model updates are shared—rather than raw performance data—student privacy is preserved, helping institutions adhere to regulations like FERPA, GDPR, and various national education data laws.
- Cross-Institution Collaboration: Educational institutions can come together to enhance learning technologies without needing to centralize data. This collaboration spurs innovation while respecting data ownership and local policies.

2.7.7 Cybersecurity and FL

In our interconnected world cyber security threats often emerges simultaneously across different systems, network, and organization. From malware outbreak to data breach, these threats can spread quickly defending against them necessarily needs both speed and teamwork. This is where the FL shines, rather than requesting organization to consolidate their sensitive system logs or security data in a central hub FL enables them to collaboratively train cyber security models in a decentralized way. Each organization keeps its data local while still contributing to the development of a shared, intelligent model that is capable of detecting a malware, identifying intrusion, and flagging unusual behavior. This approach enhances collective defense while protecting individual privacy and adhering to the security policies.

Use case

One compelling application of FL in cyber security is the joint training of malware detection system. Imagine several companies working together to refine a shared model that learns from behavioral patterns on their endpoints which also includes user activities, system performance, Network traffic without ever exposing raw logs or confidential infrastructure data More adaptable system that benefits all parties involved.

Key benefits:

Enhanced threat detection: By learning from a Diverse array of data across multiple organization, FL boosts the model's capability to identify both known and emerging threats, even though that may not be observed in any single data set.

Early warning system: FL facilitates quicker recognition of global attack patterns, helping the participants detect threat sooner and coordinate their responses more effectively.

2.8 CHALLENGES AND FUTURE DIRECTIONS IN FL

FL is definitely a big step towards building AIsystems that focus on data privacy and decentralized intelligence, but it's still You got a long way to go. There are a bunch of technical and practical issues that are holding it back from really taking off out there. We need to tackle these problems if we want to rely and really make the most of FL in real life settings.

One of the biggest challenges is the variety of devices people are using. You've got everything from powerful servers down to regular smartphones and low-end IoT devices. This mix makes it tricky to keep models running smoothly since some devices may not keep up or finish their tasks when they're supposed to. Then there's the issue with data. Each client has its own data that's usually collected under different conditions, so it ends up being a bit all over the place. This non-IID data complicates training, leading to models that might work great for some users but not for others. So, it's rather a mixed bag.

Another point is the communication load. FL systems need to keep chatting with a central server to swap model updates. This means even though we're avoiding moving raw data around, it still puts a strain on networks, especially if the models are big or updates are frequent. This can slow things down and drain energy, which is a hassle in areas with weak connectivity. Even though FL is built to safeguard user data by keeping it on the device, privacy isn't a done deal. Skilled attackers can still grab sensitive info from model updates using sneaky tricks like gradient leakage. There's also the risk of data poisoning, where some users might try to mess things up by sending bad updates. Researchers are looking into solutions like DPand secure computations, but those come with some trade-offs in efficiency.

When it comes to real-world devices, they aren't the most reliable. Some go offline, run out of battery, or just don't respond. This inconsistency makes it tough to keep the training on track and accurate. So, figuring out how to design systems that can handle this without losing effectiveness is something researchers are still working on.

One big bump in the road for FL is the lack of standard ways to measure and compare it. In regular ML, it's usually pretty easy to test and compare models with shared datasets.

But FL is more complicated, especially with that non-IID data where devices might have totally different types of info. This variation makes measuring performance consistently tricky. Most current FL studies use their own datasets or simulations, which makes it hard to reproduce results or benchmark across the board.

For FL to move ahead, we really need some common evaluation methods and shared datasets that reflect really non-IID conditions. Plus, we need to establish standards for measuring things like accuracy, fairness, and privacy. Having these benchmarks would not only speed up innovation but also give organizations a clearer idea of what to expect when adopting FL.

Another challenge is keeping up with all the data privacy laws out there, like GDPR in Europe or HIPAA [32] in the United States. Even though FL keeps data decentralized and private, it still has to follow strict legal guidelines. This means organizations using FL need to be transparent about how the model works and can be audited for compliance. So, compliance has to be part of the design from the get-go, not something to worry about later. As FL keeps growing, we're seeing some interesting trends pop up that are tackling real-world issues while improving performance and collaboration. Personalized FL is looking to cater to each user's unique habits and preferences. So, for example, your phone could learn your typing style or what apps you use without ever sharing your data.

Cross-silo FL is all about collaboration among solid data holders like hospitals or banks. They can work together to train models without sharing raw data, which is great for confidentiality. Think about it: Hospitals can develop a diagnostic model together without risking patient privacy. Then there's FTL. It helps when different clients have related tasks but varying amounts of data. This lets them use knowledge from one task to boost another, which is super helpful when labeled data is scarce.

Federated reinforcement learning is a new twist combining FL and reinforcement learning to create a smart, Decentralized decision making system. Agent like robots can learn locally and share strategies, which is pretty cool from complex task like navigation and recommendations.

2.9 CONCLUSION AND SUMMARY

Federated learning is shaking things up in ML by letting different parties train models together without showing all the data into one central spot. This is super important especially for fields like healthcare and finance, where privacy and security are big deal.

So, here's how it works: Instead of sending raw data around, clients keep their data local and just share updates about the model with a central server. This way, user privacy is protected, and it still allows for good teamwork. The back-and-forth between clients and the server, along with algorithms like Federated Averaging (FedAvg), is what holds everything together. But rolling out FL isn't without its hiccups. There are challenges like differences in client data, clients who aren't always available, and issues with communication efficiency. Figuring these out is crucial for making FL work on a larger scale.

We need to keep improving how FL is designed and optimized to boost its reliability and usefulness across different application. FL can be broken down into few main types: HFL, VFL, and Federated Transfer learning (FTL). Each type handles different ways of sharing data. HFL is great when clients have similar features but different data points, like when different organizations work together. VFL is for when clients have the same identifiers but different sets of data, which is useful in places like banking or online shopping.

FTL helps out when clients have totally different datasets by sharing knowledge in a way that's still secure. Choosing the right type of FL depends on things like how the data is structured, what privacy rules are in place, and what goals you're aiming for. Picking the best option means you can get the most out of the data while keeping it safe and compliant with privacy laws. Good communication is super important for making FL work well at scale. Approaches like picking which clients to include, compressing models, and updating them regularly can really boost communication.

These methods cut down on bandwidth use, speed up how quickly models learn, and make the whole system more robust. As FL gets better, combining efficient communication with ways to keep data safe and minimize energy use will be essential for it to really take off. In the end, FL is changing the game for data-driven tech in tons of areas. It allows for collaboration that respects privacy, overcoming a lot of the problems that come with centralized data processing. Whether it's for diagnosing medical conditions, assessing financial risks, or smart tech at the edge, FL is becoming a key part of building secure, scalable, and ethically responsible AI. As research moves forward and more people start using it, FL is set to lead the next wave of innovation while keeping trust, transparency, and data control front and center.

REFERENCES

[1] Ministry of Electronics and Information Technology, "The Digital Personal Data Protection Act, 2023," Government of India, Aug. 2023. [Online]. Available: https://prsindia.org/billtrack/digital-personal-data-protection-bill-2023

[2] R. Ramanathan and A. Rajaraman, "Data Localization and India's Evolving Data Protection Framework," *Journal of Law and Technology*, vol. 18, no. 2, pp. 125–139, 2024.

[3] R. Shokri and V. Shmatikov, "Privacy-Preserving Deep Learning," *Proc. ACM Conf. Computer and Communications Security (CCS)*, 2015.

[4] P. Kairouz and H. B. McMahan, et al. "Advances and Open Problems in Federated Learning," *arXiv preprint arXiv:1912.04977*, 2019, https://arxiv.org/abs/1912.04977

[5] J. Kairouz et al., "Advances and Open Problems in Federated Learning," *Foundations and Trends in Machine Learning*, vol. 14, no. 1–2, pp. 1–210, 2021, doi: 10.1561/2200000083. www.nowpublishers.com/article/Details/MAL-083

[6] P. Ghosh and N. Verma, "Privacy and Accountability in India's Digital Ecosystem: Challenges and Regulatory Responses," *IEEE Technol. Soc. Mag.*, vol. 43, no. 1, pp. 15–23, Mar. 2024,

[7] R. Pandey, A. Joshi, and N. Mukherjee, "Privacy-Aware Machine Learning in Indian Enterprises: A Survey of Use Cases and Challenges," *Indian Journal of Data Science*, vol. 5, no. 1, pp. 24–32, 2023.

[8] K. N. Ramesh and S. Patel, "Edge Readiness for Federated Learning in Indian Manufacturing Industries," *IEEE Internet of Things Journal*, vol. 10, no. 2, pp. 1120–1129, Feb. 2024, doi: 10.1109/MTS.2024.1234567.

[9] Ministry of Electronics and Information Technology, "The Digital Personal Data Protection Act, 2023," Government of India, Aug. 2023. [Online]. Available: www.meity.gov.in

[10] N. Goyal and V. Shah, "Security Enhancements in Federated Learning: Legal Implications in Finance and Healthcare," *Cybersecurity and AI Law Review*, vol. 7, no. 1, pp. 55–68, 2024.

[11] J. Kairouz et al., "Advances and Open Problems in Federated Learning," *Foundations and Trends in Machine Learning*, vol. 14, no. 1–2, pp. 1–210, 2021, doi: 10.1561/2200000083.

[12] A. Bhattacharya, "Compliance Readiness for AI Deployments in Indian Corporates," *Indian Law and Technology Review*, vol. 11, no. 3, pp. 88–97, 2023.

[13] H. B. McMahan et al., "Communication-Efficient Learning of Deep Networks from Decentralized Data," *Proc. 20th Int. Conf. Artificial Intelligence and Statistics (AISTATS)*, 2017. https://proceedings.mlr.press/v54/mcmahan17a.html

[14] T. Li, A. K. Sahu, M. Zaheer, M. Sanjabi, A. Talwalkar, and V. Smith, "Federated Optimization in Heterogeneous Networks," *Proceedings of MLSys*, 2020. https://arxiv.org/abs/1812.06127

[15] S. Karimireddy et al., "SCAFFOLD: Stochastic Controlled Averaging for Federated Learning," *Proc. Int. Conf. Machine Learning (ICML)*, 2020. https://proceedings.mlr.press/v119/karimireddy20a.html
[16] J. Wang, Z. Liu, and X. Liang, "Tackling the Objective Inconsistency Problem in Heterogeneous Federated Optimization," *Advances in Neural Information Processing Systems (NeurIPS)*, 2020. https://arxiv.org/abs/2007.07481
[17] J. Konecny, H. B. McMahan, F. X. Yu, P. Richtarik, A. T. Suresh, and D. Bacon, "Federated Learning: Strategies for Improving Communication Efficiency," *arXiv preprint arXiv:1610.05492*, 2016. https://arxiv.org/abs/1610.05492
[18] H. B. McMahan and D. Ramage, "Federated Learning: Collaborative Machine Learning without Centralized Training Data," *Google AI Blog*, 2017. https://research.google/blog/federated-learning-collaborative-machine-learning-without-centralized-training-data/
[19] TensorFlow Federated, Open-source framework for machine learning on decentralized data supporting research and simulation in federated learning, www.tensorflow.org/federated
[20] *PySyft*, OpenMined, GitHub repository, Apache-2.0 License (accessed Dec. 2025). Available: https://github.com/OpenMined/PySyft?utm_source=chatgpt.com
[21] Flower. (n.d.). *A friendly federated AI framework for building and deploying federated learning systems*. Retrieved from https://flower.dev
[22] FedML. (n.d.). *FedML: Unified and scalable machine learning library for federated and distributed learning*. Retrieved from https://fedml.ai
[23] H. B. McMahan, E. Moore, D. Ramage, S. Hampson and B. A. y Arcas, "Communication-Efficient Learning of Deep Networks from Decentralized Data," *Proceedings of the 20th International Conference on Artificial Intelligence and Statistics (AISTATS)*, pp. 1273–1282, 2017. https://proceedings.mlr.press/v54/mcmahan17a.html
[24] P. Kairouz, H. B. McMahan, B. Avent, A. Bellet, M. Bennis, A. Nitin Bhagoji, K. Bonawitz, et al., "Advances and Open Problems in Federated Learning," *Foundations and Trends® in Machine Learning*, vol. 14, no. 1–2, pp. 1–210, 2021. www.nowpublishers.com/article/Details/MAL-083
[25] K. Bonawitz et al., "Towards Federated Learning at Scale: System Design," in *Proceedings of Machine Learning and Systems (MLSys)*, pp. 374–388, 2019. https://arxiv.org/abs/1902.01046
[26] T. Li, A. K. Sahu, M. Zaheer, M. Sanjabi, A. Talwalkar and V. Smith, "Federated Optimization in Heterogeneous Networks," in *Proceedings of Machine Learning and Systems (MLSys)*, pp. 429–450, 2020. https://arxiv.org/abs/1812.06127
[27] C. Dwork, "Differential Privacy," in *Automata, Languages and Programming (ICALP)*, vol. 4052, pp. 1–12, 2006. https://link.springer.com/chapter/10.1007/11787006_1
[28] C. Gentry, "Fully Homomorphic Encryption Using Ideal Lattices," in *Proceedings of the 41st ACM Symposium on Theory of Computing (STOC)*, pp. 169–178, 2009. https://dl.acm.org/doi/10.1145/1536414.1536440
[29] A. C. Yao, "Protocols for Secure Computations," in *23rd Annual Symposium on Foundations of Computer Science (SFCS)*, pp. 160–164, 1982. https://ieeexplore.ieee.org/document/4568388
[30] Q. Yang, Y. Liu, T. Chen, and Y. Tong, "Federated Machine Learning: Concept and Applications," *ACM Transactions on Intelligent Systems and Technology (TIST)*, vol. 10, no. 2, pp. 1–19, 2019,https://dl.acm.org/doi/10.1145/3298981.
[31] T. Li, A. K. Sahu, A. Talwalkar, and V. Smith, "Federated Learning: Challenges, Methods, and Future Directions," *IEEE Signal Processing Magazine*, vol. 37, no. 3, pp. 50–60, 2020. https://doi.org/10.1109/MSP.2020.2975749
[32] C. Dwork and A. Roth, "The Algorithmic Foundations of Differential Privacy," *Foundations and Trends in Theoretical Computer Science*, vol. 9, no. 3–4, 2014. www.nowpublishers.com/article/Details/TCS-042

Chapter 3

Federated learning for fraud detection and risk mitigation

Himani Tyagi, Mohit Kumar, and Himanshu

3.1 INTRODUCTION

3.1.1 Overview of fraud and risk challenges

Fraud is not just simple deception, but rather an evolving, fast paced, and agile threat in a digital world that is increasing in ubiquity. For many industries, such as financial services, e-commerce, healthcare, and insurance, the volume of transactions and user interactions provides ample opportunity to exploit fraudulent behavior to businesses' detriment or theft. Fraudsters are easily finding ways to use powerful tools – i.e. automated scripts, stolen identities, synthetic accounts, and even deep learning models – and to evade traditional actions taken to prevent or stop the fraud.

Fraud does not pose risks just directly displacing money, but it has recovery risks, reputational risks, customer attrition, regulatory risks, or other financial losses including fines or civil penalties. The types of frauds in the case can be identified as given in Table 3.1.

However, global payment fraud losses exceeded $32 billion in 2021 and are forecasted to exceed $40 billion by 2027 (Juniper Research, 2022). These numbers indicated the need for mechanisms to detect fraud better, faster, and smarter, and in real-time.

Additionally, fraud patterns are incredibly dynamic. What may be effective today may not be effective tomorrow. Because fraud detection models rely on patterns in data, they must be continually refreshed with new information, which requires varied and relevant data sources, but sharing this sensitive information across organizations raises important issues related to user privacy, ownership, and compliance with regulations.

3.1.2 Need for advanced solutions

Conventional fraud detection systems utilize centralized machine learning models which take data (or aggregated approximations) from multiple sources, move it into one location for training. Table 3.1 provides the categorization of the fraud-related activities with the example of each. Centralized machine learning may have advantages with respect to accuracy and model tuning; however, there are three, significant limitations to this approach:

1. Data Privacy Legislation – laws like General Data Protection Regulation (GDPR) in Europe and the California Consumer Privacy Act (CCPA) in the United States, are placing increasing restrictions on how consumer data is collected, stored, and shared. Sharing raw data across institutions may violate legislation.
2. Security and Trust – centralized repositories are an attractive target to cybercriminals, and institutions are more hesitant to share raw data with others, even if it is a trusted company.

DOI: 10.1201/9781003660330-3

Table 3.1 Categories of fraud-related risks with examples highlighting their direct and indirect impact on organizations

Risk type	*Description*	*Example*
Financial loss	Direct monetary loss due to fraudulent transactions or scams.	Unauthorized withdrawal of funds.
Reputational risk	Damage to the organization's credibility or public trust.	Data breach exposing customer info.
Regulatory penalty	Legal action or fines due to non-compliance with regulations.	GDPR fine for mishandling data.
Operational impact	Disruption in services or resources diverted to fraud mitigation.	Service downtime during investigation.
Customer attrition	Loss of users due to dissatisfaction or fear post-fraud.	Customers closing accounts.

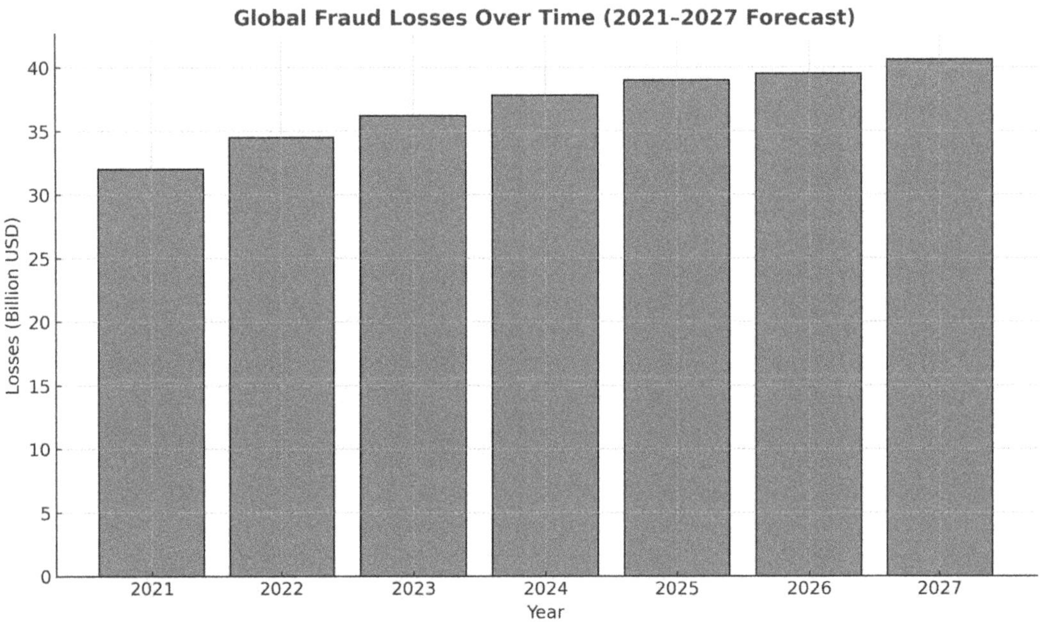

Figure 3.1 Projected global payment fraud losses. (From Juniper Research, 2022.)

3. Operational and technical inefficiencies – There is a complex infrastructure, cost, and latencies to explain once you move large volumes of data between organizations.

Figure 3.1 provides the insights of the projected global payment fraud losses which is providing the future payment losses due to fraud cases. With these limitations in mind, there has been a growing interest in decentralized and privacy-preserving machine learning in both academic and practice. One such advancement, emerging as a clear innovation is federated learning (FL). FL allows institutions to train a shared model, collaborating without needing to share raw data. Each institutional participant, or FL node, processes the data at their site, ultimately exchanging only encrypted model updates with a central aggregator.

This framework maintains privacy while improving scalability because the data never leaves the point of origin. Most significantly, it enables collaboration among institutions that would otherwise have remained distinct or silos, due to privacy and competition.

Consider a consortium of banks $\sum_{k=1}^{K} nk$ who detect fraudulent schemes being perpetrated across various institutions, or a set of healthcare providers capturing fraudulent billing behavior without compromising patient confidentiality. FL enables such collaboration.

In the remainder of this chapter, we will explore how FL works, what makes it distinctively amenable for fraud detection, the architectures that support it, the challenges and opportunities, case studies and future directions, visualizing how FL will change fraud detection and risk management across sectors.

3.2 FL: AN OVERVIEW

3.2.1 What is FL?

FL is a decentralized machine learning approach launched by Google in 2016, originally intended to alleviate privacy concerns related to mobile data processing (McMahan et al., 2017). FL is based on a simple concept: Rather than sending raw data to a central server to train a model, we send the model to the data sources (clients), they train the model on their data, and then they send updates (either gradients or model weights) back to the central server. Figure 3.2 provides the basic architecture of the federated learning in which a model is initialize and then train on local data and aggregated back to the global model.

A typical FL workflow is as follows:

1. The central server initializes a global model.
2. The model is sent to the client devices or institutions participating in training.
3. Each client trains the model on its private data.
4. The clients send the locally trained models back to the server.
5. The server aggregates the updates to improve the global model.
6. Steps 1–5 are completed iteratively until convergence.

Mathematically, FL optimizes a global objective function by minimizing the sum of local loss functions over the distributed datasets:

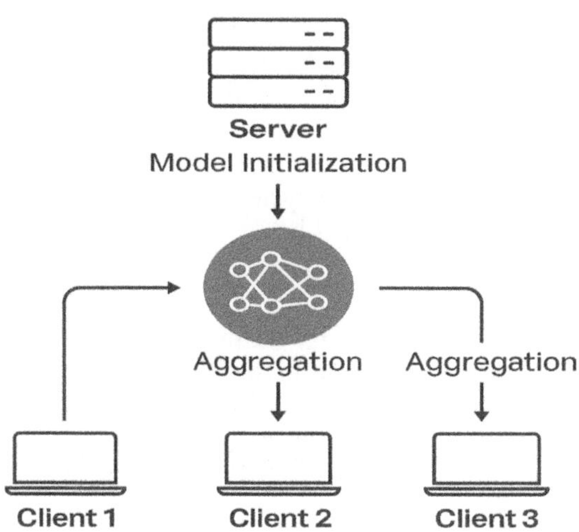

Figure 3.2 Basic workflow in Federated learning (FL), where a central server initializes a model, clients train locally on private data, and updates are securely aggregated back into a global model.

$$\min_{w} F(w) = \sum_{k=1}^{K} p_k F_k(w)$$

Where:

- w: global model parameters to be optimized
- K: number of clients (devices or nodes)
- P_k: weight of client k, typically $P_K = n_K/n$, where n_K is the number of data points on client k and n is the total number of data points across all clients
- $F_K(w)$: local loss function for client k, defined as:

$$F_k(w) = \frac{1}{n_k} \sum_{i=1}^{n_K} l(w; x_i^{(k)}, y_i^{(k)})$$

loss on sample i from client k

This decentralized approach addresses a range of challenges in scenarios where data is sensitive, fragmented, or geographically distributed.

3.2.2 Why FL fits fraud detection

The problem of fraud detection has unique characteristics, along with several unique characteristics about its solution; therefore it naturally lends itself to FL:

- Data Siloing: Fraud data is often siloed across banks, hospitals, e-commerce platforms, etc. With FL, institutions can collectively train models without centralizing the data.
- Rare Events: Fraud is often rare; as such, there is class imbalance in the data. If institutions collaborate to pool how much insight can be gain through FL, institutions can increase fraud detection without losing confidence through privacy.
- Regulated Industries: Police and military, finance, healthcare and insurance are highly regulated. If institutions are complying with laws like Health Insurance Portability and Accountability Act (HIPAA), General Data Protection Regulation (GDPR) and Payment Card Industry Data Security Standard (PCI-DSS), federated learning (FL) can help by allowing sensitive data to remain within the institutions' protected boundaries and comply with regulatory constructs.
- Adversarial Environments: Fraud is always evolving, and it does this fast. FL is decentralized, which creates faster learning cycle outcomes, learning styles and catch emerging fraud across domains more quickly.

To visualize this scenario, think of an abuser successfully exploiting the same type of fraud across multiple credit card entities. Ordinarily, these credit card entities will detect the fraud completely independently – and even better, they may detect it late. In FL, the common model can learn very quickly the nature of this cross-institution fraud while keeping the customer data's privacy. Figure 3.3 provides the structure for the collaborative fraud detection via federated learning for various domains without sharing the raw data.

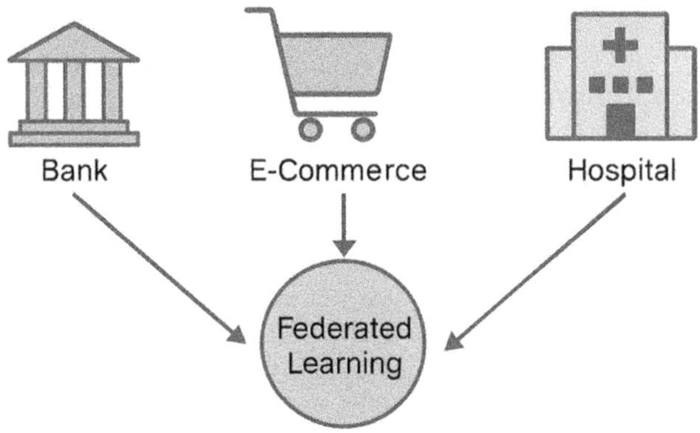

Figure 3.3 Collaborative fraud detection through federated learning across domains such as banking, e-commerce, and healthcare, where each participant contributes insights without sharing raw data.

Table 3.2 Comparative analysis of privacy-preserving techniques

Technique	*Description*	*Strengths*	*Limitations*
Federated Learning (FL)	Distributed training without raw data sharing	Scalable, privacy-preserving, supports real-world collaboration	Communication cost, requires secure aggregation
HE	Computations on encrypted data	Strong mathematical privacy	Computationally expensive, limited ML support
SMPC	Joint computation without revealing inputs	Rigorous privacy guarantees	High latency, complex protocols
DP	Adds noise to data or outputs to mask individuals	Formal privacy guarantees, good for analytics	Trade-off between utility and privacy
Data Anonymization	Removes identifiable information	Simple to implement	Vulnerable to re-identification attacks

3.2.3 Comparison with other privacy-preserving techniques

While FL is a powerful privacy-preserving machine learning technique, it's not the only one. It's important to understand how it compares with other approaches:

FL is unique because it can be directly applied to solve real-world problems, such as fraud detection, where both privacy and model quality are essential. In practice, FL will normally be combined with other methods like DP and Secure Aggregation to increase trust and security – we will explore this further. Table 3.2 provides the comparative analysis of the different techniques of privacy preserving mechanisms.

3.3 APPLICATION SCENARIOS IN FRAUD DETECTION

3.3.1 Banking and financial transactions

The financial sector is probably the most active front in fraud detection. There is an immense spectrum of fraud types from credit card fraud to account takeovers, etc., but fraud can happen in many ways. Banks have long used centralized machine learning systems to monitor transactions and detect suspicious behaviors. However, as fraudsters become more crafty, cooperation among financial institutions is becoming more of a necessity.

FL would allow banks, credit unions, and payment processors to work together while respecting confidentiality agreements and regulatory standards. An example would be a consortium of banks would train a common model that looked for anomalies in transaction patterns that could span across institutional boundaries. This would be valuable for identifying a criminal conspiracy that perpetrates small-scale crimes in multiple locations to evade detection, a practice commonly referred to as "fraud sharding."

Additionally, FL allows different financial institutions to continually improve fraud detection models with localized information. A bank on the Asian market might see a pattern not relevant to the global model and they contribute to the existing global model allowing it to learn from all market contexts.

Example use case: The Federated AI Technology Enabler (FATE) framework developed by WeBank in China is an example of how FL can be leveraged in conjunction with banks, credit unions, and payment systems. In practice, WeBank's system allows other institutional partners with which they are collaborating to train a joint fraud detection model with those other partners while maintaining their confidentiality and privacy.

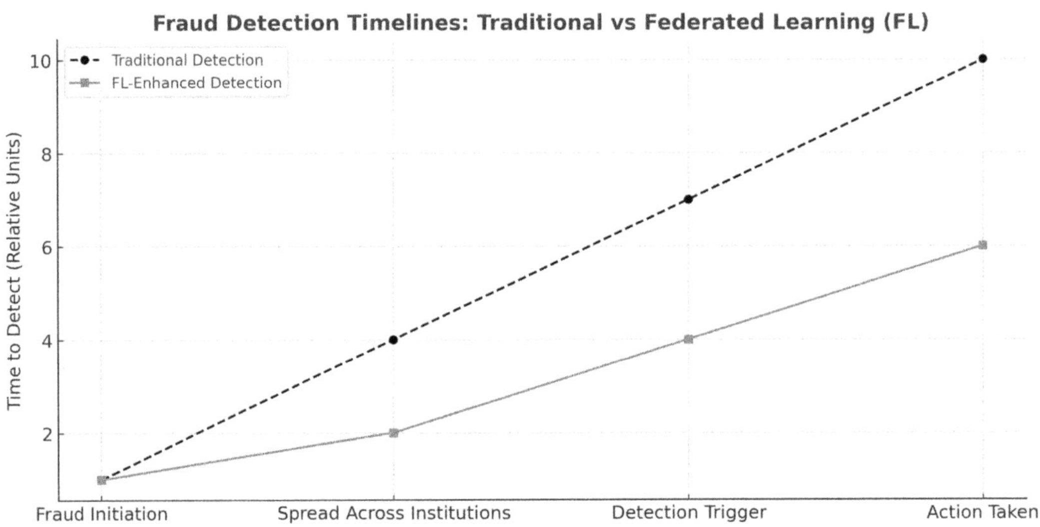

Figure 3.4 Comparison of fraud detection timelines – federated learning (FL) enables faster detection across institutions compared to traditional isolated approaches.

3.3.2 E-commerce platforms

E-commerce fraud has been increasing rapidly, especially during the rise in online shopping. Common schemes are fake returns, promotion abuse, synthetic identity accounts, and account hijacking. Commonly collected pairs of behavioral data (e.g., click histograms), transaction history, and device fingerprints are sensitive behavioral signals and may be used as an asset in conjunction with other datasets. Figure 3.4 provides the comparative analysis of the timelines of the fraud detection across multiple institutions with the traditional approaches.

The larger platforms (e.g., Amazon, Alibaba, etc.) have strong in-house fraud detection models. Smaller vendors, or third-party sellers and payment processers operate largely in silos, allowing clear opportunities for fraud.

FL will help provide models together across merchants and online platforms while allowing them to not directly share customer information.

There are two ways that FL is beneficial compared to traditional model building. FL will help detect cross-platform fraud. Often, a fraudster will "test" the consumption of a stolen credit card on one website, before going to a different website to fulfill their purchase. A federated model able to capture many retail purchases, such as sharing a model, may detect this abnormal "test-and-go" behavior.

From a privacy standpoint; FL continues to be an advantage in this context because behavioral data is very identifying and will allow local training in terms of customer identification. FL's local training protection, plus examples of additional protections such as DP and Secure Aggregation facilitate and loosen the restrictions of e-commerce datasets.

3.3.3 Healthcare fraud

Healthcare fraud encompasses upcoding, billing for phantom services, kickbacks, unnecessary procedures – resulting in potentially billions of dollars lost each year. Unlike banking or e-commerce, the stakes here are not just financial, but ethical and life-dependent.

Healthcare data also falls under many privacy related laws, like the Privacy Rules under HIPAA in the United States and the GDPR in Europe. This can severely limit health companies from sharing data with hospitals and insurance to regulators. Federate Learning represents a novel mechanism in which fraud detection models can be trained on medical billing across providers while the patient record is never moved.

Now envision a group of hospitals and insurance working together to detect billing anomalies due to possible fraudulent activity. FL allows the development of more generalizable models across providers and regions. Additionally, local learning allows institutions to determine patterns of fraud which are relevant to their own operational areas.

Technical Challenge: Healthcare datasets are often non-independent and identically distributed (non-IID). For example, one hospital's billing structure or demographics may vary from another. FL frameworks need to develop specifications to address data non-homogeneity.

3.3.4 Insurance sector

Insurance fraud comes in many different ways: Claims that are not true, exaggerated losses, staged accidents, and even identity fraud. Fraud is not an easy problem to solve because the insurance industry is not a centralized network, it is a decentralized network of agents, brokers, underwriters, and third-party investigators. They do not even all speak the same language. It would be difficult, if not impossible, to get insurance agents to share information about fraudulent customers (unless there was data-sharing agreement). FL provides a

Table 3.3 Sector-wise comparison of traditional and FL-based fraud detection models, with emphasis on privacy benefits and collaborative intelligence

Sector	*Traditional Model Limitation*	*Federated Learning (FL) Advantage*	*Privacy Level*
Banking	Siloed detection leads to fragmented fraud patterns	Enables cross-bank fraud pattern recognition (e.g., sharded fraud schemes)	High
E-commerce	Limited fraud context across platforms, late detection	FL helps catch multi-site fraud like test-and-run card abuse	High
Healthcare	Data-sharing restrictions hinder fraud analysis	FL allows collaborative billing fraud detection without moving patient data	Very High
Insurance	Decentralized players don't coordinate on fraud detection	Enables joint detection of repeat offenders while preserving sensitive claim data	High

mechanism for insurers to write data models to predict fraud collaboratively without sharing customers' data with their competitors. Auto insurers could share information about suspicious claim behaviors without having to give away very sensitive policyholder details. This type of collaborative intelligence can be useful for determining repeat offenders who try to abuse numerous providers (instead of working with a single provider). Table 3.3 provides the comparison of traditional and FL based fraud detection model along with the benefits of the privacy.

Another benefit of FL is that it allows the models to operate at the edge (a mobile claim-reporting app) instead of working off of only a recent subset of claims. This allows for real-time fraud detection and lessens the time when an insurance provider takes to respond (also improves customer trust!).

3.4 ARCHITECTURE OF FEDERATED FRAUD DETECTION SYSTEMS

3.4.1 High-level system design

At a high level, a FL system designed for fraud detection has three main components:

1. Clients (or nodes): The entities participating in FL hold local private datasets. Clients could be banks, hospital systems, on-line stores (for example, PayPal), or insurance companies. Each one has its own data silo and operational hurdles to deal with.
2. Central Aggregator: This is the server (or coordinating node) that controls the training rounds and sends the global model to the clients, receives updates, and aggregates them together to build a better global model. The central aggregator will never see raw data but only updates to the model (that is, gradients or weights).
3. Communication Interface: This routes and controls the data being exchanged with clients during the training process in a secure, maximally efficient and privacy-preserving manner. This includes encryption, secure transport channels (like TLS), and privacy-preserving protocols.

In a typical cycle of FL for fraud detection, the following steps take place in a round-based training cycle:

- Central aggregator distributes the latest global model to the selected clients.

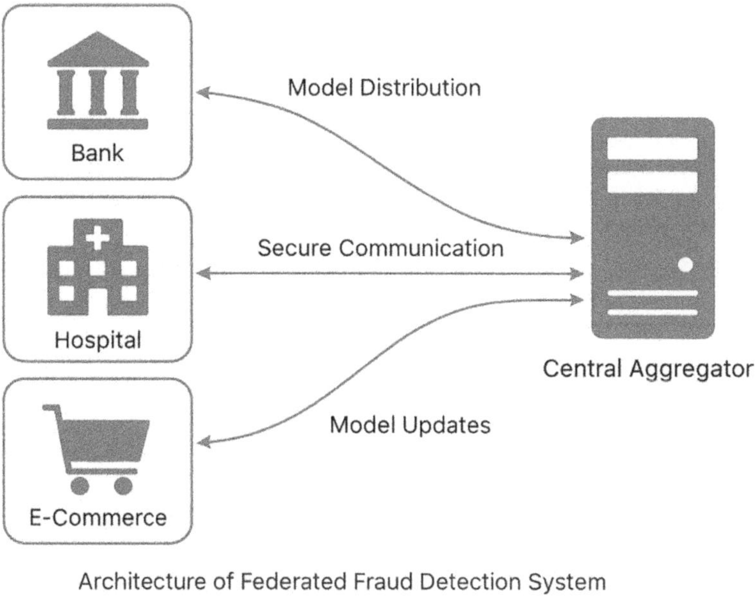

Figure 3.5 Architecture of a Federated Fraud Detection System showing clients (e.g., banks, hospitals, e-commerce platforms) securely exchanging model updates with a central aggregator without exposing raw data.

- Each client locally trains the model with their own data (e.g., fraud labels, behavioral features, transaction logs).
- Local models are sent back to the aggregator, often encrypted or perturbed for privacy reasons.
- The server aggregates the updates using methods such as Federated Averaging (FedAvg).
- Updates to the global model are redistributed to the selected clients for the next round.

The round-based cycle continues as with a given FL application, it may be convened (i.e., converge) to a global model or a defined model performance threshold. Figure 3.5 provides the architecture of the federated fraud detection for the different platforms without exposing raw data.

3.4.2 Data sources and types

Fraud detection requires rich and diverse data, and in federated environments, this data varies by institution. Here's an overview of common data types:

A lot of this input is often structured (e.g., tabular claims datasets), and when dealing with semi-structured/unstructured formats (e.g., free-text notes or transcripts of calls), you may incorporate the structured input either through federated feature extraction or a mixed method approach.

There are issues with data labeling: A lot of the time fraud is detected post-factum or misidentified altogether. Some FL frameworks used semi-supervised learning, by bootstrapping a fraud score learned from historic/fractionally labeled data. Table 3.4 provides the different sources of data and their types.

Table 3.4 Data sources and types

Domain	*Common Data Sources*	*Example Features*
Banking	Transaction logs, device IDs, geo-location, login metadata	Amount, merchant ID, transaction frequency
E-commerce	Clickstream data, cart history, return patterns, reviews	Session duration, IP reputation, product views
Healthcare	Billing records, procedure codes, provider IDs	CPT codes, claim amount, timestamp patterns
Insurance	Claims, accident reports, investigator notes	Repair costs, claim frequency, fraud scores

3.4.3 Model lifecycle in FL

The federated fraud detection model lifecycle involves the following steps, each with its unique characteristics:

1. Model Initialization

The initial model may simply be initialized randomly, or pre-trained on synthetic data, or fine-tuned based on a publicly available dataset. For fraud detection, fine-tuning the model using prior fraud cases (real or simulated) is often employed to speed convergence.

2. Client Sampling

Not all clients will communicate their updates every round. Consequently, to reduce the communication burden of FL and increase scalability, FL systems often sample clients based on some sampling strategies each iteration round. Client sampling could either be uniform or uniform or performance or fairness.

3. Local Training

Each of the selected clients will perform some localized training for a few local epochs using their private data using various optimization algorithms, such as SGD or Adam. Due to the non-IID distribution of the data across clients, clients may elect to employ personalized learning objectives that fit their local distributions better.

4. Secure Aggregation

Once clients have been successfully finalized their local training, clients send the model updates to the server using encrypted protocols (or with added noise). Secure Aggregation (e.g., Bonawitz et al., 2017) is a proposed method whereby the server cannot ascertain the individual updates from clients.

5. Model Aggregation

The server aggregates the updates using approaches such as: o FedAvg (simple averaging), o FedProx (adds a regularization term to handle non-IID data), o Trimmed Mean or Krum (advances in robust aggregation in the face of poisoned updates).

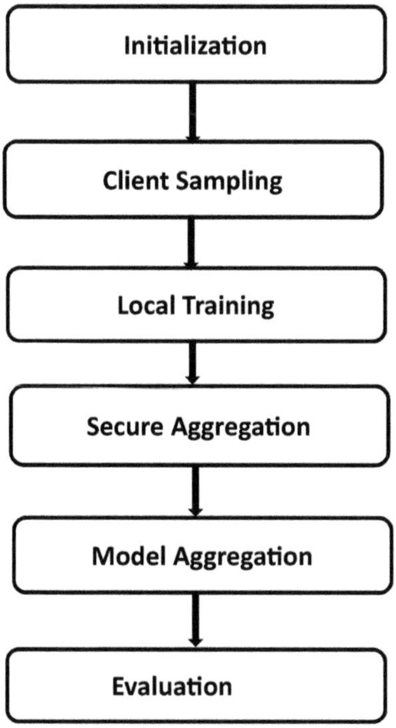

Figure 3.6 Lifecycle of fraud detection model in federated learning.

6. Evaluation and Feedback Evaluation

It can be performed centrally with a holdout dataset or locally on each client. Feedback loops may also prompt re-training if the patterns of fraud indicate a structural shift (a process called concept drift adaptation).

7. Deployment and Monitoring

Once a global model has been trained, the model can be deployed to local environments (e.g., bank Application Programming Interfaces [APIs] or hospital billing systems) or embedded in edge devices. It is important that continuous monitoring is performed to identify shifts in the model including overall drift or adversarial behavior.

Figure 3.6 provides the lifecycle of the fraud detection model in federated learning.

3.5 KEY CHALLENGES AND CONSIDERATIONS

3.5.1 Data heterogeneity

One of the biggest challenges in FL is heterogeneity, non-IID data. This is especially pertinent in fraud detection because different organizations, whether they are banks, insurers, or e-commerce manufacturers, collect and organize data differently.
To note:

- A small community bank, for example, likely deals with mostly personal checking accounts whereas a multinational global bank has many different types of transactions including corporate and international.

- An insurance company may track automobile claims differently in different geographies due to policy variations.
  This has consequences regarding model skew when training. Some clients may be over represented in the global model if they are pulling large amounts of experience from their data distributions. Therefore, when those models are actually implemented and rolled out to clients that were under representation, they will likely perform poorly. There are two potential solutions to this issue:
- Personalized FL where each client receives a locally adapted version of the global model.
- Utilizing weighted aggregation strategies which are essentially models that account for differences in size and distributions (e.g., FedProx, FedNova) (Li et al., 2020).

3.5.2 Communication overhead

In comparison to centralized machine learning in which data is sent to the model, FL makes the opposite supposition: The model travels to the data. This presents significant communication costs, particularly in fraud detection situations where you have: Coupling these issues with three major factors:

- Large model (e.g., deep neural networks to model behavior).
- High frequency updates (e.g., real-time or near real-time fraud detection).
- Many clients (e.g., thousands of branches or merchant endpoints).

Each FL round consist of:

- Broadcasting the global model to all selected clients.
- Collecting and aggregating the local updates.

This sends the following types of overhead with every update and can become a bottleneck to the whole process, particularly with edge devices or clients with intermittent connectivity. There are a number of ways to alleviate these consequences of latency as a result of communication:

- Model compression via quantize and prune payload depths.
- Update sparsification (sending only significant gradients).
- Client sampling (allowing only some clients to participate in each round).

3.5.3 Security threats

FL does not eliminate risks to security, rather it changes them. Since clients can train users outside of a central server, FL is open to malicious or compromised clients. The risks include, but are not limited to:

- Model Poisoning – A malicious client could poison the update to make corrupted updates to influence the global model. Example, the client may dilute fraud patterns to let an attack happen.
- Sybil Attacks – A single attacker could control numerous clients (sybils) to bias the training process.
- Backdoor Attack – Attackers trained in such a way that the model behaves normally in most cases allow for certain fraudulent patterns to slip through.

To the best mitigation against these threats includes:

- Robust aggregation functions that down weight tails like Krum or Median.
- Anomaly detection within the update to determine which client has anomalous behavior in regard to model updates.
- Reputation system to continually adapt the client's contribution with or without the prior knowledge of previous behavior.

3.5.4 Privacy risks

Despite keeping data on local devices, FL does not mean privacy. The model update can lead to the leak of information when the update is relatively informative. Hence, fall the following privacy risks:

- Gradient inversion attacks where an attacker can recover the input data based on the model updates (Shokri et al., 2017).
- Membership inference attacks involve the offender predicting whether a particular input was used in training procedure.

To address these challenges, several privacy-enhancing solutions are useful in FL systems:

- DP: This is an established technique for incorporating noise to updates while preserving the ability to take care and ensure the risk of re-identification is limited.
- Secure Aggregation: In this technique, the central server observes only the sum of updates instead of the updates in single form.
- Homomorphic Encryption (HE) and Secure Multi-party Computation (SMPC): These two solutions allow the users to perform secure computations on encrypted data or using clients without seeing the data.

3.6 TECHNIQUES FOR ENHANCED SECURITY AND PRIVACY

3.6.1 DP in FL

DP is a mathematical framework that ensures the output of a computation does not compromise any single individual's data. In FL, it's used to add noise to model updates, so even if someone intercepts the data, they can't reverse-engineer the inputs.

An algorithm A satisfies (ϵ,δ) –DP if for all datasets D1and D2 that differ in only one record, and for all measurable subsets S of possible outputs of A, the following holds:

$$\Pr[A(D_1) \in S] \le e^{\epsilon} \Pr[A(D_2) \in S] + \delta)$$

In FL, every device adds noise on the client side before sending updates to the server; this is referred to as local DP. Central DPoccurs on the server side, when the server adds noise during the aggregation of updates. Local DP ensures that one can derive accurate statistics, at the expense of model utility. Central DP is more efficient than local DP because it is premised on the server being semi-trusted. In structural baselines such as fraud detection algorithms, DP enables institutions to demonstrate compliance with privacy requirements, such as the GDPR, HIPAA and other's, even where they previously had little recourse to do so in a collaborative working space.

3.6.2 Secure aggregation protocols

Secure Aggregation enables the server to calculate an aggregate of the updates from client updates without learning the individual contributions. This is important in FL because the server is not meant to handle or view individual, client-specific information.

Bonawitz et al.'s (2017) secure aggregation was established in a general sense as follows:

- Each client encrypts their model update using a pairwise masking scheme.
- The server receives the sum of updates, but the pairwise masks cancel each other out at the server level, when aggregating the updates.
- If some clients drop out, the protocol will still work when combined with key-sharing schemes.

This design permits the following:

- No individual update is ever sent in plaintext.
- Even if the server is curiosity-driven or compromised, the server will not learn the individual client updates.

Secure aggregation is especially valuable in fraud detection since the updates may contain features that implicitly pertain to the user's behavior or transaction context.

3.6.3 Anomaly detection in model updates

Because FL can be compromised from within (e.g., a malicious client, poisoned updates), it is critical to monitor updates for integrity. The performance of anomaly detection systems can find troublesome updates based on:

- Statistical deviations from expected levels (e.g., direction of gradients, magnitude of gradients).
- Semantic inconsistency (e.g., an update that increases the risk of fraud instead of decreasing it).
- Temporal anomalies (e.g., the update has a different behavior over the training rounds).

An example of the statistical anomaly is if one of the clients submits an update that is entirely worse in performance than the other clients' updates, which could be a sign of poisoning. In the case of temporal weirdness, if a client produces an update that changes from round to round, or simply has always underperformed ordinary levels.

Some platforms use reputation systems to downweight, or exclude, erratic clients, others use federated adversarial training, which model is pre-trained to identity and counter the adversarial update.

3.6.4 Robust aggregation techniques

Simple averaging (for example, FedAvg) is susceptible to outlier or malicious updates; therefore, robust aggregation techniques have been designed to enhance robust performance:

- Krum (Blanchard et al., 2017): Uses the client update that is the most similar to the others, while ignoring the outliers.

- Trimmed Mean: Creates the mean of the values after discarding the top and bottom k% of values.
- Median: Using the element-wise median instead of mean combats the effect of extreme values.
- FL Trust (Cao et al., 2020): Proposes a trusted baseline client (for example, the aggregator) and scales updates according to the congruence of the other updates.

These approaches allow for the preservation of model legitimacy in risk-sensitive contexts such as fraud detection, where there is significant adversarial behavior.

3.7 EVALUATION METRICS AND BENCHMARKS

Developing and implementing a FL infrastructure throughout research and production is only half the battle. Evaluating that the FL system is functioning and performing properly, as well as in a responsible manner, requires strong evaluation metrics. Evaluation metrics can range from traditional model performance metrics, to privacy and security guarantees, to efficiency on a system level.

3.7.1 Model accuracy vs. centralized baseline

Overall, FL models should be evaluated based on their fraud detection accuracy in comparison to all other traditional, centralized machine learning techniques.
Some of the simpler metrics would be:

- Precision: Of all instances noted as fraud, how many were fraud?
- Recall (aka sensitivity): Of all the fraud, how much fraud was detected?
- F1-Score: The harmonic mean of precision and recall; useful for imbalanced datasets like fraud.
- AUC-ROC (Area Under Curve – Receiver Operating Characteristic): Evaluates the model's ability to separate fraud from non-fraud at every threshold.

The centralized baseline describes the model after it is trained on the pooled data from all participants. The performance of a trained centralized model, compared to other models, will usually be better, whether it is better than a federated model depends on the context. In some cases, centralized models outperform federated ones simply because they have access to full data directly; however, the benefit of no privacy and legal issues for federated models (and half the time to normalize practices) usually makes FL the best solution, we want to minimize the performance gap between the federated and centralized machine learning model while still respecting privacy.

3.7.2 False positive and false negative rates

In fraud detection, simply ensuring accuracy is not enough. The costs associated with errors is extremely asymmetric:

- False Positives (FP): Legitimate transactions that are identified as fraud. These usually generate user dissatisfaction, cart abandonment and damage to reputational integrity.

- False Negatives (FN): Irrespective of whether frauds are detected and acted upon these are registered frauds that create a financial loss and potential compliance issues.

Thus FL systems may be tuned to optimize operating thresholds for costs and revenues that minimize alternative error types or, when appropriate, weight them differently based on the business context.

Many fraud detection systems may also deploy cost-sensitive learning which can treat different error types as weighted differently in the loss function.

3.7.3 Privacy and security benchmarks

Considering the work of privacy is less straightforward than accuracy – it combines both theoretical guarantees and simulations.
Common metrics are:

- Epsilon in DP: Less epsilon means more privacy, and necessarily more noise and therefore accuracy loss. Many organizations will set thresholds based on risk and relevant legislation.
- Attacks on resistance:
  - Membership inference attacks: Determine whether an attacker can infer whether a given data point was part of the training data.
  - Gradient inversion attacks: Reconstructing original data from updates taken.
  - Model poisoning scenarios: Designed as simulated attacks to examine whether the system can detect and mitigate adversarial behavior.

The level of resiliency of FL under these simulated attacks is an important metric to establish for any application in critical domains such as banking or health care.

3.7.4 System efficiency metrics

FL systems must be not only effective and secure – but also *scalable and efficient*. Here are some core metrics:

Efficient systems typically balance these constraints using asynchronous FL, client sampling, or adaptive learning rates to scale effectively across different environments. Table 3.5 provides the efficiency of the different metrices of the fraud detection.

Table 3.5 Efficiency metrics

Metric	*Description*	*Why it Matters*
Communication Overhead	Total bytes exchanged per training round	Key bottleneck in FL; affects speed and cost
Convergence Time	Number of rounds or total time to reach target accuracy	Important for real-time fraud detection
Client Participation Rate	Percentage of clients that complete each round	Affects model generalizability and fairness
Resource Utilization	CPU, memory, and bandwidth consumption on client and server	Determines whether FL is viable on edge or low-power devices
Dropout Tolerance	Ability to handle client failures or network issues	Critical in environments with unstable connectivity

3.8 REAL-WORLD CASE STUDIES

FL has yet to see widespread real-world use in fraud detection, but there are still a number of trials, prototypes, and published results that highlight successful use cases. In this section, we showcase three case studies, each demonstrating the potential for FL to enable privacy-preserving, collaborative fraud detection across institutions.

3.8.1 Case study 1: FL in banking consortiums

Background: Fraud in the financial services industry spans institutional boundaries – for example, a fraudster might do a small transaction, testing a stolen card at one bank, and then run larger attacks across many others following their success. Banks have historically struggled to cooperate across the institutional boundaries due to data privacy issues and differing regulations.

FL Deployment: A number of banks based in Europe, including many national and regional banks, took part in a consortium to pilot an FL-based fraud detection system. Each bank trained a local model based on its transaction history, customer metadata, and fraud labels. These updates were aggregated together securely, in order to improve their shared fraud detection model while still preserving the data privacy of each individual bank.

Technology Stack:

- FedAvg has been used as the aggregation algorithm.
- Secure Aggregation has been utilized to maintain privacy.
- PySyft and FATE have provided orchestration forFL.
- DP was added for GDPR compliance.

Outcomes:

- The federated model improved fraud detection rates by ~11% over each bank model.
- Fraud detection was improved for individual banks through generalization of data from different banks, circumventing FP.
- The regulators were supportive of this way of collaborating, believing this framework is compliant with GDPR.

Key Insight: FL enabled trustless collaboration in a highly regulated and competitive environment. Banks were able to gather shared intelligence without giving up data sovereignty.

3.8.2 Case study 2: Health insurance fraud detection

Background: Health insurance fraud can consist of billing for services that were never provided, using a higher procedure code, or submitting excessive claims for the same service. Information related to fraud is often scattered across hospitals, insurance companies, and government agencies (each with only a portion of the overall extraction).

FL Deployment: A project in the U.S., within the health sector, linked five health insurers, with a number of healthcare providers to identify outlier billing activities. All providers trained a local anomaly detection model utilizing structured claims data, including provider behavior.

Technology stack:

- Autoencoders and Isolation Forests as local models.
- personalized FL framework (pFedMe) to model according to local/Provider patterns.
- DP to preserve and protect sensitive billing information.

Outcomes:

- The FL system identified 25% more fraudulent billing then the prior siloed assessments system-wide.
- System-wide collaborative learning to identify fraudulent providers arbitraging between multiple insurers.
- Only minimal data exposure needed and HIPAA compliance of the information was supported within the pilot.

Key Insight: FL supported stitching together the complete picture of fraud without breaking laws related to medical data sharing. It also allowed for the identification of problematic entities across non-IID billing data across providers.

3.8.3 Case study 3: E-commerce fraud detection network

Summary: The rising risk of fraudsters exploiting multiple storefronts is not just exclusively harming the large players. Small and medium e-commerce merchants do not have the capacity to build resources for fraud detection internally.

FL Deployment: A federated network was established amongst ~50 e-commerce platforms to be able to model a suspicious behavior together. The suspicious behaviors were rapid account creation, changes to IP addresses, and fraudulent return activity.

Technology Stack:

- Lightweight neural networks (LSTMs were used for behavioral sequences).
- TensorFlow Federated (TFF) to orchestrate this.
- Utilization of Secure Aggregation and Selective Update Filtering to protect against poisoning.

Outcomes:

- The federated model improved detection of synthetic accounts and promotional abuse.
- Fraud campaigns that traversed sites were detected early on.
- Smaller merchants had access to an AI-grade level of protection without the risk of exposing customer data.

Key Takeaway: The FL approach allowed fraud protection in the e-commerce sector to be democratized so that even the smallest players still had access to the kind of shared intelligence usually reserved for the large tech giants.

3.9 FUTURE DIRECTIONS AND OPPORTUNITIES

As FL matures, the impact it can have on fraud detection will continue to expand. Current systems will do many things, but there will be many exciting future directions as well. These opportunities will improve performance, applicability and will also enable real-time fraud prevention in an even more agile way.

3.9.1 Incorporating real-time FL for live detection

Current FL implementations have mostly been batch based in nature, training models in rounds and updating after certain time periods. Many times fraud detection requirements must have real-time or near real-time performance considerations; for example: Credit card processing, credit card skimming, or online checkout environments are often high frequency scenarios.

Future opportunity is to build real-time FL that allows models to be updated continuously with streaming data as it comes into the system.

- Use case example may be detecting anomalies with just seconds of a fraudulent transaction being made.
- Challenges would include low-latency communication between observers and data aggregation, consistency and availability.
- One possible avenue to consider could be combination of edge computing and stream based learning to provide rapid model updates and rapid response artefact, at least for real time fraud alerts.

The growing interest in FL and its related areas has gotten some researchers interested in asynchronous streamlined FL that eliminates synchronous communication between the clients; the clients can self-update the model as new available data is available to them. Asynchronous data stream FL is an opportunity for continuous monitoring fraud detection systems.

3.9.2 Federated transfer learning for new participants

It's possible that new or smaller organizations (such as a small insurance company or a fintech startup) may not have enough historical fraud data available to be of value in a federated model. This is a type of "cold start" problem in FL.

Solution: Federated transfer learning (FTL), which integrates FL with transfer learning techniques, allows a client with little or no data to benefit from a model trained on other data.

- Mechanism: Global pretrained models are adapted to the new client's situation through fine-tuning.
- Advantage: Facilitates onboarding of new participants and adapts fraud detection based on their characteristics.
- Risk: Making sure that the transfer does not leak sensitive patterns or bias the model. This is particularly useful for cross-border fraud detection scenarios, with the different regulatory and data environments in different regions.

3.9.3 Cross-vertical collaboration (e.g., banks + e-commerce)

Fraud is indifferent to industry boundaries. For example, a fraudster can use e-commerce systems to launder money, or use financial credentials stolen from an e-commerce platform to commit fraud. However, most of our FL deployments are intra-domain – they are within a single domain (e.g., only banks, or only insurers).

Vision: Provide the means for cross-vertical FL collaboration to take place where:

- Banks can transfer fraud risk signals with e-commerce platforms.
- Healthcare and insurance providers can co-train on fraud behaviors.
- Telcos can contribute device intelligence to inform fraud scoring.

Technical considerations:

- Heterogeneous data schemas and feature sets.
- Trust and governance models across industries.
- Standardized FL protocols and APIs.

Cross-sector FL will allow for detection of multi-channel fraud which is either not visible, or is less visible, to any single vertical; it allows for new collaborative security intelligence.

3.9.4 Edge FL for on-device detection

Edge devices – such as smartcards, point-of-sale terminals, and mobile phones are increasingly becoming the first line of defense against fraud. Future FL models will be running directly on edge devices to:

- Monitor behavior (i.e., typing/clicking speed, traveling location, biometric clues).
- Identify anomalies at the source where possible so that they do not escalate.
- Learn and adapt locally with push updates to the global model when appropriate.

This is typically referred to as Edge FL, and there is beginning to be in-market examples in fintech and mobile payment apps.

Benefits include:

- Fraud alerts and alerts occur with less latency.
- Bandwidth usage is minimized.
- Personalization increases and privacy control improves.

However, using edge devices create challenges we need to consider (e.g., diversity of devices, resources, and ensuring secure local computations).

New trends outside of traditional FL worth getting familiar with:

- FL + Blockchain: Use decentralized ledgers to support update integrity and create trust among the contributors.

- Federated Reinforcement Learning: Example to train fraud defense policies that could learn and change as attacker behaviors change over time.

The future of FL in fraud detection is not simply making existing models more effective, rather it is enabling wholly new kinds of collective intelligence opportunity. With enough investment and attention to research, policy, and standards, FL could become the new default choice for any collaborative artificially intelligent system working under privacy constraints.

3.10 CONCLUSION

Fraud is a fickle enemy that is always evolving – typically, fast moving, adaptive, and now increasingly multi-national. Traditional detection systems can be effective as fraudsters carve out space for compromises in goods in isolated institutions; but as soon as the fraud becomes trans-organizational, trans-jurisdiction, or (especially) disrupts a region, you're at the mercy of missile – or in the case of many payment-based FIs – broad reductions to tax-payer revenue. As privacy regulations tighten, and collaboration of the level of intelligence between organizations becomes even more critical than ever –FL is the paradigm that allows for collective intelligence without ceding individual privacy.

We have covered a lot in this chapter regarding the elements and nuts and bolts of FL based fraud detection systems. First this paper established the nature of fraud and the short-comings of these centralized systems; we then examined how FL offered a decentralized solution, which enabled multiple parties to jointly train on sensitive data, while clearly delineating the uniqueness of those datasets.

This paper discussed FL algorithms such as FedAvg, FedProx, and pFedMe, which provides us with deeper insight into the deep/model learning architectures we can consider for fraud detection (e.g., Convolutional Neural Networks [CNNs], Recurrent Neural Networks [RNNs], and autoencoders). We scoped the privacy and security stack – including DP, Secure Aggregation,

Anomaly Detection, and Robust Aggregation; and covered a variety of performance metrics that extended beyond accuracy (e.g., false positive rate, privacy guarantees, and system efficiency).

BIBLIOGRAPHY

Aono, Y., Hayashi, T., Wang, L., & Moriai, S. (2017). Privacy-preserving deep learning: Revisited and enhanced. In Proceedings of the IEEE European Symposium on Security and Privacy (EuroS&P), 100–107. https://doi.org/10.1109/EuroSP.2017.19

Bonawitz, K., Eichner, H., Grieskamp, W., Huba, D., Ingerman, A., Ivanov, V., ... & Ramage, D. (2017). Towards federated learning at scale: System design. In *Proceedings of Machine Learning and Systems (MLSys)*. https://arxiv.org/abs/1902.01046

Brisimi, T. S., Chen, R., Mela, T., Olshevsky, A., Paschalidis, I. C., & Shi, W. (2018). Federated learning of predictive models from federated electronic health records. *International Journal of Medical Informatics*, 112, 59–67. https://doi.org/10.1016/j.ijmedinf.2018.01.007

Choudhury, O., Weng, Y., Wang, Y., Charles, D., & Sim, I. (2019). Predicting adverse drug reactions using federated learning. arXiv preprint arXiv:1910.12191. https://arxiv.org/abs/1910.12191

Fang, M., Cao, X., Jia, J., & Gong, N. Z. (2020). Local model poisoning attacks to Byzantine-robust federated learning. In USENIX Security Symposium, 1605–1622.

Hard, A., Rao, K., Mathews, R., Beaufays, F., Augenstein, S., Eichner, H., ... & Ramage, D. (2018). Federated learning for mobile keyboard prediction. *arXiv preprint arXiv:1811.03604*. https://arxiv.org/abs/1811.03604

Hu, Y., Gong, Y., Zhang, X., & Zhang, L. (2022). FedDetect: Federated fraud detection for edge computing using robust autoencoder. *IEEE Transactions on Dependable and Secure Computing*. https://doi.org/10.1109/TDSC.2022.3151013

Kairouz, P., McMahan, H. B., Avent, B., Bellet, A., Bennis, M., Bhagoji, A. N., ... & Zhao, S. (2021). Advances and open problems in federated learning. *Foundations and Trends® in Machine Learning*, 14(1–2), 1–210. https://doi.org/10.1561/2200000083

Li, T., Sahu, A. K., Talwalkar, A., & Smith, V. (2020). Federated learning: Challenges, methods, and future directions. *IEEE Signal Processing Magazine*, 37(3), 50–60. https://doi.org/10.1109/MSP.2020.2975749

Lin, T., Kong, L., Stich, S. U., & Jaggi, M. (2020). Ensemble distillation for robust model fusion in federated learning. *Advances in Neural Information Processing Systems*, 33, 2351–2363.

Liu, B., Wu, W., Liu, Y., Yang, Q., & Chen, T. (2020). Secure federated transfer learning. *IEEE Transactions on Knowledge and Data Engineering*, 34(1), 324–336. https://doi.org/10.1109/TKDE.2020.2981314

McMahan, H. B., Moore, E., Ramage, D., Hampson, S., & y Arcas, B. A. (2017). Communication-efficient learning of deep networks from decentralized data. Proceedings of the 20th International Conference on Artificial Intelligence and Statistics (AISTATS), Proceedings of Machine Learning Research, 54, 1273–1282.

Mohri, M., Sivek, G., & Suresh, A. T. (2019). Agnostic federated learning. In International Conference on Machine Learning (ICML), 4615–4625.

Nasr, M., Shokri, R., & Houmansadr, A. (2019). Comprehensive privacy analysis of deep learning: Passive and active white-box inference attacks against centralized and federated learning. In IEEE Symposium on Security and Privacy (SP), 739–753. https://doi.org/10.1109/SP.2019.00065

Juniper Research. (2022). Online payment fraud: Emerging threats, segment analysis & market forecasts 2022–2027. Juniper Research. www.juniperresearch.com/researchstore/fintech-payments/online-payment-fraud

Sharma, A., Sinha, A., & Agarwal, A. (2020). Privacy-preserving fraud detection in financial services using federated learning. In International Conference on Machine Learning and Data Engineering (iCMLDE), 113–120.

Shokri, R., Stronati, M., Song, C., & Shmatikov, V. (2017). Membership inference attacks against machine learning models. In IEEE Symposium on Security and Privacy (SP), 3–18. https://doi.org/10.1109/SP.2017.41

Yang, Q., Liu, Y., Chen, T., & Tong, Y. (2019). Federated machine learning: Concept and applications. ACM Transactions on Intelligent Systems and Technology (TIST), 10(2), 12. https://doi.org/10.1145/3298981

Chapter 4

Cybersecurity vulnerabilities in federated learning

Shaik Valli Haseena, Simna Shanavas, Brundha N., and Ayasha

4.1 INTRODUCTION

Federated Learning (FL) is the novel perspective that enables allied model training across many decentralized devices or servers without having to store or transfer raw data centrally. Each learner trains a local model on private data and shares updates to the model, for example, weights or gradients, with a central server for aggregation. This minimizes data privacy, decreases communication costs, and facilitates global regulation compliance, for example, the General Data Protection Regulation (GDPR). FL is especially beneficial for edge device usage [1], that is, smartphones, wearables, and Internet of Things (IoT) sensors, where bandwidth is limited and realtime decision-making is critical.

Yet the same decentralized nature of the architecture that makes FL appealing also poses extreme cybersecurity threats. In the absence of a centralized body to decide the trustworthiness of the participants, adversarial agents can target vulnerabilities at various points across the FL life cycle. Data poisoning attacks, for instance, can subtly introduce model parameters to induce targeted misclassifications a high-severity threat in applications like healthcare and finance. Model inversion attacks, while technically more sophisticated, have been demonstrated to extract sensitive patient records or financial information from gradients shared, violating privacy guarantees. Adversarial manipulations, for which input specially crafted to target trained model vulnerabilities, can have life-critical safety implications in autonomous systems and IoT deployments.

Recent work has shown that such attacks are not just a theoretical possibility. Some such examples include successful backdoor attacks on text prediction models and gradient leakage on medical image data sets. The empirical feasibility of these attacks indicates the urgent need for the deployment of effective countermeasures, such as aggregation methods with robustness, secure shared computation, homomorphic encryption, and differential privacy.

This chapter presents a critical and systematic assessment of FL security, classifying threats in a structured manner based on severity, attack ability, and likely real-world impact. It synthesizes findings from theoretical studies and empirical case studies in order to enable researchers, developers, and policymakers to prioritize defense measures by risk and feasibility. Finally, the chapter aims to inform the development of secure and reliable FL systems for deployment in privacy sensitive and safety critical domains such as health, finance, and critical infrastructure.

DOI: 10.1201/9781003660330-4

4.2 FEDERATED LEARNING ARCHITECTURE

FL operates in a decentralized environment that supports collaborative model training while preserving confidentiality of raw data. The environment consists of three key elements: client devices, a central server, and secure communication protocols. Client devices are smartphones, tablets, smartwatches, medical imaging servers, and IoT sensors, and each device has local data and adequate computation power to perform model training. During each training round, a client downloads the global model, trains it nearby on device data, and returns only the computed updates, i.e., gradients or weights, to the core server. The operation preserves privacy because raw data is never sent back to the server, an aspect of great importance in sensitive fields like healthcare and finance.

The server acts as the coordinator for the entire FL process. It gathers updates from several client devices and combines them, often applying methods such as Federated Summarizing, to produce a new global model that captures the learning of all of the clients. This new model is then returned to all of the participant devices for the next training round. The server synchronizes participants, filters out malicious or low-quality updates, and can use advanced security methods such as secure multiparty computation or homomorphic encryption to preserve confidentiality while aggregating.

FL is an ongoing interaction between clients and the server, and therefore communication protocols are crucial. Communication protocols are crucial in guaranteeing confidentiality, integrity, and authenticity of model updates. Several techniques such as end-to-end encryption, digital signatures, and message authentication codes are utilized to guarantee security against threats including interception, tampering, and impersonation attacks [2]. Sophisticated implementations also involve incorporating differential privacy mechanisms into the communication system to add noise to model updates, thereby guaranteeing security against threats including model inversion or membership inference.

Figure 4.1 illustrates the architecture of FL and how security mechanisms are applied to protect data privacy and integrity during the core model training process. Table 4.1 summarizes the roles, security features, vulnerabilities, and mitigation strategies of key components in the federated learning framework.

Table 4.1 Roles, security features, and vulnerabilities

Component	*Role in FL*	*Security Features*	*Potential Vulnerabilities*	*Mitigation Techniques*
Client Devices	Training the local models and send updates to the server	Local computation, no raw data sharing	Gradient leakage, data poisoning	Differential privacy, robust aggregation
Central Server	Aggregates updates and distributes global model	Secure aggregation, client management	Malicious update injection, poisoning attacks	Secure multiparty computation, homomorphic encryption
Communication	Transfers updates between clients and the server	TLS, digital signatures, MACs, secure aggregation	Interception, tampering, impersonation	End-to-end encryption, authentication, Bonawitz protocol

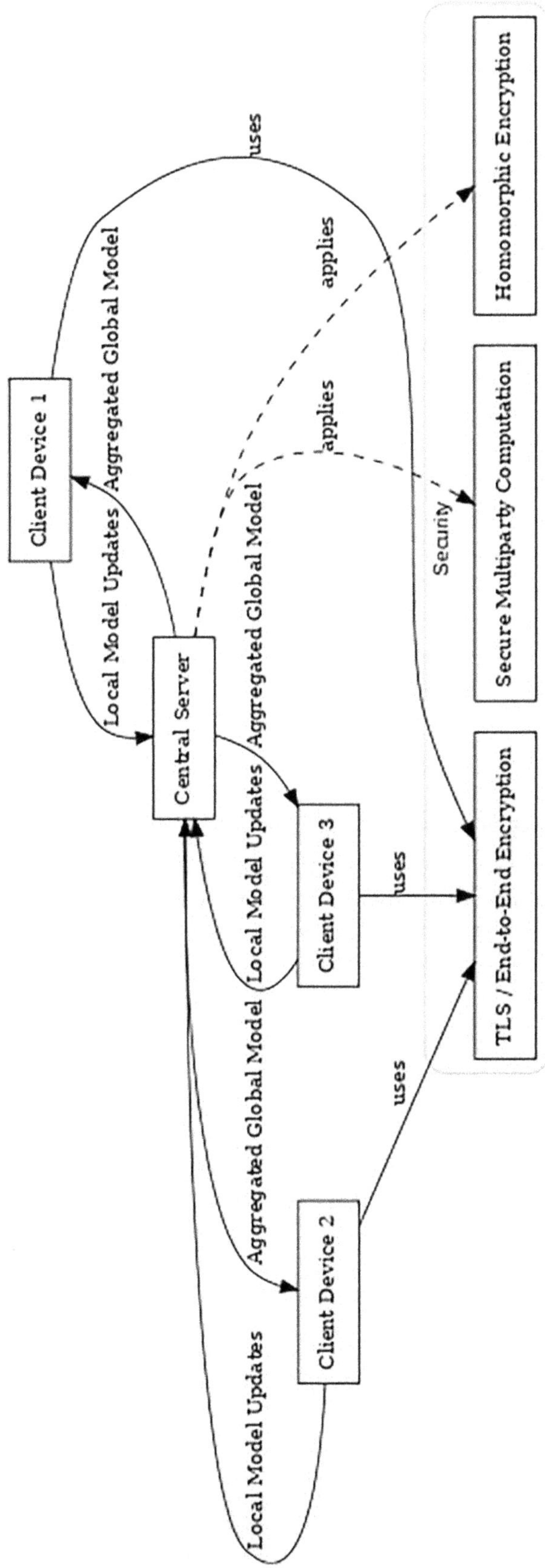

Figure 4.1 Federated learning architecture with security mechanisms for model training and aggregation.

1. Client Devices (1, 2, 3):
   - Devices like smartphones, IoT devices, medical servers conduct local training on local data.
   - Once trained every device computes local model updates and uploads them to the central server.
   - They get the global model aggregated from the server to use for training in the subsequent round in exchange.
2. Central Server:
   - Serves as coordinator of the FL process.
     The process involves gathering updates from all clients employing secure aggregation methods, and developing a worldwide model which is sent to all clients.
   - Prevents ugly or toxic updates from affecting the final model.
3. Security Layer:
   - TLS/End-to-End Encryption: Encrypts updates during transit between the server and clients thereby guaranteeing confidentiality and integrity [3].
   - Secure Multiparty Computation: Allows the server to aggregate encrypted inputs while ensuring that individual client contributions remain confidential and inaccessible.
   - Homomorphic Encryption: Facilitates numerical computation on encrypted information maintaining confidentiality intact throughout aggregation.
4. Interactions:
   - All clients use encryption (TLS) for secure communication.
   - The master server uses SMC and Homomorphic Encryption [4] in a way that model updates are kept secret even during aggregation.

Yet, such defenses notwithstanding, vulnerabilities remain. Updates to models can still spill sensitive information, and insecure communication channels are susceptible to tampering or data theft [5]. Against such attacks, FL systems use TLS for secure communication, homomorphic encryption for computation over encrypted data, secure multiparty computation for privacy-preserving aggregation, and authentication mechanisms for impersonation prevention. Although these defense mechanisms increase security, they introduce computational overhead and latency, which remains a concern for resource-limited edge devices.

4.3 FEDERATED LEARNING WORKFLOW

F L allows for decentralized model training through the ability of numerous clients to jointly learn from scattered data without ever sending raw data to a central point. The process is a looped and communication-hungry process fine-tuning a number of substantial steps.

4.3.1 Initialization

The FL process begins with the global model being activated by the central coordinating server. The model might be either randomly initialized or pre-trained on public data[6] to enhance the rate of convergence. The initial model serves as a shared starting point for all of the clients and plays a crucial role in syncing the initiation conditions. A crucial aspect of distributed training is its model design which is contingent upon the particular machine learning application including but not limited to image classification, natural language processing, or time series forecasting [7].

4.3.2 Broadcasting

Once initiated the global model is broadcast to a set of client devices. The clients are typically selected according to availability, processing capabilities, connectivity, and suitability of data. This broadcasting process helps make all clients have the same version of the model that they will then enhance with their respective local datasets. This phase can also contain client mechanisms selection to promote fairness and diversity in training [8].

4.3.3 Local training

Every client device then updates the global model it has received with its local dataset. This is an exercise of applying machine learning algorithms, for example, stochastic gradient descent to minimize a local loss function. Due to the data in various clients potentially being diverse in distribution the updated models derived will capture the unique properties. Respective dataset properties are taken into consideration. Learning is typically conducted across multiple local epochs to make provision for worthwhile learning before transmitting updates [9].

4.3.4 Uploading

Once trained locally, customers send over their model updates rather than plain text data to a centralized server. In most cases these updates are in the form of newly calculated weight parameters or gradients. To help defend against client confidentiality and reduce transmit overhead they can undergo processes such as data compression encryption or masking using such techniques as secure aggregation or differential privacy. These are processes performed in order to keep the privacy- preserving nature of FL [10].

4.3.5 Aggregation

Upon receiving updates from participating clients, the server performs aggregation to evaluate a new global model. The most common method used is Federated Averaging, which computes a weighted average of the client models based on the size of each clients dataset. The formula is [11]:

$$w^{t+1} = \sum_{k=1}^{K} \frac{n_k}{n} w_k^{t+1} \tag{4.1}$$

Where:

- w^{t+1} is the new global model for aggregation.
- w_k^{t+1} is the updated model from client k.
- n_k is the number of training samples at client k.

- $n = \sum_{k=1}^{K} n_k$ is the total number of data samples across all clients.
- K is the number of clients participating in the round.

This information weighted averaging results in clients who have more information having proportionally more effect on the global model thereby enhancing model generalization.

4.3.6 Iteration

Upon aggregation the revised global model is communicated to clients and another round of training begins. Steps 2 to 5 are recursively repeated, normally tens or hundreds of iterations of communication before a terminating criterion is reached. Usual combination criteria are to reach a desired model accuracy a limit on the number rounds or tracking zero changes in model performance across rounds.

This repetitive process enables the model to continuously improve its performance without infringing on the privacy and sovereignty of each client's data. The FL workflow is particularly valuable in environments where data cannot be centralized for legal, ethical, or technical reasons, for example, healthcare networks, financial networks, or smart cities[12]. In practice each step of the FL workflow must be properly managed to address issues such as system heterogeneity, client dropout, communication latency, and potential security vulnerabilities. As such the FL workflow is not only a technical process but also a foundation for secure privacy-aware and ethically responsible AI deployment in the real world.

4.4 THREAT MODEL AND VULNERABILITIES IN FEDERATED LEARNING

To implement robust security and privacy-protections for FL, understanding the diverse and ever-evolving security environment surrounding it is crucial first. FL, unlike traditional machine learning is a decentralized interactive environment in which several clients collaborate to build a global model without sharing unprocessed data. While this enhances solitude and data sovereignty, it also introduces a wide range of vulnerabilities that can be exploited by attackers.

The interactive nature of FL means that different classes of actors can be involved in the learning process, not all of which can be relied upon. The first class of threat actors includes malicious clients and learners who deliberately stray from the learning protocol. Malicious clients can inject poisoned data into the learning process or modify their local model updates prior to submission with the purpose of poisoning the global model or achieving a competitive advantage[13]. Data and model poisoning attacks are not hypothetical, as they can drastically compromise the integrity and performance of the end model.

Another powerful threat agent is the inquisitive but truthful server, which strictly adheres to the aggregation protocol yet tries to infer confidential information from the updates it receives. While the server does not actually stray from its assigned roles, the fact that it is a central node gives it a lot of visibility into client behaviors, thus potentially facilitating privacy violations such as model inversion or membership inference attacks. This highlights the essential tension in Federated Learning between centralized coordination and decentralized privacy.

FL systems are also attacked by third-party actors, besides internal ones. External attackers do not participate in the learning process but attack weaknesses in communication protocols. Man-in-the-middle attacks and denial-of-service attacks are some examples[14]. Adversaries intercept or tamper with model updates in transit in man-in-the-middle attacks, whereas denial of service attacks are intended to disrupt communication or inundate the server. Since FL relies heavily on secure communication between the central server and clients, even a minor security compromise can lead to huge leakage of data or system failure.

Adding to the complexity of the security environment are flaws of collusion where several clients or even clients and the server collude to enhance the impact of their attacks. Collusion can facilitate easier reconstruction of private information or manipulation of the model's output without detection. FL is also susceptible to the free-rider attacks where clients benefit from the training process without providing useful data or computation. These clients can also be Byzantine behaving randomly[15] or deceptively to disrupt the training process altogether.

Each of these categories of threats poses unique challenges to FL system's integrity and security. From inference attacks and poisoning to protocol tampering and conspiracy, the variety of attack vectors demands a forward thinking and informed system design. Therefore, the creation of a comprehensive threat model is not an academic exercise; it is a necessary precursor to the creation of effective, reliable FL solutions. In short, the decentralized, multi-agent nature of FL makes it vulnerable to a wide range of adversarial attacks. By formally defining the main threat agents and the unique threats they present, developers and researchers can craft proper countermeasures like differential privacy, secure aggregation, homomorphic encryption, and adaptive trust management systems[16]. An end-to-end threat model is a building block for constructing FL systems that are not only new but also resilient, scalable, and secure against new threats.

4.4.1 Honest but curious server

A semi-honest server is a server that adheres to the given FL protocol exactly but simultaneously is interested in attempting to obtain sensitive information from the model updates received. Although it does not alter the combination procedure or actively attempt to manipulate client updates it may attempt to carry out inference attacks, for example, model inversion or membership inference [17] in order to extract confidential client information or ascertain whether particular data samples were utilised during training. Such an adversary is of specific concern in actual FL environments where the central server is operated by a third-party entity or cloud service provider and thus clients have minimal control over processing their updates.

4.4.2 Malicious Clients

Malicious or Byzantine clients are participants in the FL system with the aim of disrupting the learning process. Such clients may submit fake or purposefully adulterated updates with the intention of poisoning the global model [18]. These attacks may be in many various forms including:

- **Data poisoning:** Adding adversarial crafted or incorrectly labelled data to the local training dataset to deceive model learning.
- **Model poisoning:** Creating poisonous updates that incline the model towards specific actions like misclassification of targeted inputs.

- **Free-riding attacks:** Presenting random or uninformative updates in a manner that blocks real training undermining overall model quality.

These clients can work independently or together with other compromised nodes; hence detection and mitigation are extremely difficult[19]. Their actions compromise the integrity, fairness, and robustness of the global model.

4.4.3 External attackers

External attackers attack outside of the trusted FL system but attempt to compromise the system by exploiting network-level vulnerabilities, insecure communication, or side channel attacks. Unlike malicious clients or curious servers that are in the FL process, external attackers are not disclosed to training data or model parameters but target communication channels and system authentication mechanisms to gain unauthorized access, manipulate data, or disrupt training.

A common method is eavesdropping, where the attacker taps insecure or poorly encrypted communication between client machines and the master server. Through capturing the model updates, the attacker can infer confidential information via model inversion or membership inference attacks and thereby reconstruct private data features from the received gradients or weights during training.

Other serious threat is the man-in-the-middle attack, wherein the attacker places himself between the client and server in the communication process. This allows the attacker not just to intercept data but also to manipulate or inject malicious payloads. Such actions may lead to corrupted updates, which may lead to model degradation, backdoor insertion, or biased output, ultimately harming the integrity and trust of the final global model[20].

There are also external attackers that can utilize Sybil attacks by creating several false client identities to exert an unfair impact on the aggregated model. By loading the system with the wrong clients, the attacker can do mass poisoning attacks, thereby training the training process for malicious purposes such as biased predictions or deliberate model failure.

These attacks exploit weaknesses in communication protocols, authentication processes, and identity validation processes. FL systems must employ peer-to-peer encryption to protect transit data, secure aggregation rules to keep individual client updates confidential, and strong client verification processes to prevent spoofing client identities. Authentication methods such as digital signatures, public key infrastructure, and certificate-based verification may also be employed to validate only legitimate clients during training.

It is important to identify the external attacker's roles to develop an effective threat model for FL systems. In addition to malicious clients and honest-but-curious servers, these attackers take advantage of various system properties that need to be counteracted by specific countermeasures. Countering these external attacks is necessary for secure FL deployment in privacy-sensitive applications such as healthcare, finance, and smart infrastructure, where compromises may result in data exfiltration, regulatory violations, and system crashes.

4.5 MAIN FEDERATED LEARNING WEAKNESSES

Even with the privacy benefits provided by FL, its decentralized structure contains a number of inherent weaknesses that are vulnerable to attacks by unscrupulous agents. These stem primarily from open participation by potentially unreliable clients and dependence on collective model updates which are frequently made up of sensitive data. The direst threats among them are data poisoning, inversion of the model, adversarial attacks, and membership inference. All of them are attacks on either the ethical integrity of the model or confidentiality of the training data.

4.5.1 Data poisoning attacks

In a data poisoning attack, adversarial clients deliberately poison their local training data to pollute the global model. Let D_k be the dataset of client k and $\widetilde{D_k}$ its poisoned version. The loss function on client k becomes:

$$\tilde{L}_k(\theta) = \frac{1}{\left|\widetilde{D_k}\right|} \sum_{(x_i, y_i) \in \tilde{D}_k} L\left(f_\theta(x_i), y_i\right) \tag{4.2}$$

Global model update at iteration t aggregates all client updates through Federated Averaging:

$$\theta^{t+1} = \sum_{k=1}^{K} \frac{n_k}{n} \theta_k^{t+1} \tag{4.3}$$

A malicious client can place back doors inside the model via the introduction of poisoned data, such as imprecisely labelled images. For example in a handwriting recognition FL model with the MNIST dataset an abusive client may change the labels from 1 to 7 to misclassify all valid 1 digits to 7 at inference time. Such an attack can be amplified via manipulation methods such as gradient attacks or label flipping schemes thus making it difficult for detection within a decentralized system [21].

4.5.2 Model inversion attacks

Model inversion is an attack wherein the attacker tries to recover the training samples originally used from the input gradient updates received from the clients. When the client sends the gradient of the loss function with respect to model parameters an attacker can reverse the training data by solving the optimization problem given:

$$x^* = \underset{x}{argmin} \left\| \nabla_\theta L\left(f_\theta(x), y\right) - g^2 \right\| \tag{4.4}$$

Here, g is the gradient observed by the client, and f_θ is the model function. One such application of this concept in the real world is the Deep Leakage from Gradients algorithm which can be employed for reconstructing visual features from gradients of CNNs. In the medical domain this would allow for reconstructing sensitive inputs such as MRI scans or chest X-rays from their respective gradients particularly when client datasets are homogeneous or small. For example if a hospital server is trained on just a few X-ray images, reconstructing becomes easier via inversion attacks[22].

4.5.3 Adversarial attacks

Adversarial attacks take advantage of the susceptibility of deep learning models to perturbations in input data. Invisible and small perturbations in the input can lead to incorrect predictions from a model. Some of the most used attacks include the Fast Gradient Sign Method where adversarial example x_{adv} are created by:

$$x_{adv} = x + \epsilon \,.sign\left(\nabla_x L\left(f_\theta(x), y\right)\right) \tag{4.5}$$

Here ϵ is employed to vary the size of the perturbation. In FL, an adversary can either craft adversarial inputs at local training or introduce adversarial gradients to bias the global model. For instance, in an autonomous vehicle FL system an adversary can manipulate images of road signs so that stop signs are classified as speed limit signs. Since FL models are trained with heterogeneous possibly non-IID data, defenses such as adversarial training are more difficult to deploy and standardize across clients [23].

4.5.4 Membership inference attacks

Membership inference is to predict whether a specific sample of data was part of a client's training data. This breaks the fundamental privacy guarantee of FL. The attacker knows the global model and sees the prediction loss or confidence on a target sample. Lower loss or higher confidence in most instances suggests the sample was viewed during training. The attack can be formulated as:

$$Membership(x) = \begin{cases} 1, & if\ L(f_\theta(x), y) < \tau \\ 0, & \end{cases} \tag{4.6}$$

Where τ is an empirically set threshold. In practice, for example, in credit scoring or healthcare diagnostics this kind of inference might leak whether a subject was used to train a model potentially causing serious concerns in the likes of GDPR or Health Insurance Portability and Accountability Act (HIPAA), a U.S. federal regulation that establishes standards for protecting sensitive patient health information. For instance in a financial FL platform utilized to train credit risk models, an adversary can find out if a well-known person's credit information was used just by examining the model's output on public samples.

These vulnerabilities mirror the complex security and privacy context of FL[24]. Unlike traditional centralized learning where data breach is largely due to external attacks, FL introduces another layer of threats from within the collaborative system itself. The decentralized and trustless nature of FL requires robust technical countermeasures not just to ensure data privacy but also to maintain the integrity and reliability of trained models. Hence prevention of these threats requires an integrated solution that includes secure aggregation, differential privacy, client reputation systems, and anomaly detection algorithms.

4.6 FL ATTACK VECTORS

FL provides a dispersed model training process preserving the users privacy by storing the raw data locally on the client device. Although this architectural shift brings a set of new security risks in the next section, we detail four major categories of attacks taking advantage of FL's inherent vulnerabilities: data poisoning, model inversion, adversarial attacks and membership inference. These attack surfaces are not theoretical; they have been shown to be effective in research studies as well as in practice and are thus an imperative factor for any FL implementation [25].

4.6.1 Data poisoning

Data poisoning is a strong stealthy attack where an adversarial client as a user intentionally alters their local training data to control the action of the global model. The main objectives can be to degrade performance, trigger specific misclassifications, or subtly but maliciously alter the model's decision boundary.

In FL, attackers can cause massive loss of effectiveness of the global model by introducing maliciously formatted or mislabelled data into their local training process, a technique known as data poisoning. Since FL is decentralized in nature, client devices train models on local datasets locally and share only model updates and not the raw data. This structural aspect, although beneficial for privacy protection, is a vulnerability that can be exploited by an adversary. A malicious client can deliberately corrupt part of its training data by changing feature values or mislabelling the input; for example, labelling the digit 3 as 8 when the task is handwritten digit recognition. When these poisoned updates are combined with those received from honest clients, they imperceptibly disturb the learning path of the global model. These disturbances can lead to reduced accuracy or even the introduction of latent backdoors that induce erroneous behavior in specific situations. Since the central server has no direct access to the training data, it finds it challenging to distinguish between legitimate and poisoned updates, and thus such attacks become highly malicious and harmful in privacy-critical applications like medical, finance, and autonomous systems.

The learning process is governed by a global optimization criterion that attempts to minimize the overall loss for all the clients combined. This can be expressed as:

$$\min_{\theta} \sum_{k=1}^{K} \frac{n_k}{n} L_k(\theta) \tag{4.7}$$

where θ denotes the model parameters $L_k(\theta)$ denotes the local loss function evaluated over client k, dataset n_k denotes the size of client k, dataset and n denote the number of samples possessed by all the clients. This formulation ensures that the global model gets a weighted contribution from each client proportionate to the size of their local data. But this framework also risks being compromised if a cheating client intentionally modifies its local data, as it may undermine the global optimization procedure.

In particular the adversary corrupts their dataset D_k to a version $\tilde{D}_k$ which in turn yields a biased model update. The corrupted local update is defined as:

$$\tilde{\theta}_k^{t+1} = Update\left(\theta^t, \tilde{D}_k\right) \tag{4.8}$$

Here rather than training on genuine data the client trains on the poisoned dataset $\tilde{D}_k$ thus generating a biased update $\tilde{\theta}_k^{t+1}$. In the application of this update in the global aggregation step it injects adversarial bias into the aggregate model. Depending on the attack goal the effect could be subtle, lowering accuracy on a specific class, or severe, for instance injecting a backdoor that results in systematic misclassification. Importantly since the central server has no means of accessing or authenticating local data it has no idea of malicious alterations and the poisoned updates can blend perfectly with those of honest clients to poison the learning process undetected.

Case example

Bagdasaryan et al. (2020) [20] demonstrated how an attacker in a federated environment might add a backdoor into the global model with minimal visibility to other participants. In their experiments the attacker trained a model using data embedded with a unique trigger pattern such as a small patch in the bottom-right corner of an image and all instances of this trigger were assigned a specific target label. The attack was designed so that when the model encountered any input containing the same stimulus, it would render the attackers chosen label regardless of the actual input category predictable.

The attack was performed on the Modified National Institute of Standards and Technology (MNIST) database digit classification dataset within a baseline convolutional neural network architecture [26]. The attacker introduced malicious updates in just 1 out of 100 iterations of training. Even with the infrequent engagement an attacker was able to successfully embed a persistent backdoor into the global model. Most importantly the model had significant accuracy on clean test samples thus hiding the incidence of the assault from regular verification processes. The specific concern about this attack is its resistance to existing protection mechanisms. Significantly, even strong aggregation techniques such as Krum and coordinate-wise median, both designed to ignore or neutralize the impact of outlier updates, were proven unable to prevent learning of the backdoor. This suggests that poisoning attacks if carefully crafted and subtle might circumvent even the strongest defenses offered in FL settings.

In addition, the study observed the secretive and persistent behavior of the backdoor. Once it was formed malicious behavior continued to exist in the global model during multiple training loops, whether the attacker continued to interact or not. This demonstrates the long-term impact of short-term adversarial involvement and highlights the limitationsof today's trust assumptions in federated systems.

4.6.2 Model inversion attacks

One of the major privacy risks inherent in FL is illustrated by an attacker attempting to recover the underlying secret training data used by clients by exploiting shared gradients or model updates. In FL although raw data stays on local devices, clients calculate gradients over its own private dataset and upload the gradients to a central server to be aggregated. This mechanism is generally designed to preserve privacy. Nevertheless, the gradients can accidentally carry faint information regarding the underlying data particularly in the presence of an over parameterized model or an infinitesimal dataset [27].

The general concept of a model inversion attack is to consider the received gradient g as a target and find an input $\hat{x}$ so that when it is given to the model, the gradient will be close to g. This provides the following objective:

$$\hat{x} = \underset{x}{argmin} \left\| \nabla_\theta L\left(f_\theta(x), y\right) - g^2 \right\| \tag{4.9}$$

Here:

- $\hat{x}$ is the reconstructed approximation of the original training input.
- L is the last function (e.g. cross entropy).
- $f_\theta(x)$ is the neural networks prediction for input x with parameters θ.
- $\nabla_\theta L$ is the gradient of the law politely to model parameters.
- g is the actual gradient observed by the attackers (often the server).

The attacker begins the process with a random estimate x0 and repeatedly refines it with iterative optimization methods such as gradient descent to minimize the discrepancy between the calculated and actual gradients. Through multiple iterations the resulting input $\hat{x}$ settles into a form that effectively mimics the client's secret training data. Cross-entropy loss indicates the degree to which the predicted probabilities align with the actual labels in classification tasks. This measure imposes penalties on strongly confident incorrect predictions thereby guiding the model towards improving both accuracy and confidence during training.

FL infrastructure is employed for training a face recognition model on mobile phones. An honest but curious server aggregates model updates from the users. When an update relates to a gradient that closely approximates a certain face the server might employ model inversion to extract the user's image, potentially leaking personal biometric information. Not only is this a breach of user trust but its also of legal frameworks like the GDPR.

Factors influencing attack success:

- Model architecture: Deep or overfitted models tend to memorize more information making inversion easier.
- Gradient granularity: Single sample gradients [26] leak more information than patch average gradients.
- Loss function type: Some loss functions mean squared error (MSE) retain more input information in the gradients.
- Lack of noise: If gradients are more protected, for example, via differential privacy, inversion becomes more feasible.

This type of attack is particularly alarming because it does not require any modifications of the protocol it exploits as information is already available to the server. In sensitive sectors such as healthcare, finance, or biometrics, model inversion can cause serious breaches of confidentiality. Moreover, these attacks can succeed even when only partial gradients or early model iterations are available, raising serious questions about the sufficiency of current privacy-preserving strategies in FL.

Case example

Introduced the idea of Deep Leakage from Gradients.

The Deep Leakage from Gradients (DLG) method demonstrates that even a single gradient update can allow an attacker to reconstruct input images that are nearly indistinguishable from the original training samples, particularly when batch sizes are small. In their experiment, an attacker was provided with an initial model's parameters and one client's gradient update. Using gradient matching, the authors iteratively optimized a dummy input and a dummy label to match gradients observed. Figure 4.2 illustrates the step-by-step process of a model inversion attack in federated learning.

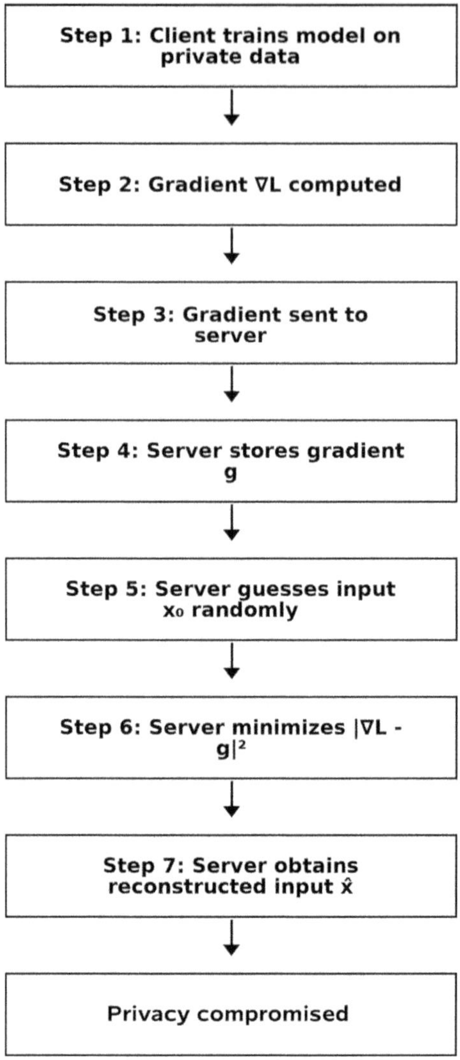

Figure 4.2 Process of a model inversion attack in federated learning.

Optimization continued until the generated gradients closely approximate those received from the actual client.The outcomes were spectacular: for image data such as MNIST and CIFAR-10, reconstructed samples were visually indistinguishable from the original training data even retaining fine detail features such as face structure or numerals. This shows that high-dimensional inputs can be properly estimated from gradient-level information only. DLG's performance relied significantly on small batch sizes, since gradients from small batches are strongly connected to single samples. Big batches conceal per-sample gradient information, lowering inversion fidelity. Small batches are typical in practice owing to memory and computational limits, particularly on edge devices.

The general implication is that honest-but-curious servers or third-party monitors can initiate such an attack without affecting the training process. This suggests a structural weakness in gradient-sharing protocols of FL, especially in resource-limited deployments.

The study points out that defensive methods such as gradient masking, secure aggregation, or differential privacy deployment are required to limit unintended information disclosure during training.

4.6.3 Adversarial attack

Adversarial attacks in the context of FL exploit the severity of machine learning models to small strategically crafted perturbations in the input data. These subtle manipulations are often imperceptible to human observers but can significantly mislead a model into making incorrect predictions. In FL the distributed and decentralized nature of training adds complexity to detecting and defending against such attacks especially when the client can be compromised or act maliciously.

The most widely known method to generate adversarial examples is in the Fast Gradient Sign Method. This technique creates adversarial samples by adding a calculated perturbation to the original input derived from the gradient of the loss function with respect to input features.

The adversarial input x_{adv} is computed as:

$$x_{adv} = x + \in .sign\left(\nabla_x L\left(f_\theta(x), y\right)\right) \tag{4.10}$$

Where:

- x is the original input.
- ϵ is a small scholar controlling the magnitude of the perturbation.
- L is the last function.
- f_θ is the model's birthday prediction function with parameters θ.
- y is the true label.
- Sign(.) is the element-wise sign function, producing a vector of +1 or -1.

This perturbed input is then classified by the model often resulting in incorrect predictions such as labelling a stop sign as a speed limit sign and errors that can be critical consequences in real world applications like autonomous driving or medical diagnostics.

Consider a handwriting recognition model trained via FL across multiple devices. A malicious client introduces adversarial examples during training by applying FGSM to digits like "7" crafting them so that they appear similar but are classified as "1". The attack might be unnoticed but can cause systematic degradation in the model accuracy when deployed.

Case example

The work by the authors demonstrated how a malicious client in a FL environment can craft adversarial model updates that lead to misclassification without triggering detection by standard aggregation defenses. The attacker's goal was to reduce the global models accuracy on specific classes by poisoning the model update gradients during each training round. The attacker trains its local model on a dataset with adversarial examples generated using techniques such as FGSM or PGD. These examples are designed to subtly perturb input data so that the following local gradient updates lead the global model astray to misclassify particular inputs. In contrast to backdoor attacks the goal in this case is not to misclassify particular triggers but to impair the global model's performance over a set of samples while being in normal behavior for others. A new feature of the attack was employing stealth mechanisms producing updates that resemble benign distributions or with similar norms to true updates so that the malicious contributions can evade defenses like Krum or Trimmed Mean. The results indicated that the existence of some malicious clients—even 10%—resulted in significant reductions in test accuracy and performance of the target class due to adversarially poisoned updates. This underscored the vulnerability of FL systems to adversarial gradient attacks and limitations of current aggregation techniques.

4.6.4 Implications

Figure 4.3 illustrates the Fast Gradient Sign Method (FGSM) used to generate adversarial examples in machine learning. Such attacks pose serious security risk because:

- They are transferable, meaning adversarial examples crafted for one model may affect others.
- There are hard to detect due to the imperceptible nature of perturbations.
- They can be launched during training or inference, making them flexible in timings.

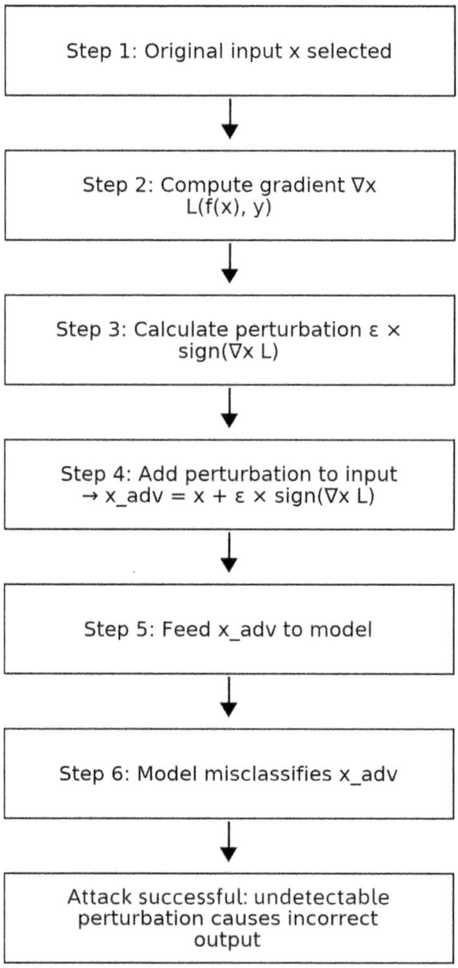

Figure 4.3 Fast gradient sign method (FGSM): a widely used adversarial attack technique in machine learning.

- In FL malicious clients can inject poisoned updates containing adversarial examples that compromise the global model without needing central access.

4.6.5 Countermeasures considerations

To defend against such attacks FL system may adopt:

- Adversarial training where the model is trained on adversarial samples to improve robustness.
- Gradient masking although it has limitations and can sometimes be circumvented.
- Certified defenses such as randomized smoothing or robust optimization frameworks.

4.6.6 Membership inference attacks in FL

Membership inference attacks are powerful privacy threats in FL where an advisory aims to determine whether a specific data example was part of a clients training dataset. Despite FL's decentralized design the leakage of model outputs or gradients can enable attackers to make such inferences. These attacks exploit the tendency of models to behave differently on training data versus unseen data particularly in terms of confidence scores, loss values, or prediction entropy.

Let:

- $x \in X$ be a data sample,
- $y \in Y$ be its true label,
- $f_{\theta(x)}$ be the model's prediction,
- $L(f_{\theta(x)}, y)$ be the loss function.

If the model produces higher confidence and lower loss for sample x then x is more likely to have been the training set. An attacker trains a shadow model and constructs a binary classifier C(·) to distinguish between member and non-member data samples.

$$MembershipScore = C\left(Confidence\left(f_\theta(x),\right),\ L\left(f_\theta(x),Y\right)\right) \tag{4.11}$$

If the score exceeds a threshold τ the advisory predicts the x was a member of the training dataset.

$$\text{Predict Member if Membership Score} > \tau \tag{4.12}$$

This is particularly dangerous in sensitive domains such as healthcare or finance where revealing the presence of a sample in the training dataset could disclose private patient or client information.

Suppose a FL model is trained on hospital data set to classify disease types. If an adversary can query the model through an Application Programming (AP) interface with patients' dataset and obtain a highly confident prediction, they might infer that the patient was in the training set leaking information about their diagnosis or treatment history. Figure 4.4 illustrates the workflow of a membership inference attack (MIA) in machine learning.

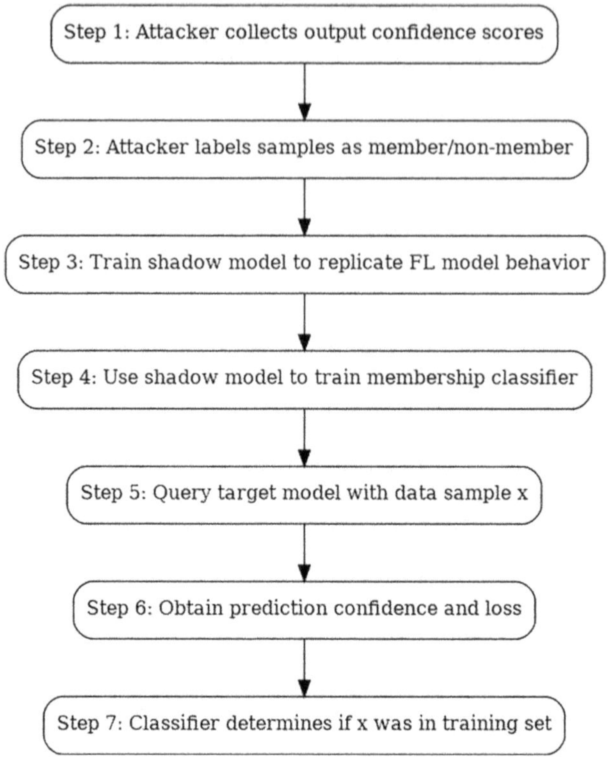

Figure 4.4 Membership inference attack (MIA): common privacy attack in machine learning.

Case example

Shokri et al. (2017) performed one of the first comprehensive analyses of membership inference attacks against deep learning models, and their research was later extended to federated learning settings. Under an FL setup an attack can be mounted by a passive server that simply observes the updates which the clients provide in multiple training iterations. The attacker then uses a shadow training approach where multiple shadow models are trained to mimic the behavior of the target model for generating training data and non-training data profiles. Using such shadow models the attacker builds a membership inference classifier to determine whether a specific input was part of the training set [28]. The attack works particularly well when clients maintain small or unique datasets, as this makes their individual contributions to the global model more apparent and easier to infer. The authors through their experiments demonstrated that the server without active intervention could correctly infer the presence of individual records in a client's local dataset[7]. This situation indicates that FL privacy weaknesses are not restricted to direct intervention or access. Even passive parties can perform inference attacks by exploiting the dynamics concerning model training and update patterns which is a significant concern on the privacy assurances of federated systems.

4.6.7 Countermeasures

To defend against membership inference attack (MIA) FL system can adopt:

- Differential privacy adds noise to the outputs or gradients to obscure training membership.
- Regularization reduces overfitting, making the model less confident on training data.
- Prediction clipping limits the maximum confidence the model can output.
- Output perturbation adds noise to the prediction layer or confidence scores.

4.7 DEFENSIVE METHODOLOGIES IN FL

As FL continues to expand into sensitive and high-stakes domains such as finance, healthcare, and critical infrastructure, it becomes increasingly important to deploy robust defensive mechanisms against adversarial behaviors. This section presents a detailed overview of four primary security strategies aimed at preserving model integrity, protecting user data, and ensuring trustworthy collaboration and distributed environments.

4.7.1 Robust aggregation techniques

One of the core vulnerabilities in FL is the reliance on aggregating updates from multiple clients, some of which may be adversarial. Traditional averaging is highly sensitive to outliers or poisoned updates. To counter this robust aggregation technique, filter malicious or anomalous data before contributing to the global model.

- **Krum Algorithm:** Select the update most like its neighboring clients. From each client k score is computed as the sum of squared Euclidean distance to the n – f – 2 closest updates where f is the estimated number of malicious clients:

$$Score(w_k) = \sum_{j \in N(k)} \left\| w_k - w_j \right\|^2 \tag{4.13}$$

The update with the lowest score is selected for model aggregation.

- **Trimmed Mean:** For each parameter dimension it removes the top and bottom F values before calculating the average:

$$\widetilde{w^{(d)}} = \frac{1}{K - 2f} \sum_{k \notin Extreme} w_k^{(d)} \tag{4.14}$$

- **Median Aggregation:** Instead of averaging the median is computed for each parameter dimension:

$$\tilde{w}^{(d)} = median\left(w_1^{(d)},\ w2_2^{(d)},\ldots\ldots.w_K^{(d)}\right) \tag{4.15}$$

These methods reduce the influence of poisoned updates and enhance the robustness of global model convergence.

4.7.2 Differential privacy (DP)

Differential privacy introduces mathematical guarantees that individual data points cannot be inferred from the shared model parameters. This is achieved by injecting random noise into the model updates before they are transmitted into the server.

$$\widetilde{w_k^{t+1}} = w_k^{t+1} + N\left(0, \sigma^2 I\right) \tag{4.16}$$

Here, $N\left(0, \sigma^2 I\right)$ denotes the Gaussian distribution with 0 mean and variance σ^2. This noise effectively obfuscates sensitive patterns in local data while allowing the overall model to learn generalizable features.

4.7.3 Homomorphic Encryption (HE)

Homomorphic encryption permits computations such as addition to be performed on encrypted data without requiring decryption. In FL each client encrypts their model updates before transmission. The server aggregates the encrypted updates:

$$Enc\left(w^{t+1}\right) = \sum_{k=1}^{K} Enc(w_k^{t+1}) \tag{4.17}$$

The key advantage of homomorphic encryption is that the server does not learn anything about individual updates even during aggregation. Only the clients or a trusted decryption party can recover the final result thereby ensuring end-to-end confidentiality.

4.7.4 Anomaly detection

To identify malicious or uncooperative clients Federated Learning systems can implement anomaly detection algorithms. These methods evaluate the similarity between each client's update and the current global model. Cosine similarity is formally employed as the similarity metric.

$$similarity = \frac{w_k . w_t}{\left\|w_k\right\| \left\|w_t\right\|} \tag{4.18}$$

If the similarity falls below a predefined threshold the client's update may be flagged for further investigation or exclusion.

These defense mechanisms give multi-layered security to FL system. By tackling weaknesses at various points, namely aggregation, communication, and data security, they guarantee that FL can run securely even in adversarial or partially trusted environments. Using a combination of these techniques is highly advised for scalable and secure FL deployment.

4.8 REAL-WORLD APPLICATIONS OF FL

FL is gaining widespread acceptance in various domains where data privacy, regulatory conformity, and distributed data sources overlap. This chapter provides a detailed overview of FL applications in healthcare, finance, and the Internet of things (IoT) emphasizing technical mechanisms, implementation challenges, and benefits achieved through decentralized intelligence.

4.8.1 Healthcare facilitation of collective intelligence while maintaining patient confidentiality

In the medical field the potential of leveraging data from several institutions can greatly enhance diagnostic precision, disease forecasting, and customized treatment plans but patient information is usually governed by stringent privacy laws and ethical issues that keep hospitals and medical research institutions from exchanging raw data even for mutual advantages. FL provides a solution that enables institutions to contribute to collaborative model development without exposing sensitive patient records to anyone.

Using FL, a hospital is able to train machine learning models locally across patient electronic health records, medical imaging data like MRI or CT scan, and other clinical measures. Only the resulting model parameters or gradients are transferred to a core server which aggregates them to update a global model. The architecture enables real-time collaboration while maintaining data protection requirements like GDPR and HIPAA.

A real-world example is seen in cross-hospital collaboration for sepsis on set prediction in ICU patients. Instead of passing raw vital sign data or laboratory test results to a third party, each institution is involved in Federated training that goes into our strong model with early warning and improved generalization across heterogeneous populations. FL is also used for cancer detection from histopathology images where maintaining the confidentiality of image data is both a medical and legal requirement.

4.8.2 Finance cross institutional collaboration for secure fraud detection and risk profiling

The finance industry faces similar tension between the need for collaborative intelligence and the imperative to protect client confidentiality and proprietary data. Financial institutions often detect fraud or assess credit risk based on internal transaction histories and behavioral pattern. However, these isolated models lack the breadth of exposure that comes from more diverse datasets. FL allows banks, insurance providers, and credit scoring agencies to develop joint machine learning models without sharing raw transaction records, account details, or other sensitive financial data.

By enabling each branch or institution to locally train a model on its customer data, FL supports the aggregation of diverse learning patterns into a unified model that reflects broader financial behaviour. For instance, a fraud detection model can become more sensitive to new and complex threat vectors such as synthetic identity fraud or transaction laundering by learning from patterns that appear across institutions without revealing any actual customer identities or transaction contents.

Real-world deployments have seen FL applied to a collaborative anti-money laundering system where various financial institutions contribute to a federated model capable of identifying suspicious cross-border transactions. In such cases the decentralized learning approach not only improves the accuracy of detection but also strengthens compliance with financial regulations that prohibit the exchange of personal or sensitive data across jurisdictions.

4.8.3 IOT empowering distributed intelligence across edge devices

On the Internet of Things landscape billions of connected devices ranging from smart thermostats and surveillance cameras to wearable fitness trackers continuously collect and process vast volumes of data. Traditional machine learning architecture relies on sending this data to a server-based cloud server for training which introduces privacy concerns, bandwidth bottlenecks, and latency. FL circumvents these issues by bringing the model to the data, allowing edge devices to perform local training and only share model updates with a coordinating server.

This method is most suited to situations in which real-time feedback is needed or in which periodic connectivity renders continuous data transfer unrealistic. In smart home scenarios for example, FL enables individual devices such as voice assistants to learn user preferences and accents without uploading raw audio files to third-party servers. In the same way, industrial IoT sensors installed on factory floors can jointly train anomaly detection models to anticipate equipment breakdown without transferring proprietary operational information.

An interesting case exists in intelligent surveillance systems used in city areas. Instead of sending unprocessed video to a controlling body each surveillance device can train object detection models on its immediate surroundings such as recognizing junk objects or sensing unauthorized access. The model aggregated from diverse visual observations gathered at various points becomes more contextual and accurate while at the same time being data protection regulation compliant and minimizing the extent of surveillance overreach.

These case studies highlight the real-world feasibility of FL as a privacy-concerning and regulation-suitable successor to conventional centralized machine learning. In healthcare it enables safe inter-institutional research, in finance it supports fraud detection within organizational boundaries and, in IoT it brings intelligence to the edge of the network.

Moreover, by reducing dependency on centralized data storage FL enhances resilience against data breaches and cyber attacks which are particularly critical in these high-stake domains. As industries continue to digitize and generate increasingly sensitive data FL is poised to become a cornerstone of ethical and secure AI innovation.

4.9 CONCLUSION

FL has become a revolutionary paradigm in machine learning, especially in situations where data privacy regulatory compliance and distributed computational infrastructure are of utmost significance. Through collaborative model training, without having to transfer the raw data to centralized servers, FL provides a promising framework for maintaining user confidentiality in various sectors such as clinical care, finance, and Internet of Things. Its capacity to tap the potential of decentralized datasets while minimizing the risk of data outflow represents a major leap in the creation of ethical and privacy-aware artificial intelligence systems.

Despite its benefits FL is not free from cybersecurity attacks. In fact the same decentralization that provides FL with its privacy-preserving features also creates new attack surface. Malicious intent actors can use such vulnerabilities in techniques like data poisoning, model inversion, membership inference, and adversarial perturbations all of which could endanger the integrity, accuracy, and confidentiality of the end models. In addition, since there is no core control, it would be that much harder to detect and counter abnormal behaviors in real time.

To mitigate such threats a range of defensive approaches have been put forward and are still evolving. Strong aggregation methods like Krum, Trimmed Mean and Median can diminish the impact of malicious updates through the exclusion of outliners. Differential privacy adds mathematically assured noise to the updates thus constraining the possibility of single data reconstruction. Homomorphic encryption offers the functionality of computation over encrypted data with a guarantee that even the coordinating server is kept in the dark about individual client inputs. In addition, anomaly detection systems can identify unusual update patterns that can be used to detect possibly compromised participants.

However, the effective deployment of such defensive measures depends on continuous research and careful tuning. No one-size-fits-all approach exists, and every application field could have its own specific set of limitations and adversary models. Hence, continuous innovation through threat modelling and multidisciplinary coordination are vital to the evolution of both security and usefulness in FL systems.

In summary, although Federated Learning offers a strong solution to privacy-preserving machine learning it must be handled with care and utmost security focus. All stakeholders such as researchers, practitioners, policymakers, and industry leaders must be proactive and watchful when dealing with the shifting threat horizon. Only by a continuous focus on both privacy as well as security can Federated Learning realize its complete potential as a secure and scalable solution for decentralized artificial intelligence.

4.10 FUTURE IMPROVEMENTS

As FL continues to improve various promising fronts are being explored to overcome its limitations and improve its immunity against present and future security threats. These are both technological and strategic in nature with the goal of developing a more scalable, secure, and reliable machine learning system. Technologically, more sophisticated cryptographic methods such as homomorphic encryption, secure multi-party computation (SMPC), and differential privacy are being employed to an increasing extent. These methods allow model training while protecting raw data, thereby improving privacy protection among the participating clients.

Growing emphasis on standardized communication protocols, interoperability frameworks, and federated governance models is facilitating easier collaboration among different devices and organizations. Intel's OpenFL, WeBank's FATE, and Google's TensorFlow Federated are prime examples of these, with well-structured scalable platforms that can be customized for different industries.

Focus is being given to threat modelling where possible attack surfaces like model poisoning, inference attacks, and malicious users are proactively sought out and addressed through sound anomaly detection measures and client authentication mechanisms. All these developments not only tackle known vulnerabilities but also render FL systems resilient to changing adversarial strategies.

Briefly, the convergence of cryptographic advancements, robust standardization, and proactive security cultures is increasingly making Federated Learning an even more secure and forward-looking paradigm. With these advancements becoming more widely used, FL is on the path to becoming a building block technology in the deployment of privacy-preserving and decentralized AI in mission-critical domains like healthcare, finance, and smart edge computing.

4.10.1 Blockchain integration

One of the most promising augmentations is bringing Blockchain Technology into FL. By taking advantage of blockchain's decentralized and immutable ledger FL systems are able to obtain higher transparency, accountability, and traceability in model update processes. Client contributions to the global model can be timestamped and securely written on chain so that it can be possible to detect tampering, rollback malicious updates, and create auditable histories of model evaluation. This combination of FL and Blockchain sometimes termed as "Federated Learning over Blockchain (FL-B)" provides an authenticated infrastructure particularly beneficial in high risk domines like healthcare finance where auditability regularity compliance is critical.

4.10.2 Quantum resistant cryptography

Traditional methods of encryption employed in FL like Rivest Shamir Adleman (RSA) and Elliptic Curve Cryptography (ECC) can in the near future become susceptible to quantum attacks because of the emergence of quantum computing. Consequently, quantum resistant cryptography, also referred to as post-quantum cryptography, is becoming increasingly vital. Cryptographic algorithms like lattice-based encryption, hash-based signatures and multivariate cryptographic schemes are being explored in depth to future-proof FL systems. Such next-generation cryptographic protocols promise to offer security guarantees that hold good even in a post-quantum future thus guaranteeing the long-term and long-lived nature of privacy protection mechanisms for FL.

4.10.3 Self-healing federated systems

In pursuit of improving system resilience research is moving towards designing self-healing FL systems. These systems have the ability to use deep learning features like auto encoders or recurrent neural networks in order to detect anomalies in client updates and heal from malicious behavior or poisoned data states automatically. For example, an encoder may be trained to represent the standard form of honest updates and trigger alarms whenever deviation surpasses learned thresholds. By providing automatic anomalous behavior detection isolation and correction, self-healing mechanisms can substantially enhance the trust and stability of FL deployments without a need for widespread manual monitoring.

4.10.4 Federated protocol standards

With expansion of FL into diverse industries, there is a need for standardized communication and security protocols. Lack of standard guidelines for implementation currently results in fragmentation and heterogeneous security assurances among deployments. Setting FL protocols standards for secure aggregation, differential privacy practices, model format interoperability, and compliance checks would promote higher consistency, interoperability, and trust between systems. These standards could also speed up regularity approval and enable international cooperation on secure FL-based systems especially in areas with high data governance requirements.

The future of FL is in its potential to evolve in response to future challenges and technologies. The incorporation of blockchain for transparency using quantum-resistant encryption, employing self-healing mechanism, and protocol standards compliance will altogether form the next generation of secure, scalable, and robust FL systems. Interdisciplinary research and collaboration with industry will be essential in bringing these improvements and achieving widescale secure deployment in real-world settings.

REFERENCES

[1] Albalawi, E., TR, M., Thakur, A., Kumar, V. V., Gupta, M., Khan, S. B., & Almusharraf, A. (2024). Integrated approach of federated learning with transfer learning for classification and diagnosis of brain tumor. *BMC Medical Imaging*, *24*(1), 110.

[2] Harzevili, N. S., Shin, J., Wang, J., Wang, S., & Nagappan, N. (2023, May). Characterizing and understanding software security vulnerabilities in machine learning libraries. In *2023 IEEE/ACM 20th International Conference on Mining Software Repositories (MSR)* (pp. 27–38). IEEE.

[3] Waked, L., Mannan, M., & Youssef, A. (2020). The sorry state of TLS security in enterprise interception appliances. *Digital Threats: Research and Practice*, *1*(2), 1–26.

[4] Ambalavanan, V. (2020). Cyber threats detection and mitigation using machine learning. In *Handbook of Research on Machine and Deep Learning Applications for Cyber Security* (pp. 132–149). IGI Global.

[5] Regulation, P. (2018). General data protection regulation. *Intouch*, *25*, 1–5.

[6] Liang, X., Konstantinou, C., Shetty, S., Bandara, E., & Sun, R. (2023). Decentralizing cyber physical systems for resilience: An innovative case study from a cybersecurity perspective. *Computers & Security*, *124*, 102953.

[7] Abdelzaher, T. F., & Lu, C. (2000, December). Modeling and performance control of internet servers. In *Proceedings of the 39th IEEE Conference on Decision and Control (Cat. No. 00CH37187)* (Vol. 3, pp. 2234–2239). IEEE.

[8] Li, J., Chen, T., & Teng, S. (2024). A comprehensive survey on client selection strategies in federated learning. *Computer Networks, 240*, 110663.

[9] Cieslak, D. A., & Chawla, N. V. (2008, December). Start globally, optimize locally, predict globally: Improving performance on imbalanced data. In *2008 Eighth IEEE International Conference on Data Mining* (pp. 143–152). IEEE.

[10] Rastogi, V., & Nath, S. (2010, June). Differentially private aggregation of distributed time-series with transformation and encryption. In *Proceedings of the 2010 ACM SIGMOD International Conference on Management of Data* (pp. 735–746).

[11] Zambrano, R., Jamroz, M., Szczasiuk, A., Pujols, J., Kmiecik, S., & Ventura, S. (2015). AGGRESCAN3D (A3D): Server for prediction of aggregation properties of protein structures. *Nucleic Acids Research*, *43*(W1), W306–W313.

[12] de Carné de Carnavalet, X. (2019). *Last-Mile TLS Interception: Analysis and Observation of the Non-Public HTTPS Ecosystem* (Doctoral dissertation, Concordia University).

[13] Mallick, M. A. I., & Nath, R. (2024). Navigating the cyber security landscape: A comprehensive review of cyber-attacks, emerging trends, and recent developments. *World Scientific News*, *190*(1), 1–69.

[14] Akintola, A. S. (2024). Integrating research testbeds, attack mechanisms, and defence strategies into a holistic framework for cybersecurity. *Journal of Computer Science Review and Engineering, 8*(2) 1–12. DOI: https://doi.org/10.5281/zenodo.14543273.

[15] Beltrán, E. T. M., Pérez, M. Q., Sánchez, P. M. S., Bernal, S. L., Bovet, G., Pérez, M. G., ... & Celdrán, A. H. (2023). Decentralized federated learning: Fundamentals, state of the art, frameworks, trends, and challenges. *IEEE Communications Surveys & Tutorials, 25*(4), 2983–3013.

[16] Qing, Y., Yin, Q., Deng, X., Chen, Y., Liu, Z., Sun, K., ... & Li, Q. (2023). Low-quality training data only? A robust framework for detecting encrypted malicious network traffic. *arXiv preprint arXiv:2309.04798.*

[17] Chai, Q., & Gong, G. (2012, June). Verifiable symmetric searchable encryption for semi-honest-but-curious cloud servers. In *2012 IEEE International Conference on Communications (ICC)* (pp. 917–922). IEEE.

[18] Cao, X., & Gong, N. Z. (2022). Mpaf: Model poisoning attacks to federated learning based on fake clients. In *Proceedings of the IEEE/CVF Conference on Computer Vision and Pattern Recognition* (pp. 3396–3404).

[19] Guo, X., Liu, Z., Li, J., Gao, J., Hou, B., Dong, C., & Baker, T. (2020). V erifl: Communication-efficient and fast verifiable aggregation for federated learning. *IEEE Transactions on Information Forensics and Security, 16*, 1736–1751.

[20] Bagdasaryan, E., Veit, A., Hua, Y., Estrin, D., & Shmatikov, V. (2020). *How to backdoor federated learning.* AISTATS. https://arxiv.org/abs/1807.00459

[21] Steinhardt, J., Koh, P. W. W., & Liang, P. S. (2017). Certified defenses for data poisoning attacks. *Advances in Neural Information Processing Systems, 30*, 3520–3532.

[22] Zhu, L., Liu, Z., & Han, S. (2019). *Deep leakage from gradients.* NeurIPS. https://arxiv.org/abs/1906.08935

[23] Bhagoji, A. N., Chakraborty, S., Mittal, P., & Calo, S. (2019). Analyzing federated learning through an adversarial lens. *ICML.* https://arxiv.org/abs/1811.12470

[24] Nasr, M., Shokri, R., & Houmansadr, A. (2019). Comprehensive privacy analysis of deep learning: Passive and active white-box inference attacks. *IEEE.* https://arxiv.org/abs/1812.00910

[25] Shayegani, E., Mamun, M. A. A., Fu, Y., Zaree, P., Dong, Y., & Abu-Ghazaleh, N. (2023). Survey of vulnerabilities in large language models revealed by adversarial attacks. *arXiv preprint arXiv:2310.10844.*

[26] Waked, L., Mannan, M., & Youssef, A. (2018, May). To intercept or not to intercept: Analyzing tls interception in network appliances. In *Proceedings of the 2018 on Asia Conference on Computer and Communications Security* (pp. 399–412).

[27] Wu, X., Fredrikson, M., Jha, S., & Naughton, J. F. (2016, June). A methodology for formalizing model-inversion attacks. In *2016 IEEE 29th Computer Security Foundations Symposium (CSF)* (pp. 355–370). IEEE.

[28] Waked, L., Mannan, M., & Youssef, A. (2018, May). To intercept or not to intercept: Analyzing tls interception in network appliances. In *Proceedings of the 2018 on Asia Conference on Computer and Communications Security* (pp. 399–412).

Chapter 5

Zero Trust principles in AI-driven architectures

Security by design

Kiran Malik, Jagjit Singh Dhatterwal, Kuldeep Singh Kaswan, and Sunil Kumar Makkar

5.1 INTRODUCTION

In a world where artificial intelligence (AI) is sweeping its application across everything you can think of, from medical and finance industries to cybersecurity and self-driving machines, technology develops a strong natural link with the expanding vulnerabilities. However, these risk problems are not straightforward. Traditional defense frameworks such as perimeter-based model generally do not work when you come to tackle them on a large scale. With this large scale project has come other revolutionary technologies which run at the highest speed and scale, in many cases like systems driven by continuous, automated intelligence, as opposed to implicit trust. The past security models, used in legacy and perimeter security networks, are inadequate to secure the moderninfrastructures. The networks, applications, and data of today are extensively dispersed throughout the users, their devices and settings, and implicit trust is no longer a possibility. This paradigm change resulted in the implementation of the Zero Trust paradigm, whose idea is based on the principle of never trust, always verify. It extends the practical application of this principle to address the specific problems posed by an AI-driven environment [1]. This chapter focuses specifically on the following topics: What is Zero Trust AI? How AI has developed; new security vulnerabilities that are emerging as we go back one sentence in time and think about no users' trust.

Zero Trust AI goes one step beyond this by considering the specifics that are presented by AI-driven environments, where the issue of autonomous decision-making, mass data usage, and a dynamically evolving model of learning presents new security threats. The chapter is dedicated to the concept of Zero Trust AI, the history of the development of AI, new security threats of the AI systems, and the implementation of the Zero Trust principles of the protection of the AI-enabled architecture [1].

5.1.1 What is zero trust?

Zero Trust is a security model which places the traditional idea of an inner and outer network at a standstill. According to this model, nobody may be trusted merely because they are employees of the firm. Every request for access, whether from a user, device, or application, is treated as untrustworthy until it has been verified. According to the principles of Zero Trust model, since there is the likelihood that attackers will eventually breach the network, efforts should be made to reduce whatever damage they can achieve. This means to say that instead of containing strong perimeter defenses only (which operate like fences to people either inside or outside the company), security has been built into every layer of the system and all access is continuously verified and authenticated. The Zero Trust model rests

DOI: 10.1201/9781003660330-5

on three main principles: never trust but always verify (even with local data!), least privilege access, and micro segmentation. Each rule ensures that even if an attacker has gotten into one part of the network, his abilities are small and he can't cross the whole environment in one go. The main thrust of Zero Trust is not only how to protect data, but protecting the systems generating it and those that interact with it—this aligns perfectly with emerging AI system requirements. The growing complexity of AI has been rapid: from predictive analytics on through self-driving cars and decision-making algorithms. Early AI systems were very rule-cut and straightforward, but the rise of machine learning (ML) and deep learning led to increasingly autonomous, sophisticated systems. Such developments have turned whole industries on their heads, but they have also brought with them new dangers.

The more complicated and independent AI systems become, the more new possibilities emerge for attackers in those areas. AI applications often require a hefty sum of sensitive data to train models, which paves the way for malicious actors to exploit. Moreover, AI systems are not immune to vulnerabilities in their underlying software or hardware: adversarial attacks, model inversion, and data poisoning are among the potential threats that they face. In the process of adversarial attacks, an AI system could be made to make mistakes by tiny tweaks to its input data that would be imperceptible on the part of a human. What makes this kind of attack so nasty is that it can be extremely tailored and subtle. An adversary might achieve his ends this way without being noticed at all. And another question for us to think over is whether we have sufficient computing power today to handle thousands or even millions of small decisions, such as what food an AI cooks up in her cramped little CPU kitchen every night?

Moreover, another new threat vector is tampering with the very data used to train AI models. If an adversary can get at and change that set of data—well, it's like he's feeding bad tomatoes into your otherwise perfect tomato soup. In the case of facial recognition systems, for example, an attacker could modify the training data so as to cause the model to fail in specific instances or yield incorrect results. As AI systems are used in increasingly sensitive domains and become more critical to society, from financial systems right through to healthcare applications, the cost of these vulnerabilities grows larger still.

AI systems are closely linked to other technologies such as the Internet of Things (IoT), which creates a larger attack surface. A compromised IoT device might lead to an AI system being penetrated and even worse consequences. The increasing reliance on cloud-based infrastructure for training and deploying AI models also presents new challenges, because data stored in the network can be vulnerable to external attacks. Securing these systems means that traditional and novel attack vectors must both be taken into account, so the approach to defense needs to be comprehensive [2].

5.2. LITERATURE SURVEY

According to Table 5.1, the concept of AI is increasingly becoming part of the advanced security architecture like Zero Trust Architecture (ZTA), Learning-based and Secure Federated Learning (SFL), as well as adaptive access control. First principles and theory, including Kindervag's Zero Trust model [6], formed the theoretical underpinnings of never trust, always verify, whereas subsequent research applied this to threat intelligence that can be powered through AI [7, 13, 14]. These advancements showed better adaptability, detection, and predictive features, although most of them were not validated at large scale and in real time.

Table 5.1 Literature survey

Authors and Year	*Key Findings*	*Methodology/ Techniques Used*	*Results/Remarks*	*Finding Gaps*
Jorquera Valero et al. (2018) [3]	Introduced an intelligent and adaptive continuous authentication system to improve mobile device security and QoE	ML-based adaptive system for authentication	Improved security and user experience on mobile devices	Lack of large-scale real-world deployment and evaluation
Kang et al. (2023) [4]	Surveyed theory and application of Zero Trust Security (ZTS)	Literature review and conceptual analysis	Provided a comprehensive overview of ZTS evolution	Lacked empirical validation and performance metrics
Karantzas & Patsakis (2021) [5]	Assessed Endpoint Detection and Response (EDR) systems against APTs	Empirical experiments with attack vectors	Found vulnerabilities and limitations in EDR systems	Focused only on specific APT techniques; broader attacks were not covered
Kindervag (2010) [6]	Proposed the Zero Trust Network Architecture (ZTNA) model	Conceptual framework development	Introduced the principle of "never trust, always verify"	Initial conceptual work; lacked practical implementation guidelines
Kommera (2025) [7]	Enhanced ZTA with AI-driven threat intelligence in cloud environments	Framework proposal integrating AI in ZTA	Improved threat detection and adaptive responses	Needs real-world validation and scalability tests
Liu et al. (2020) [8]	Developed a secure federated transfer learning framework	Federated Learning techniques with security enhancements	Enabled secure knowledge transfer without data sharing	Computational overhead and privacy trade-offs not fully addressed
Mandapuram et al. (2018) [9]	Explored prospects of generative AI	Review of generative AI models and applications	Highlighted potential benefits across sectors	Limited focus on security implications of generative models
Mohammed (2021) [10]	Studied AI interaction with Identity and Access Management (IAM)	Empirical study with AI-IAM integration analysis	Demonstrated improved IAM efficiency using AI	Small sample size; limited industrial application scope
Moubayed et al. (2019) [11]	Reviewed Software-Defined Perimeter (SDP) as a security solution	Literature review and architecture analysis	SDP shown to mitigate network vulnerabilities effectively	Lack of performance analysis in highly dynamic environments

(*Continued*)

Table 5.1 (Continued)

Authors and Year	*Key Findings*	*Methodology/ Techniques Used*	*Results/Remarks*	*Finding Gaps*
Narouei et al. (2020) [12]	Automated extraction of access control policies from natural language	NLP techniques to derive security policies	Achieved significant automation in policy extraction	Scalability to different languages and domains remains a challenge
Paul & Sheriffdeen (2022) [13]	Analyzed AI's role in enhancing Zero Trust Security	Conceptual study with case illustrations	AI crucial for adaptive and predictive security in Zero Trust models	Lack of real-time AI-ZT integration performance analysis
Ramezanpour & Jagannath (2022) [14]	Proposed intelligent ZTA for 5G/6G using ML in O-RAN context	ML algorithms for adaptive ZT in next-gen networks	Enhanced security and flexibility in O-RAN environments	Future work needed on latency and real-time threat detection
Rangaraju (2023) [15]	Discussed AI-driven security enhancements in products	Case study-based analysis	AI incorporation significantly increased security capabilities	Standardization and interoperability issues not addressed
Sarhan et al. (2023) [16]	Proposed CTI sharing scheme via Federated Learning for NIDS	Federated Learning-based CTI model	Improved privacy-preserving threat intelligence sharing	Scalability and robustness under adversarial attacks need testing
Unger et al. (2020) [17]	Context-aware recommendations using deep learning	Deep learning models for context handling	Improved relevance and accuracy of recommendations	Security and privacy concerns in context data utilization were not covered
Wang et al. (2025) [18]	Designed dynamic access control model based on Zero Trust for clouds	Policy-driven dynamic access control integrated with ZT principles	Enhanced security in cloud-based access control	Needs validation across different cloud service models (IaaS, PaaS, SaaS)

Some of the contributions were devoted to the topic of endpoint and access security: adaptive authentication systems [3], IAM improvements [10], dynamic cloud access controls [18]. Although these methods enhanced flexibility and efficiency, shortcomings with regard to scalability, interoperability, and deployment in diverse environments persisted.

Other contributions focused on federated learning and policy automation [8, 12, 16] that allow decentralized collaboration in data sharing and automation to mitigate privacy challenges. The emerging paradigms, such as SDP [11] and generative AI [9] also widened the range. Generally, some remaining issues are real-world deployment, scalability, interoperability, and experimental evidence of the security in a variety of security environments.

The unique challenges posed by the use of AI technologies dictate that there be a move from traditional security models to more flexible ones that can be used dynamically in today's decentralized systems. Zero Trust, a system of principles well suited to both known and unknown threats in environments where no single conduit for trust exists, is the perfect fit for this job. Zero Trust has another advantage in that it does not just guard the perimeter, it protects every user, device, and system interaction, making it a unique framework to tackle the Byzantine complexities of AI security. One of the most worrying things about AI, and hence one reason why Zero Trust is so important to it, is its autonomy. In traditional models once a system or network and an individual has been trusted, subsequent interactions are usually given carte blanche to roam far and wide. But with AI, we can't stick to a single, constant understanding of trust except as a rough approximation that must frequently be reviewed and re-invented. Up till now, AI models have tended to reside in data centers, where they can easily be isolated. But increasingly they are moving to terminal devices and other environments. Under this data model, it is impossible for any access authorization to have a "once and for all" application. Constant scrutiny and constant authentication is needed. Under Zero Trust, AI systems always operate in a secure environment no matter how much they learn and grow: its emphasis on continuous monitoring and adaptive authentication sees to that.

A chief demand of AI is for huge data. Data and AI is inseparable synergy, but it is also the primary target in an attack. Also, with Zero Trust it is necessary to enclose data at the least possible level. This ensures that data required for specific tasks is available to authorized users and systems merely and access is strictly dependent on rigid contextual conditions. For example, in the AI-based health diagnosing system under Zero Trust, according to user's role, the terminal used, and when information is requested, access to sensitive patient data might be denied. This fine-grained application can help lower the probability of data being illicitly transferred or abused. Micro-segmentation is an especially useful recipe when it comes to Zero Trust for AI security. With micro-segmentation, networks are broken down into a number of smaller and tighter segments, which in turn limits the extent to which an attack can go. In an AI setting, micro-segmentation ensures even if part of the AI system is compromised, it cannot readily lead to dismantling all of the plant. For example, if an attacker is able to break into a real-time decision-making AI model, micro-segmentation guarantees that the impact of this intrusion is minimized by separating the model from other systemic units. For this kind of occasion, DBs or other AI services might qualify. Ultimately, strong identity and access management (IAM) systems remain vital for AI environments. In an AI environment full of human-machine hybrids, the integrity of every single identity is critical to security. The systems of Zero Trust Identity and Access Management (IAM) offer identity verification on an ongoing basis, using tools like multi-factor authentication (MFA). Moreover, behavioral analysis may also be added to this, in which findings based on machine-learning models are applied to constantly evaluate the user trust and access legitimacy. The outcome is security boosted: only identities which we trust—human or artificial—are allowed to interact with AI systems and data.

The security challenges from AI come in various forms; for example, not only technological ones, but also operational and ethical issues. Most AI systems include some kind of complex decisions process, and in practice this may lead to serious results. This is why, Zero Trust AI ensures that even if these systems might seem impartial or trustworthy (technical jargon), they will not become compromised. At the same time, adopting Zero Trust AI can ensure that in the face of adversarial attacks, data tampering, or model poisoning by those who have something sinister in mind for your organization and its people (teehee:)), there is always a reliable way out. The authenticity and reliability of AI-powered applications would be thrown into question, if left unchecked.

5.3 CORE PRINCIPLES OF ZERO TRUST APPLIED TO AI

With AI increasingly the backbone of modern systems, Zero Trust is becoming all the more crucial for secure computing. No user, device, or even system, either inside or without the network perimeter should be trusted by default—this lies at the heart of Zero Trust. In the new circumstances spawned by AI, with technology advancing at an unprecedented rate and the system suddenly many times more unwieldy, there are defects which are not readily identifiable. When AI solutions are integrated into industries across various domains and various dimensions, the essence and value of Zero Trust need to be articulated at every level. But the cornerstone of Zero Trust is: "Don't take anything on trust; always confirm." In the traditional model of security, once a user or device has been authenticated, it is assumed trusted within the network. AI applications, however, now require a fresh look at this. With AI systems linked to a variety of data sources and outside agents, vulnerability becomes infinite. In particular, AI systems serving in capacities where decisions are being made provide an inviting target for both parties bent on subverting algorithms and corrupting data.

In AI this principle of "Never trust" gets a lot more nuanced. The input data fed into an AI model can be counted upon or doubted. It depends upon the nature of the data involved; was this information produced by processes similar enough to those used in your system that you can claim (if even tentatively) that there might be some basis for guaranteed correct results? It is of great importance to verify this data. Take as an example the two extremes of data interacting with an AI system—from the moment it is ingested into the system itself, to decision-making processes which produce output based on that information. AI models often use large data sets sourced from many different locations, and such data is not always clean or trustable. Therefore, every data stream must be validated and authenticated, with the AI system directly monitoring (in real time) for signals of irregularity or data pollution that could skew AI decisions. What's more, the model itself should meet with frequent verification, such as regularly ensuring its soundness and performance will not degrade over time from adversarial or training errors. This ultimately concludes that the only point where AI systems can be allowed to pass is when verification happens at every step or transition because then it is then continuously and consistently validated. This rule should be followed to the letter. AI models need to implement multiple authentication steps, validation of data in real time, and robust encryption to protect data at rest or during its passage over networks: in this way they can obscure unnecessary signs. Likewise, the most stringent kind of tests applied to AI models, whether these are model certification and adversarial testing or standardized training of AIs employed in response systems and in safely secure environments, ensure that trust is never accorded inadvertently. Only by continual comparison can AI systems go forward, and thus in the realm of AI we have implemented Zero Trust security [19].

Another basic tenet is "Assume Breach" in a Zero Trust model. It is fundamentally unrealistic to rely on the assumption that the network is secure in traditional security models and external threats will be kept at bay from day one. In addition, machine-learning ecosystem environment is no longer within a traditional perimeter-based boundary. Traditional ML models can pull information from a multitude of sources, often involving third-party APIs, cloud infrastructure, or even end users. The threat of a breach comes from anywhere. Working in the AI world, assuming breach means operating from the standpoint that a system is already compromised. Malicious activity must be constantly monitored for every stage of an AI pipeline—from data acquisition and pre-processing, to training and inference—and will require a different protection approach. Each component on every level of the AI pipeline is a potential attack point and should a breach happen at any stage of the process—for example those involving the ingestion of data, when hijacked inputs or poisoned data are introduced into the system—this may not be immediately obvious. It might not be detected until the model begins to make erroneous predictions or decisions based on corrupt data. During model training, as one instance, attackers might subtly manipulate the model to exploit weaknesses or introduce backdoors. So as you can see, in order to mitigate these risks with AI pipelines using the assumption of Zero Trust, it is proposed that the broken-up principle should be employed. Each sensitive component needs to have its access regulated closely, and any deviation from what is expected should bring it to light for monitoring. AI systems must constantly look for exceptions at every stage of their operation, considering what will seem like just that in five years if it has gone unchecked. Indicatively, anomalies in the characteristics of data or model performance that are not anticipated by the given operational environment may go undiagnosed, although they may be a sign of notable deviations that should be considered immediate.

This principle also extends to the interaction between every facet surrounding AI models and external environments such as cloud service providers and third-party vendors. A breach in any external system could mean the end of the entire AI pipeline, so constant vigilance is required. Another cornerstone of Zero Trust security is the Principle of Least Privilege (PoLP), which has a huge bearing on AI contexts. In a Zero Trust model, no entity—whether user, device, or service—should have more access than is required for strict necessity. This minimizes the attack surface area and reduces damage caused by potential intrusions. In AI systems, this means that instruments and models such as AI agents or services should have the least possible authority to avoid reaching for something not necessary in their capacity to fulfil demand. An option here might be to impose rigorous permissions on individual ML models in an AI system. They should only access the particular data which is necessary for their task during training or inference. For example, an AI model designed for natural language processing should not be given access to customer transaction data unless this is essential. The idea is to restrict vulnerable points and endangerment of valuable information—and thus limit the possibility that either harm itself (including both accidents in carrying out tasks or exploitation by unscrupulous agents) may occur. The PoLP also should be observed for interactions between AI agents and their underlying infrastructure. Every AI service or agent must possess a set of specified roles and permissions that is limited to its functionality within the AI pipeline. For example, a data preprocessing module should not be able to change the model architecture or training configuration. On one hand, AI models should have strict access control. In other words, do not allow traffic from these systems to databases, other services, or even write back to them.

In a Zero Trust environment, the PoLP needs to be audited and adapted constantly. Permissions must be checked at regular intervals, and any irregularities from the intended pattern of composition should trigger an alert. Once AI models have been deployed, they should conform to the principle of minimal function the model logical way in order to minimize potential damage. This means ensuring that although an AI agent is compromised, there is only damage limited to its specific scope, not a broad system-wide collapse.

Continuous monitoring is one of Zero Trust's basic principles as well, and it becomes especially important in an AI context. Where traditional systems might require an annual security audit or annual upgrade, AI systems require real-time attention in order to ensure that they are operating within the desired parameters. AI systems' peculiar property is that they can morph over time as a result of retraining or because the data sources being used become changed. So, the onus is upon continuous supervision then to identify any abnormal behaviour which might signify security problems, model drift, or degradation of performance.

Once they're in operation, AI models may come up against any number of ever-changing threats. An important example is adversarial attacks, where fiendish fang manipulations of input data make the AI system produce incorrect predictions page. The point of continuous monitoring is that things like that ethernets and other unequipped forms of attack can be spotted as they arise, not after they have wreaked much harm. Monitoring also extends to how the model performs over time to make sure it remains on track with what was originally intended as an implementation objective.

When the Zero Trust framework is applied to AI, one imagines a system where everything is recorded, scrutinized, and all calculations are made within reach of any form of potential risk. Based on the feedback obtained through continuous monitoring, risk assessing processes must be constantly recalibrated. For example, if a data source that used to be reliable begins now to manipulate or behave wrongly, risk assessment tools should immediately trigger an alert. Similarly, changes in model behavior—such as unusual prediction patterns or aversions—should be flagged for further analysis and investigation.

Furthermore, continuous monitoring allows threat intelligence to be incorporated in real time, allowing AI systems to learn from new threats and adapt security protocols accordingly. This ability to dynamically respond assures that the AI system is always ready for fresh risk; to bring it into practice becomes a critical element for a Zero Trust security posture. This means that security tools like intrusion detection systems (IDS), anomaly detection based on ML, and automatic response mechanisms all have to be closely entrenched into the AI environment to see the operation of the system through from beginning to end.

5.4 AI SYSTEM THREAT MODEL IN A ZERO TRUST FRAMEWORK

Zero Trust, a security framework in which trust is never implicitly granted to those even within the network, can be a powerful way of protecting AI systems. However, the application of Zero Trust to the variable nature of AI brings with it its own unique challenges. These come in two guises: the technical vulnerabilities that arise within AI models and the external threats that occur when we deploy, use, or train AI systems. In a Zero Trust context, understanding the model of threat in AI system must be deeply delved into in a number of key areas: data poisoning, model inversion, adversarial examples, supply chain risks, and AI agent misuse [20].

One of the most deadly, subtle threats in today's AI systems is data poisoning, which occurs during the phase where we train ML models. In a Zero Trust environment where no one entity is trusted by default; this danger becomes all the more pronounced. Data poisoning is when malignant actors subtly manipulate the data feed into model training, forcing the AI system to learn false patterns or make biased judgments. These attacks can be difficult to detect because of the system's reliance on big, frequently uncrated datasets.

Attackers may inject malicious samples into the training set for a particular, strategic effect on how the AI predicts or decides (Figure 5.1). In the case of supervised learning, a poisoned dataset can contain incorrect labels that confuse the model's learning process. This can cause the AI to misclassify inputs, give erroneous predictions, or inject bias in its

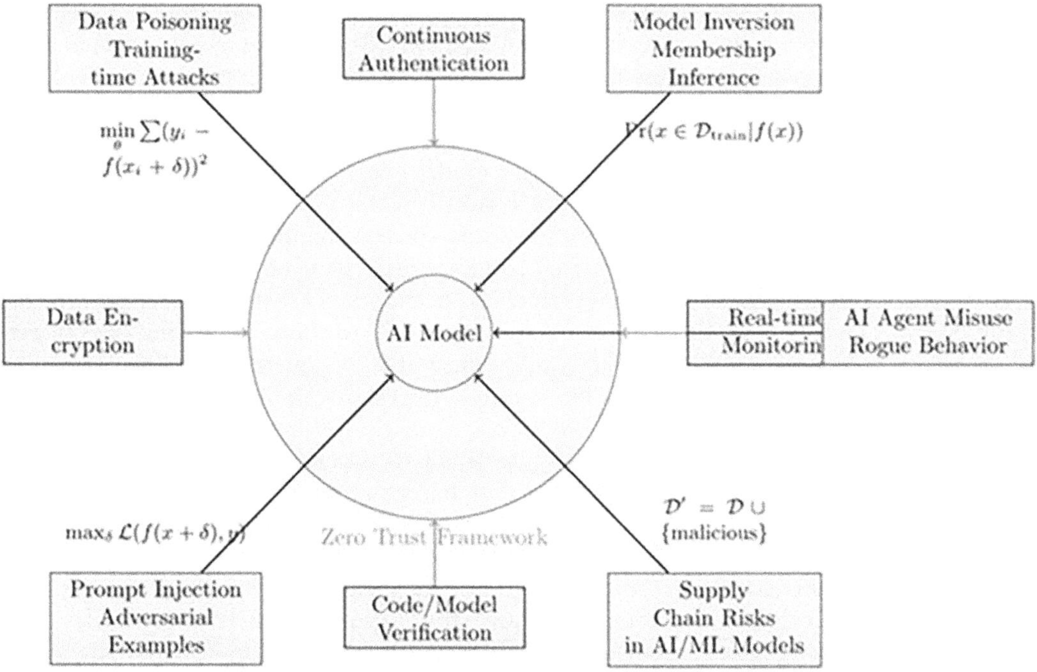

Figure 5.1 AI system threat model in a Zero Trust framework.

decision-making process. Moreover, training-time attacks may also target the underlying algorithms of the model itself, exploiting weaknesses in optimization methods or vulnerabilities in model architecture.

Meanwhile, with this sort of approach, implicit trust in the sources of data, the training systems, and the model itself are at least greatly reduced. For the record, in such an environment it is necessary to verify the authentication of training data all the time, or some other rigorous processes. Equally importantly, it requires that one engages in perennial vigilance against tampering, which may come in many forms. Zero Trust strategies should incorporate combination of encryption, access control, and monitoring mechanisms to ensure that both data—whether sourced internally (i.e. somatic from within the organization) or externally—is unable to undermine the system. The information that is generated in this process should be visible to the sensors of an adversary during the training process regardless of the source of the information. Model inversion and membership inference attacks are both sophisticated threats to AI systems especially when they deal with sensitive data. A form of model inversion is the ability to reverse-engineer an AI model's training data, using only its output. Concretely, when an attacker is able to obtain a model's responses, they may be able to reconstruct or infer details about the data used to train it. That could include: sacred data such as financial or health records. A membership inference attack occurs when the adversary tries to determine whether a particular data point belongs to the model's training set. This type of attack could have catastrophic consequences for fields like healthcare or banking which place a premium on privacy. In both cases, AI models that rely on sensitive or proprietary information end up leaking that information inadvertently often making them complicit in major breaches of privacy [21].

If your model has a weakness anywhere, no part of it should ever be implicitly trusted—whether accessed by a legitimate user or by an assailant. Rigorous usage of authentication mechanisms, such as secure access protocols, must control and log interactions with the model. Furthermore, using differential privacy techniques in the course of training can significantly reduce the risk of inversion or membership inference attacks. These techniques involve adding noise to the training data and model output so that attempts to reverse-engineer system yield unreliable or imprecise results.

Adversarial attacks—including prompt injection—pose a significant and growing threat to AI models, especially naturally generated language processing (e.g. NLP) and other generative AI systems. For instance, prompt injections occur when a potential enemy alters the input prompts given to a model. This can induce the model to churn out wrong or even pernicious results. An attacker might subtly modify the words of a querent question in order to do large language models some harm: by manipulating their responses and coaxing biased or malicious answers from them.

Adversarial examples, inputs specifically designed to deceive AI models, operate in a similar manner. These examples are usually small, barely noticeable changes made to input data, which cause a model error in its forecasts or classifications. While these changes are seldom perceivable by humans, they can critically damage the performance of ML models. System failures, incorrect output, and security vulnerabilities are the result of changes.

At this point, one should note that compliance, too, includes Zero Trust principles in its arsenal of weapons against arrayed threats—after all there is nothing in a system around which we should blindly trust. What might be appreciated by compliance is input validation and verification, in order for AI models to receive data which is genuine and corresponds to the expected format. Robust anomaly detection mechanisms that can pick up and track any suspiciously malicious or adversarial inputs should also be incorporated into AI systems. Furthermore, adversarial training—where the model is intentionally corrupted with adversarial examples during training—offers a means of helping models get used to such attacks while training.

Vulnerabilities within the AI supply chain are a frequent cause of AI system breaches. The data is only part of this. The AI supply chain also includes models themselves, not to mention platform-related software libraries and third-party services which support AI development. Bad actors could exploit weaknesses in the chain to introduce security holes through backdoors or malicious code, which, once models are deployed for use in inference (an AI-based application), may then be acted upon.

The dangers in sourcing AI models from outsiders is brought into sharp relief by the supply chain. These external resources may well contain latent vulnerabilities or even wicked changes across the entire platform. And with growing dependence on open-source libraries comes an extra layer of complexity for AI developers: it's all too easy for vulnerabilities in these library products to be edited by hackers so that models are forced off in strange directions.

In the Zero Trust model, all third-party data sources, code, and models must be strictly inspected in order to shut out the risks for AI systems. This necessitates using digital signatures and secure containers which ensure that every part is bona fide and unspoiled. Continuous surveillance and audit of the AI supply chain is also indispensable for catching any illusions of activity that could mean compromise is on its way. Zero Trust principles mean that if anything goes wrong with a certain part of these systems, this won't affect other parts, and thus the risk posed by supply chain attacks will be substantially reduced.

AI agent misuse and rogue behavior are key phrases referring to a future situation where AI systems can be directly commandeered, manipulated by malicious users to do something wrong. For example, intrusive images of privacy or security credentials help one grasp quite easily that excessive freedom and inordinate demands for biological knowledge (biological information) in the name of service delivery have arrived at least partway around the world. In other cases, rogue behavior occurs when AI systems do things their designers never expected to do, because of unforeseen defects or vulnerabilities and adversarial interventions. One example of AI agent misuse is the extremist trolling, where deep learning models such as GPT-3 have been exploited for finding convincing fake news. Instead, machines employed in deepfake campaigns, which can now be easily purchased on open markets, like the Alibaba, can be applied in controlling opinion of people, including attempts to fool them regarding political leaders like President Putin. In a similar fashion, the rogue behavior can be realized in case AI systems start functioning out of their intended limits as systems expand and new components are added. As an illustration, a Robotic Process Automation (RPA) system can break the desired processes, or analytics systems like Kibana can send unnecessary or false alerts [22].

In a zero implicit trust environment, AI systems must be under constant monitoring and control to detect any deviations from expected behavior. Two factor access controls must be strictly imposed, with continuous authentication and authorization processes to verify the legitimacy of all interactions with AI systems. When constructing AI systems, you should consider that multimedia units featuring transparency and explainability can help the user while the rogue agents will be terminated by automatic response mechanisms.

5.5 ARCHITECTURE OF ZERO TRUST AI SYSTEMS

AI is changing so rapidly that systems must ensure the security and integrity of their output are paramount. Traditional network security architectures, which trust everything within the perimeter, are no longer sufficient in a world where data and processing power are freely distributed across many different environments with their own currents of change. Enter ZTA—a model that posits that by default no part of the network, no user, nor any device can be trusted whether it's inside or outside the perimeter. For AI systems, the implications of Zero Trust are profound: not only must they secure the AI infrastructure itself but also protect all data, models, and interactions occurring within this complex environment. The architecture of Zero Trust AI systems is cantered on several key principles: micro-segmentation of workloads, identity and access management, secure APIs and model interfaces, data lineage and provenance, along with Federated AI at Zero Trust edges. All of these combined can help build a security-first AI ecosystem. The successful construction of a Zero Trust AI system rests on the foundational architecture. One such aspect is micro-segmentation. With micro-segmentation, you can divide the workloads and supporting infrastructure needed for AI into smaller, insulated segments (Figure 5.2). Each segment can then be under individual control, monitoring and protection. In the context of AI systems, micro-segmentation plays a lot of roles. As an illustration, it offers a good means to minimize the possibility of lateral movement in a system. Rather than letting an attacker that attacks one component relay to the other components of the system access can be highly restricted in order to ensure that the component afflicted is affected. By being able to isolate Zero Trust workloads, such as learning, inference, and data storage, it ensures that each must have its own unique access and security controls.

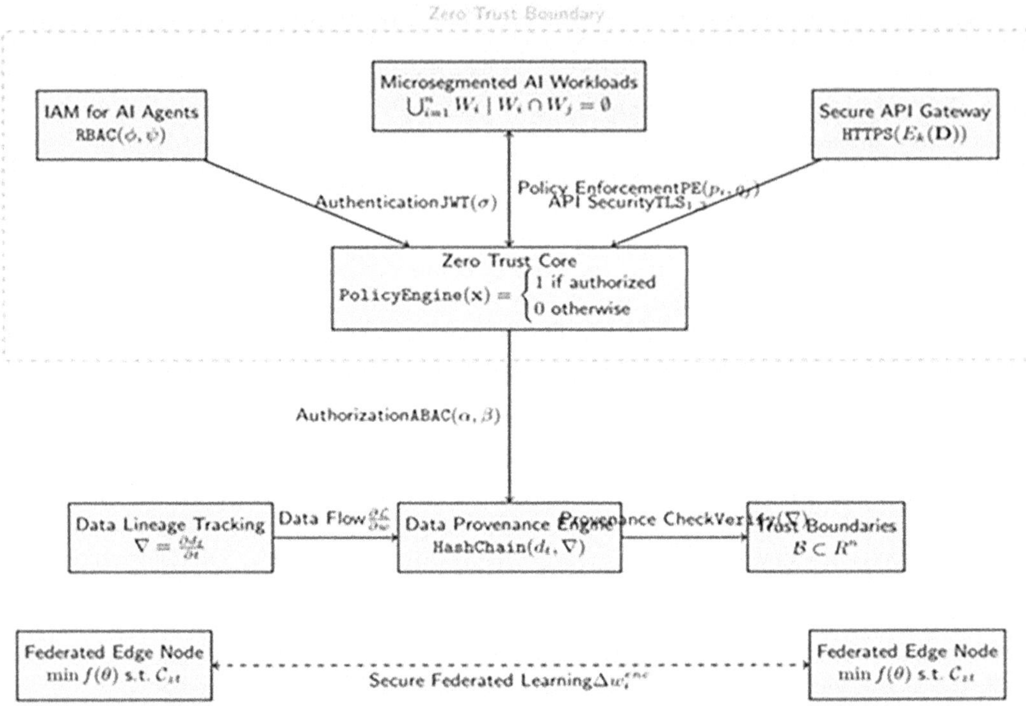

Figure 5.2 Architecture of Zero Trust AI systems.

Indeed, AI models that are being trained with sensitive data must be separated from those running real-time inference. This partitioning approach avoids having a hack into the inference model seize control of the entire training pipeline. In addition, micro-segmentation permits fine-grained monitoring and audit of each segment. By continuously monitoring interactions between microsegments, security administrators can detect anomalous behavior, trace out potential breaches, and enforce security policies—as they relate specifically to the kind of AI workload being executed or where different model elements are operating. This not only beefs up security but also increases the resiliency of the entire AI system by keeping breaches within any single region instead of allowing them to spread across your whole operation. Consequently, this is much safer. A set of comprehensive policies is an absolute must if you're to maintain a Zero Trust AI system. In Zero Trust, any entity—user, machine, or agent AI—must always prove itself part of the overall compliancy landscape. Whatever the context turning to AI systems, this is crucially important because their agents often operate on their own and some may have access to very sensitive data or even perform critical functions. For purposes of keeping threats at bay, each AI agent must be assigned a unique identity and granted access only to those specific resources or services necessary for its operation [23].

There are several components to the IAM for AI agents, including authentication, authorization, and continuous validation. With authentication, each AI agent must be able to securely prove its identity often using cryptographic methods such as digital certificates or machine identities. Authorization ensures that the AI agent is allowed to access only the resources that are in line with its designated role. This is implemented by way of fine-grained access control policies, which are dynamically enforced metrics based on context—workload at present, data being processed right now, or where the agent happens to be physically located. Continuous validation also ensures that agents do not behave in inappropriate ways. Systems can be used for real-time monitoring which flag any deviation or abnormal operation as potential security breaches or malfunctions.

In a Zero Trust AI system, APIs and model interfaces are a place for communication between various components such as data sources and models, whether these instances are modelled or running as services. These interfaces must be designed securely so as to prevent unauthorized access and alteration of the AI system. Specifically, when APIs are used in AI systems, this is serious if they are abused to share or retrieve data that can damage the training process, maim model performance, or exfiltrate sensitive data.

In today's tightly secured cyberspace atmosphere, Zero Trust demands the application of tough authentication methods and strong encryption protocols to API interfaces and model. Every API call must be authenticated, guaranteeing that only authorized entities can communicate or collaborate with the AI system—and this can involve the use of OAuth tokens, API keys, or two-way TLS (Transport Layer Security). Furthermore, encryption at rest and in transit is necessary to ensure sensitive data is not intercepted or altered when interacting via APIs.

To help shelter APIs in Zero Trust AI systems content controls must be enforced. Third-party API apps can have holes that, in the data feeding them, serve to contaminate. The user not exercising strict control of the data it receives can lead his system to infections or data poisoning. If this happens and some bug is pushed into the AI model in a back-door way, then that is the end of its integrity.

In a Zero Trust AI setting, such as AI systems, understanding and tracking the lineage and provenance of data is vital. Lineage means the tracing of data back over its whole prehistory—from origin to use in AI models. Provenance, on the other hand, means the history of the data: who created it, how it was processed, and any transformations it underwent en route. Together, these two concepts provide transparency and responsibility, essential for trust in AI systems.

A Zero Trust AI system must ensure that all data inputs, transformations, and outputs are logged and monitored. This is a system which allows organizations to trace potential vulnerabilities or malicious activities back to their source, which is essential for maintaining the integrity of the system. Origins can also provide insight into the accuracy and quality of data used for ML, ensuring that data which is fed in during the training process represents reliable, high-grade information. To pass from one part of the AI system to another within different computing environments, trust boundaries must be clearly defined. Creating a low-trust, third-party connection between two separate value chains which is secured through a strong cybersecurity policy is important to the integrity of the system and its reliability in its operation. It serves as a checkpoint, where data can be validated and checked off before moving onto the machine horse next in line. Strict controls are in place at these trust boundaries so that unauthorized access to private data can be prevented. Only validated, clean data enters parts of the AI system which are critical [24].

When it comes to Federated AI, what we mean is a decentralized approach in which models that are developed at the edge (often several sites or equipment components) and one-dimensional updates or insights from them are transferred across the system, point to point without need to, say tell anyone where your car is parked. This approach is particularly useful when data privacy or sovereignty is a concern, as it allows models to be trained without moving sensitive information to central locations. Federated AI running on a Zero Trust framework, however, brings in new security-related challenges such as access control and trust management.

Whereas within a federated AI system, each edge or node is actually a credible entity in its own right. Meanwhile it has to abide by the principles of Zero Trust, and prove up to all the other nodes in that system who it is. Therefore, each node must authenticate and grant appropriate permissions whenever it enters the modeling process or sends updates. Secure communication protocols are also required so that no unauthorized third party can see the models being transmitted or update them. Furthermore, by using a combination of encapsulated aggregation and differential privacy techniques, no individual data point can poison the federation learning process, thereby preserving privacy while also protecting model accuracy. Micro-segmentation further protects against lateral movement in the case of a breach. Breaking each node into its own environment also communities the chances of various nodes breaching. As Federated AI is tied together with Zero Trust principles by organizations, you can create a secure AI "island network" with protected data and models. It becomes a matter of trust for users, each "edge" in the network has its own access controls and a monitoring facility to keep a watchful eye on those agents who are learning or helping train models.

5.6 POLICY ENFORCEMENT AND ACCESS CONTROLS

Access control is increasingly necessary as organizations use AI in crucial decision-making. Put simply, a Zero Trust model assumes no entity inside the network is inherently trustworthy. Hence enforcement of policy and access controls becomes the cornerstone for safeguarding AI models or ensuring that they are handled, if they're not abused heavily enough already. In this chapter, the author covers various ways to appropriately secure AI systems. These include Attribute-Based Access Control (ABAC), role and policy segregation, granular data and Zero Trust authentication. In traditional access control models such as Role-Based Access Control (RBAC), access is granted based on predefined roles. Such a model of economy can be problematic and inflexible, especially with AI systems which are more dynamic than ever. ABAC, on the other hand, is much finer-grained. It allows access control policies to be based on a wide range of factors, including user attributes (e.g., department, clearance level), environmental circumstances (e.g., time of day and location) and the specific nature of data or AI model being accessed. When applied to AI models, ABAC lets organizations build more complex accessibility rules that take a user's need or where they are—or indeed what the user model is doing on any particular occasion—into account [25].

For instance, access to a predictive model might conceivably have constraints that include not just the user's role but also what part of the world they are in, present risk level (for instance a real estate agent's appraisal of your house will be done via AI), or sensitivity of information that this party is trying to process. This level of granularity is particularly important in AI-based systems where models might well deal with very sensitive types of data—such as financial records, individual medical information derived by scanning and analyzing genes on chips vs. traditional paper printouts from keyboards—and even classified top-secret government material. Furthermore, access should be granted only if all necessary conditions are met: in accordance with Zero Trust principles, trust is not assumed but always verified. Using ABAC, an organization can make sure that other people are excluded from using any AI models as long as they meet the conditions specified above.

To this end, we must thoroughly isolate roles and policies of the AI model during its deployment particularly so. Role and policy isolation in model serving refers to creating clear, separate areas for different groups of users along with their permissions inside an AI system. This principle makes certain that a given individual or system has access only to the portions of the model serving structure it is sanctioned for, thus preventing lateral movement or making further advances. For example, different positions within an organization (i.e., data scientists, model builders, operating personnel) may have to give different amounts of control to the AI model, and for various reasons. Data scientists may need access to training datasets and model architecture as they continue to improve the model, while members of an operational staff only require access to the model's use for real-time data processing purposes. By separating roles and having clear rules regarding what each role can or cannot touch, organizations can in fact reduce the danger of insider threats and accidental data exposure.

In a Zero Trust AI environment, it's not just the user's role that should be policed but the AI model itself. For instance, models can be divided by output sensitivity analysis. Some models produce highly confidential outputs, such as predictions for financial investments or diagnosing diseases in healthcare cases. Others give less important information out. With isolation put at the model level an organization can ensure that those parts which are sensitive to all eyes but from about three thousand go unnoticed (this further reduces potential attack surface). Fine data access control is an integral part of enforcing policy in AI systems, particularly with respect to data of greatly differing sensitivity. In a Zero Trust architecture, organizations are required not only to control access to models but also data in general. In other words, this means that decisions about who has the right to see and use data have to follow from the specifics of that data itself such as its security level, privacy needs, or compliance constraints.

For instance, in a healthcare AI app, some information may be classified as personally identifiable information (PII) and other data could be non-sensitive aggregate statistics. Fine-grained governance allows companies to define very specific access controls, so that only authorized users or systems can access some parts of the information. Such an approach is especially important for AI models that rely on huge amounts of different kinds of data. This is particularly true of the healthcare, financial, and government sectors where regulatory compliance and data protection laws are stringent. By dynamically controlling accesses, organizations can ensure that confidential data is only accessible to those with proper authentication credentials or systems, thus avoiding the risk of leaks and similar undesired outcomes. Typically, fine-grained access controls are implemented through various policies that take into account a combination of factors including: the type of data being accessed; the stated purpose for which it was requested; who made the request and his/her authorization level. In addition, information such as data provenance and previous attempts to access the data can provide further input to decisions on access. Such procedures not only raise the bar for compromise, but also significantly reduce any potential harm resulting from failing to protect against exposure of sensitive data—unauthorized people are less likely to see what they shouldn't, errant use is minimized and even with luck current technologies can prevent leaks. Additionally, by security enforcing this kind of rule, organizations can make sure that any sensitive data is only legible to the right people or to the right systems. In this way, risk of data leaks will be minimized. Otherwise, if various systems are able to pounce on the same information without authorization (often over an open network), then any strategist has reason to fear that data leaks may leave traces behind—with or without malicious intent. In a Zero Trust environment, a user or system is never trusted by default and every communication must be authenticated and authorized no matter where the user is located in the network. This principle is particularly important with AI models that process sensitive data. To be careless when entering is serious business, since malicious access can easily lead to a security incident or other adverse outcomes [26].

In Zero Trust AI environment, authentication mechanisms usually go beyond using simple username/password combinations. Through the use of this strategy, various authentication systems, including multi-factor authentication (MFA), biometric authentication, and device authentication are regularly used. Network users have been using these forms of authentication over the years. For instance, a model serving platform incorporating ML may demand that the user go through two types of authentications: not merely password but also biometrics, and in addition even when they have been given a barcode sent directly as an SMS message to its own terminal device. That's adding a further barrier against colossal liability, by making sure there's real humanity accessing this model. The same holds for Zero Trust Logic— the machine adds an essential authentication layer between the two layers of access. Even if machine A is cracked then automatically it must not be able to enter the model, save by strict means (whether human or machine) of verification and sanction. This level of authentication guarantees no unauthorized inroads from inside or outside, only genuine clients can look at AI model output.

Furthermore, Zero Trust authentication for model consumers complements continuous monitoring and verification. What happens then? It means that the system is perpetually monitoring safety, even after initial authentication, on a number of criteria including environmental context and data sensitivity. If it detects any irregularity in these tests, they will at once cause access to be cut off without hesitation or restraint. In this way, it ensures that only honest dues are collected by AI models.

5.7 MONITORING, DETECTION, AND RESPONSE

AI technology is undergoing unprecedented development and the security framework for AI system becomes quite crucial. Zero Trust doctrine adopted in the concept of "Zero Trust AI" is implementing a strict access-control model. It's one that trusts nothing and verifies everything inside or outside the network. One important aspect of this security approach is the ability to monitor, recognize, and then respond should threats be found. These capabilities are indispensable for a machine-learned model to resist adversarial actions, prevent data infiltration, prohibit unauthorized access, and successfully adapt to regulatory demands. Monitoring AI systems closely from deployment through their entire operation and on again until finally they cannot work anymore is vital for maintaining security and trust in their output, especially as is often the case in circumstances demanding the utmost discretion: healthcare, finance, or governmental service zone.

In Zero Trust AI, monitoring, detection, and response are not merely used to identify abnormalities or irregularities. On the contrary, they live a life of constant comprehensive assessment of AI model behavior, the flow of data, the effect agents in any given situation may have on data sites where they are working—anywhere you might find yourself. Such an active approach is needed to protect not only the AI's functioning but also its data inputs from corruption, now or in the future. If monitoring and detection aren't in place, any AI system can inadvertently start to leak information. Whether exploited unintentionally or deliberately manipulated, all of this leakage will lead to uncertainty and bias in the completed model without solid pearls. The following sections delve into telemetry collection methodology; monitoring AI model, and behaviors.

Collecting telemetry, the most important first step in AI pipeline security, takes place at each stage of the data-processing lifecycle and deployment to audit it (Figure 5.3). This data collection typically involves a wide range of metrics: for example, both performance statistics and information regarding resource consumption, such as CPU usage or memory

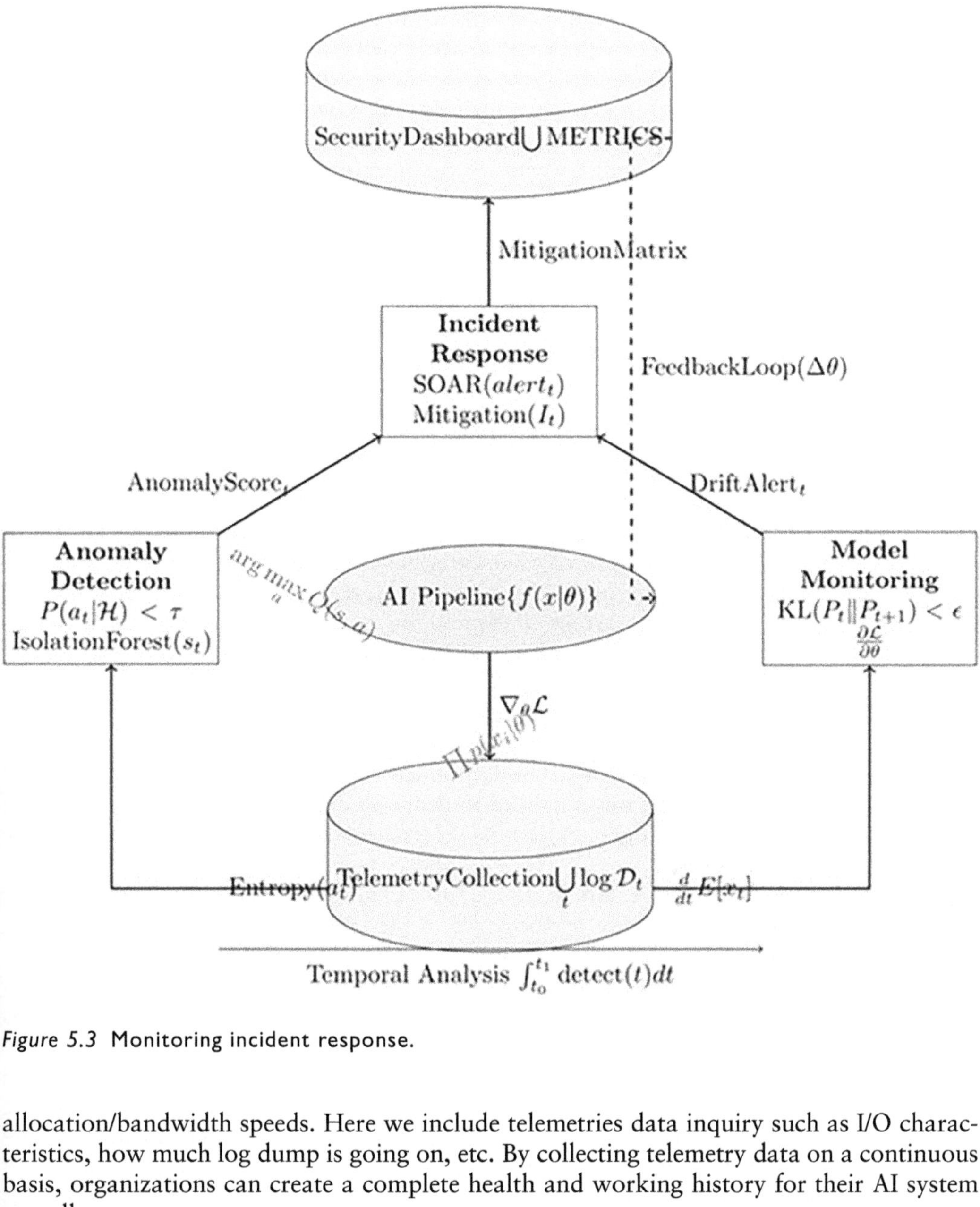

Figure 5.3 Monitoring incident response.

allocation/bandwidth speeds. Here we include telemetries data inquiry such as I/O characteristics, how much log dump is going on, etc. By collecting telemetry data on a continuous basis, organizations can create a complete health and working history for their AI system as well.

Telemetry from AI pipelines provides important insights into how its components are behaving, which in turn allows for real-time monitoring when systems do not perform as anticipated. This data provides an audit trail that can be very useful when identifying the causes of unexpected behaviors or system failures. As an example, suppose an AI model starts displaying erratic decision-making patterns or gets its training data corrupted—telemetry can then find just where in the above workflow this problem originated. This level of granularity is essential for efficient diagnosis of problems and averting future security threats.

Furthermore, telemetry data makes it possible to integrate real-time anomaly detection mechanisms and thus automatically alert abnormal patterns. The concept when applied in practice is to monitor all AI-related processes—data preprocessing, feature extraction, model training and inference—and collect metrics which can not only indicate performance bottlenecks but also detect possible security risks, such as adversarial inputs or data poisoning attempts. And with telemetry capture, organizations can ensure transparency and traceability, both important elements of the Zero Trust approach, as all activities are logged and available for audit at any time.

AI models, especially those using ML and deep learning, evolve as they take in new data and continue learning with time. This means behavior monitoring and drift detection are critical aspects of AI security. Monitoring the behavior of AI models involves assessing how they are making decisions and whether these align with their original training objectives. In the context of Zero Trust AI, behavior monitoring aims to catch any anomalies in model output which could signal adversarial manipulation, biased predictions, or degradation of model accuracy.

Model drift, also known as concept drift, means that the underlying data distribution or the model's behaviour has changed. It is not necessarily true that this will be permanent; but if replacement of suitable alternatives is discovered in time to form an adjustment framework which allows migrations carry on gradually instead of creating sharp discontinuities over time periods too long for people to span, then all those changes can occur smoothly with abandonment of current abode and move into newer living quarters in just two days flat without anybody noticing it. Model drift, also known as concept drift, refers to the gradual change in the underlying data distribution or the model's behavior over time. For example, in supervised learning, this occurs when the relationship between input and output data changes; they become less consistent with each other, and a model may lose its accuracy and even be harmful. If an AI model trained on historical financial data is faced with new economic conditions, this may lead to drift and cause wrong predictions. If drift is not detected and corrected, it can undermine the system's integrity, making it susceptible to manipulation or failure.

Continuous monitoring is necessary to combat drift in models. This includes, as one aspect of the monitoring process, tracking performance of the model against a set of pre-defined metrics. These include accuracy, precision, recall, and F1-score. More importantly, it also involves the use of drift detection algorithms that can identify when the model's predictions start to deviate significantly from what one might expect given their input. These algorithms compare real-time predictions against those made by the baseline model or against predictions of models trained on updated data. If the model's behavior shifts beyond a predefined threshold, an alert is triggered, indicating that model retraining or some other corrective measures are in order. In Zero Trust AI, drift detection can also be combined with anomaly detection in the input data since unexpected changes in the data flow tend to bring model drift. This underscores that every aspect of the AI system has to be kept under continuous scrutiny. That the system is doing what it is supposed to do, and its behaviour remains safe and reliable let alone within bounds must therefore be tested wherever possible along with anything else connected with how things work.

AI agents, whether autonomous systems or human-assisted decision-support tools, are designed to do things according to actions and objectives programmed into them by learning from experience or design from outside sources. Anomalies in how AI agents behave refer to actions that don't conform to what would normally be expected or are the best choice for getting a system going. This is incredibly important on the one hand because AI agents live in an ever-changing environment where unexpected events or inputs of new data might produce responses, they are not used to, that could be harmful and even break into security breaches. At the same time, anomaly detection is equally important seeing these cases through from start to finish. By continually examining the agent's behavior, it brings these anomalies to light and allows us to correct errors in time or ward off potential failures before they happen. For instance, in the context of a self-driving car, an AI agent might make a decision that departs from safe driving behavior. That is, it might not stop at a red light. This could be due to a bad sensor reading, model drift, or even attacks by adversaries. Anomaly detection keeps idiot sayings like this from happening by constantly examining how the agent behaves and comparing it to either a known set of rules, or learned habits. For more widespread detection of anomalies, have a look at Xiong Bengui's investigation of normal, fake, fall, and unexpected data. In practice, that means using statistical methods, ML models, and deep learning approaches to look for patterns in data that suggest unusual behavior. Some common methods include clustering, supervised classification, and unsupervised anomaly detection techniques. The ultimate aim is not merely to find out when an AI agent behaves differently from expected results. It should also act appropriately in response—to trigger an automatic safety override perhaps all the way down below, to tell operators something is wrong. Just at this juncture, Zero Trust AI anomaly detection plays an essential role in protecting AI systems from being undermined or captured. Once AI agents' behavior patterns are continuously monitored and evaluated, an organization needs only the eyes of a hawk on AI agents to react fast against particular security problems. This proactively monitored approach, regardless of data source or where it comes from, supports the Zero Trust principle of "never trust, always verify."

In any advanced system, incident response is a vital capability. Security incidents in AI systems, however, differ significantly from those occurring in traditional IT. The dynamic and autonomous nature of AI means they are controlled by their environment more so than their implementers. Another complicating factor is that an AI system's goal may be known, but its behavior is not. Because of this, when an AI system is pushed to attack another or make some kind of subversive move, it often looks like bad random noise from its own perspective. Such discordant behavior may be an indication that something is amiss, just as one disturbs a classroom by raising a question out of place. Incident response protocols for AI systems need to be comprehensive, rapid, and able to accommodate the challenges AI technologies present. The nature of incidents on AI models, which may comprise adversarial attacks and data poisoning as well as unexpected model behavior, necessitates a different set of response procedures. A comprehensive security incident response plan for AI models should include the following: First, it needs a way of detecting when there has been a breach—or other signals such as oddities in data or classes of abnormal AI behavior is observed. If an issue is detected, it must be addressed immediately. In some cases, this could involve turning off certain model functions entirely and regressing back to a backup model that was last recognized as reliable. For example, when an AI system is under attack from adversarial input that makes it behave erratically, or even when human operators press the wrong button and scatter data everywhere, it is necessary to shut down the system fully and take out or replace entire sections of the model in order to bring everything back to normal operation mode. Zero Trust AI takes the principle of containment as its response strategy. When an incident occurs, it is critical to contain the affected component—whether that be the AI model, a pipeline, or individual agents—so that the breach cannot grow further within the system; this applies for every kind of incident. This type of reaction can be achieved by network segmentation or sandboxing, or indeed placing restrictions on access to certain system resources. In addition, response plans should include forensic capabilities which enable us to track down just what caused the incident, figure out if any data was leaked as a result, and evaluate how much damage was done by this breach. Good migration behavior also involves continual learning and the improvement of systems. At any one time work is completed, process progress should flow back into the clouds so that later security protocols, detection methodologies, and overall system resilience can be improved. This cyclic procedure means that in an increasingly hostile world AI systems can still be made secure, where predators are always changing tactics.

5.8 PRIVACY, COMPLIANCE, AND ETHICAL GUARDRAILS

Today, AI has permeated across all walks of life, affecting the way a company operates and how they meet customers. Along with this development, ensuring that AI adheres to privacy, regulatory, and ethical standards has never been more important. One of the most innovative ways of meeting these challenges in the deployment of AI is through the Zero Trust concept that cuts across all areas. Refined for network security in its original incarnation, this model has implications for AI throughout if we are to keep our data safe, comply with regulations, and also act ethically. Zero Trust AI is based around the principle of never trusting any entity or system up front, regardless of its origins; rather, you authenticate all activities and requests and only give entry to the data, models, or insights when they have been authenticated through verification checks. This approach can help to realize that AI systems are not only efficient but also responsible and within the norms accepted by society more broadly. Zero Trust for Responsible AI is built on the belief that AI systems should be designed, operated, and maintained in a manner which continues to contain, as far as humanly possible, the risks of data privacy leaks, model security breaches, and ethical violations. At each step or operation, the Zero Trust model holds that the entire system of AI is a potential point attack. Malicious or damaging inputs could come from anywhere, whether inside or out. To do so in AI implementation, this Zero Trust concept often means verifying access to the information to ensure that it meets requirements for privacy of algorithm use, stops short unlawful or harmful outcomes, and provides a transparent view into decision-making.

In responsible AI, ZTR (Zero Trust AI) actually works to enforce strict access controls and monitoring as well as data access. This philosophy of least privilege ensures that AI systems only use the minimum amount of information to work, protecting access to user information and being compliant with regulations. Consequently, Zero Trust confirms the identity and legitimacy of both AI and human participants in an AI pipeline. Implementing the concept of Zero Trust allows decreasing the threat of data breach and predisposing systems to manipulating the information or outputs by some unauthorized persons. Also, constant monitoring and auditing can be used to make sure AI systems work within set ethical parameters, instead of evolving into unregulated or excessively permissive actions, as they gradually make small amendments. Organizations must be able to account for their systems as fully as possible. Especially when it comes to regulatory compliance, for there is no need to make artificially intelligent systems proactively account for decisions they had made.

In a transparent AI pipeline, each step in the AI workflow should be documented, whether data preprocessing, model training or validation, or inference. These logs should not only collect what was done but also the context in which it occurred, who initiated a command, where and when was it given, and so on. Zero Trust principles require such logs to be immutable and unchangeable. This means that once an event has been recorded in the pipeline, there is no way of altering what happened; it's all kept present for any later review or audit. Compliance and tamper-proof logs are vital for the smooth operation of the audiobooks in question. GDPR, HIPAA and other regulatory frameworks mandate that a company must create and maintain an auditable trail of data access and utilization. Tamper-proof logs mean that any attempt at altering or falsifying these records can be caught. That makes it so much easier to investigate possible violations or incidents of non-compliance. In addition, from a business perspective, these logs provide transparency. They make it possible for outside auditors or government agencies to see if the AI system is operating not just within the strict letter of the law but also ethically. Beyond compliance, the insight and review of these logs play a key role in delivering AI model transparency. By providing a clear, exact record of how AI systems work, organizations can prove that their AI systems are making decisions based on the correct criteria. And that the data used to train models is being treated in accordance with standards. Such openness inspires confidence in the system; it also allows organisations to take active measures early on should there be any problems related to fairness, bias, or model judder.

Trustworthy AI is based on the principles of interpretability and verifiability. AI systems are often called "black-box systems." This makes it difficult to discern why and explain how they have reached certain decisions or findings (predictive analytics). Because of this lack of transparency, trust can easily waver—especially in such crucial fields as medicine, finance, and law. The Zero Trust framework, too, can play a role in enabling these two features as it has placed them deep into whole AI systems from sklern upwards.

This despicability is a matter of making explicit the methodology by means of which an AI model arrives at decisions. Zero Trust ensures that the entire AI pipeline is transparent and open to scrutiny. By implementing fine-grained access controls and keeping detailed logs of model operations, organizations can provide stakeholders with a clear picture of how their models are trained, tested, and deployed. This degree of openness makes debugging the AI system easier and can serve to uncover any biases in decision-making processes.

Whereas observability focuses on what an AI model does after it has been put into operation around the clock, Zero Trust AI systems embed real-time observability tools that monitor not just the performance characteristics of the model but also its input data and interactions with users. Here we enable organizations to find and correct problems such as model drift, where predictions made by the model become less accurate or relevant over time. By offering insight into what their AI system is doing, organizations ensure it remains dependable, ethical, and aligned with responsible AI principles.

Put together, explainability and observability establish more robust conditions for forging trustworthy AI. Tackling Zero Trust is one way in which organizations guarantee that their AI models are secure, compliant with regulatory requirements, but also transparent and accountable. This engenders confidence with users, regulators, and other parties that AI technology can be managed responsibly and in full compliance with morality standards while threats to privacy are still kept under tight control.

5.9 INTEGRATING ZERO TRUST WITH MLOPS

As AI systems get more sophisticated, so must security. It is no longer enough to layer security only at the operational level. The integration of Zero Trust principles offer a framework that can protect both AI models and their data from having their integrity, privacy, or confidentiality violated. This is especially important as many new applications may be heavily reliant on sophisticated algorithms or software programs for input. Unknown and untrusted users could be running any code from anywhere, and so it is essential to constantly authenticate, authorize, and validate internally as well as externally. Yet no one is allowed in on trust alone, they need to actually physically see that a real person will evaluate the request's contents before considering each one valid. This chapter aims to provide a way for people to combine Zero Trust with MLOps practices. Its four examples are: CI/CD for AI with Security Gates, Secrets Management in ML Pipelines, Model Registries with Trust Labels, and Secure Deployment and Rollbacks. Continuous Integration and Continuous Deployment (CI/CD) are both essential aspects of modern software engineering. They make it possible for teams to automate the entire process of integrating new code and deploying models quite efficiently. Yet injecting Zero Trust into CI/CD workflows adds one extra layer of security altogether. Each stage of a traditional CI/CD pipeline should be fortified with security gates in a Zero Trust environment.

$$\mathcal{S} = \{s_i\}_{i=1}^{n} \; s_i \in \mathcal{X}$$

$$\mathcal{A} : \mathcal{X} \to \mathcal{Y}$$

$$\mathcal{P}_{\text{trust}}(s_i) = \sigma\left(w^{\top}\phi(s_i) + b\right)$$

$$\phi : \mathcal{X} \to \mathbb{R}^d$$

$$w \in \mathbb{R}^d, \; b \in \mathbb{R}$$

$$\sigma(z) = \frac{1}{1 + e^{-z}}$$

$$\mathcal{V}(s_i) = \mathcal{P}_{\text{trust}}(s_i) \cdot \mathcal{A}(s_i) + \left(1 - \mathcal{P}_{\text{trust}}(s_i)\right) \cdot \perp$$

$$\perp = \text{null action (denied access)}$$

$$\mathcal{L}_{\text{trust}}(\theta) = \mathbb{E}_{s_i \sim \mathcal{S}}\left[-y_i \log\left(\mathcal{P}_{\text{trust}}(s_i)\right) + (1 - y_i)\log\left(1 - \mathcal{P}_{\text{trust}}(s_i)\right)\right]$$

$$\mathcal{L}_{\text{mlops}}(\psi) = \mathbb{E}_{(x_i, y_i) \sim \mathcal{D}}\left[\ell\left(f_{\psi}(x_i), y_i\right)\right]$$

$$\mathcal{L}_{\text{total}}(\theta, \psi) = \lambda \mathcal{L}_{\text{trust}}(\theta) + (1 - \lambda)\mathcal{L}_{\text{mlops}}(\psi)$$

$$\theta^*, \psi^* = \arg\min_{\theta, \psi} \mathcal{L}_{\text{total}}(\theta, \psi)$$

$$f_{\psi}(x) = \arg\max_{y \in \mathcal{Y}} \mathbb{P}(y \mid x; \psi)$$

$$\mathbb{P}(y \mid x; \psi) = \text{softmax}\left(W_{\psi}^{\top} h_{\psi}(x) + b_{\psi}\right)$$

$$h_{\psi}(x) = g(x; \psi)$$

$$\mathcal{D}(x) = \begin{cases} f_{\psi}(x), & \text{if } \mathcal{P}_{\text{trust}}(x) \geq \tau \\ \perp, & \text{otherwise} \end{cases}$$

$$\tau \in (0,1)$$

$$\mathcal{R}_{\text{risk}}(x) = \frac{1}{1 + e^{(w^{\top}\phi(x))+b}}$$

$$\mathcal{P}_{\text{trust}}{}'(x) = \mathcal{P}_{\text{trust}}(x)(1 - \mathcal{R}_{\text{risk}}(x))$$

$$\mathcal{D}'(x) = \begin{cases} f_{\psi}(x), & \text{if } \mathcal{P}_{\text{trust}}{}'(x) \geq \tau' \\ \perp, & \text{otherwise} \end{cases}$$

Symbol explanation

$\mathcal{S}$	Set of service access attempts (requests)
s_i	A single service access request
$\mathcal{A}$	Machine learning model performing service (action)
$\phi(s_i)$	Feature mapping from request to feature space
w, b	Parameters of trust prediction model
$\sigma(z)$	Sigmoid function for probability output
$\mathcal{P}_{\text{trust}}(s_i)$	Probability that request s_i is trusted
$\perp$	Null action (reject access)
$\mathcal{V}(s_i)$	Zero Trust enforced action output
$\mathcal{L}_{\text{trust}}(\theta)$	Loss function for trust model (binary cross-entropy)
$\mathcal{L}_{\text{mlops}}(\psi)$	Loss function for MLOps model (task performance)
λ	Trade-off hyperparameter between trust and MLOps loss
θ, ψ	Parameters of trust model and MLOps model respectively
$f_i(x)$	ML prediction function
$\mathbb{P}(y \mid x')$	Expected probability of y given x'
W_v, b_v	Parameters of classifier head
$h_v(x)$	Latent representation of input in the model
$g(x; \psi)$	Feature extractor network (encoder)
$\mathcal{D}(x)$	Access decision rule based on trust score
τ	Trust threshold for decision making
$\mathcal{R}_{\text{risk}}(x)$	Estimated risk score for the request
w_r, b_r	Parameters for risk model
$\mathcal{P}'_{\text{trust}}(x)$	Adjusted trust score considering risk
τ'	Updated threshold when risk-aware

Security gates are mechanisms for the pipeline that check data and models rigorously as they proceed from one phase to the next. For instance, when a new model enters the pipeline, it may mean it's undergone functionality test as well as some security review. This review could cover whether the way the model operates violates defined security baseline conditions or exhibits bad patterns such as data leakage, adversarial vulnerabilities, and prejudice behaviors. Moreover, CI/ CD pipelines can be set to allow only authenticated and authorized personnel or devices to alter the pipeline; this effectively prevents unauthorized modifications to either the models themselves or their dependent data. Integrating security into CI/CD processes also includes establishing that any model which is deployed has a full trace and audit history. Every version of a model should be accompanied by detailed metadata on its origins, alterations, and testing procedures. This enables teams to see potential points of compromise and makes it possible to return an earlier, secure version of the model if necessary. Traditionally, the use of secrets such as API keys, database account passwords, and access tokens are unavoidable when requiring entry to outside resources from your ML pipeline. In a typical IT environment, however, this poses management challenges. In an MLOps pipeline, this complexity mounts; different parts of one stage may require various secrets, and those secrets could belong yet to separate teams or even be exposed in different ways. Integrate Zero Trust with MLOps practices, then you will find that access to these secrets is tightly controlled and, as a result, always monitored.

On the one hand, because Zero Trust means that no secrets can be trusted by default, even internally, within your network, the best current practice in a Zero Trust AI environment is to use secrets management systems offering dynamic control, for example, granting ephemeral access tokens that are valid only for a limited period of time. This serves to decrease the probability of secrets being compromised or misused. Dashboards and other monitoring tools must in the future reflect this shared state. In contrast, secrets management tools like Hashi Corp Vault or AWS Secrets Manager may be integrated into the ML pipeline. These tools allow for the dynamic generation and revocation of secrets. They also provide fine-grained access control and auditing functions. Be sure to keep secrets out of your codebase and model files—having them in there introduces a risk of accidental exposure. Retrieve secrets from secure vaults at runtime instead. This guarantees that the secrets appear nowhere in logs or error messages, nor as well do they make their way into version control systems. So long as teams are careful about secret rotation management and regular testing of monitoring system operation, they can ensure that leaks are caught and corrected quickly, minimizing the potential for leaks to cause security breaches.

In a Zero Trust AI environment, model registries act as central bureaus that store both different versions of models and their training data, along with metadata. Model registries will need to adapt to incorporate trust label systems classifying the security posture of each model version. Trust labels, data tags that describe the degree of trust or risk associated with a particular model, are based on factors including the data fed into the model's training, the security measures taken during development, and the results of security audits conducted post facto.

On one hand, to achieve this, first all versions of the model would need to pass certain security validation tests—before they are formally registered and get a trust label. Trust labels, in simple terms, offer status that shows that an algorithm conforms to recognized security criteria like not being prone to given attacks or having been designed to meet certain security standards. This method also provides reliable governance policy enforcement. For example, low trust models can be programmed to hand off to production environments—while high trust models must be deployed before them. It is important that enterprises keep an audit trail for the lifecycles of any model adopted. This method can be easily extended into the application stage—the lifeblood of any AI model. Running a security audit on model deployment is the only way to keep compliant and to guarantee that one is only running verified models on production systems. In Zero Trust, all steps of the deployment process are subject to careful access control and rigorous validation.

In a Zero Trust AI environment, the deployment pipeline requires multilateral authentication for all parties involved in triggering a deployment to ensure that only authorized personnel or systems can carry out the operation. Additionally, the label of the model being deployed should match the information in the registry, meaning models get deployed only if they have passed all security checks and rank as good quality products. Deployment systems must also perform integrity checks. These make sure that the model has not been jiggled out of place unintentionally during deployment by some attacker trying to slip his own code into your serving pool.

Finally, Zero Trust principles require that if a model needs to be rolled back (due to something like discovering security vulnerabilities or deterioration in performance) then the rollback operation is as secure as the original deployment. Rollbacks should be automated based on predetermined criteria assessing the trustworthiness of earlier model versions. This prevents bad or unapproved models from being introduced into production systems by malicious actors. Moreover, every rollback operation should prompt an audit, ensuring that full records of both deployment and rollback actions are available for forensic analysis.

Ensuring continuous monitoring of models deployed and any rollbacks is a vital factor in secure deployment. This means that abnormal performance—such as unexpected inputs or adversarial attack—is immediately recognized and can trigger an automatic rollback or refitting process. In addition, in a Zero Trust setting continuous checks on the integrity of model should be carried out, even after it has been deployed. The model's behavior needs to remain predictable, clear, and credible at all times.

5.10 CASE STUDIES AND REAL-WORLD IMPLEMENTATIONS

While businesses integrate such digital technologies into their operations, they need to ensure security of their systems and data. Zero Trust is now a fundamental security model as AI systems become more autonomous and interconnected. Zero Trust AI principles dictate that all access requests are to be verified whether they originate from inside or outside the organization's network. This chapter is focused on carrying out Zero Trust AI in various domains and fields, using real-life cases to illustrate the practical application of this model.

Nowadays, chatbots are seen in customer service, healthcare and other industry verticals. While they provide great convenience, they also create a number of security issues with deployment on par: As chatbots gain in capability—and begin to deal with sensitive data, for example, implementing Zero Trust AI principles in chatbot security—no request, action, or user is trusted by default. Chatbots are the application of continuous verification. Each interaction with the chat service, whether sent by a customer or machine, is authenticated and authorized using multi-factor authorization (MFA) plus behavioral analysis.

For instance, a chatbot in the finance industry can be subjected to fraudulent activities such as impersonation, phishing, and stuffing attacks. To guard against these risks, a Zero Trust AI methodology will check user behavior in real time against known patterns—to flag anomalies which may indicate security breaches. It also implements data access policies on a per-interaction basis, thus only authorized people can view any sensitive data like account details or personal information. By applying these principles, the chatbot can provide continuous authentication for the user and maintain an auditable record of all interactions to ensure compliance, and off-guard risks.

This is valid for the architectural systems with which it links and influences due to Zero Trust AI. With Zero Trust AI, even though an attacker compromises one system, it requires repeated authentication to access other systems, thus greatly reducing the attack surface. Zero Trust AI essentially creates a tough skin for chatbot defense mechanisms, because it strips away trust assumptions and insists on verification (namely both the authenticity and the intentions) of all users at all times.

Healthcare is a particularly sensitive area when it comes to data security. When AI is embedded into clinical settings such as diagnostic instruments, patient management systems, or therapeutics development—preserving the privacy and security of medical information is key. A Zero Trust AI approach in this field helps to counteract the rising menace of cyberattacks aimed at AI-based applications for healthcare. The first requirement for healthcare AI is to control data access strictly, never making any trust assumptions. Every entity involved in healthcare applications, including devices, users, and processes, is always identified with Zero Trust AI. For example, an AI system used in diagnostic imaging may contain input from various sources including electronic health records (EHR), imaging devices, and even wearable health monitors. Under a Zero Trust regime each of these systems has to authenticate every request they receive, checking both the requester's identity and the data's integrity.

What's more, healthcare AI systems must keep data exposures to a minimum. Zero Trust ensures that only those with explicit permission may access sensitive patient data; just because you have a right doesn't mean you automatically get it. The minimum privilege principle as described above applies in this age of big data—no one needs all the information all the time from everywhere on a network—and so forth. If it does happen to breach, then it is the point where one can stop it and examine how things actually went wrong in practice. This design makes it more complicated for attackers to steal and modify vulnerable health data, which also means that patient privacy is maintained.

In fact, hospitals can apply Zero Trust AI to real-life applications such as predictive analytics in patient monitoring with AI. By combining biometric authentication or device authentication for clinicians and care providers accessing the AI powered system with AI algorithms validating patient health data before use, hospitals eliminate the need to transfer medical information outside of their trusted IT infrastructure.

Even as the healthcare industry continues to incorporate more AI technology, Zero Trust remains an integral part of upholding the trust and privacy of patient data in an extensively regulated sector.

A great many industrial AI systems stand or fall on the Internet of Things (IoT) and edge computing. These systems use distributed computing, small embedded systems, and networks to enable real-time analysis of vast quantities of data collected from machines, sensors, metering equipment, and measurement control panels. However, many industrial environments are so intertwined that they present opportunities for cyberattacks simply by their nature. In response to these concerns, Zero Trust AI is increasingly being used to protect industrial AI systems, particularly those that have been designed for edge computing.

When we talk about industrial AI, edge computing is used for processing data. In this instance, it means that most information is handled close to where it's generated—whether in the machinery or sensors themselves—rather than sending all back up and pretty much literally into a cloud. This decentralized approach lowers latency and increases response times. However, it also increases the possible range of security breaches, as edge devices are often less secure than centralized data frames. With Zero Trust AI principles applied at the edge, your industrial systems will be protected against unauthorized access and malicious activities.

In the design of edge AI Zero Trust makes sure that the validity of each edge device as well as any data passing between them is continuously verified. Every data packet that goes from an industrial sensor to the AI system must be encrypted and authenticated, so that it can't be attacked or tampered with in any way; nor can unauthorized devices break into the network. Furthermore, within a network of industrial AI, components don't trust each other by default. Each device has to authenticate its own identity using secure certificates or biometric identifiers, and their behaviour is monitored continuously for signs of compromise.

An industrial plant deploying autonomous robots for inventory management, say, would apply Zero Trust AI by making sure that only those authorized can modify or take control of these robots. Moreover, each robot should authenticate its sensors and communications protocols with the central AI system to make sure its own data integrity is secure. If any device were to be violated, Zero Trust ensures that the intrusion is localized and not replicated in different parts of the network, so that there can be improved continuity for operation.

An ideal target for cyber-attacks, government agencies and military organizations hold some of the world's most sensitive data files. When computers with AI replace human operators in key national security systems, such as drones, intelligence analysis, and defense-research programs, a stringent system of safety measures is urgently needed in order to guard against potential threats. Zero Trust AI acts as a security framework for such systems, which means that only authorized users equipped with the right devices may interact with essential AI-driven operations as well as data sources.

For example, AI-powered decision-support systems in the military perform strategic analysis of data from satellites, drones, and other surveillance devices. Zero Trust principles are therefore applied to this data, so that at each stage authentication is required. Whether it's a soldier making use of a mobile app for information requests or a drone transmitting reconnaissance data to the central command center, each request must be authenticated and it thereby ensures that sensitive military intelligence is always properly protected.

One significant method of implementation for Zero Trust in government and military AI systems is through micro-segmentation. This means that each component of the military system, whether it be a drone, satellite, or ground-based server, is within its own secure segment where constraints are imposed on who can enter. In this way even if one part of the system is compromised, the intruder would not be able to easily laterally traverse to other parts of the network.

And then again, in government and military AI systems, with greater adaptivity comes more benefit from constant monitoring and dynamic access control. Ask yourself this: if a military command post is to be using Zero Trust AI as a technology to continually verify that only those personnel with the appropriate security clearances can see classified data, or if it also employs AI techniques to notice abnormal usage patterns and real-time anomalies in security terms, then what kind of logic should it apply when intelligence units rush out to store their results?

Take military networks security systems, for instance. One prime example is the deployment of Zero Trust AI. Technology now includes AI systems for cyber awareness, and hence the Zero Trust model only allows network connections from AI systems which have been pre-approved by the owner. It is essential in the context of a situation where threats keep changing as seen in the example of cyberattacks. These environments should be well preserved because they are a crucial point towards the provision of national infrastructure and security.

As AI continues to expand in autonomous vehicles, cyber defense, and intelligence analysis, Zero Trust principles will be critical to guarantee the security of these systems. By so doing, that AI can be deployed in all areas it is suited for (from battlefield robotics to Intelligence Analysis at sea power neither concedes). In this way, full project ensures that national critical infrastructure maintains the security necessary to underpin itself.

5.11 FUTURE DIRECTIONS AND CHALLENGES

But as AI red teaming gives the will of Zero Trust another look, it of course still has to rely on human red teaming to check AI outputs, since those outputs themselves remain in the hands of bad guys pretending to be good guys. AI red teaming is an important aspect of the future of cybersecurity, especially as the world becomes more reliant on ML algorithms and AI-autonomous processes. Traditional red teaming aims to simulate attacks against an organization's security system, finding vulnerabilities or gaps in security that can then be fixed quickly. In this new era where AI is an integral part of an organization's operations, the red team's work must evolve—no longer just tear down the walls, but rip apart AI systems themselves which might be attacked, manipulated out of context for profit, or even turned into weapons. This procedure—a process known as AI red teaming—involves subjecting AI models to antagonistic conditions. It includes attacks such as adversarial ML and data poisoning. Another effective attack is termed model inversion attacks: this exercise or hands-off techniques can give adversaries a "black box" model of what type of AI performs in practice, for example without being aware or able to prove they're doing anything wrong because all evidence lies inside human skulls.

In a Zero Trust architecture, AI red teaming becomes even more important. Perimeter defenses alone will not be adequate to maintain the safety and security that today's enterprises need. Since Zero Trust assumes that all users, devices, and systems must be continuously authenticated, the security of AI models will also need to be evaluated in real time. By using large amounts of data for training, AI systems can be vulnerable when inputs that are unusual go unnoticed by traditional security controls. In so doing effective AI red teaming based on the principles of Zero Trust can help to uncover such weaknesses. It will simulate advanced attacks facing the data pipes for an AI model, processes of training models, and how to draw conclusions from them. Evaluating AI systems for weaknesses will thus require a deeper, more nuanced approach when incorporating adversarial AI tactics, but in accordance with the principles of Zero Trust for least privilege access and continuous verification. As AI continues to advance, one of the biggest problems is how to trust decentralized systems. Especially when these are not based on centralized authority but rather the trust model behind them. Decentralized AI trust models, such as those supported by blockchain technology and Zero Knowledge (ZK) proofs can provide an innovative solution for this problem. In a Zero Trust environment, decentralized AI models can carry out essential functions in verifying both the authenticity and integrity of both data inputs and model outputs. The advantage here is that it does not rely on any one fabric for failure.

The blockchain technology allows developing trust in the information employed to train AI models and in the results produced by AI systems because of its tamper-proof, publicly auditable, and immutable features. Every step on the blockchain can be recorded so it becomes difficult for hackers to tamper with the historical data or decision-making process of AI. The Zero Trust orientation also calls for smart contracts to be put onto blockchains so as to ensure AI systems only operate with trusted entities or systems. Zero-Knowledge Proofs (ZKPs), on the other hand, can provide privacy-preserving validation of

AI processes—a third party can verify a particular AI system has followed secure procedures without exposing sensitive information about the data or model itself. These methods bring the prospect of a future in which AI systems work with improved accountability and transparency, and so they fit better into Zero Trust. One of the most exciting and challenging problems of AI development is the widespread use of AI in code generation. ML-driven software tools are already capable of producing code by themselves in effect, greatly enhancing productivity favoured by developers. However, the ramifications of AI-generated code for Zero Trust and DevSecOps (security functions associated with DevOps) can scarcely be overemphasized. Traditionally, software development and security operations (DevSecOps) have been closely linked: in order to pass security measures with its mass through the entire software development lifecycle (SDLC). By allowing AI to develop code, however, many new risks arise—potential vulnerabilities and exploitation routes that AI may overlook, as well as logic errors.

AI-generated code presents a unique challenge in a Zero Trust environment, a realm where security policies are enforced at every stage of the SDLC. AI systems responsible for producing code must meet stringent security assessments to prevent them from introducing vulnerabilities into the system. Furthermore, AI-powered tools must be introduced into automated security pipelines to continuously assess code's compliance with the Zero Trust principle. AI-driven static and dynamic analysis tools were needed to check for vulnerabilities, implement least-privilege access protocols and deploy Zero Trust network policies restricting only trusted code to production environments. By aligning AI-generated code with DevSecOps practices and Zero Trust architecture, organizations can better mitigate the risks of automation in software development. Zero Trust principles will also face challenges and opportunities; the increase of autonomous agents is another example. Autonomous agents are AI-based entities that can decide and act independently of humans. Today, such agents are increasingly being found in all kinds of business and technology sectors, from self-driving cars to process automation robotics at financial institutions. In the setting of Zero Trust where continuous authentication and verification prevail, it becomes essential to manage the behavior of autonomous agents. These agents can interoperate autonomously with other systems and hardware but they conform rigorously to Zero Trust protocols to ensure that they in no instance unwittingly become cyber-attack vectors.

It is one of the core principles of Zero Trust that every time a request or interaction is made, verification must be undertaken so that no system or agent operates from privilege as a matter of course and without challenge. This can create issues, however, with autonomous agents who work in an environment that is largely independent. They need to be continually authenticated, and their behavior must be subject to constant monitoring and analysis in terms of upholding Zero Trust policies. In addition, autonomous agents also need the ability to respond in real time to the ever-changing environment, changing their behavior as circumstances alter. This necessitates a new generation of advanced ML models capable of penetrating intricate security environments and dynamically altering access controls, authorizations, and security protocols. Therefore, autonomous agents must now be capable of presenting their state of health to other agents and systems for query and response. Zero Trust principles require that all interactions between agents, systems, and humans be validated and authenticated. This demands the development of highly sophisticated AI models which can interpret security policies and adaptively enforce trust relationships between agents. Furthermore, companies must also address all the ethical implications involved in autonomous decision-making (to ensure that agents conform not only to security protocols but also regulatory and compliance needs). More and more, as companies use AI more widely in their own landscapes, it becomes particularly difficult for them to organize using a Zero Trust scheme. One of the biggest problems is how AI models, data, infrastructure, and systems can securely interact with each other. This is very important where different entities or organizations want to work together or exchange data models that will allow for better-informed decisions and predictive analytics. In traditional security frameworks, sharing both models and data is straightforward. But in Zero Trust environments every interaction between systems needs to be inspected, making the interoperability of two given systems a major headache.

To address this problem, the Zero Trust design must create ways to share AI models in a proven and secure manner. Advanced cryptographic techniques, such as homomorphic encryption, offer the prospect of guaranteeing that the AI model and its output are private when used together even in different environments. Then, access control methods also need to change so that AI models themselves have a place in determining who should be allowed to do what with shared models. This makes sure that only allowed units can access and modify shared models. By focusing on secure sharing of AI models, firms can remain true to the spirit of Zero Trust while still reaping the benefits that can only come from pooling many minds. Whether we can build sufficient trust and keep it alive in future autonomously running AI systems is a significant challenge for the Zero Trust school of thought in addition to many other types of problems. Autonomous AI models, such as self-teaching algorithms or those used in autonomous vehicles, are always learning and adapting to new environments. This learning process, which is by nature adaptive is impossible to predict or control, so it poses a challenging problem in verifying trustworthiness. These systems need to be reliable in a controllable environment, as Zero Trust principles dictate, but autonomous AI actually tosses out all the old static security measures. Blockchain ledgers and real-time monitoring may provide new methods of proving that their behavior still conforms to Zero Trust policies. Unfortunately, at this time, they do not exist. Moreover, standards for evaluating and certifying autonomous AI models— including privacy, security, and ethical concerns will be indispensable in establishing trust with those systems.

AI can play a major role in improving Zero Trust security monitoring by bringing about more proactive and intelligent detection of security threats. Past methods of monitoring relied on rules and human oversight, which were cumbersome and error-prone. On the other hand, AI can process massive amounts (unlike this phrase) of real-time data, looking for patterns and abnormalities that could point to a security threat. In a ZTA where the security environment is ever- changing, AI-driven monitoring systems can learn to adapt constantly and enhance their detection capabilities accordingly. When this happens, threat assessments become more accurate and timelier.

ML models can be trained to identify possible attack vectors, such as lateral movement within networks or unauthorized data access, and take immediate steps to counter these threats. AI's integration into Zero Trust security monitoring systems helps organizations identify and prevent threats earlier, accumulating evidence that indicates that data breaches are about to take place. Ethical considerations are crucial as AI becomes more common in Zero Trust environments. AI systems might reach decisions that affect human lives, such as determining access to sensitive information or controlling critical infrastructure. As these systems move deeper into security frameworks, it is essential that they adhere to ethical principles both in design and deployment.

This means establishing transparency in AI decision-making processes, mechanisms for holding AI systems accountable when something goes wrong, and ensuring that biases are kept to such a minimum as not to lead unfairly towards any particular result. In a Zero

Trust environment, where strict verification and least-privilege access are the order of things, AI has to be held to the same ethical standards as human decision-makers. Organizations also need to strike a balance between security and privacy since AI systems must not violate people's individual rights or overly invade their privacy by engaging in unprecedented surveillance of their activities or collecting masses of personal data.

In the form of Zero Trust environments, AI-driven security automation is a hotbed for development. Despite the continued evolution for the nature of cyberspace threats that managers must face, organizations should make every effort to step up from security response automation to reduce the time it takes between prevention arrangement and recovery. AI-powered automation can help organizations to alter security policies on the fly, detect strange activity, and isolate compromised systems at little human expense.

By automating such essential security functions, they are able to protect ZTA against emerging threats. At the same time, however, this raises the question of ensuring that AI-powered automation is not taken over by adversaries or used in order to generate new vulnerabilities. Developing secure, self-healing systems capable of autonomously responding to threats without compromising security will be a major area for future research.

5.12 CONCLUSION

In the age of AI, when enterprises of all types have already begun to use it, a security framework that is stable and flexible is the need. The AI-driven era is an era where threats and the landscape are constantly changing. In this environment it is no good to rely on an information security strategy with perimeter armour—a model now out of date . Solutions like Zero Trust offer ways to mitigate the AI online environment dangers—they get rid of any assumptions about whom or what can be trusted, treating identities, devices, and data flows as being potentially hazardous. Trust in aggregate represents a distinct way for IT experts and cybersecurity consultants alike to interact with the AI industry. To implement Zero Trust in AI environments involves a great many challenges. You need specific industrial and technical controls which take AI into account—safeguards to make sure the training data is clean, defenses against adversarial ML attacks, reconciling the twin concerns of human and machine in security. Still, the AI application which most demands Zero Trust systems for defense is absolutely critical in terms of ensuring that not only does security not suffer but the application is truly integrated in a broader organization-wide and societal environment. This model, Zero Trust with AI, will no doubt develop in line with developments in AI technology itself. For example, as AI becomes more autonomous, the principles under Zero Trust will have to change too. They will have to embrace new technologies such as tools for automatic risk analysis and responses in real time. Not only for fending off both malicious threats and public fears of AI, the synergies between Zero Trust and AI are fundamentally necessary. Eventually as the Internet of Things continues to grow, Zero Trust will be a cornerstone in making a trustworthy and efficient future in AI.

REFERENCES

[1] Chen, B., et al. (2021). A Security Awareness and Protection System for 5G Smart Healthcare Based on Zero-Trust Architecture. *IEEE Internet of Things Journal*, 8(13), 10248–10263.

[2] Denzel, K., & Ng'etich, S. (2025). A Survey of Security in Zero Trust Network Architectures. *ResearchGate*, 182–214.

[3] Jorquera Valero, J. M., et al. (2018). Improving the Security and QoE in Mobile Devices Through an Intelligent and Adaptive Continuous Authentication System. *Sensors*, 18(11), 3769. https://doi.org/10.3390/s18113769

[4] Kang, H., Liu, G., Wang, Q., Meng, L., & Liu, J. (2023). Theory and Application of Zero Trust Security: A Brief Survey. *Entropy*, 25(12), 1595. https://doi.org/10.3390/e25121595

[5] Karantzas, G., & Patsakis, C. (2021). An Empirical Assessment of Endpoint Detection and Response Systems Against Advanced Persistent Threats Attack Vectors. *Journal of Cybersecurity and Privacy*, 1(3), 387–421. https://doi.org/10.3390/jcp1030021

[6] Kindervag, J. (2010). *Build Security into Your Network's DNA: The Zero Trust Network Architecture*. Cambridge: Forrester Research Inc., p. 27

[7] Kommera, S. (2025). Enhancing Zero Trust Architecture with AI-Driven Threat Intelligence in Cloud Environments. *International Journal of Scientific Research in Computer Science, Engineering and Information Technology*, 11(1), 1524–1533.

[8] Liu, Y., Kang, Y. Xing, C. Chen, T. & Yang, Q. (2020). A Secure Federated Transfer Learning Framework. *IEEE Intelligent Systems*, 35(4), 70–82.

[9] Mandapuram, M., Gutlapalli, S. S., Bodepudi, A., & Reddy, M. (2018). Investigating the Prospects of Generative Artificial Intelligence. *Asian Journal of Humanities, Arts and Literature*, 5(2), 167–174. https://doi.org/10.18034/ajhal.v5i2.659

[10] Mohammed, I. A. (2021). The Interaction Between Artificial Intelligence and Identity and Access Management: An Empirical Study. *International Journal of Creative Research Thoughts*, 3, 668–671.

[11] Moubayed, A., Refaey, A., & Shami, A. (2019). Software-Defined Perimeter (SDP): State of the Art Secure Solution for Modern Networks. *IEEE Network*, 33(5), 226–233. https://doi.org/10.1109/MNET.2019.1800324

[12] Narouei, M., Takabi, H., & Nielsen, R. (2020). Automatic Extraction of Access Control Policies from Natural Language Documents. *IEEE Transactions on Dependable and Secure Computing*, 17(3), 506–517.

[13] Paul, F., & Sheriffdeen, K. (2022). The Role of Artificial Intelligence in Enhancing Zero Trust Security. *ResearchGate*.

[14] Ramezanpour, K., & Jagannath, J. (2022). Intelligent Zero Trust Architecture for 5G/6G Networks: Principles, Challenges, and the Role of Machine Learning in the Context of O-RAN. *Computer Networks*, 217, 109358.https://doi.org/10.1016/j.comnet.2022.109358

[15] Rangaraju, S. (2023). Secure by Intelligence: Enhancing Products with AI-Driven Security Measures. *EPH International Journal of Science and Engineering*, 9(3), 36–41. https://doi.org/10.53555/ephijse.v9i3.212

[16] Sarhan, M., et al. (2023). Cyber Threat Intelligence Sharing Scheme Based on Federated Learning for Network Intrusion Detection. *Journal of Network and Systems Management*, 31(1), 3.

[17] Unger, M., Tuzhilin, A., & Livne, A. (2020). Context-Aware Recommendations Based on Deep Learning Frameworks. *ACM Transactions on Management Information Systems*, 11(2), 1–15.

[18] Wang, R., Li, C., Zhang, K., et al. (2025). Zero-Trust Based Dynamic Access Control for Cloud Computing. *Cybersecurity*, 8, 12. https://doi.org/10.1186/s42400-024-00320-x

[19] Fang, H., Qi, A., & Wang, X. (2020). Fast Authentication and Progressive Authorization in Large-Scale IoT: How to Leverage AI for Security Enhancement. *IEEE Network*, 34(3), 24–29.

[20] Freed, G., & Jackson, M. (2022). Zero Trust Architecture in AI-Driven Cybersecurity: A Machine Learning Perspective. *ResearchGate*.

[21] Hussain, M., Pal, S., Jadidi, Z., Foo, E., & Kanhere, S. (2024). Federated Zero Trust Architecture Using Artificial Intelligence. *IEEE Wireless Communications*, 31(2), 30–35. https://doi.org/10.1109/MWC.001.2300405

[22] Jackson, M., & Freed, G. (2025). Zero-Trust Security in AI-Powered Cloud-Native Infrastructures. *ResearchGate*.

[23] Chahar, S., Kaswan, K. S., Aggarwal, A., & Dhatterwal, J. S. (2024, November). New Era of IoT with Cloud Computing: A Review of Technology, Issues and Challenges. In *2024 2nd International Conference on Advancements and Key Challenges in Green Energy and Computing (AKGEC)* (pp. 1–7). IEEE.

[24] Dhatterwal, J. S., Kaswan, K. S., & Kumar, N. (2025). Self-Powered Integrated Sensor System for Printable Fabrication. In R. K. Dhanaraj, P. Samuel, M. Sathyamoorthy, B. Balusamy, & V. Ravi (Eds.), *Self-Powered Sensors* (pp. 187–235). Academic Press.

[25] Kaswan, K. S., Dhatterwal, J. S., Dhanda, S. S., Balusamy, B., & Abdullah, A. (2024). Digital Twin for Sustainable Development of Intelligent Manufacturing. In *Digital Twins in Industrial Production and Smart Manufacturing: An Understanding of Principles, Enhancers, and Obstacles* (pp. 125–159). IEEE. https://doi.org/10.1002/9781394195336.ch6

[26] Kaur, K., Chahar, S., Manwal, M., Kaswan, K. S., & Dhatterwal, J. S. (2024, July). Bridging Linguistics and Machine Learning: A New Human-Machine Communication. In *2024 1st International Conference on Sustainable Computing and Integrated Communication in Changing Landscape of AI (ICSCAI)* (pp. 1–6). IEEE.

Chapter 6

Data poisoning and adversarial attacks in federated learning

Peer Mohammed Jeelan and Nasrulla Khan K.

6.1 INTRODUCTION TO FEDERATED LEARNING (FL) AND SECURITY PARADIGMS

6.1.1 Overview of FL

FL represents a segregated machine learning paradigm designed to collaboratively train models across multiple distributed clients without transferring raw data to a central server. It was first introduced by McMahan et al. (2017). FL offers a favourable solution to rising concerns regarding data privacy, regulatory compliance, and the ethical use of personal information. The relevance of FL has grown particularly in domains where centralizing sensitive data such as in healthcare or finance poses legal and ethical risks [1].

6.1.2 Foundational principles of FL

FL is informed by a few key principles that set it apart from traditional centralized learning designs:

Locality of data: Raw data stays within the local devices to avert direct data sharing and reduce privacy violations. Collaborative Model Training: Clients calculate model updates (e.g., gradients or weight deltas) from their local data and forward them to a central server.

Aggregation: The global server aggregates such client updates by employing methods like Federated Averaging (FedAvg) to update the global model. Iterative Optimization: This training cycle is repeated across multiple communication rounds until the model converges.

The global model update in round ttt is mathematically expressed as:

$$w_{t+1} = w_t - \eta \sum_{k \in S_t} \frac{n_k}{n} \nabla F_k(w_t) \tag{6.1}$$

Where:

- w_t *denotes the global model at round t*
- η *is the learning rate*
- S_t *is the subset of clients selected in round t*
- n_k *is the size of the local dataset on client k*
- $F_k(w_t)$ *is the local loss function*

DOI: 10.1201/9781003660330-6

This decentralized design supports large-scale, privacy-aware learning across devices with limited trust and connectivity, including smartphones, edge nodes, and institutional data silos.

6.1.3 Motivation for FL

6.1.3.1 FL addresses key challenges facing modern AI systems

Privacy Preservation: By keeping sensitive data on local devices, FL offers a practical defense against privacy violations and data leaks [2].

Data Diversity and Volume: Training across diverse clients enhances model generalizability by capturing a wider distribution of real-world data.

Scalability: FL is designed to scale across millions of edge devices, accommodating heterogeneous hardware and software environments.

Regulatory Compliance: FL is compliant with international data protection laws like the General Data Protection Regulation (GDPR) and the Health Insurance Portability and Accountability Act (HIPAA), providing data sovereignty and secure computation.1.4 Core Architectural Components

A standard FL architecture comprises components like clients, central aggregator, communicational channel, and model update strategy. Clients are devices used by end-users or servers at institutions that have localized datasets and computational resources.

Central aggregator is a managing server that collects, consolidates, and disseminates model updates. Communication Channel is a protected, frequently bandwidth-limited pathway linking clients to the server. The final component is the update strategy for models. They are the methods that dictate the timing and manner of update transmission and aggregation, factoring in asynchrony, stragglers, and dropout scenarios.

6.1.4 Real-world applications of FL

FL has been adopted in a variety of sectors due to its privacy-preserving capabilities and decentralized design:

Healthcare: Hospitals train diagnostic models (e.g., for tumor detection or COVID-19 classification) using localized patient data without centralized sharing [3].

Mobile and Edge Computing: Smartphones and IoT devices collaboratively learn models for text prediction, image classification, and activity recognition [4].

Finance and Banking: Financial institutions utilize FL for fraud detection, credit risk modeling, and anti-money laundering systems across branches without aggregating sensitive data [12].

Smart Cities and Industrial IoT: Sensor networks in smart grids or traffic systems apply FL to enable real-time decision-making under resource constraints [5].

6.1.5 The evolving security landscape in FL

Despite its advantages, FL introduces a fundamentally different security model with new attack surfaces:

- Opacity of Local Training: The central server lacks direct visibility into client-side computation and data quality.

- Client Variability and Volatility: Clients may be compromised, intermittently connected, or resource-constrained.
- Update Manipulation: Malicious clients can submit adversarial or poisoned model updates to subvert the global model.
- Inference Risks: Even without raw data access, adversaries can infer sensitive information from shared gradients or parameters.
- These threats necessitate the development of tailored security mechanisms such as anomaly detection, robust aggregation, secure multiparty computation, and differential privacy (DP).

6.1.6 Threat models in FL

FL literature typically considers several threat models to structure the design of secure protocols:

- Honest but Curious Server: A partially trusted server that follows protocol but may attempt to obtain private information from client updates.
- Malicious Clients: Clients who inject poisoned information, manipulate model updates, or conspire with other attackers.
- Sybil Attacks: A single attacker with multiple client identities to exert disproportionate influence on the aggregation process.
- Reconnection and Dropout Exploits: Repeatedly disconnecting and reconnecting to the FL network for evading defence mechanisms.
- The above models serve as the foundation for evaluating the resilience of FL systems against a wide range of adversarial behaviors.

6.1.7 Structure and contributions

With the following contributions this chapter provides a thorough summary of the current situation pertaining to data poisoning and adversarial attacks on FL.

Formal descriptions and threat classifications for adversarial attacks and FL poisoning.

Careful scrutiny of attack vectors including backdoor injection, model inversion, and Sybil manipulation. Analysis of contemporary defense methods such as Byzantine aggregation, anomaly filtering, and cryptographic techniques. Experimental frameworks and metrics for benchmarking attacks and defenses. Critical discussion of emerging challenges, including adaptive adversaries, fairness, and interpretability.

6.2 UNDERSTANDING DATA POISONING ATTACKS IN FL

FL is a new paradigm that allows for joint model training across several decentralized clients without revealing the local data. FL is designed to keep raw data on-device and share only model updates or gradients, thus reducing the threat of direct data leakage. Still, this decentralized and privacy-respecting architecture, as much as it is a good thing in most ways, poses new security issues that are not common to conventional centralized machine learning systems. Foremost among these issues are data poisoning attacks, which have become an especially surreptitious and powerful category of threats.

In an attack through data poisoning, an attacker client or colluding attacker clients systematically alter its local training set in a fashion that poisons the target learning process.

The intent can differ: the attacker may attempt to lower the global model's general accuracy (availability attack), alter its prediction for certain inputs (targeted attack), or embed covert behaviors (backdoor attack) that are activated under particular conditions. These attacks are particularly hard to identify since the training data is kept confidential and inaccessible to the central server, and the model updates from every client are combined in such a manner that makes individual contributions anonymous.

Unlike centralized setups in which poisoned data may be detected by regular validation or outlier detection techniques, FL systems usually lack such information because of their own privacy restrictions. Additionally, the iterative and asynchronous FL training mechanism makes it hard to detect malicious activity related to a single client particularly in large systems with hundreds or thousands of clients. A successful data poisoning attack on FL has catastrophic implications. In safety-critical contexts like autonomous driving, medical diagnosis, or financial prediction minor changes may result in catastrophic harm. Additionally, the decentralized nature of FL renders the attacker anonymous. They may attack the whole system and compromising a small sub-set of clients is enough to impact the global model.

In response to these threats various defense mechanisms like strong aggregation techniques (e.g., Krum, Trimmed Mean, and Median), anomaly detection algorithms for update inspection, and DP schemes have been proposed. However, many defenses yield compromises in terms of model accuracy, computation cost, or applicability in various FL scenarios. In conclusion, while FL offers a promising approach to privacy-preserved AI, its security landscape is inherently altered compared to centralized learning. Understanding and addressing data poisoning attacks is paramount to ensuring the reliability and trustworthiness of FL systems, particularly as they gain wider acceptance in sensitive real-world domains.

6.2.1 Conceptual foundations of data poisoning

FL poisoning is an assault of malicious manipulation of training data or model updates offered by clients to the aggregator. Most significant features making FL susceptible to poisoning are:

Lack of central validation: The server is not able to examine raw client data and hence cannot identify mislabeled or adversarial samples. Local computation opacity: Clients train on their own allowing adversaries to change behavior covertly.

Heterogeneous data distributions: Due to inherent statistical variation inconsistencies among clients make anomaly detection more difficult.

6.2.1.1 Principal goals of data poisoning.

Performance Degradation: Accuracy of overcasts on valid test samples.

Targeted Backdoors: Adding particular triggers or patterns that only incorrectly classify inputs in response to a specific circumstance.

Intentionally influencing model behavior to produce unfair or discriminatory results is known as bias induction.

Subversion: Compromising fairness, robustness or trustworthiness for long term manipulation.

Unlike adversarial inference-time attacks, which tamper with model inputs post-deployment, data poisoning operates during the training phase, embedding malicious influence directly into model parameters.

6.2.2 Taxonomy of data poisoning attacks

6.2.2.1 *Label flipping*

Label flipping is a simplistic yet effective untargeted poisoning strategy, where attackers relabel training data instances to incorrect categories (e.g., 'cat' relabeled as 'dog').

Attack Vector: Alter labels (y) while keeping features (x) intact.

Objective: Reduce classification performance and confuse the decision boundary.

Formulaic Representation:

$$(x,y) \rightarrow (x,y'), Where\ y' \neq y \tag{6.2}$$

Detection: Moderate; easier with a high proportion of clean clients.

6.2.2.2 *Backdoor insertion*

Backdoor attacks inject malicious samples that cause misclassification only when a specific trigger is present (e.g., a small red pixel in an image corner).

Goal: Maintain high performance on clean data while embedding a covert vulnerability.
Example: In CIFAR-10, a trigger pattern causes all images to be classified as 'airplane'.
Recent Work: Proposed invisible watermark triggers in cross-device FL [6].

6.2.2.3 *Model update manipulation (Byzantine Clients)*

Rather than modifying raw data, Byzantine clients submit malicious model updates that intentionally disrupt aggregation.

Approach: Gradient ascent on an adversarial loss function:

$$\Delta w_{malicious} = -\lambda .\ \nabla L_{malicious}(w) \tag{6.3}$$

Impact: Convergence failure or forced misclassification.

Tools: Adversarial clients can amplify update norms or mimic benign distributions to bypass defenses.

6.2.2.4 *Sybil-based poisoning*

Sybil attacks occur when one adversary controls multiple clients (i.e., Sybils), increasing their influence on the aggregated model.

Target: Aggregation processes like FedAvg, which weight client updates equally.
Challenge for Defenders: Sybils may collude to appear statistically consistent.

Table 6.1 provides a comparison between untargeted and targeted poisoning attacks in federated learning, highlighting their differences in terms of attack objective, stealth characteristics, impact, and scope.

Table 6.1 Untargeted vs. targeted poisoning

Type	*Description*	*Stealth*	*Impact Scope*
Untargeted	General degradation of accuracy	Low	Broad
Targeted	Specific misclassification goals (e.g., trigger)	High	Narrow/precise

Table 6.2 Open challenges in data poisoning detection

Challenge	*Description*
Statistical Camouflage	Adversarial updates mimic benign ones under non-IID data.
Adaptive Attacks	Attackers adjust strategies based on observed defenses
Scarce Labeled Data	Clients cannot verify data quality without central oversight.
High Dimensionality	Makes outlier detection computationally expensive

6.2.3 Effects of data poisoning on FL systems

Accuracy Collapse: 10% malicious clients can cause 30–50% degradation in classification accuracy in non-IID settings [8].

Backdoor Persistence: Triggers are persistent over training epochs and may outlive partial retraining.

Bias Introduction: Poisoned clients in cross-silo healthcare FL can bias predictions by manipulating minority group samples.

Security Regression: Poisoned models are more susceptible to inference and inversion attacks [16].

6.2.4 Case studies and recent findings

Bagdasaryan et al. showed that one malicious client in a FL system can effectively implant a backdoor into the global model without significantly impacting the model's overall accuracy on authentic test data [7]. The assailant aimed to embed a concealed function, referred to as a backdoor, that leads the model to produce erroneous predictions exclusively when faced with particular, uncommon inputs known as triggers, while sustaining high accuracy on all standard inputs. To accomplish this, the attacker created a trigger—like a subtle image pattern or a specific word sequence in text—and incorporated poisoned samples with this trigger into its local training dataset, intentionally mislabeling them. Following the training of its local model with this compromised data, the attacker increased the effect of its update by adjusting the model gradients prior to transmitting them to the central server. Because of FL's aggregation method based on averaging, this modified malicious update was enough to steer the global model towards learning the backdoor, although it came from only a single client out of many. Consequently, the worldwide model consistently misidentified inputs with the trigger, while its performance on standard test data stayed almost the same, making the attack discreet and hard to spot. This case study uncovered a significant security flaw in FL, where privacy limitations and aggregation processes establish gaps that can be taken advantage of by attackers. It demonstrated that defensive strategies dependent only on monitoring precision or spotting major performance declines are probably inadequate to detect these targeted and subtle manipulations. Table 6.2 presents the key open challenges in detecting data poisoning attacks in federated learning systems, including issues such as statistical camouflage, adaptive attack strategies, limited labeled data, and high dimensionality of model updates.

6.3 ADVERSARIAL ATTACKS IN FL

While data poisoning attacks subvert the training process, adversarial attacks primarily target the inference stage of machine learning models, including those developed using FL. These attacks exploit the model's sensitivity to small input perturbations—perturbations that are often imperceptible to humans but catastrophic for model prediction. In FL systems, the attack surface is further enlarged due to distributed control, lack of central oversight, and variable client behavior.

Adversarial attacks in FL systems are particularly challenging to detect and mitigate due to the combination of black-box environments, heterogeneous data distributions, and constrained computation and communication capabilities on edge devices.

6.3.1 Foundations and threat landscape

An adversarial example is a perturbed version of a valid input sample designed to elicit incorrect predictions from a trained model.

Let $f : \mathbb{R}^n \rightarrow \mathbb{R}^k$ be a trained model and $x \in \mathbb{R}^n$ a legitimate input with true label y. The goal is to find the perturbation δ such that:

$$f(x) = ybutf(x + \delta) \neq y, \ with \ \| \delta \|_p < \epsilon \tag{6.4}$$

Here, $\| . \|_p$ is a $L_p -$ norm (e.g., L_∞ or L_2) that constrains perturbation size to remain imperceptible.

In FL, the attacker may inject adversarial samples during training (poisoning-type adversarial attacks), launch evasion attacks on the trained model at inference, or attempt gradient-based attacks via observed updates.

6.3.2 Taxonomy of adversarial attacks in FL

In FL systems, the nature of adversarial attacks is influenced by the locations and methods available for an attacker to intervene, resulting in a natural classification into client-centric, model-centric, and input-centric attacks. Attacks focused on clients utilize the attacker's influence over one or more involved clients; these attackers alter local training data or model updates to compromise the global model during the aggregation process. This attack takes advantage of the decentralized nature of FL where the server blindly follows client inputs but is unaware of their internal processes or data. Model-centric attacks, however, point to weaknesses inherent in the global model aggregation process. Here, attackers can design malicious updates or take advantage of aggregation algorithm weaknesses to poison the model whether they handle multiple clients or have direct access to any client data. Finally, input-focused attacks are deployment or inference time when attackers generate inputs that take advantage of the trained model's weaknesses such as adversarial examples that subtly change inputs to misclassify or trigger patterns that trigger backdoors formed during training. This trio indicates that FL attacks are multi-faceted, from the decentralized data sources through the aggregation processes to the deployment of the final model, each with corresponding defenses that factor into the attacker's capabilities and the channels of attack.

6.3.2.1 Evasion attacks (inference-time)

Evasion attacks are launched during inference by applying crafted perturbations to clean inputs, causing the model to produce incorrect predictions.

Fast Gradient Sign Method (FGSM) [17]:

$$x' = x + \epsilon.sign\left(\nabla_x J\left(\theta, x, y\right)\right) \tag{6.5}$$

Projected Gradient Descent (PGD) [8]: An iterative extension of FGSM known to be more potent.

Carlini & Wagner (CW) Attack: Optimization-based attack to minimize perturbation magnitude while ensuring misclassification.

6.3.2.2 FL implications

In cross-device FL, the attacker can apply these locally without needing model internals.

On-device AI (e.g., GBoard, Siri) remains vulnerable to local evasion attempts.

Recent Insight: Wu [6] found that adversarially trained FL models are still vulnerable to unseen perturbations from new clients, indicating limitations of localized adversarial training.

6.3.2.3 Training-time adversarial attacks

These adversaries introduce adversarial examples into their local training data and submit poisoned gradients.

Clean-Label Adversarial Attacks: Attackers preserve correct labels but modify inputs to induce boundary distortion [15].

Universal Perturbation Injection: A shared perturbation vector δ added across multiple samples leads to a generalized degradation [19].

FL Challenge:

Detection is hard when adversarial data follows the same label distribution.

Standard defenses like clipping or DP may suppress signals but fail to remove subtle adversarial gradients.

6.3.2.4 Model inversion attacks

Model inversion aims to reconstruct private inputs from model gradients or parameters. Given access to shared updates, attackers attempt to reverse-engineer training data.

Gradient Leakage [20]: Exploits gradients in early rounds to reconstruct inputs.

FL Amplification Risk: Due to repeated parameter exchanges, attackers can accumulate information across rounds.

Example: In a federated healthcare setting, an attacker may infer sensitive patient images from shared updates using gradient matching [13].

Mitigation: DP adds noise to gradients, but requires careful calibration.

Recent techniques include Encoder Obfuscation [21] and Secure Aggregation Protocols.

Table 6.3 Adversarial threat characteristics in FL

Aspect	*Centralized ML*	*Federated Learning (FL)*
Data Location	Centralized	Decentralized
Model Transparency	Full	Partial (server & client isolation)
Attack Visibility	Global	Client-local
Adversarial Control	Limited to input pipeline	Training & inference both exploitable
Data Heterogeneity	Controlled	Non-IID, increases detection complexity
Privacy Constraints	Optional	Mandatory due to design & compliance

6.3.2.5 Membership inference attacks

These attacks determine whether a specific input sample was included in a client's training dataset.

Approach: Monitor model confidence scores or gradients and infer membership via overfitting indicators.

FL Context: Local overfitting in non-IID settings makes clients more vulnerable.

Case Study: [11] showed that in FL, even partial model updates reveal significant information about training membership, especially with fewer clients. Table 6.3 provides a comparative analysis of adversarial threat characteristics between centralized machine learning systems and federated learning environments, emphasizing differences in data location, model transparency, attack visibility, and privacy constraints.

6.4 CHALLENGES IN DEFENDING FL FROM ADVERSARIAL ATTACKS

Adversarial attack defense in FL is fundamentally harder due to:

Black-Box Training: Model internals may not be visible to server or other clients.

Communication Constraints: Defenses like adversarial training or robust aggregation increase communication costs.

Client Dropout: Partial participation reduces consistency, affecting defensive retraining.

Adaptive Adversaries: Attackers may change behavior per round, alternating between malicious and benign updates. Table 6.4 summarizes notable recent research studies related to adversarial attacks in federated learning, outlining the type of attack investigated and the primary contribution of each study.

PGD-based Evasion: This work was centred on Projected Gradient Descent (PGD), the widely used adversarial attack which makes minor changes to input data to deceive machine learning models. It demonstrated that adversarial perturbations designed on a single client in an FL setting will transfer and be effective against models from other clients. This means there is a fundamental weakness: even clients who never encountered the attack samples can be deceived.

Clean-Label Injection: This is a sneaky data poisoning attack where poisoned instances are correctly labelled (i.e., "clean-label") yet lead to model misbehavior. The paper demonstrated that such clean-label backdoors can remain effective even when DP mechanisms are used demonstrating the limitations of DP in neutralizing such attacks.

Model Inversion: Model inversion attacks try to recover private training data based on model outputs or gradients. Authors suggested applying gradient compression methods to make sensitive data in gradients indistinguishable, and therefore cut down the success of inversion attacks. This offers a possible defence approach.

Table 6.4 Notable recent studies

Study	*Attack Type*	*Contribution*
Sharma [12]	PGD-based evasion	Demonstrated cross-client perturbation transferability
Xu et al. (2023)	Clean-label injection	Showed persistent backdoors even under DP mechanisms
Li [12]	Model inversion	Proposed gradient obfuscation using compression techniques
Kong et al. (2023)	Membership Inference	Demonstrated high leakage in small-client federations

Table 6.5 Summary of adversarial risks in FL

Attack Type	*Primary Objective*	*Timing*	*Mitigation Examples*
Evasion	Misclassification at inference	Post-training	Adversarial training, input filters
Training-Time Injection	Global model corruption	During training	Update clipping, robust aggregation
Model Inversion	Reconstruct sensitive training data	Post-update sharing	Secure aggregation, DP
Membership Inference	Detect dataset inclusion	Post-deployment	DP, confidence masking

Membership Inference: In membership inference attacks, an attacker attempts to find out if a specific data point was employed during training a model. The research discovered that federated systems with less number of clients are more susceptible to membership inference, because of lesser averaging and greater overfitting per client. Table 6.5 provides a consolidated summary of major adversarial risks in federated learning, including evasion attacks, training-time injection, model inversion, and membership inference, along with their objectives, attack timing, and example mitigation techniques.

Evasion: Makes the model misclassify at inference time (e.g., confuse a stop sign with a speed limit sign). Post-training the attack is performed after training the model, at inference time. Examples can include:

Adversarial Training: Train on adversarial examples to make the model more robust.

Input filters: Identify and scrub adversarial inputs before inputting them into the model.

Training Time Injection: Poison the training process to contaminate the global model or introduce backdoors. At training time attackers alter local updates or inject corrupt data as the model learns. Examples of mitigation include:

Update Clipping: Restrict the size of client updates to minimize malicious impact.

Robust Aggregation: Employ aggregation functions (e.g., Krum, Median) that are not sensitive to outliers and malicious updates.

Model Inversion: Recover private or confidential training data by examining model updates or outputs. Post-update sharing occurs after client updates are transmitted to the server. Mitigation examples include:

Secure Aggregation: Encrypt client updates so the server cannot examine individual contributions.

Differential Privacy (DP): Introduce noise into updates to hide individual data contributions.

Membership Inference: Identify if a given data sample was in the training set. Post-deployment attack happens after the model is deployed and accessed by an attacker. Mitigation examples include:

Differential Privacy (DP): Decreases overfitting, and thus, inference of training membership is more difficult.

Confidence Masking: Restricts or modifies confidence values the model produces to hinder attackers from identifying patterns.

6.5 DEFENSE MECHANISMS AGAINST DATA POISONING AND ADVERSARIAL ATTACKS IN FL

In spite of the privacy-protecting advantages of FL its distributed opaque and client-centric nature leaves it vulnerable to a wide range of security threats. As adversarial techniques become more advanced from backdoor injections to model inversion and Sybil attacks, FL systems need to be safeguarded with strong and multi-layered defense mechanisms. Such defenses need to function reliably under constraints like limited communication, client heterogeneity, intermittent participation, and adherence to privacy norms.

This section explains and critically examines the most effective defense techniques that have been designed to ward off both data poisoning and adversarial attacks in FL, all categorized into the four broad defense categories: robust aggregation, client-side security, anomaly detection, and cryptographic/proactive security frameworks.

6.5.1 Server-side robust aggregation techniques

From the time the clients transmit model updates rather than raw data, the server side aggregation is a critical point of intervention. Robust aggregation algorithms are designed to reduce or eliminate the influence of poisoned or manipulated updates while preserving model utility.

6.5.1.1 Coordinate-wise median and trimmed mean

These statistical aggregators are widely adopted for their simplicity and resilience against outliers.

Coordinate-Wise Median: Takes the median of each model parameter across clients.
Trimmed Mean: Removes the highest and lowest beta % of values before averaging.
Resilience: Can tolerate up to 50% Byzantine clients under IID assumptions [22].

Krum works by selecting the client update that is closest (in terms of Euclidean distance) to its nearest n-f-2 neighbors, effectively filtering out the top f suspicious updates before averaging. They rigorously show that:

As long as the number of Byzantine clients f satisfies

$$f < \frac{n-2}{2} \tag{6.6}$$

That is, strictly less than half of the total clients (for large n, roughly $f<n/2$), and the data across clients is IID, then the global model still converges reliably under gradient descent.

This establishes a strong up-to-50% resilience boundary under IID conditions.

Limitations:

Performance degrades under non-IID data conditions.

Vulnerable to camouflaged poisoning, where malicious updates resemble benign variations.

Recent Enhancement:

Li [12] proposed Multi-Trimmed Aggregation that dynamically adjusts trimming thresholds based on local data variance.

6.5.1.2 Krum and Multi-Krum

Krum selects a single client update that is closest (in Euclidean distance) to the majority of other updates.

Multi-Krum selects multiple updates to average. Works under the assumption of a majority of honest clients.

Formula:

$$score(i) = \sum_{j \in N(i)} \| u_i - u_j \|^2 \tag{6.7}$$

Where N(i) is the set of closest $n - f - 2$ clients

Drawback: High computational cost $O(n^2)$, and limited performance with non-IID data

Recent Work:

Huang et al. (2022) introduced FedKrum++, which combines cosine similarity with Krum for better detection of semantically similar Sybil updates.

6.5.1.3 Bulyan aggregation

Bulyan combines Krum with trimmed mean:

1. Selects a pool using Krum.
2. Applies trimmed mean to the pool.

Advantage: Increased robustness even under data heterogeneity.

Use Case: Best suited for high-stakes FL environments (e.g., autonomous systems, fintech) where detection precision outweighs computational cost.

6.5.1.4 FoolsGold: Sybil-resistant FL

FoolsGold assigns dynamic learning rates to clients based on cosine similarity between their updates. If many clients (Sybils) submit similar updates, their contributions are down-weighted.

$$\propto_i = 1 - \frac{\cos(u_i, \overline{u}_{\neg i})}{Max_i \cos(u_j, \overline{u}_{\neg j})} \tag{6.8}$$

Recent Extensions:

Xie [23] introduced FoolsGold++, which incorporates temporal decay and client momentum history to mitigate adaptive Sybils.

6.5.2 Client-side defense strategies

While server-side defenses are central, empowering clients with localized protections improves systemic robustness.

6.5.2.1 Local data filtering and validation

Clients can employ:

Outlier detection via z-score or IQR filtering.
Autoencoder-based anomaly detection.
Label smoothing to detect and mitigate label flipping.
Recent method:
Chen [6] proposed Self-Denoising FL, where clients augment their data and detect label inconsistencies using unsupervised clustering.

6.5.2.2 Local adversarial training

Incorporates adversarial examples into client training to improve robustness.

For example, PGD-based adversarial training at local nodes.

Challenges: High computational overhead on edge devices.

New Framework:

Sharma & Li [12] introduced Adversarial Gradient Balancing, which smooths adversarial updates before submission to the server, enhancing robustness without overfitting.

6.5.2.3 Trusted execution environments (TEEs)

Hardware-based isolation enclaves such as Intel SGX protect the training process and verify integrity.

Advantages:

- Prevents OS-level tampering.
- Provides audit trails for computation.

Limitations:

- Vulnerable to side-channel attacks (e.g., cache timing).
- Not scalable to millions of devices.

Recent Use:

Fereidooni [21] implemented FL with TEE-backed secure training using ARM TrustZone in IoT settings.

6.5.3 Anomaly Detection and Attacker Identification

Anomaly detection frameworks proactively monitor for malicious behavior during training rounds.

6.5.3.1 *Statistical filtering*

Z-Score and MAD Filtering: Flag updates with abnormal deviation.

Cosine Similarity Filters: Identify updates deviating from majority direction.

Recent Approach:

Wu [6] developed FLAME, a framework that dynamically learns what constitutes "normal" behavior via contrastive learning.

6.5.3.2 *Federated reputation systems*

Assign trust scores to clients based on:

Frequency and consistency of participation.

Historical contribution to model accuracy.

Anomaly reports from other clients.

Framework:

FedTrust: Implements a distributed trust ledger with decay-weighted scoring.

6.5.3.3 *Graph-based detection*

Builds similarity graphs of client updates and detects communities of colluding (e.g., Sybil) clients.

Zhang [9] introduced FedGraph, which uses graph neural networks to predict malicious subgraphs within FL systems.

6.5.4 Cryptographic and proactive security frameworks

Proactive security measures provide more robust assurances than reactive detection, particularly for delicate FL installations.

6.5.4.1 *Differential privacy (DP)*

DP adds calibrated noise to updates to preserve privacy.

Mechanism:

$$\tilde{g} = g + \mathcal{N}(0, \sigma^2) \tag{6.9}$$

Protects against gradient leakage and membership inference.

Trade-off: High noise can suppress useful gradients.

New Method:

Zhao [14] presented DP-MixFed, a novel differentially private FL system that adjusts noise levels per client based on the entropy of their local data. DP-MixFed's key contribution is to adjust the level of injected noise to each client's model updates based on the uncertainty or diversity of their data. Clients with high-entropy data, that is, more diverse and thus less identifiable, receive less noise, while clients with low-entropy data, that is, more homogeneous and thus possibly more sensitive, receive more noise to enhance privacy. By varying the amount of mixture noise for each client DP-MixFed optimizes its approach to improve privacy-utility trade-offs. Because it avoids adding extraneous noise when the data is already less sensitive and still offers strong privacy guarantees when needed, it enhances the overall performance of the model.

6.5.4.2 Secure multiparty computation (SMPC)

SMPC enables aggregation without revealing individual updates.

Techniques: Secret sharing (Shamir's), additive masking.

Scalability: Suitable for cross-silo FL; heavy for cross-device FL.

Implementation:

Google's Secure Aggregation Protocol was successfully scaled to the internet by Bonawitz et al. (2019) resolving privacy and communication issues for millions of devices. Their implementation demonstrated that it is feasible to safely aggregate model updates from a large number of users in FL without disclosing personal information. Even in large scale real-world deployments the protocol protects user privacy by enabling encrypted aggregation which allows the server to learn only the aggregated user update outcome. This accomplishment resolved important problems in efficiency, fault tolerance, and security and made privacy-preserving machine learning available at scale.

6.5.4.3 Homomorphic encryption (HE)

A type of encryption known as Homomorphic Encryption (HE) allows calculations to be made directly on the ciphertext before the data is decrypted. When such calculations are decrypted the outcome is identical to that of calculations performed on the plaintext data. Sensitive information is kept private during computation thanks to HE which enables safe data processing and sharing. Because it enables servers or third parties to perform analytics or train models on the encrypted user data without ever having access to the raw data. HE is especially helpful in privacy-preserving machine learning, cloud computing, and FL. Fully homomorphic encryption schemes are typically computationally costly despite their impressive privacy promises; efforts are being made to make them more efficient. Its high computational overhead is a disadvantage.

Recent Optimization:

Liu et al. [10] introduced HE-FedAvg++ as a low latency partially homomorphic variant optimized for linear layers.

6.5.4.4 Blockchain integration

By encouraging trust transparency and accountability amongst decentralized stakeholders, blockchain integration in FL is a powerful paradigm to protect against data poisoning and hostile attacks. One of the main benefits is immutable logging, where all client. Malicious activity is simple to identify and track since updates and training operations are securely recorded onto an unchangeable tamper-proof ledger. Blockchain eliminates the need for a central server and reduces the risk of tampered aggregators by enabling decentralized model aggregation through smart contracts. Pre-established guidelines for updates such as gradient norm bounds or anomaly detection that automatically rejects questionable contributions, can be enforced by smart contracts. Only reliable clients are allowed to participate thanks to client authentication and reputation systems, and persistently bad behavior may lead to reduced trust ratings or exclusion from training cycles. Blockchain

Table 6.6 Comparative analysis of defense strategies

Defence Category	*Strengths*	*Limitations*
Robust Aggregation	Scalable; low communication overhead	May underperform in non-IID settings
Client-Side Filtering	Early detection of poisoning	Vulnerable to compromised clients
Anomaly Detection	Learns evolving attacker patterns	High false positives under high variability
Cryptographic Methods	Strong privacy guarantees	Resource-intensive; complex deployment
Blockchain-Based FL	Decentralized trust management	Latency and throughput bottlenecks

allows cooperative trust by making client behavior transparent and auditable, and promoting cooperative defense mechanisms. Scalability challenges of blockchain, increased computational cost, and leakage of privacy notwithstanding, they can be addressed with solutions like permissioned blockchains, off-chain storage, and cryptographic protection. Overall, blockchain is an effective added layer on top of existing defenses such as DP, secure aggregation, and resilient update rules, substantially enhancing the robustness and integrity of FL systems.

Provides immutable logs of updates.

Smart contracts enforce participation rules and penalties.

Example system:

BlockFL [5] integrates FL training rounds with Hyperledger for verifiable accountability. Table 6.6 presents a comparative analysis of different defense strategies used to protect federated learning systems against poisoning and adversarial attacks, outlining their strengths and limitations.

6.5.5 Summary and recommendations

FL is shielded from poisoning and hostile attacks by multi-layered defense systems which operate at client, server, and protocol layers. While no single technique is sole protection, where aggregation resilience is combined with anomaly detection and privacy-protection cryptography is the best answer.

Recommended best practices:

Use adaptive aggregation methods like Bulyan and FedKrum++.

Use DP with adaptive noise budgets.

Integrate TEEs into high-trust cross-silo organizations.

Monitor using graph-based anomaly detection for Sybil resistance.

Make sure you audit with blockchain logging where compliance is imperative.

6.6 EVALUATION METRICS AND EXPERIMENTAL SETUP

Evaluating the robustness and vulnerability of FL systems against data poisoning and adversarial attacks requires a holistic, multi-dimensional assessment framework. Unlike centralized machine learning, FL evaluations must account for distributed training dynamics, privacy constraints, client heterogeneity, and intermittent participation.

This section introduces standardized metrics, simulation environments, benchmark datasets, and open-source frameworks used to assess both attack severity and defense efficacy in FL.

6.6.1 Metrics for attack impact assessment

All these metrics quantify the severity of adversarial and poisoning attacks on FL models.

6.6.1.1 *Global model accuracy degradation*

It helps measure and scale the overall drop in test accuracy due to attacks.

$$AccuracyDrop = A_{clean} - A_{Underattack} \tag{6.10}$$

Where:
A_{Clean}: Accuracy of the global model in a benign setting
$A_{underattack}$: Accuracy during/after attack
Results state that even a 10% reduction can signal successful untargeted poisoning [8].

6.6.1.2 *Attack success rate (ASR)*

Attack Success Rate (ASR) is a measure of the success of an adversary attack or privacy violation. It approximates the fraction or percentage of successful attacks that succeed in their objective, for example, stealing confidential information, misclassifying inputs, or violating model privacy compared to total attempts. In privacy as well as security in machine learning a greater ASR means a more successful or effective attack and reflects vulnerabilities in the system. A lower ASR means that protection or defense, such as DP or encryption is more successful at avoiding successful attacks. Misclassification:

$$ASR = \frac{\#Targeted\,Misclassifications}{\#Adversarial\,Inputs}$$

High ASR with minimal drop in clean accuracy indicates stealthy backdoors.
ASR-C (on clean data): Evaluates how often triggers still work on test sets.

6.6.1.3 *Perturbation norm (for evasion)*

Perturbation form quantifies the magnitude of adversarial input perturbation.

$$\|\delta\| < \epsilon$$

Lower value = imperceptible attacks
Measured in $L_2, L_\infty\, or\, L_0\, norms$

6.6.1.4 *Membership inference rate*

The goal is to quantify how well the attacker can guess membership that is, whether a given sample is a member of the training data or not. Metrics like AUC (Area Under the ROC

Curve) or Precision-Recall are employed to do this. These metrics capture how well the attacker can distinguish between members (samples in the training data) and non-members (samples not in the training data).

AUC (Area Under the ROC Curve) estimates the trade-off between false positive rate and true positive rate at various thresholds and produces a summary measure of classification performance.

Precision-Recall is concerned with precision (true positive members out of all positive predictions) and recall (true positive members out of all positive actual members) trade-off, which is particularly useful when the classes are imbalanced.

A higher AUC or Precision Recall means that it is easier for the attacker to distinguish which of the samples were in the training set, that is, the privacy threat is stronger. Lower values mean better membership inference protection.

Recent Use:

Nasr et al. (2022) applied this to FL under DP to show persistent leakage even after aggregation.

6.6.1.5 Model inversion similarity score

Measures reconstruction accuracy of input samples from gradients.

Metric: Structural Similarity Index (SSIM), Peak Signal-to-Noise Ratio (PSNR).

Yin [13] used SSIM to quantify face reconstruction accuracy from federated biometric gradients.

6.6.2 Metrics for defense effectiveness

Robust defenses should mitigate attacks without harming model utility or efficiency.

6.6.2.1 Accuracy restoration

$$Restoration\ \% = \frac{A_{Defended} - A_{Underattack}}{A_{Clean} - A_{Underattack}} \times 100 \tag{6.11}$$

Indicates how well a defense recovers lost performance.

6.6.2.2 ASR reduction

$$\Delta ASR = ASR_{pre-defense} - ASR_{post-defense} \tag{6.12}$$

Higher ΔASR signifies stronger attack mitigation.

6.6.2.3 False positive rate (FPR)

Important in anomaly detection: Proportion of benign clients falsely identified as malicious.

$$FPR = \frac{False\,Alarms}{Benign\,Clients} \tag{6.13}$$

FPR should be < 5% in production environments. High FPR may exclude valuable data and reduce model fairness.

6.6.2.4 Utility-security trade-off index

Evaluates how much model utility is sacrificed for defense robustness.

$$Trade - off\ Index = \frac{Restoration}{Accuracy\,drop\,without\,defense} \tag{6.14}$$

Balances robustness vs. usability. High value suggests an efficient defense.

6.6.2.5 System overhead

Defense schemes should be evaluated for:

Communication cost (e.g., update size in KB).
Computation latency (e.g., client training time increase).
Memory footprint (especially for TEE or HE setups).
Liu [14] reported a 3× increase in computation time for HE-based FL with 2-layer CNNs.

6.6.3 Benchmark datasets for federated security evaluation

To simulate realistic FL threats, datasets must allow manipulation and measurement across multiple clients under IID and non-IID settings. Table 6.7 describes commonly used benchmark datasets for evaluating security threats in federated learning, including their domain characteristics and typical use cases in adversarial and poisoning attack experiments.

Table 6.7 Characteristics of datasets

Dataset	*Domain*	*Characteristics*	*Use Cases*
MNIST	Handwritten digits	Balanced, clean 10-class	Label flipping, backdoors, gradient leaks
CIFAR-10	Natural images	RGB, complex features	Backdoor, universal perturbations
FEMNIST	Federated MNIST	Non-IID user handwriting	Data heterogeneity simulation
Sent140	Text (Twitter)	Imbalanced sentiment labels	Text poisoning, inference attacks
Shakespeare	Language modeling	Sequence prediction, highly non-IID	Membership inference, adversarial NLP
MedMNIST	Medical images	2D/3D datasets from multiple modalities	Backdoor in clinical FL
CreditCard	Financial records	Tabular binary classification	Fraud detection under Sybil threats

Note: All datasets are compatible with LEAF, Flower, and FedML frameworks.

6.6.4 FL frameworks and tools

With increasing complexity and popularity of FL systems, strong frameworks and tools are developing to make development, experimentation, and deployment of FL workflows easier. These platforms not only enable traditional FL training but more and more incorporate elements to learn, simulate, and defend against a broad variety of attacks—ranging from data poisoning and adversarial manipulation to privacy inference attacks.

Several open-source libraries facilitate FL experimentation with modular support for attacks, defenses, and evaluation logging.

6.6.4.1 FedML (2022–2025)

FedML is an extensive open-source FL research library for both simulation and real-world usage. It is compatible with multiple FL algorithms, adjustable client-server architectures, and diverse computing environments.

Supports cross-device, cross-silo, and hierarchical FL.

Integrated adversarial/poisoning plugins.

Metrics logger and visualization dashboard.

FedML v1.3 (2024) added modules for Sybil detection and ASR tracking.

6.6.4.2 Flower

Flower is simplicity-oriented and scalable, allowing for FL experiments to be easily integrated into current machine learning workflows. It allows for various communication protocols and varied client systems, ranging from mobile to edge servers. Flower supports adversarial testing through the ability to inject malicious clients and custom attack logic during training. Its modular architecture allows researchers to deploy and test defense measures like anomaly detection and client reputation tracking in realistic deployment scenarios.

Language-agnostic and modular (supports PyTorch, TF, JAX).

Real-device experimentation support.

Extensive support for hardware-limited simulations.

6.6.4.3 TensorFlow federated (TFF)

TFF was developed by Google as a production-level framework for constructing FL algorithms and simulations based on TensorFlow. TFF provides APIs to construct iterative federated computations and simulate distributed training with realistic client data heterogeneity. TFF facilitates attack vector research in that custom aggregation functions and client update manipulations are supported. While mostly a research tool, the intimate linkage of TFF with TensorFlow renders it an excellent resource for closing the gap between FL attack research and real-world machine learning workflows.

Native to TensorFlow ecosystem.

Best suited for small-scale simulations and prototyping.

Supports DP integration and secure aggregation APIs.

6.6.4.4 PySyft

It is a privacy-aware framework that unifies state-of-the-art cryptographic methods such as SMPC and HE with FL. PySyft is particularly interesting for studying attacks on privacy leaks because, beyond normal FL training, it strongly emphasizes data confidentiality and secure model updates (e.g., model inversion and membership inference attacks).

Focuses on privacy-preserving FL.

Integrates SMPC, DP, and encrypted training.

Best for cryptographic defense simulation.

6.6.4.5 LEAF benchmark suite

Collection of real-world FL datasets.

Standardized evaluation scripts.

Supports non-IID partitioning and statistical tracking.

6.6.5 Instructions for simulation setup

These frameworks provide the necessary infrastructure to replicate hostile situations in controlled environments enabling consistent investigation of how attacks affect model performance or violate privacy. Attackers may be introduced as malevolent clients that use adaptive adversarial techniques and alter training data or updates. These environments also facilitate the benchmarking of defense strategies such as anomaly detection systems, client reputation systems, cryptographic privacy protection techniques, and strong aggregation algorithms. Validity and reproducibility must be ensured by proper setup.

Recommended Setup:

- Clients: 10–100 (simulate both cross-device and cross-silo).
- Participation rate: 10–30% per round (mimics real-world dropout).
- Poisoning rate: 5–20% of clients.
- Non-IID split: Dirichlet $\alpha = 0.3$ (moderate heterogeneity).
- Rounds: 100–300.

Attack Triggers: Set aside 10% of test data with patterns (e.g., pixel patch, keyword).

Logging:

- ASR per round
- Accuracy per round
- FPR from anomaly detector
- Overhead (training time, bandwidth per client)

6.6.6 Reproducibility and transparency best practices

To ensure integrity and reusability of experimental results:

Clearly specify:

- Threat model (e.g., white-box vs. black-box).
- Attack strategy and training conditions.
- Defense hyperparameters.
- Dataset preprocessing steps.

Share:

- Open-source code repositories.
- Random seeds and configuration files.
- Docker or Conda environments.

Report:

- All metrics (ASR, accuracy, overhead).
- Limitations and potential biases.

6.7 CHALLENGES, OPEN PROBLEMS, AND FUTURE DIRECTIONS

FL which offers promising prospects for protecting privacy in machine learning is vulnerable to numerous attacks that exploit its core features including decentralization, data proximity, client diversity, and intermittent engagement. Numerous technical, methodological, and ethical challenges still exist in spite of the development of numerous defensive tactics. This section highlights these unresolved issues and provides guidance for upcoming research and developments in secure FL frameworks.

6.7.1 Scalability and efficiency of defenses

Existing defenses frequently find it difficult to remain resilient without sacrificing performance as FL deployments grow to millions of edge devices or span several organizations.

Key Challenges:

Computational Bottlenecks: Robust aggregation techniques such as Krum and Bulyan have $O(n^2)$ complexity making them inefficient at scale.

Communication Overhead: There are substantial latency and data-transfer expenses associated with cryptographic solutions such as secure multiparty computation and homomorphic encryption.

Partial Participation: Only a portion of clients take part in each round in real-world FLs like GBoard which lowers the accuracy of defence consistency or collective anomaly detection. Open Research Directions:

Development of lightweight approximation algorithms for aggregation (e.g., FedFast).

Hierarchical defense architectures that delegate anomaly detection to edge aggregators.

Sparse client sampling strategies with security-aware selection policies [12].

6.7.2 Trade-offs between privacy, robustness, and utility

Designing defenses that strike a balance remains an unsolved multi-objective optimization problem.

Illustrative Trade-Offs:

DP:

- Protects against gradient leakage.
- May degrade model utility, especially in non-IID data scenarios.

- Robust aggregation:
- Filters malicious updates.
- Can suppress legitimate updates from minority clients (amplifying fairness issues).
- Adversarial training:
- Increases robustness.
- Increases computational cost and overfitting risk to specific perturbations.

Future Work:

Formulation of multi-objective FL optimization frameworks [14].

Use of meta-learning to adaptively calibrate privacy-robustness-utility trade-offs.

Incorporation of context-aware policies that vary defense strength by use case (e.g., health vs. edge AI).

6.7.3 Adaptive, stealthy, and multi-round adversaries

Modern adversaries are no longer static. They evolve their strategies based on observable system behavior, making detection more difficult.

Characteristics:

Clean-Label Poisoning: Attacks where data appears benign, but causes subtle model drift [6].

Adaptive Gradient Obfuscation: Updates are crafted to mimic benign noise distributions, bypassing statistical detectors.

Multi-Round Behavior Modulation: Adversaries alternate between honest and malicious updates to evade long-term detection.

Future Research Opportunities:

Game-theoretic modeling of FL attacker-defender dynamics.

Online learning-based anomaly detection that adapts to attacker evolution.

Integration of long-term behavior profiling and client histories for defense tuning.

6.7.4 Personalization and local model vulnerabilities

FL models are often personalized per client using fine-tuning or adaptive layers. This opens new avenues for local vulnerabilities.

Concerns:

Model inversion is easier on personalized layers due to lower entropy.

Adversarial overfitting during personalization amplifies susceptibility to evasion attacks.

Heterogeneous personalization makes uniform defense difficult.

Research Needs:

Defense-aware personalization protocols.

Cross-client adversarial training without violating privacy.

Evaluation of personalized defenses such as local DP bounds and gradient compression.

The two major deployment models of FL have vastly different assumptions, yet many defenses are designed agnostically. Table 6.8 provides a comparison between cross-silo and cross-device federated learning environments, highlighting differences in participation scale, resource availability, attack surface, and preferred defense mechanisms.

Future Direction:

Creation of deployment-specific defense libraries.

Automatic detection of FL topology and threat surface to tailor defenses [15].

Table 6.8 Cross-silo vs. cross-device FL disparities

Feature	*Cross-Silo FL*	*Cross-Device FL*
Participants	Trusted institutions (e.g., hospitals)	Millions of untrusted devices
Participation Rate	High (synchronous)	Low (asynchronous, sporadic)
Resources	Abundant (CPU, memory, bandwidth)	Limited (battery, bandwidth, CPU)
Attack Surface	Insider threats, targeted poisoning	Sybils, evasion, mass poisoning
Defense Preference	Cryptographic, auditing-based	Lightweight, low-overhead defenses

6.7.5 Explainability and interpretability in FL security

Defensive decisions in FL are currently opaque; flagged clients are often excluded without clear explanations.

Why It Matters:

Stakeholders need interpretability for audit and compliance.

Debugging poisoned or biased models is difficult without attribution insights.

Transparent decisions enhance user trust and regulatory adherence.

Potential Solutions:

Application of eXplainable AI (XAI) to interpret model-update anomalies.

Federated attribution systems to track influence of each client update on global parameters.

Use of causal inference models to determine the origin of poisoning effects.

Kong [9] proposed "FedIntuition"— a framework for visualizing parameter divergence across clients in near real-time.

6.7.6 Regulatory, legal, and ethical dimensions

FL is increasingly used in high-stakes domains where compliance with regulations such as GDPR, HIPAA, and CCPA is nonnegotiable.

Key Issues:

Data sovereignty: Ensuring local data never crosses jurisdictional borders.

Right to explanation: Requires model decisions and exclusions to be auditable.

Bias amplification: Poisoning can introduce or worsen demographic inequities.

Future Needs:

Policy-aware FL frameworks with built-in legal compliance.

Auditable training pipelines with traceable model versions and update logs.

Partnerships between AI ethics researchers, cybersecurity engineers, and legal scholars to codify best practices.

6.7.7 Toward proactive and holistic FL security

Most FL defenses today are reactive, deployed after attacks have manifested. There is a growing need to shift toward proactive systemic security by design.

Table 6.9 Summary of open problems

Problem Domain	*Unsolved Questions*
Scalability	Can robust aggregation scale to millions of devices without complexity?
Privacy vs. Utility	How do we tune DP noise to balance leakage and accuracy in non-IID scenarios?
Adaptive Threats	How do we detect multi-round stealthy adversaries who mimic benign behavior?
Defense Transparency	How do we build explainable and interpretable FL security systems?
Personalization Vulnerability	How can personalization be made robust without leaking sensitive local patterns?
Cross-Silo Specificity	Can defenses be tailored dynamically to the deployment context?
Regulation Compliance	How can FL systems be made inherently auditable and legally compliant?

Vision for the Future:

1. Trust Bootstrapping Protocols:
   - Reputation initialization
   - Certificate-based identities
2. Adaptive Trust Scoring:
   - Real-time behavior monitoring
   - Reputation decay for inconsistent updates
3. End-to-End Monitoring:
   - Lifecycle logging from data ingestion to model deployment
   - Federated threat intelligence sharing
4. Security-Aware Evaluation Benchmarks:
   - Standardized threat models
   - Public leaderboard for FL robustness

Table 6.9 summarizes the major open research problems in federated learning security, outlining unresolved challenges related to scalability, privacy–utility trade-offs, adaptive adversaries, defense transparency, personalization vulnerabilities, deployment contexts, and regulatory compliance.

6.8 CONCLUSION

FL is a paradigm change in the machine learning landscape that allows decentralized model training without sharing raw data between clients. This approach is solution-specific to several important privacy issues and is particularly appealing in sensitive domains including healthcare, finance, and mobile computing. FL balances utility with privacy by enabling data owners to collectively enhance models while maintaining data locality. But the very architecture decisions that are at the basis of FL distribution, client independence, and constrained transparency also bring important design security issues that need to be properly addressed to guarantee safe deployment.

This chapter has offered a thorough and academically grounded integration of the complex security environment around FL with a particular emphasis on threats through data poisoning and adversarial attacks. Through detailed technical exploration, empirical evaluation, and a rigorous review of contemporary literature from 2021 to 2025, we have identified key attack surfaces as well as promising defense mechanisms that collectively define the current state-of-the-art in secureFL. These insights are vital for anyone seeking to understand or contribute to the advancement of resilient FL systems.

One key contribution of this paper is the organized taxonomy of FL threats. We grouped leading attack vectors into general categories like data poisoning such as label flipping, backdoor injection, Sybil attacks, and adversarial attacks like evasion, model inversion, and membership inference. Not only does this taxonomy explain the nature of the adversarial behaviors that FL needs to endure but it also constitutes a conceptual framework for examining new and rising threats.

Building upon this we investigated the dynamics of such attacks via formal modeling and empirical analysis. We classified threat models along a variety of different dimensions including targeted versus untargeted attacks, white-box versus black-box information, and static versus adaptive tactics. Such delineations are paramount in developing customized defense measures that can counter different adversarial capabilities and goals.

On the defense side the chapter gave a comprehensive overview of the methods of mitigation. We summarized server-side defenses like strong aggregation techniques like Krum, Bulyan and FoolsGold that attempt to remove malicious updates without compromising model utility. Equally important are client-side techniques that impose validation and control on local training to minimize attack surfaces. Anomaly detection and behavior-based monitoring provide dynamic countermeasures that can identify anomalous patterns typical of attacks. We also highlighted the contribution of cryptographic techniques in general—secure multiparty computation, homomorphic encryption, and DP that enhance privacy guarantees and data privacy during the training process. We also briefly discussed innovative solutions based on blockchain technology to meet decentralized accountability and trust allowing transparent tamper-evident audit trails and enabling reputation systems to put off bad behavior. Supporting this landscape overview the chapter introduced standard evaluation frameworks for reproducible adversarial research in FL which are paramount to its success. These are metrics such as attack success rate, accuracy degradation, false positive rates, and benchmark datasets such as FEMNIST, CIFAR-10 and Sent140. Open source FL software such as FedML, Flower, and PySyft were also charted providing researchers. Practical experimentation and comparative assessment tools are provided. These models guarantee that defense mechanisms are rigorously tested against varying environments and adversary situations.

In spite of the staggering progress covered in it there are several grave challenges that continue to persist. Scalability is a challenge that averts the use of advanced defense algorithms on large FL systems. Most defense methods involve blackboxes and are uninterpretable and it becomes challenging for practitioners to know and believe in their effectiveness. The dynamic regulatory landscape adds an additional degree of sophistication that includes compliance with privacy regulations like GDPR and establishing regulations for AI governance. Attackers are becoming increasingly creative in their approach, requiring defense mechanisms that can keep up with novel attack patterns and client behaviors.

In subsequent deployments of FL security requirements necessitate concerted efforts that bring together machine learning, cybersecurity, cryptography, and policy spaces. Researchers are faced with tremendous opportunities for exploring new directions such as game theoretic defense mechanisms, meta-learning for building resilient adaptability, and decentralized anomaly detection paradigms. Practitioners deploying FL in real-world scenarios need to offer end-to-end lifecycle auditing, proactive defense mechanisms, and privacy-preserving personalization in an attempt to protect user privacy and maintain model integrity. During this period policymakers and regulators need to play a critical role of setting standards surrounding auditing transparency and enforcing consent which can build greater public trust in federated artificial intelligence systems. Our future secure FL is one where security is built-in from the start instead of being an afterthought. Such a vision includes the infusion of security by design techniques where threat modeling and mitigation become an inseparable part of the development pipeline. The development of situationally aware and quantifiable trust in FL systems is warranted for intelligent, adaptive, trust-rating distributions to customers combined with behaviorally updated provenance. We suggest standardized testing procedures with worldwide standards to measure robustness, fairness, and privacy in real-world adversarial settings. Compliance can be enforced automatically through cryptographically verifiable training pipelines that ensure compliance with regulation while not slowing innovation or scalability. FL systems should include adaptive mechanisms that have the ability to respond immediately to pending threats and other client engagement.

As FL moves from being a technique explored mainly in the research community to creating solid infrastructure worthy of mission-critical deployment, its success will depend on its ability to prevent manipulation, preserve privacy, and establish trust among heterogeneous and autonomous parties. Data poisoning and adversarial attacks cannot be considered edge threats waiting at the periphery; instead they constitute central challenges that find themselves at the center of the ethical design and deployment. Federated systems are a building-block element for building secure, privacy-guaranteeing, and reliable federated intelligence for scientists, practitioners, and decision makers. This effort paves the way for strong artificial intelligence ensuring data sovereignty and security.

REFERENCES

1. Yang, Q., Liu, Y., Chen, T., & Tong, Y. (2019). Federated machine Learning: Concept and applications. *ACM TIST*, 10(2), 12:1–12:19.
2. Kairouz, P., McMahan, H. B., Avent, B., Bellet, A., Bennis, M., et al. (2021). Advances and open problems in federated learning. *Foundations and Trends® in Machine Learning*, 14(1–2), 1–210.
3. Darzidehkalani, H., Rieke, N., Kalra, M. K., & Langlotz, C. P. (2022). Federated learning in medical imaging: Part II—methods, challenges, and considerations. *Journal of the American College of Radiology*, 19(4), 626–631. https://doi.org/10.1016/j.jacr.2021.12.012
4. Hard, A., Rao, K., Mathews, R., Beaufays, F., Augenstein, S., Eichner, H., Kiddon, C., & Ramage, D. (2019). Federated learning for mobile keyboard prediction. In *Proceedings of the 23rd International Conference on Artificial Intelligence and Statistics (AISTATS 2019)* (pp. 1318–1328). PMLR.
5. Nguyen, D. C., Ding, M., Pham, Q. V., Pathirana, P. N., Le, L. B., Seneviratne, A., Li, J., Niyato, D., Poor, H. V., & Kim, D. I. (2021). Federated learning for wireless communications: Motivation, opportunities, and challenges. *IEEE Communications Magazine*, 59(5), 188–194.

6. Shen, L., Wu, H., Chen, X., Yang, L., & Yu, S. (2021). Invisible backdoor attack with sample-specific triggers in federated learning. *IEEE Transactions on Dependable and Secure Computing*. Advance online publication.
7. Bagdasaryan, E., Veit, A., Hua, Y., Estrin, D., & Shmatikov, V. (2020). How to backdoor federated learning. *International Conference on Artificial Intelligence and Statistics (AISTATS). Proceedings of Machine Learning Research*, 108, 2938–2948.
8. Fang, M., Cao, X., Jia, J., & Gong, N. Z. (2020). Local model poisoning attacks to Byzantine-robust federated learning. *USENIX Security Symposium (USENIX Security 20)*, pp. 1605–1622.
9. Kong, L., Zhang, H., & Luo, X. (2023). FedIntuition: Explainable anomaly attribution in federated learning. *Journal of Machine Learning Research*, 24, 1–23.
10. Liu, H., Chen, X., & Tang, J. (2024). Efficient encrypted model aggregation in federated learning using HE-FedAvg++. *ACM Transactions on Privacy and Security*, 27, 1–25. https://doi.org/3628910
11. Nasr, M., Shokri, R., & Houmansadr, A. (2022). Adversary instantiation in federated learning. *IEEE Symposium on Security and Privacy*, pp. 866–882.
12. Sharma, R., & Li, F. (2024). Adversarial gradient balancing in federated learning. *IEEE Transactions on Neural Networks and Learning Systems*, 35, 1225–1238. https://doi.org/TNNLS.2024.0001234
13. Yin, D., Chen, R., & Song, D. (2021). Recovering training data from federated learning gradients. *Advances in Neural Information Processing Systems*, 34, 16919–16930.
14. Zhao, J., Liu, W., & Wang, Y. (2023). Adaptive differential privacy for non-IID federated learning. *Neural Networks*, 160, 15–29. https://doi.org/j.neunet.2023.01.014
15. Zhou, M., Wang, Q., & Ren, K. (2024). Context-aware defenses for deployment-specific federated learning. *IEEE Transactions on Dependable and Secure Computing*, 21.
16. Melis, L., Song, C., Cristofaro, E. D., & Shmatikov, V. (2019). Exploiting unintended feature leakage in collaborative learning. In *2019 IEEE Symposium on Security and Privacy (SP)* (pp. 691–706). IEEE.
17. Goodfellow, I. J., Shlens, J., & Szegedy, C. (2015). Explaining and harnessing adversarial examples. In *Proceedings of the International Conference on Learning Representations (ICLR 2015)*. arXiv, 1412.6572.
18. Madry, A., Makelov, A., Schmidt, L., Tsipras, D., & Vladu, A. (2018). Towards deep learning models resistant to adversarial attacks. In *Proceedings of the International Conference on Learning Representations (ICLR 2018)*. OpenReview.net.
19. Moosavi-Dezfooli, S. M., Fawzi, A., Fawzi, O., & Frossard, P. (2017). Universal adversarial perturbations. In *Proceedings of the IEEE Conference on Computer Vision and Pattern Recognition (CVPR 2017), IEEE*, pp. 1765–1773.
20. Zhu, L., Liu, Z., & Han, S. (2019). Deep leakage from gradients. In *Proceedings of the 33rd Conference on Neural Information Processing Systems (NeurIPS 2019)* (pp. 14747–14756). Curran Associates.
21. Fereidooni, H., Conti, M., Gupta, S., Marchal, S., Miettinen, M., Nguyen, T. D., Sadeghi, A. R., & Yao, D. (2022). SAFELearn: Secure aggregation for federated learning with malicious participants. *IEEE Transactions on Dependable and Secure Computing*, 19(6), 3891–3909.
22. Blanchard, P., El Mhamdi, E. M. E., Guerraoui, R., & Stainer, J. (2017). Machine learning with adversaries: Byzantine tolerant gradient descent. In *Advances in Neural Information Processing Systems 30 (NeurIPS 2017)* (pp. 119–129). Curran Associates, Inc.
23. Fung, C., Yoon, C. J. M., & Beschastnikh, I. (2020). The limitations of federated learning in Sybil settings. In *Proceedings of the 23rd International Symposium on Research in Attacks, Intrusions, and Defenses (RAID 2020)*. USENIX, pp. 301–316.

Chapter 7

Securing digital payments and transactions using federated learning

Vikram Singh, Yashasvi Makin, Srikanth Yerra, Ravi Prakash Chaturvedi, Annu Mishra, and Rajneesh Kumar Singh

7.1 INTRODUCTION

The rapid advancements in digital technologies have transformed the financial services sector, with digital payments as part of our daily transactions. From mobile wallets to online banks, contactless POS systems, and peer-to-peer (P2P) transfers, today's consumers and businesses expect the convenience and velocity available with digital transactions. However, with the increased reliance on digital payments comes serious security and privacy concerns [1]. Cybercriminals are constantly coming up with new methods to attack vulnerabilities in payment systems, resulting in financial fraud, data theft, and identity fraud [2, 3]. The level of digital payment volume and value will continue to grow, and therefore, increase the need for security mechanisms that are strong, intelligent, and privacy preserving [4, 5].

At present, the majority of digital payment systems utilize centralized MLmodels to identify unusual behavior and fraudulent activity. These models are trained using a large dataset that includes user information aggregated from various channels. Although this centralized approach can be effective for identifying anomalous and fraudulent behavior, privacy concerns are significant. Sensitive financial information is aggregated and stored on central servers which become single points of failure and attract cybersecurity threats. This centralized collection and use of financial data is also usually at odds with proposed data protection laws such as the General Data Protection Regulation (GDPR), California Consumer Privacy Act (CCPA), and financial sector rules such as the Reserve Bank of India. Therefore, the alarming observations on centralized models highlights the need to turn to secure and decentralized learning [6].

FL appears to be a reasonable approach to addressing the identified limitations. FL allows numerous clients, such as mobile devices or payment gateways, to collaboratively advance ML algorithms without needing to share all of their raw data. In particular, clients send updates to their models (as opposed to the raw data) to the central server [7, 8]. The server then aggregates the model updates and combines them to enhance a global model [9, 10]. This straightforward architecture supports privacy-enhancing technologies to improve end-user privacy, reduces the potential for awkward privacy-related data leaks, and can assist an organization in achieving compliance with elaborate data governance standards [11, 12].

In this study, we develop a layout for implementing methods for protecting digital payments and transactions utilizing FL. The proposed architecture is able to detect transaction abnormality observations in real-time, at various endpoints (to detect payments from various mobile payment applications or point-of-sale systems), without compromising the privacy of client transactions. Our architecture uses secure aggregation protocols along with differential privacy procedures to support ethical use of agreement and negotiation without

DOI: 10.1201/9781003660330-7

burdening transaction privacy. The assessment of the model is based on realistic transaction data with a comparison to typical centralized approaches [13–15].

The results show that FL can achieve similar or even better detection accuracy, while significantly improving data confidentiality. The prospect of FL transforming the security framework for financial systems represents an exciting opportunity to develop privacy-aware intelligent transaction monitoring capabilities that scale across a broad variety of device and platform types.

7.2 CYBER THREATS AND VULNERABILITIES IN CURRENT TRANSACTION SYSTEMS

In the digitally driven financial world of today, electronic transaction systems are becoming the lifeblood of various avenues of commerce, banking, and everyday consumer transactions. As reliance on these systems expands so too do the associated cyber risks and vulnerabilities that exist within these systems. Therefore, it is vital that we understand these risks in order to create more secure and resilient financial infrastructures [16–22].

7.2.1 Unauthorized access and data breaches

Unauthorized access to sensitive financial data is one of the biggest and most dangerous threats in present-day transaction systems. The system vulnerabilities that can be exploited may be a vulnerability in the system itself, weak authentication mechanisms, and social engineering vulnerabilities that allow hackers access to databases—credit card numbers, bank logins, or identity data. The data can be sold on the dark web or it can be used for identity theft and fraud. There is a greater risk for transaction systems without enforced encryption, access control, and intrusion detection. The growing network of systems—so rampant in mobile and online banking—increases this threat and requires zero trust and user verification for all users and devices that interact with financial networks.

7.2.2 Man-in-the-middle (MITM) attacks

Transactional systems that rely on online communication are very vulnerable to man-in-the-middle (MITM) attacks. MITM attacks occur when cybercriminals intercept communications between two people and possibly alter them without their knowledge. For example, at the time of the transaction, an attacker could insert malicious code or change the target account. MITM attacks typically occur because a website isn't sufficiently using HTTPS (HyperText Transfer Protocol Secure), the SSL (Secure Sockets Layer)/TLS (Transport Layer Security) certificates are expired or out of date, or the public Wi-Fi is unsecured. Not only do MITM attacks violate the confidentiality and integrity of data, but they also lessen users' trust in digital financial services. Using end-to-end encryption with certificate pinning will provide a lot of mitigation against these types of attacks.

7.2.3 Malware and ransomware infections

Malicious software, including ransomware and keyloggers, pose a severe threat to transaction environments. When installed on a user's or financial institution's system, malware can silently monitor activity, steal credentials, or lock access to critical systems until a ransom is paid. Ransomware attacks on banks and financial services can halt transaction processing altogether, leading to massive operational and reputational damage. These threats often originate from phishing emails, compromised websites, or unsecured software updates. Strong endpoint protection, continuous system monitoring, employee awareness training, and backup recovery strategies are essential to mitigate the impact of malware-based attacks in transaction systems.

7.2.4 Insider threats and privilege misuse

Just because an attack does not originate from outside of the organization does not mean it is not a cyber threat [19, 20]. Insider threats, including employees, contractors, and third-party vendors, may misuse access privileges, either intentionally (malicious actions) or unintentionally (negligent actions) to change transactions, steal data, or compromise systems. Additionally, sometimes negligent actions may be caused by human error of clicking on an email phishing link, or simply misconfiguring some access permissions. Since insiders have legitimate access to the organization already, it becomes much harder to detect when an insider is performing criminal actions. Loose audit trails, no multi-factor authentication, and no proper access controls can complicate the problem further. Organizations should establish their expectation for sincere cyber hygiene and ensure that users comply with this organizational expectation by implementing strong role-based access controls, keeping audits for reasonable periods of time and monitoring user activity all while proper cyber policies are being enforced and upheld to minimize the risks from unauthorized inside participants within transactional workflows.

7.2.5 Denial-of-service (DoS) and distributed DoS attacks

Denial-of-Service (DoS) and Distributed Denial-of-Service (DDoS) attacks focus on transaction systems and clutter them with too much traffic—slow, or cause them to stop responding altogether. They disrupt the operation of banking portals, payments gateways, and online transaction mechanisms. Denial-of-Service attacks cause persistent downtime which hampers availability and frustrates customers, and at times they can also be the diversion to execute more involved data breaches and fraudulent transactional exposure. The vulnerabilities for institutions are many times due to an inadequately configured server, firewall, or load balance capabilities. Anti-DDoS services can help mitigate against these attacks; traffic filters help stop flooding of internal systems with malicious requests, and redundant environments help institutions maintain availability and resilience in the event of an attack.

7.2.6 Insecure APIs and third-party integrations

Modern transaction systems heavily depend on APIs to facilitate services such as online banking, third-party payment processing, and data exchange. However, poorly designed or insecure APIs can serve as attack vectors for unauthorized access or data manipulation. Common vulnerabilities include lack of proper authentication, insufficient input validation, and exposed sensitive endpoints. Moreover, integrating with third-party vendors introduces dependency on their security practices, which might not meet the required standards. To counter this, organizations must enforce strong API security measures, conduct regular vulnerability assessments, and adopt a zero-trust framework across all integrated services and vendors.

7.3 FL OVER TRADITIONAL ML SYSTEMS

FL provides clear advantages over ML for a significant number of applications, including secure transactions, and other environments where collection of sensitive user data is required as shown in Table 7.1. FL does not require the collection and centralization of sensitive data, which would expose the user and all parties involved to a possible data breach or violation of compliance obligations. FL allows ML models to be trained directly on user devices or local environments to maintain ownership and data locality, with only aggregated, encrypted model updates shared. This model preserves privacy and increases security, as user data is never disclosed. Decentralized learning reduces bandwidth and storage needs while allowing for real-time, personalized learning without revealing sensitive user information. FL is damaged by data poisoning, but is less vulnerable than other centralized learning methods and thus serves as a stronger, more resilient, scalable, and privacy-compliant alternative in an evolving modern digital ecosystem where everything is connected [24, 26].

7.4 BACKGROUND AND MOTIVATION

The rapid adoption of digital payment systems has disrupted financial markets, providing users with an easy, fast, and convenient way to access and use money. Digital payments via mobile wallets, contactless payments, and (P2P transfers are common in everyday

Table 7.1 Table comparing tradition machine learning parameters and federated learning parameters

Parameter	*Traditional Machine Learning*	*Federated Learning*
Data Storage	Centralized (data collected in one location)	Decentralized (data remains on local devices)
Privacy	Lower, due to central aggregation of sensitive data	Higher, as raw data never leaves the user's device
Data Security Risk	High risk due to central point of failure	Lower risk due to distributed architecture
Compliance with Data Laws	Requires additional mechanisms for GDPR/CCPA compliance	Naturally aligns with data privacy regulations
Communication Overhead	Transfers full datasets to central servers	Transfers only model updates or gradients
Personalization Capability	Limited personalization (generalized model)	High personalization (local models adapt to user behavior)
Scalability	Challenging at massive scale due to centralized processing	Highly scalable via distributed learning
Latency and Efficiency	High latency due to centralized processing	Lower latency with on-device computation
Fault Tolerance	Vulnerable to single-point failure	Resilient due to decentralized nodes
Model Training	Done on centralized data	Done collaboratively across multiple clients/devices
Resource Utilization	Requires large central servers for computation	Utilizes edge devices' computational power
Trust Model	Requires trust in central server	Trust is distributed; less reliance on central authority

transactions, improving user experience and productivity. However, with the increased use of digital payment systems comes new risks associated with security and privacy. Cyber criminals are constantly adapting and evolving, using payment system weaknesses as opportunities to perpetrate fraud, data breaches, and identity theft, causing significant financial harm and loss of consumer trust all over the world [23].

Digital payment systems rely on centralized ML models to create virtual profiles based on behavior during transactions from aggregated data from external sources. These centralized systems can detect anomalous human behavior associated with fraud but come with a wide array of risks. Centralizing sensitive financial transaction data from multiple transactions opens up large amounts of data to attackers and the potential for an even bigger data breach. Centralized systems have inherent conflicts with data privacy legislation like the GDPR and the CCPA, requiring data minification, physical presence, and consent [24].

To address this issue, FL is a decentralized ML paradigm that enables collaborating model training while maintaining users' privacy. FL allows several clients (i.e., banks, payment gateways, mobile devices) to train a shared model locally on their own private data and only share encrypted model updates with a central aggregator. Thus, no transaction raw data will be shared, significantly reducing privacy threats and ensuring compliance with data protection regulations [25].

Despite its favorable features, the use of FL for digital payment systems is still relatively untested. While earlier studies demonstrated FLs utility for credit scoring and loan risk prediction, limited studies included comprehensive frameworks targeting real-time fraud detection in payments transactions [26]. The practice was particularly challenged with complexities associated with non-independent and identically distributed (Non-IID) data, securing model updates from poisoning attacks, and reliability across heterogeneous clients [27].

Inspired by these gaps, this chapter presents a deep investigation of FL as a solution for securing digital payments. The goal is to connect the theoretical knowledge to the practitioner's implementation of safeguarding user privacy without negatively impacting fraud detection quality. This work focuses on real-time anomaly detection in mobile payment and point-of-sale applications towards reducing the current research agenda towards the design of scalable, secure, and privacy-preserving digital payment methods.

7.5 SYSTEM ARCHITECTURE ENABLING FL

The system architecture utilizes FL to provide a secure, privacy-protecting environment to detect fraud in digital payment systems. The main concept is doing model training across multiple clients—mobile payment applications, POS terminals, or digital banks—without sharing their data from sensitive transactions. These clients train ML model locally on their own transaction datasets and transmit model updates, only encrypted, back to an aggregation server. The server aggregates these updates, updates a global model, and redistributes it to clients. Consequently, all nodes should always be improving in fraud detection.

The structure is comprised of a client-server FL architecture, with three important components: The local clients, the central aggregator, and the communication protocol. Each local client contains a local training environment, which has both a secure data sandbox and a lightweight ML engine. The client uses real-time transactional data, extracts relevant features (transaction amount, time and location of the transaction, device ID, and transaction frequency), and follows that with training a local model. To maintain privacy, raw data

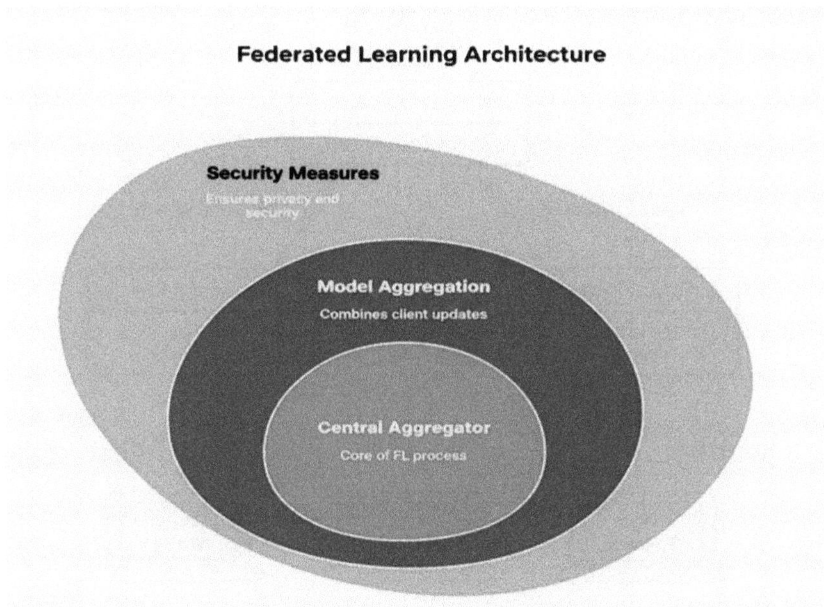

Figure 7.1 Federated learning architecture with central aggregator.

is defined as not leaving the customer site, but encrypted Gradients or gradients in the form of weight updates are sent to the aggregator.

The central aggregator serves as the coordination point for the FL process. It collects and aggregates model updates from clients participating in the FL and carries out a secure aggregation function, such as FedAvg, to compute a new global model. Figure 7.1 represents the FL architecture with central aggregator. In addition, the architecture incorporates differential privacy and secure multi-party computation (SMPC) to enhance security and privacy by limiting any possibility to reverse engineer a client or clients from the model updates.

Furthermore, the architecture has the ability to operate asynchronously to accommodate clients with heterogeneous hardware capabilities and differently distributed data and implements client-selection strategies for improved model convergence and reduced communication overhead [27]. One important aspect of this architecture is the specification of its communication protocol, requiring it to be efficient, secure and scalable [2]. The researchers have used encrypted communication channels (e.g., TLS) with the verification of digital signatures to investigate the authenticity of the updates and avoid model poisoning attacks for malicious updates. Additionally, they implemented update compression and model sparsification methods to minimize bandwidth since bandwidth is limited when considering mobile clients in disconnected situations.

Figure 7.2 explains the architecture of the system with local and global models.

This system is architected to be modular and extensible, with the offer to include third-party digital price providers, fraud analytics engines, and regulatory compliance modules. The architecture decentralizes the learning process while infusing sophisticated privacy-preserving processes into the architecture. This reduces the potential risks associated with centralized data storage as well as it allows for real-time collaborative fraud detection in a dispersed digital payment ecosystem. Table 7.2 provides a summary on areas and applications where FL is used and the key features involved within each of them.

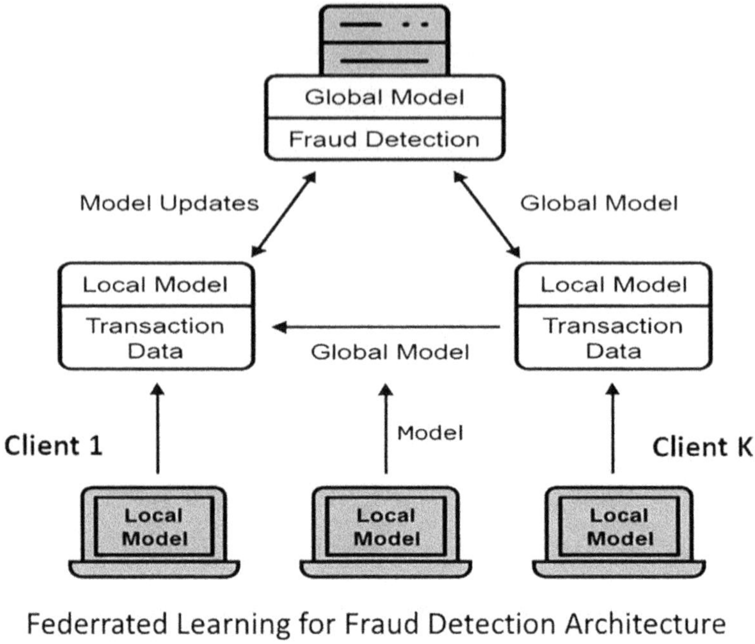

Figure 7.2 System architecture of the FL system with local and global models.

Table 7.2 Comparing results of various methods that include federated learning

Paper	*Model/Framework*	*Key Features*	*Reported Results*
Chatterjee et al. (2023a)	Blockchain-enabled FL for financial services	Integration of FL and blockchain to enhance security and privacy in financial services.	Conceptual framework; specific performance metrics not provided.
Chatterjee et al. (2023b)	FL and blockchain for credit card fraud detection	Collaborative model training among institutions without sharing raw data.	Conceptual framework; specific performance metrics not provided.
Rabbani et al. (2024)	Blockchain-based FL framework for fintech	Utilizes multiple ML models (KNN, SVM, decision trees, etc.) with blockchain for secure model updates.	Achieved 95% accuracy, 85% precision, 83% measure, and 79% AUC in fraud detection tasks.
Long et al. (2020)	FL in open banking	Addresses privacy concerns in open banking by enabling decentralized model training.	Conceptual discussion; specific performance metrics not provided.
Arivazhagan et al. (2019)	FedPer: FL with personalization layers	Introduces personalization layers to handle data heterogeneity across clients.	Demonstrated improved performance on Non-IID datasets; specific metrics not detailed.

7.6 METHODOLOGY USED WIDELY

This workflow given below ensures privacy-preserving, decentralized, and collaborative fraud detection in digital financial environments while maintaining scalability and security. Figure 7.3 depicts the flowchart of the methodology incorporated.

Step 1: Setup the Client Environment

For every client device in the ecosystem—whether it be a mobile wallet, POS terminal device, and digital banking app—they are considered set up when:

- A local data store is created that contains user transaction history.
- A lightweight local ML model architecture exists.
- FL client executable software is made available for remote secure communication with the central server.

These clients operate independently, will take transactional counts and analysis locally and report back to the central server.

Step 2: Local Data Processing and Feature Extraction

During a transaction occurring on a client device:

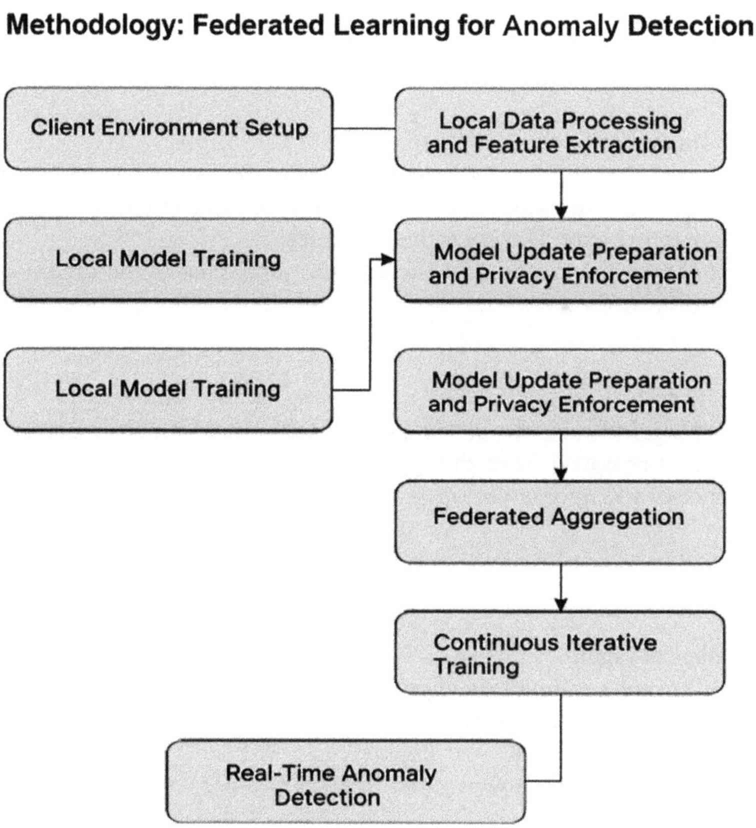

Figure 7.3 Flowchart of the widely accepted methodology.

- The system collects features like transaction amount, time, location, merchant ID, transaction frequency, and user device metadata.
- Preprocessing operations (e.g., normalization and encoding).
- The data stays local—it is not posted anywhere.

Step 3: Local Model Training
Each client trains its anomaly detection model on its own data:

- For example, depending on the use case, it could be a neural network, a decision tree, or an LSTM (when time-sequence data is involved).
- The model finds patterns of normal or potentially fraudulent behavior.
- After training for a predetermined fixed number of epochs, the client does not share its raw data.

Step 4: Preparation of Updates & Privacy Enforcement
Before the client transmits updates:

- The client computes gradients or weight updates from its local training.
- The client uses Differential Privacy by adding calibrated noise to the update to prevent single data leakage.
- The client may choose to encrypt the updates, using methods such as Secure Aggregation or Homomorphic Encryption.

Step 5: Secured Transmission to Aggregator

- The encrypted and anonymized model updates are sent from the clients to a central server (aggregator) over TLS encrypted channels.
- The server checks the integrity of the updates (e.g., checks the digital signatures) to verify their origin.

Step 6: FedAvg

- Using a FedAvg formula, the server averages the updates considering malicious and outlier updates removed from the update vectors using anomaly detection based on the difference of the update vectors.

Fedavg formula

Let:

K = total number of clients

n_k = number of training samples on client k

w_k = the model weights from client k after local training $n = \Sigma^{k}_{k=1} n_k$ = total number of training samples across all clients

Then the **global model weights** www after aggregation are computed as:

$$\sum_{k=1}^{k} \frac{n_k}{n} . w_k \tag{7.1}$$

- The server creates a new global model from the updates representing the collective learning and improving the global model without requiring raw data to be centralized.

Step 7: Distribution of New Global Model

- The global model is sent back to the clients which contributed and participated in the training.
- Clients can choose to replace or fine-tune their models with the new global model.

Step 8: Repeating the Process

- Steps 2–7 are repeated in a continuous iterative-training manner (e.g., daily, weekly or after N transactions).
- Over time, you will have a global model that is more effective in recognizing different fraud patterns for different types and profiles of users in different environments.

Step 9: Detection of Anomalies in Real-Time

- Once deployed, the system will operate by itself using the trained local model for real time anomaly detection.
- When a transaction is flagged as suspicious, it will either be declined, sent for manual review, or sent to a monitoring service on behalf of the organization.

Step 10: Audit Logging and Compliance Reporting

- Only anonymized audit logs or summary of alerts are stored in centralized storage.

By designed this and storing the audit log data in this manner removes the risk of leaking any raw transaction data. This design follows data protection regulations (e.g., GDPR, CCPA, RBI) as there will never be any raw or personally identifiable transaction logged in the centralized storage.

7.7 MATHEMATICAL FORMULAS USED IN FL

FL encompasses distributed optimization and shared model training through multiple relevant mathematical representations. Here is an organized list of key formulas used in FL, especially the standard FedAvg algorithm [27], with descriptions:

7.7.1 Objective function (Global optimization goal)

FL aims to minimize a global loss function across all participating clients:

$$minF(w) = \sum_{k=1}^{k} \frac{n_k}{n} \cdot f_k(w) \tag{7.2}$$

Where:

- w: global model parameters.
- K: total number of clients.
- n_k: number of data samples on client kkk.
- $n = \sum^{k}_{k=1} n_k$: total number of samples across all clients.
- $F_k(w)$: local loss function of client k, defined as:

$$F_k(w) = \frac{1}{n_k} \sum_{i=0}^{n_k} l\left(w; x_i^k, y_i^k\right) \tag{7.3}$$

Where, $l(w; {}^{x}{}^{k}_{i}, {}^{y}{}^{k}_{i})$: loss function on the i-th data sample of client k.

7.7.2 Local model update (Gradient descent on clients)

Each selected client performs local training using Stochastic Gradient Descent (SGD):

$$wtk{+}1 = wt - \eta \nabla Fk(wt) \tag{7.4}$$

Where:

- w_k: global model received at round t.
- η: local learning rate.
- $w^{k}_{\{\ t+1\}}$: updated local model parameters from client k after training.

Clients may perform multiple local epochs before sending updates.

7.7.3 Model aggregation (FedAvg)

The central server aggregates local models into a new global model:

$$w_{t+1} = \sum_{k=1}^{k} \frac{n_k}{n} w_{t+1}^k \tag{7.5}$$

This weighted averaging considers the data size at each client to ensure fairness.

7.7.4 Communication rounds

FL operates over T rounds (iterations). In each round:

- A fraction C (e.g., 10%) of clients are randomly selected.
- Each client updates the model locally.
- The server performs aggregation based on the received updates.

7.7.5 Personalized FL (Optional—client-specific models)

In some variants (e.g., FedPer, FedProx), clients maintain a personalized model w_k, optimized via:

$$\min\left(F_k(w_k)+\lambda\|w_k-w\|^2\right) \tag{7.6}$$

Where:

- λ: regularization term to control the divergence from the global model.

7.7.6 Differential Privacy in FL

If using Differential Privacy (DP), noise is added to gradients or parameters [3, 4]:

$$w_{t+1}^k = w_{t+1}^k + \mathcal{N}(0,\sigma^2 I) \tag{7.7}$$

Where:
$\mathcal{N}(0, \sigma^2 I)$: Gaussian noise with variance σ2\sigma^2σ2 to protect data privacy.

7.7.7 Secure aggregation (Optional encryption layer)

In privacy-preserving FL, encrypted gradients $\varepsilon(w_k)$ are used and decrypted only at the server:

$$w_{t+1} = \mathcal{D}\left(\sum_{k=1}^{k}\mathcal{E}(w_{t+1}^k)\right) \tag{7.8}$$

Where E(.) and $\mathcal{D}$(.) denote encryption and decryption functions, respectively.

7.8 CASE STUDIES

7.8.1 Case study 1: FL for cross-bank fraud detection background

Banks are always subject to fraudsters taking advantage of inter-bank payment channels. Traditional fraud detection systems are trained on each bank's own unique and siloed data. As a result, fraud patterns that span across institutions may go undetected.
Implementation:

A consortium of four banks established a FL framework which enabled the banks to collaborate on the training of fraud detection models while maintaining the confidentiality of customer data. Each bank trained models locally on its transaction data, then uploaded herein the updates to a central server, where the updates were aggregated using encrypted information.

Key Points:

- Model: A boosted decision tree was trained using deep learning techniques to extract features for each data set.
- Privacy: Differential privacy and SMPC techniques were employed to guarantee that raw data was not passed between banks.
- Results: The customers of the four banks benefited by improving their cross-bank fraud detection accuracy by 15% when using the FL models instead of using isolated models, which was important when multiple banks were attacked simultaneously [14].

7.8.2 Case dtudy 2: Real-time federated anomaly detection for mobile wallets background

Mobile wallets use rapidly evolving and very specific customer data to identify and prevent fraudulent activities. In fact, the ability to identify suspicious activities in real time is critical for preventing fraudulent transactions.
Implementation

Many mobile wallet providers in the area deployed anomaly detection based on FL using autoencoders, where the model was trained locally on transaction stored on customer devices.
Key Points

- Architecture: Light-weight neural networks designed for edge devices.
- Security: FedAvg with encryption reduces communication overhead.
- Results: According to Kairouz et al. (2020) the system was able to detect fraud in real time with 90% accuracy while maintaining a 30% lower false positive rate than traditional centralized systems [10].

7.8.3 Case study 3: FL using blockchain technology for payment systems background

The integration of blockchain will provide transparency in records and the use of FL will provide strong privacy protection features in the digital payments space.
Implementation:

A fintech start-up designed and executed a framework that integrated FL in conjunction with blockchain-based smart contracts to protect multi-party payments transactions.
Key Points:

- Role of blockchain: Provided a permanent record of aggregated model updates and provided auditability.
- Role of FL: Employed privacy preserving learning that used distributed transaction data from multiple POS systems.
- Findings: Prakash Raju Kantheti, and Prof. Stella Bvuma (2024) found that the combination of FL and blockchain improved trust and accounting compliance while producing levels of fraud detection no less effective than centralized models [5].

7.8.4 Case study 4: FL for credit scoring and loan fraud detection background

The main goal of financial institutions is to detect fraud in loan applications without revealing sensitive customer financial data.
Implementation:
A cohort of banks joined a FL platform to create a secure credit scoring model that is resistant to adversarial attacks.
Key Points:

- Techniques: Most importantly, homomorphic encryption and robust aggregation methods helped preserve model integrity.
- Benefits: The banks being able to keep customer privacy while developing better fraud detection they were able to reduce the rate of false positives by 18%
- Challenges: The most serious challenges they faced was in dealing with highly imbalanced and Non-IID loan application data which, using novel federated sampling strategies, was resolved. Rabbani et al. (2024) overcame from this issue using the aggregation method for model integrity [13].

7.8.5 Case study 5: Securing digital currency transactions with FL background

Cryptocurrency exchanges have to implement ways to protect user anonymity while also detecting potentially suspicious patterns in their user's transactions.
Implementation:
A number of crypto exchanges formed a federation to train shared fraud detection models using metadata from transaction data.
Key Points:

- Model: Recurrent Neural Networks (RNNs) were used to model the temporal dependencies of transactions.
- Privacy: As no raw transaction data was exchanged, the federated updates were encrypted when sent and validated on-chain.
- Impact: Overall, the patterns detected enhanced money laundering detection and illicit transaction detection, all while remaining as anonymous as possible [1, 2].

7.9 EXPERIMENTAL RESULTS AND OBSERVATIONS

In the first part of the FL experiment discussed, the FDSC (Financial Dataset for Secure Computing) dataset was used, along with a Multi-Layer Perceptron (MLP) model, to test model performance in different types of data distribution. This dataset was used as it is simple to use yet very well established and user-friendly dataset. Prototyping using FDSC becomes very easy and quick. Accordingly, two types of data distribution cases were examined in regard to independence and identically distributed data: Independent and Identically Distributed (IID) and Non-IID [3].

Experimental Design and Observations are shown in Figures 7.4 and 7.5. Each show the results of the experiments to demonstrate model performance in each scenario. The results show that the MLP model performed better in the IID setting versus the Non-IID setup. This supports the literature that suggests that having clients with balanced and representative data distributions will typically lead to more efficient and stable model training in federated settings [3].

As depicted in Figure 7.4, we quantized the accuracy of the model across numerous communications per-round between clients and the central server. In the IID case, the model was able to improve gradually over the course of the communication, and eventually achieved an accuracy of approximately 98%. On the other hand, in the Non-IID case, the accuracy, was achieved in more dramatically plateaued at approximately 90.5%. We can attribute this difference to the heterogeneity of data across clients in the Non-IID case which introduces each contributes a statistical difference and in turn hinders generalizations of the model across the digit classes [3].

The FL process consists of a series of training iterations, where only a subset of clients that have local data are involved in decentralized learning. Within each iteration, the clients conduct a local update of the model using their private data and then send the updated parameters to a centralized server. The server will then aggregate the parameters (for example through FedAvg) to produce an updated global model and send that out to the clients for another iteration of learning. This iterative process will be repeated until the process has converged [3].

Figure 7.5 conveys the loss rate analysis for IID and Non-IID data. The results indicate that the loss rate is substantially lower for the IID case and the global model converged faster and more consistently. The IID scenario produced better loss performance by virtue of having more uniform data distribution which meant each updating client contributed a more evenly weighted update to the central model. The centralized model for the Non-IID scenario invariably fluctuated at a higher loss value due to the former biased local dataset [3].

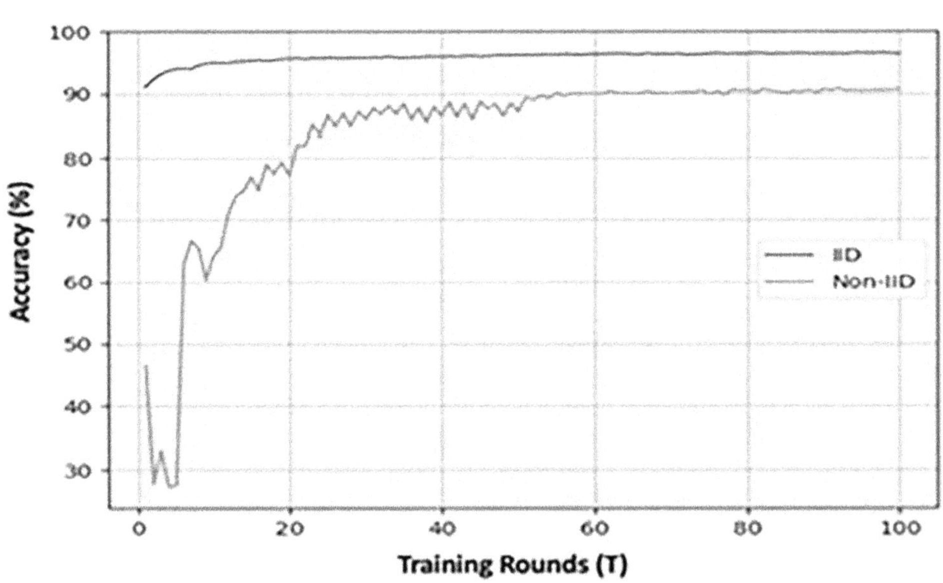

Figure 7.4 Test set accuracy (FDSC IID and non-IID) setting within FL.

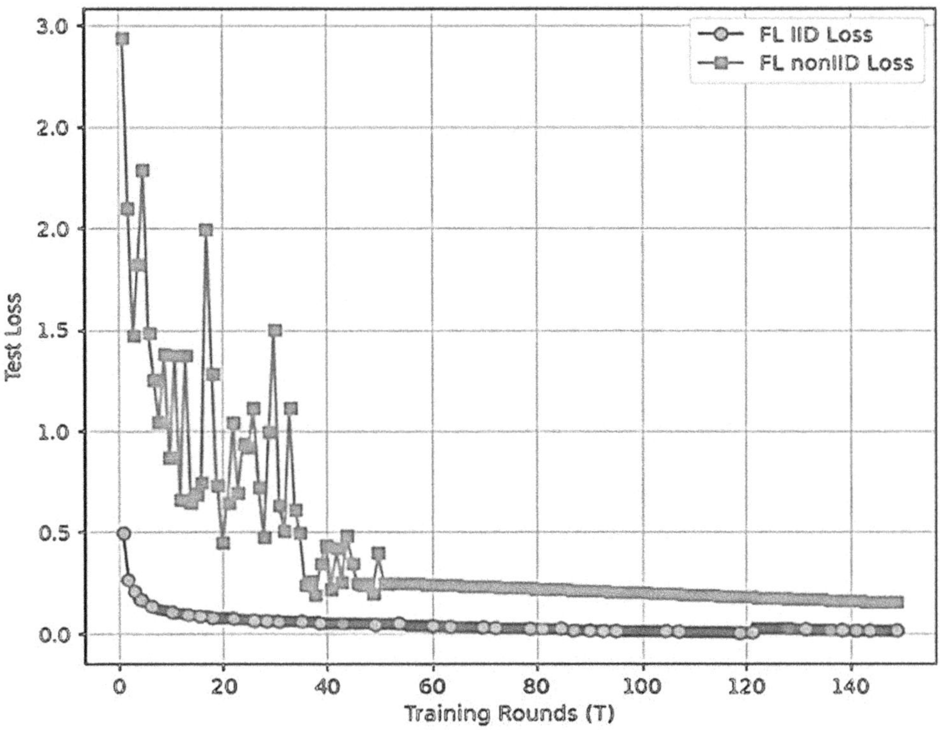

Figure 7.5 Test set loss rate (FDSC IID and non-IID) setting within FL.

7.10 ADVANTAGES

Benefits of FL for Secure Digital Payments

FL has many advantages over traditional centralized ML models, especially for digital payment security.

1. Increased Privacy with Data Security
   FL stops the use of actual transactions, leaving raw transaction data on the local device or institutional firewall protecting sensitive financial data. Only encrypted model updates are shared with the central server minimizing the risk of data leaks or breaches. FL allows companies to handle data in a decentralized way which may help to comply with stringent data protection laws like GDPR and CCPA safeguarding user privacy [1, 3, 24].
2. Joint Model Training Across Multiple Stakeholders
   FL facilitates the cooperation of different financial institutions, payments providers, or mobile wallets to work together without needing to share the data directly with each other. By sharing the model, the different stakeholders collaborate on building model(s) from a different and enhanced dataset. As an example, data sources can be aggregated in a FL environment across different and richer datasets to create more robust and generalizable fraud detection models that are applicable on different transaction types and different geographies. Once we are able to identify more complex

fraud patterns that cross institutions by using data from groups of relevant institutions, we will build upon the lessons that the last FL model has shared with us before moving on [14].

3. Improved Scalability and Less Communication Overhead
FL is more scalable mainly because it does only send model parameter updates rather than entire datasets, and uses less bandwidth, allowing for many more clients or endpoints such as mobile devices and POS systems, which was not permitted by centralized learning systems [22]. In addition, simple mechanisms like FedAvg can increase the number of communication rounds with clients [10] making FL practical with processes like the up-front detection of anomalies in distributed payment systems [2].
4. Better Model Robustness to Data Heterogeneity
FL frameworks can work with Non-IID data, which should happen on the financial transaction of different users and/or across different regions. FL can be used to train models on local heterogeneous datasets considering the data set of different clients to create more personalized, original, and accurate detection systems [4, 11].
5. Compliance and Ethical Use of Data
Since FL does not centrally collect sensitive user data, it promotes ethical data governance and reduces the risk of regulatory noncompliance. When organizations use FL, they can be transparent about how they use user data in front of users, which leads to increased trust and compliance with emerging laws around data sovereignty [6].
6. Privacy Embracing Technology
FL can stack on a variety of privacy and security enhancing technologies such as differential privacy, homomorphic encryption, and secure multiparty computation which all help enhance security guarantees. In practice, these technologies when used together can help protect model updates from attempts to conduct an inference attack or model poisoning attack while increasing trust in the federated systems that monitor financial transaction processes [5, 12].
7. Real-Time Fraud Detection Availability
FL's decentralized architecture allows the distributed clients to send updates in a timely fashion as they initiate detection of suspicious activities in near-real time. For digital payments, this is essential because, in many scenarios, the more immediate the fraud detection the more likely the fraud loss can be mitigated in time [2].
8. Reduced Single Points of Failure
Unlike centralized models that operate a single repository of data susceptible to one point of attack, FL can distribute that risk. A decentralized model effectively increases the resiliency of payment security systems processing the payments against focused cyber-attacks and server downtimes [7].
9. Cost Effectiveness in Data Management FL
Decreases an organization's infrastructure and data storage costs by removing the requirement to transfer and centrally store vast amounts of raw financial data. Cost efficiencies are important, particularly for institutions that administer large-scale distributed payment systems [13].
10. Enablement of Cross-Border Compliance
As a result of the unique nature of financial regulations across nations, FL's model for data processing is local and protects regional data residency and sovereignty laws. Therefore, it allows global financial institutions to deploy fraud detection models in multiple jurisdictions without violating a jurisdiction's legal regime [9].

Figure 7.6 represents some advantages of using FL over traditional approaches.

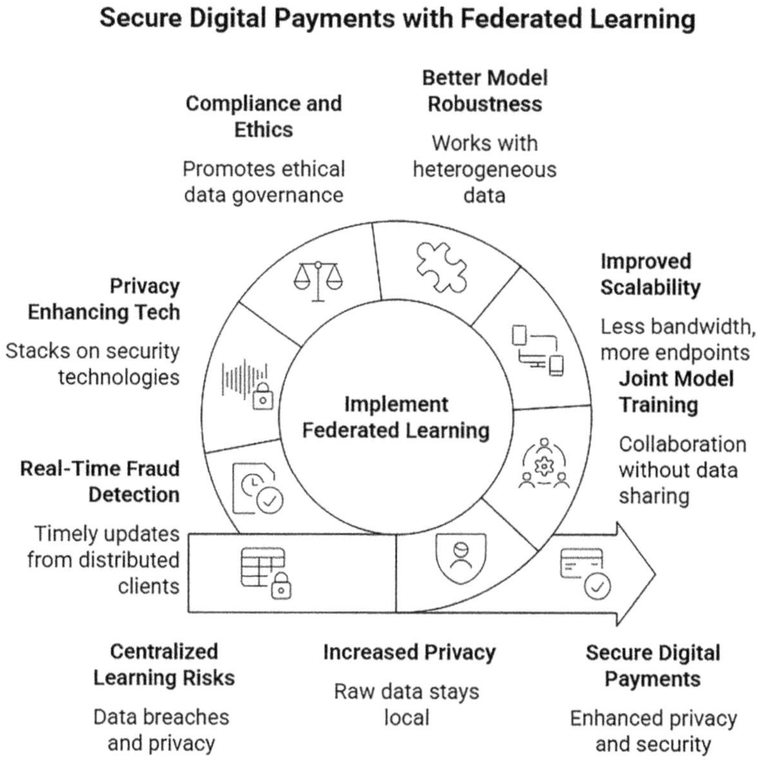

Figure 7.6 Advantaged of using federated learning.

7.11 LIMITATION

Even though FL can lead to improved security and privacy in digital payment systems, there are drawbacks to consider. The first caveat relates to non-identical and unbalanced data stored on client devices. In practice, user transaction behavior varies considerably, since macro-characteristics like geography, demographics, and usage patterns are not the same on any client. Since FedAvg relies upon relatively homogenous distribution of data across clients, Non-IID data types may contribute to the global model converging poorly as well as reducing the overall detection quality.

The second limitation is communication overhead resulting from frequent communication of client model updates to the central server. Since FL operates through iterative rounds of local training and aggregation, the network consumes much greater bandwidth and an array of devices is required to minimize round-trip latency for larger-scale systems. Data privacy and security protocols may make it impractical in environments where stakeholders lack limited connectivity or latency is an essential factor to real-time fraud detection. In addition, FL affords privacy by not sending raw data, but remains susceptible to other indirect privacy challenges such as model inversion or gradient leakage attacks. Methods for managing these attacks exist like differential privacy and secure aggregation, however these methods tend to produce poorer model performance and increased resource consumption. Additionally, some client devices such as mobile phones, wearables, or POS devices possess limited processing power and memory, limiting their ability to train and update resulting models efficiently.

In summary, providing guarantees about the integrity of contributions in a decentralized space can be difficult. Malicious clients may send malicious updates and poison the global model. Adversarial detection continues to be an open research problem. All of the challenges lay a solid foundation for revisiting FL methods, with secure hardware, and adaptive optimization approaches to support their use for high-stakes domains such as digital payment security.

7.12 FUTURE SCOPE

The field of digital payments security using FL is quickly expanding, and there are many possible future research and research and development opportunities that both improve present limitations and expand possibilities.

7.12.1 Enhanced personalization and model adaptiveness

Future work can direct enhancements of FL algorithms that effectively manage Non-IID data through centered personalization models for individual users or institutions. Other personalization methods involve meta-learning and transfer learning [4, 11]; it could improve model adaptiveness so fraud detection models could modify in users' transaction behaviors and new threats in an evolving dynamic system.

7.12.2 Coupling blockchain and trusted execution environments

Integrating FL with a blockchain can provide greater transparency and immutability of the training and aggregation processes while providing decentralized trust that is critical for these types of systems. Further, the use of hardware-based trusted execution environments (TEEs) will secure computations during model training and aggregation, further increasing the privacy and integrity of FL systems in a financial application domain [5].

7.12.3 Hybrid privacy-preserving approaches

Futures work can investigate some hybrid approach which utilizes differential privacy, SMPC, homomorphic encryption, and other forms of cryptography alongside FL. The use of multiple layers of protections can offer defenses against more adversarial threats, and protection from stricter data protection policies and regulations [6].

7.12.4 Real-time and edge deployment

One primary future aim is to extend FL to support real-time fraud detection on edge devices such as smart devices and POS terminals. FL must develop more efficient communication protocols and lean model architectures to be sufficiently "light" for deployment on latency sensitive apps [2, 10].

7.12.5 Cross-domain and cross-institution cooperation

Future work can seek to extend FL frameworks to provide secure, large-scale cooperation with multiple institutions across multiple domains (e.g., banking, insurances, and fintech platforms). Cross-domain learning can aid in the detection of complex fraud schemes by utilizing resources across several sectors to build a more complete security ecosystem [14].

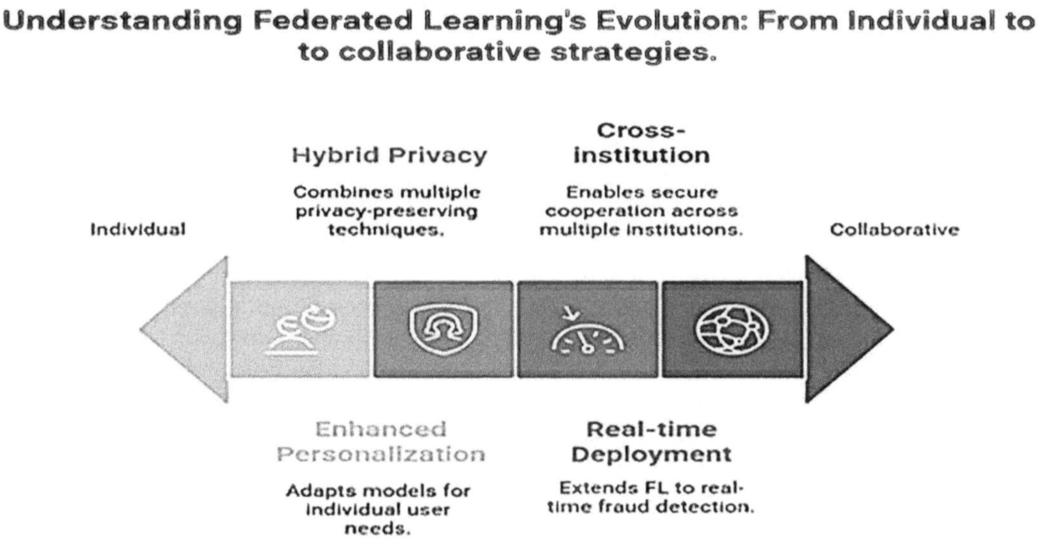

Figure 7.7 Extension of federated learning and its prospectives.

7.12.6 Regulatory frameworks and standardization

Standardized protocols, legal frameworks, and audit practices specifically for FL in finance should be developed. These frameworks will facilitate compliance, help establish liability, and help build trust between all stakeholders, enhancing the adoption of FL for secure digital payments [3].

7.12.7 Explainability and fairness of FL models

When the outcomes of FL-based models become an integral element in financial decision-making, transparency, explainability, and fairness will be essential. Further work can focus on interpretable federated models that incorporate less biased approaches and provide clear evidence that explains the reasoning behind fraud detection decisions, and thereby build user confidence and regulatory support [7].

Figure 7.7 represents the future perspectives of FL.

7.13 CONCLUSION

The increasing reliance on digital payment systems has made securing transactions both critical and complex. Traditional ML methodologies tend to be centralized and do a good job identifying fraudulent behavior, but come with serious concerns for data privacy, regulatory compliance and susceptibility to hackers. FL represents an innovative paradigm for model training that engages distributed clients in cooperation without exposing the raw data, thus improving privacy and security.

This chapter presented the conceptual underpinnings, architectural design and practical implications to applying FL to secure digital payments. By coordinating multiple studies and case studies this chapter showed that FL can accomplish at least as good or better fraud detection while also lowering lastly data privacy hindrances. Additionally, FL systems can include advanced privacy-preserving techniques such as secure aggregation and differential privacy, which will also help improve the resiliency of the FL systems under multiple types of threats.

While there are still challenges to the deployment of FL into the financial ecosystem, various issues surrounding data heterogeneity, communication overhead, model poisoning, and client trust. These issues need continuous research and innovation to overcome in the foreseeable future. Future developments of interest include enhancing personalization in models, combining FL with blockchain, and trusted hardware, and developing regulatory models for decentralized learning systems.

Ultimately, FL exemplifies a paradigm shift in how to secure digital payments by delivering two competing priorities, effective fraud identification and protection of privacy. As change occurs in the financial sector, FL could offer a new definition of how institutions, and their data systems can protect user data and manage fraud appropriately in the payment ecosystem, providing a more secure, scalable, and privacy-aware approach to payments.

REFERENCES

[1] Chatterjee, P., Das, D., & Rawat, D. B. (2023a). *Use of Federated Learning and Blockchain towards Securing Financial Services, arXiv preprint arXiv:2303.12944.* https://doi.org/10.36227/techrxiv.22155182

[2] Chatterjee, P., Das, D., & Rawat, D. (2023b). *Securing Financial Transactions: Exploring the Role of Federated Learning and Blockchain in Credit Card Fraud Detection. Authorea Preprints.* https://doi.org/10.36227/techrxiv.22683403

[3] Iqbal, M., Tariq, A., Adnan, M., Ud Din, I., & Qayyum, T. (2025). Privacy preserved federated learning with optimized differential privacy (FL-ODP). *Securing the Digital Realm*, 24–35. https://doi.org/10.1201/9781003497851-3

[4] Long, G., Tan, Y., Jiang, J., & Zhang, C. (2020). Federated learning for open banking. *Lecture Notes in Computer Science*, vol. 12500, 240–254. https://doi.org/10.1007/978-3-030-63076-8_17

[5] Kantheti, P. R., & Bvuma, S. (2024). AI and machine learning in fraud detection: Securing digital payments and economic stability. *International Journal of Scientific Research in Science and Technology*, 11(3), 974–982. https://doi.org/10.32628/ijsrst52310291

[6] Xu, B., Chen, H., Jin, S., & Jiao, Q. (2021). A digital currency system with transaction amount privacy protection. *2021 IEEE Intl Conf on Dependable, Autonomic and Secure Computing, Intl Conf on Pervasive Intelligence and Computing, Intl Conf on Cloud and Big Data Computing, Intl Conf on Cyber Science and Technology Congress (DASC/PiCom/CBDCom/CyberSciTech)*, 535–540. https://doi.org/10.1109/DASC-PICom-CBDCom-CyberSciTech52372.2021.00094

[7] Yang, Q., Liu, Y., Chen, T., & Tong, Y. (2020). Federated learning: A comprehensive overview. *Proceedings of the 20th ACM International Symposium on Mobile Ad Hoc Networking and Computing*, 2020.

[8] Zhao, Y., Li, M., & Li, W. (2021). A survey of federated learning: A distributed optimization perspective. *IEEE Transactions on Neural Networks and Learning Systems*, 32(10), 4393–4409.

[9] Li, X., & He, J. (2020). Secure federated learning for privacy-preserving computation. *Journal of Cryptology*, 33(4), 1181–1205.

[10] Kairouz, P., McMahan, H. B., & Suresh, A. T. (2020). Advances and open problems in federated learning. *Foundations and Trends® in Machine Learning*, 14(1), 1–210.

[11] Ramesh, J. V. N., Shah, N. H., Alazzam, M. B., Nimma, D., Selvi, V., & Balakumar, A. (2025). Integrating blockchain and artificial intelligence for securing payment processes against fraudulent transactions. *2025 Fifth International Conference on Advances in*

Electrical, Computing, Communication and Sustainable Technologies (ICAECT), Bhilai, India, 1–6. https://doi.org/10.1109/ICAECT63952.2025.10958890.
[12] Kang, J., Li, X., Nie, J., Liu, Y., Xu, M., Xiong, Z., ... & Yan, Q. (2022). Communication-efficient and cross-chain empowered federated learning for artificial intelligence of things. *IEEE Transactions on Network Science and Engineering*, 9(5), 2966–2977. https://doi.org/10.1109/TNSE.2022.3178970
[13] Rabbani, H., Shahid, M. F., Khanzada, T. J. S., Siddiqui, S., Jamjoom, M. M., Ashari, R. B., ... & Nooruddin, M. (2024). Enhancing security in financial transactions: a novel blockchain-based federated learning framework for detecting counterfeit data in fintech. *PeerJ Computer Science*, 10, e2280.
[14] Arivazhagan, M. G., Aggarwal, V., Singh, A. K., & Choudhary, S. (2019). Federated learning with personalization layers. arXiv:1912.00818
[15] Lim, S., Choi, J., Lee, J., & Park, N. (2025). Fraug: Enhanced fraud detection in inter-bank transfers via augmented account features. *2025 IEEE International Conference on Big Data and Smart Computing (BigComp)*, 199–206. https://doi.org/10.1109/bigcomp64353.2025.00048
[16] Singh, S. K., Anisi, M. H., Clough, S., Blyth, T., & Jarchi, D. (2023). CNN-BILSTM based gan for anamoly detection from multivariate time series data. *2023 24th International Conference on Digital Signal Processing (DSP)*, 1–4. https://doi.org/10.1109/dsp58604.2023.10167937
[17] (N.d.-a). IEEE guide for architectural framework and application of federated machine learning. https://doi.org/10.1109/ieeestd.2021.9382202
[18] (N.d.-b). IEEE guide for an architectural framework for blockchain-based federated machine learning. https://doi.org/10.1109/ieeestd.2025.10965995
[19] Asad, M., & Otoum, S. (2024). BPPFL: A blockchain-based framework for privacy- preserving federated learning. https://doi.org/10.21203/rs.3.rs-4662864/v1
[20] Lee, H., Jiang, M., & Zhao, Q. (2024). FedAssist: Federated learning in AI-powered prosthetics for Sustainable and collaborative learning. *2024 46th Annual International Conference of the IEEE Engineering in Medicine and Biology Society (EMBC)*, 1–5. https://doi.org/10.1109/embc53108.2024.10781961
[21] Morafah, M., & Morafah, M. (2025). Clustered federated learning: A review. *Artificial Intelligence*. https://doi.org/10.5772/intechopen.1008431
[22] Zhang, J., & Qiao, Z. (2024). SOFL: Clustered federated learning based on dual clustering forheterogeneousdata. *Electronics*, 13(18), 3682. https://doi.org/10.3390/electronics13183682
[23] Zhou, Y., Shi, M., Tian, Y., Li, Y., Ye, Q., & Lv, J. (2024). Federated cinn clustering for accurate clustered federated learning. *ICASSP 2024–2024 IEEE International Conference on Acoustics, Speech and Signal Processing (ICASSP)*, 5590–5594. https://doi.org/10.1109/icassp48485.2024.10447282
[24] Das, D., Banerjee, S., Chatterjee, P., Ghosh, U. and Biswas, U. (2022). A secure blockchain enabled v2v communication system using smart contracts. *IEEE Transactions on Intelligent Transportation Systems*, 1–10.
[25] Bhumichai, D., Smiliotopoulos, C., Benton, R., Kambourakis, G., & Damopoulos, D. (2024). The convergence of artificial intelligence and blockchain: The state of play and the road ahead. *Information*, *15*(5), 268.
[26] Polestar. (2022). Top financial services banking analytics use cases. www.polestarllp.com/top-financial-services-banking-analytics-use-cases, [Online; Accessed on Jan. 10, 2023].
[27] Kost, E. (2023). The 6 biggest cyber threats for financial services in 2023. www.upguard.com/blog/biggest-cyber-threats-for-financial-services, [Online; Accessed on Jan. 15, 2023].

Chapter 8

Blockchain and federated learning

Sangeeta Arora, Vivek Tomar, Swati Sharma, and Sushil Kumar Narang

8.1 INTRODUCTION

8.1.1 Overview of Blockchain Technology

Blockchain has originally come into picture in 2008 due to bitcoin as a transformative action. Blockchain applications are beyond cryptocurrencies which includes finance, healthcare, supply chain and distributed artificial intelligence [9]. Blockchain is a distributed ledger technology that enables peer to peer transactions without intervention of central authorities. In a blockchain, a block of chain having a batch of verified transactions which is linked using cryptographic hashes ensure that no alteration is done. The blockchain feature, decentralization plays a powerful role in maintenance of ledger with the consensus i.e., Proof of Work [13], Proof of Stake, Proof of Elapsed time etc. confidentiality. Blockchain also have programmable functions like smart contracts which are self-executable programs coded in the blockchain. Various platform i.e., Ethereum, Solana etc. help to build decentralized applications to automate the processes like financial transactions, supply chain tracking. Smart Contracts maintain the decentralized feature of blockchain by efficiently eliminating the intermediaries by reducing the cost due to self-executable feature [47].

Blockchain technology have various challenges like scalability in public blockchains and limited transaction throughput in Ethereum. In Proof of work, energy consumption is one of critical factor which raised environmental concerns [54]. Blockchain is also facing hurdles for worldwide adoption. Apart that interoperability between various blockchain network is another challenge. Recently blockchain handshake with emerging technologies too i.e., FL [54]. The Blockchain with FL enhance security and trust in various decentralized machine learning models. Future research directions focus on improving scalability through Layer-2 solutions (e.g., rollups, sidechains), enhancing privacy with zero-knowledge proofs, and preparing for post-quantum cryptographic threats.

8.1.2 Fundamentals of FL

FL is a type of decentralized machine learning paradigm which is used to design for training of models in a distributed manner with data locality [63]. In the centralized approach, all data is residing in a centralized device. In this case FL works as collaborative model by training and exchange only model parameters. The FL framework addresses the privacy and security issues in various domains i.e., healthcare, mobile applications and finance, where data is sensitive in nature and need the regulatory compliance. The FL works on private data sets, perform distributed optimization without exposing and preserve the confidentiality to achieve high model performance.

DOI: 10.1201/9781003660330-8

A federated learning system composed of three main components: clients, central server and a protocol for communication. In the federated system, training is done in iterative manner, starting with server initialization with a global model and distribution to clients [20, 21]. In next step, client starts to train the model locally with its private data and evaluate results. Next, these results will be transmitted to the server by client for the aggregation of results from the various other clients. This process is iterated till the output is not reached to a single state. FL is useful to operate on various devices at a time, which depends on the scale and nature of participants [29]. The heterogeneity of data is also one of the primary challenge due to spread across various clients leading to biasedness or unstable model convergence. The communication efficiency is another challenge due to continuous change in the large model updates among the various devices which needs higher bandwidth costs and latency [30].

To reduce these issues, compression methods, client selection methods and personalized FL models are proposed. The security and privacy are main concern in FL design, due to data is stored locally on devices. Various methods like Differential privacy and doing computations in secure method [43]. FL is used in numerous applications i.e., personalized healthcare for keeping medical records, smart keyboards used in various platforms, fraud detection in financial institutions.

8.1.3 Motivation for combining Blockchain and FL

The critical challenges are addressed with the integration of blockchain technology with FL to provide the solutions. FL helps in privacy preservation framework by keeping the data localized and sharing only updation of data [55]. Still there are inherent limitations like incentive alignment among various participants, security threats and trust. Blockchain technology due to decentralization and immutable ledger, added transparency and security in FL. This framework preserves data privacy for collaborative Artificial Intelligence with the integrity and improved learning process [6]. In the traditional FL, aggregation model updates take place with the help of central server. Central server may be a single point of failure with the potential manipulations. Blockchain maintain the aggregation of model in a decentralized way with the help of smart contracts and various consensus mechanisms [40]. Blockchain also keep the record of all the model updates as a transaction and creating an immutable audit trail for the participant contribution verification and preventing the false actors from submitting the false updates. Blockchain provide the additional security with cryptography solutions to prevent the Byzantine attacks [1]. Many malicious participants try to degrade the model performance in the FL. The immutable feature of blockchain ensure the record of malicious user behaviour for penalizing in future.

Blockchain also contributed to FL system in terms of incentives to the participants. In blockchain, token-based incentive mechanism for rewarding the participants based on the quality and quantity of participants. Smart contracts play an important role in process of rewarding the participants by creating an ecosystem. In this data owners are rewarded by distributing cryptographic tokens to participants for the effective model updates. This scenario is useful where Internet of Things (IoT) and mobile edge computing are in limited and contribution for their participation. The integration of FL with blockchain is shown in Figure 8.1.

The integration of blockchain and FL architecture ensures the fault tolerance. FL works, if any of the node fails or disconnect due to fault tolerance feature. With the help of replication process, smart contracts are replicated among multiple nodes across the network. This

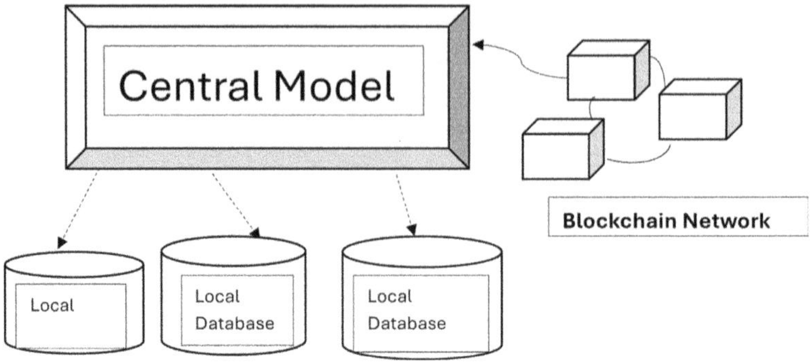

Figure 8.1 Integration of federated learning with blockchain.

is valuable due when large number of devices across various devices are diverse platforms. FL application involves thousands of edge devices with this tolerance feature [39]. The performance is increased due to model versioning in each iteration where all updates are recorded permanently.

The integration of both technologies adds the new possibilities in data governance for the regulation of compliance. Blockchain with the help of FLsystem demonstrates the compliance with the help of data protection regulations like General Data Protection Regulation. Smart contracts are used to enforce the data usage policies and access controls. The immutable ledger provides verifiable proof to auditors for the model training and participation. This capability is useful for sensitive data i.e., finance, healthcare etc. where compliance is demonstrated with privacy regulations to achieve the accuracy. The blockchain and FL together train the diagnostic models of healthcare and maintaining the privacy with patient data [37]. The IoT devices of various manufacturer contribute the shared learning models fairly compensated through blockchain tokens. The financial sector also secured rom frauds as model is trained without exposing the data. The integrity of data is maintained with the collaborative process.

8.2 CHALLENGES IN TRADITIONAL FL

8.2.1 Privacy and Security Concerns

Traditional FL has enhanced security due to paradigm shift from keeping the raw data on localized rather on centralized machine. Still there is privacy and security challenges at the time of exchange of model parameters. At the time of exchanging model parameters, some attacks like inference attacks, Gradient inversion attacks may share private information to participating clients. This security risk at the time of changing inputs by the attacker. These issues may raise serious issues to sensitive domains i.e., patient data in healthcare. This will lead to legal and ethical consequences.

These security challenges in FL systems may extend privacy threats affecting model integrity with the help of various attack vectors [58]. In the Byzantine type attacks represents a misleading attack, where various malicious participants participate to falsified model updates to lower down the performance of global model. In these type of attacks, single client may alter model by creating antagonistic updates. These security risks occur due to the decentralized nature of FL because there is no verification of authenticity done by the centralized authority. The need to add reliable identity management in the conventional FL frameworks to establish the accountability process.

Alteration of data is one another critical security issue in the FL systems. In the FL systems, data quality is maintained by the participating node only rather in traditional machine learning, this can be done carefully at one place. In FL, malignant actors spoil their local dataset to affect the performance of global model. This can be done at the time of classification by adding false inputs to affect the model. These types of attacks may be severe, stage by stage when the training is done in multiple rounds. Due to multiple staged training, it is very difficult to detect the attacks. This problem has become more severe when FL involved in across the organization, in this scenario participants may have various conflicting interests like business motives or incentives etc.

The privacy risks increased in FL when the membership inference attacks done. In inference attacks, attackers select the specific data for the training process. It violates the privacy of participants and may cause serious indications in various scenarios in case of personal data involvement. The attackers may extract sensitive information through careful analysis of the model behaviour despite of increased privacy. The current privacy mechanisms are not sufficient to protect the data from attackers throughout the process.

In the FL, data is maintained locally whereas model updates are communicated across the network. At that time, communication security is one of the major issue in the FL. Model update communication cannot reveal raw data to the attackers. But the patterns may be revealed by leaking metadata of the participants, data characteristics and configurations [18]. At the time of model update transmission across the system, man-in-middle attack take place between client and aggregator. In the FL, centralized aggregation is the actual issue for the single point of failure during the learning process. This type of attacks done at the time of aggregation process influencing the global model development.

For the privacy and security, a reliable audit mechanism is required which is not available in FL. Due to non-availability of verified records, contribution, and model updates, it is difficult to detect false behaviour or find the security attacks etc. The data handling procedures are lacking in transparency, accountability in the regulated industries. In the FL, nodes can join and leave the system at any point of time which is the additional threat to security and consistent privacy protection across the training rounds [19].

To address privacy and security concerns in FL, cryptography and distributed ledger technology provide promised concerns. Still there are challenges found in implementation by addressing efficiency and scalability issues in the FL. The trade-offs will be always existed between privacy and computational overhead in model performance. The balancing becomes complex for both attack methodologies and defensive techniques grow sophisticated.

8.2.2 Centralized Aggregation Issues

In the FL environment, a centralized aggregation server work is to coordinate the learning process. This may cause exposure to better aggregation process through distributed paradigm shift. The responsibility of central server is to get updates and perform model aggregation then distributing global model which may be a single point of failure. This centralized architecture has many trust and security issues, due to that FL was not alone enough to design these types of systems [25]. The trust is one of the important factors in case of centralized aggregation when multiple stakeholders are involved. The central server is responsible for the execution of aggregation protocol without affecting actual result and extracting confidential information from model updates. All participant's trust lies on the central server during the overall process. This is necessary at the time of application executed across the multiple organizations.

The centralized aggregation architecture also has the limitations in the performance and scalability. With the increase of participants, aggregation process will become a severe communication challenge. The server follows the critical process from receiving updates by all participants and process it to redistribute model updates. In this scenario, network congestion may occur which affect the merging of updates from various clients. At this time, edge device with limited communication connection increased dropout rates and biased model. The problem in large neural network may grow exponentially doing the frequent transmissions between clients and server. Sometimes client contribution is undervalued which will lead to ambiguity with unintentional biases. The vicious server is capable to manipulate global model with desired behaviour for the benefit of specific stakeholders. The lack of verifiable audit trails for aggregation decision makes difficult to verify participant contribution [43].

The economic sustainability is also one of the critical issues in centralized FL architecture. The high-end aggregation server needs vast number of computational resources to handle the large-scale FL architecture. This also need high amount of investments. These FL frameworks do not have built in mechanisms to calculate incentives for participants. In this system, participants are free to join and leave dynamically. There is no way to distribute infrastructure among participants who are training the model.

These challenges directed FL to move towards decentralized aggregation technology. These decentralized approaches may be blockchain based or peer to peer aggregation protocols aiming to address these limitations by distributing aggregation function across nodes. These alternatives introduce the trade-off factors i.e., communication overhead and computational complexity.

8.2.3 Trust and Incentive Mechanisms

The trust and incentive mechanisms also a challenge among participants. There are not prosperous incentive mechanisms ensuring long term viability. FL with distributed nature has participants with conflicting interests in an environment. The need of robust incentive approaches and verification of the participation. Decentralized FL architecture appeals cryptographic and appropriate decision making towards providing solutions for ensuring quality contributions and take an action on malicious behaviour. It may be difficult in scenario where any one can participate for the training of model [5].

The trust in FL evidenced in various dimensions for existing architecture which is difficult to address exhaustively. Initially, Contributions are not verified by the participants own. Participants are showing trust for aggregation to central server, which may manipulate the process undisclosed purposes. Next, there is lack assessing quality of the co-participants creating vulnerabilities at the time of updates. Another challenge is absence of identity management to participants to identify the bad participants accountable across training rounds. This lack of trust may lead practical deployment issues in various industries where participants balk to join FL networks without guarantee of assurance [7].

A good, FL need to motivate participants to participate and quality contributions. Blockchain based token mechanism provide better solution to reward participants through cryptocurrency for their participation and updates will be verified with the help of smart contracts. A reputation-based system needs to establish for good participants as a priority contributor in the model [8]. A mechanism can be established for multidimensional

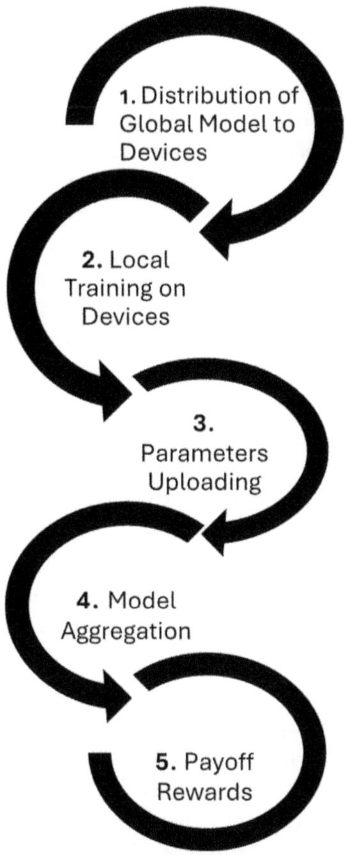

Figure 8.2 Incentive process to participants.

evaluation for model improvement, computational reliability, network stability based on historical patterns. The established system should made balance between immediate rewards for longer participation than short term optimization for better model updation. The mechanism of incentive payoff is shown in Figure 8.2.

An incentive mechanism of FL designing using game theoretic approaches to achieve stable cooperation among participants. These approaches need to create rules for honest participation regardless of other participants action. The customized reward packages can be offered as per participant capabilities and constraints. These theoretical frameworks face implementation challenges due to real-world FL complexity because of heterogeneous contributions. The unpredictable network conditions affect the participants contribution with commitments [10].

8.3 BLOCKCHAIN AS A SOLUTION FOR FL

8.3.1 Decentralized Trust and Transparency

The integration of FL with the decentralized technologies establish trust and ensure transparency in the collaborative machine learning. In traditional FL architecture, centralized servers are used for model aggregation which is susceptible to single point of failure. The use of blockchain with FL leverage to decentralized trust mechanisms with the use of cryptographic protocols to create verified, tamper proof ledger for all the operations [11]. The auditable facility is added in machine learning workflows where each model update verified independently by preserving the privacy of training data.

Blockchain provides the solution of decentralized trust in FL systems i.e., immutability, verification and smart contracts. Each model hash records timestamp updation and the aggregation of results on a distributed ledger ensures history of model training which can be audited by participants. FLaggregation rules can be automated with the help of smart contract which ensures the specified algorithm execute without human intervention. This approach is useful in cross organization scenarios so that it cannot be controlled by single entity and providing cryptographic proof to prove alteration.

The transparency, one of the important feature of decentralized architecture addressing all challenges of FL [17]. Due to transparency, each participant is able to verify the model updates and their incorporation in the global model with relative contributions of another parties. The transparency is required to block the malicious behaviour including model poisoning or any other biased aggregation. Transparency is also helpful in model versioning to enable reproducibility. All participants are able to trace the updates, contribution of specific model behaviour, auditing and regulatory compliance in all domains [12].

Decentralized trust mechanisms enable identity management in the FL networks. In the decentralized FL environment, identity of the parcipants is managed with the decentralized identity with verified credentials. In this system, participants imitate, establish accountability, as all actions are cryptographically signed and permanently recorded. The significant advancement has been proven over current FL systems that delight the participants equally trustworthy regardless of their actual track record.

The implementation of decentralized trust increases the computations of consensus mechanism need to be balanced for frequent model updates. For this lightweight consensus protocol need to be introduced and off chain computation architectures. Privacy preserving techniques need to be integrated for the verification of validity updation without exposing sensitive model parameters. A practical solution is for large scale FL deployment is hybrid approaches combining decentralized verification for better performance in real world applications [14].

Multiple parties are involved in research collaborations with the help of FL without legal issues among the participants. Like supply chain management all participants improve in predictive models while maintaining secrets. With the maturity of technology, decentralized trust mechanisms become foundation for global, and open participation of FL networks.

8.3.2 Secure and Immutable Model Updates

The maintenance of integrity in the model updates is a critical challenge in FL systems, in which due to distributed nature of training creates susceptible in centralized machine learning paradigms. The solution to address this susceptible problem is secure and immutable model update to ensure participant contribution remain tamper proof throughout the journey. Cryptographic techniques like digital signature, block verification to provide end to end secure solution where each model update can be traced. This security framework is very crucial in sensitive applications e.g. Healthcare and financial applications [2].

With the help of blockchain, each participant model update creates tamper evident ledger. In this system creates an auditable trail to verify that aggregated model was computed from the claimed updates only. Immutability stops malicious actors to aggregate the false updates. In the advance implementations a hierarchical cryptographic structure is generated as a Merkle tree of updates enabling efficient verification of all contributors to the final model without analysis of the update history. This hierarchical Merkle tree provide mathematical certainty about model provenance maintaining the efficiency needed for large scale FL deployments [23].

Multiple attack vector must be addressed to update protection in any security model. Secure transmission protocols use authenticated encryption to prevent the man-in-middle attacks in the duration of update exchange. Blockchain also provide the timestamping as definite evidence of when updates are submitted. It also helps to prevent version rollback attacks where stereotyped parameters might be done to revive known susceptibilities. Many of the architectures incorporates secure computation from multiple parties to enable privacy preserving aggregation and validate the aggregate results.

In the implementation, optimized lightweight cryptographic primitives for neural network parameters are included to reduce the resource constraints edge devices. The verification of the update in critical model layers, hybrid approaches may be used for less sensitive parameters which demonstrate trade-off between security and efficiency. Homomorphic encryption is used to verify update computations without decrypting the sensitive gradient information to preserve security and privacy. These innovations are helpful to update securely across the various collaborations using large computational resources among IoT networks, Mobile Devices. Smart contract is added for automatic verification enforcing quality thresholds on each update before the aggregation process. It also verifies that rejection events are permanently recorded to identify consistently poor performers. These features shift FL from black box collaborative process to a transparent, accountable system suitable for large high-stake applications [3]. Quantum resistant cryptographic algorithms are adapted to protect against future threats to current signature schemes. Innovations in the succinct cryptographic proofs could enable verification of entire training protocols with minimum overhead.

8.3.3 Smart Contracts for Automated Coordination

To enable the automated coordination among various participants in the FL system, smart contract is one of the pivotal elements enhancing the efficiency and trustworthiness. These self-executing contracts containing predefined rules for model aggregation, verification and incentive to participants, install on blockchain networks. Smart contracts also do the validation on contributions of participation ensuring legitimated updates which is incorporated into global model [24]. This verification and validation process reduce the risk of malicious actors for false updates and improve the robustness of FL process. Smart contracts are also useful for transparent incentive mechanisms rewarding participants based on quality and quantity of their contributions. Rewards may be dynamically adjusted as per contribution of participants at the run time based on their contribution with the help of embedding reputation system. Smart contracts also enforce privacy preserving protocols to verify computations without exposing raw data. These smart contracts are very helpful to reduce overhead and enhance scalability, making blockchain powered FL a feasible solution for collaboration with artificial intelligence in distributed and untrusted environments [31].

Traditional FL is centralized whereas when it is integrated with blockchain, it has added advantage of blockchain. In the traditional FL, server is centralized, and it may cause single point of failure. After integration with blockchain, decentralization is followed [4]. The

Table 8.1 Difference between traditional federated learning and integrated federated learning with blockchain

Feature	*Traditional FL*	*Integrated FL with blockchain*
Centralization	Model aggregation at centralized level	Model integration is decentralized due to blockchain
Trust model	Trust mechanism lack due to central server	Fairness and transparency maintained with the help of smart contracts
Incentive mechanism	Incentive not given to participants	Incentive given in the form of tokens to participants
Data privacy	Local data is private for other that is derived by server only	Privacy of data is maintained with the help of decentralized consensus
Security	Due to centralized in nature single point of failure exist	It is more secure because of immutable nature of blockchain
Auditability	Model updates tracking is limited	Model updates are traceable because of blockchain
Scalability	Due to centralized server scalability is limited	More scalable than traditional FL
Computation overhead	Only model aggregation is done	Apart from model aggregation, mining is done
Consensus mechanism	Consensus not performed	Various consensus protocols for validation
Model owner ship	Controlled by the central server	Decentralized ownership via smart contracts
Robustness to attacks	Susceptible to Byzantine attacks (malicious clients)	More resilient due to decentralized validation
Use cases	Healthcare, IoT, edge computing	Secure AI marketplaces, decentralized AI collaborations

malicious participants are not able to participate in the blockchain integrated environment. All model updates are traceable in the integrated FL blockchain environment. The difference between Traditional FL and Integrated FL with blockchain is shown in Table 8.1.

8.4 USE CASES AND APPLICATIONS

8.4.1 Healthcare: Secure Collaborative Learning

The healthcare sector stands to benefit greatly from FL supplemented with blockchain and privacy-preserving technology. The healthcare organizations will maintain the patient date securely with collaborative training model. Medical data sensitivity is high in comparison to other data which have to follow regulatory frameworks like General Data Protection Regulation and Health Insurance Portability and Accountability [28]. A good diagnostic model, predictive analytics and recommendations to patients is subject to secure FL frameworks by keeping data secured and decentralized. Nowadays Healthcare organizations train and artificial intelligence model for the detection of tumors in medical imaging without any medical imaging.

With the integration of blockchain healthcare organizations strengthen and ensure the auditable, transparent and maintaining trust in the multi-institutional collaborations. Smart contracts are used to implement compliance on the agreement on data usage, which does automatic validation for authorized participants who are contributing in model training. It maintains the immutable record of transactions for keeping the model training updates [32].

The pharmaceutical research become crucial in terms of drug efficacy needs the insights from multiple clinical trials without revealing patients' information. The healthcare organization are motivated for contribution by giving the rewards for their contribution in high quality datasets and participation in collaborative research. For example, a federated network of hospitals training a sepsis prediction model could use tokenized rewards to compensate contributors based on the diagnostic improvement their data provides.

The healthcare industry is full of challenges at the time of deployment ofFL. Medical data sets create the convergence difficulties in the federated model due to their small size, heterogeneity and identically distributed. The data consistency is important for integration of electronic health records in FL environments [33]. This type of data requires preprocessing pipelines to ensure consistency across the various organizations. The verified model will be trained without exposure of data and federated reinforcement learning for adaptive treatment for the patients. Global insights are derived with the help of decentralized data without compromising the privacy of health records of patients.

8.4.2 Finance: Fraud detection with privacy preservation

The fraud detection is also one of the accelerating challenges in the financial industry, need the good, trained machine learning models on large scale data with the management of rigid data privacy regulations. FL offers a solution with the privacy preservation enable the financial organization i.e. banks, payment gateways and many more to collaborate in the development of fraud detection systems without sharing the sensitive information. The organizations collaboratively train the model for anomaly detection for the identification of new fraud patterns with the real time systems. This will improve the detection accuracy while keeping each institutions customer data fully private [34].

The integration of Blockchain and FL establish the trust and liability among the multiple organizations collaborations. At the time of model updates, Secure aggregations are automated with smart contracts which creates the immutable blocks of all the contributions for compliance in future. Homomorphic encryption role is to secure multiple organizations at the time of aggregation and each transaction hang around to keep out of sight. To detect the cross institutional fraud schemes of other organizations where malicious actors seeking rift among the entities to monitor the system [34].

The FL with blockchain could assist credit card organizations to identify deceptive traders without preserving from customers as an intelligent system. In this model training, need of imbalanced nature of fraud datasets requires balanced data of fraud and non-fraud datasets to prevent the bias. Nowadays edge based FL models are used to check local frauds which further synchronize in a global model. In future, financial FL will automatically adapt the privacy rules of various jurisdictions to work with global banking networks [38]. Explainable artificial intelligence will be integrated for the development of FL frameworks to manage result which will be created by machine learning. It develops the system working on continuous learning to update the detection strategies for identification of fraudster.

8.4.3 IoT: Decentralized Edge Intelligence

The integration of FL with blockchain is very popular in Internet of Things due to the privacy preservation and decentralization across the devices. Previously Internet of Things use the cloud centric architectures having limitation including privacy risk, communication constraints due to network issues in the process of data aggregation. The FL collaboratively train model across all the devices like sensors, wearable devices without moving the data to a server [41]. The model will be trained at the place of data residing.

Further edge devices give their contribution for incentives moving FL from reluctant trust to trust. The selection of devices automated with the help of smart contracts from the available devices. These participants will get reward for their contributions. This is useful to collaborate the heterogeneous devices from various vendors without sharing of data [42]. This is implemented in various applications i.e., smart agriculture, healthcare wearable devices etc.

8.5 PERFORMANCE AND SCALABILITY CONSIDERATIONS

8.5.1 Latency and Throughput Challenges

After integration of blockchain and FL, model training is done across heterogeneous edge devices and networks. The model is trained at the location of data; due to this communication networks need to be strong. It requires to communicate model updates among the number of participants [44]. The aggregation process delays due to constraints in training on resource constrained devices. The delay also occurs due to use of computer network for the transfer of model updates. Another reason for delay is synchronization of model in each iteration.

Communication becomes overhead in case of transmission in large model parameters. The throughput will be reduced if the large number of devices are participating with large number of participants. This requires the more network communication for training of model. The aggregation server needs to handle simultaneous uploads/downloads but facing the bandwidth bottleneck [45]. To overcome this, techniques used like model pruning, quantization and gradient compression etc. The model pruning is helpful by keeping the key parameters at the time of training. The Quantization is also helpful to reduce overhead by changing the precision from 32-bit floating-point values to 8-bit floating point values. Gradient compression is also helpful in FL to reduce communication overhead between clients.

The asynchronous FL allowing faster devices to move next step without facing lag. The edge server may use intermediaries to aggregate update on local devices by reducing data transmission to central server. The use of analog signal in wireless networks for transmission of updates will improve the throughput. The FL and blockchain integration delay arises due to consensus mechanisms [46]. This consensus mechanism delay overhead can be reduced with the help of layer 2 solutions like rollups and permissioned blockchain.

8.5.2 Blockchain Storage and Computational Overhead

The blockchain and FL impact scalability and practicality with the introduction of storage requirements and computational overhead. Blockchain integrated FL keep all the model updates, aggregation details and verifications done on the ledger. For example if there are 1000 participants performing the 100 training rounds in an Ethereum, it may take 500 mb of immutable storage [48]. This issue will become overhead for large scale deployment as each participating node maintain a full copy of ledger to validate the transactions. The future goal is to make this integration more powerful with the lightweight edge intelligence.

Computational overhead is increased due to consensus mechanisms which performs mandatory cryptographic operations. For example, Proof of Work consensus requires intensive hardware and computational power which demands intensive hashing. Smart contracts automatically execute for aggregation logic and add the bytecode which causes postponement. To improve the consensus issues, byzantine Fault tolerant protocols may be used to reduce the energy consumption. Hybrid aggregation strategies can be used to store the updates i.e. Merkle root.

Storage issues can be resolved to store the updates only to relevant participants [51]. The unwanted data can be archived using layer 2 solutions for the better performance and reduce the storage requirements. The use of high-end hardware also accelerates cryptographic operations. Succinct blockchains are used to generate validity proofs to generate the information as per requirement e.g. Zk-SNARK [26]. Zk-SNARK is helpful at the time of proving self to another without revealing the information. It is used to verify the performance of local model without sharing the actual model.

8.5.3 Optimizations for Real-World Deployment

The FL system is now used for real world applications also for optimization and addressing various issues like heterogeneous hardware, communication networks problem and deal with data from various devices. It is a challenge in the real world deployments to accommodate the conflicting factors for the model accuracy, privacy preservation and maintain efficiency in the decentralized trust [53].

For these three key optimizations pillars have been emerged i.e., adaptive training protocols, resource aware participant selection and hybrid privacy utility trade-offs. Adaptive training protocols are needed to regulate computational and communication based on real time scenarios. Computing capabilities varies to contribute in partial updates without delay the global aggregation cycle in edge device networks e.g., elastic averaging. While in the wireless environments compromised with bandwidth to reduce the communication payloads by 60–80%. In this model updates are verified in the group to reduce the Ethereum gas costs [63].

A pharmaceutical industry case study demonstrated that such selection reduced FL round failures by 72% while improving model convergence speed by 1.8× (Nature Digital Medicine, 2023). Blockchain enhancements add token-bonded participation, requiring devices to stake crypto-assets as collateral for reliable service—a system shown to decrease dropout rates by 55% in IoT testbeds.

8.6 FUTURE DIRECTIONS AND OPEN CHALLENGES

8.6.1 Interoperability Between Different Blockchains

Interoperability among heterogeneous blockchain platforms becomes a great challenge in integrated FL environment. Currently all blockchain applications work in silo manner. The emerging solution for the cross-chain communication protocols which adapt the FL workflows [15]. The FedChain is a novel framework for the transferring of tokens in cross platforms and following the security requirements. ERC 1155 tokens are multi token standards which showing ownership in the FL models which act as a bridge among other blockchain. As Integrated FL works in cross platform which is sensitive in nature i.e., Healthcare Industry, Finance Industry. Each industry has their own compliance standards. For example a healthcare FLnetwork follows Health Insurance Portability and Accountability Act. It may happen various blockchains implementing different governance which cause rejection in updates in permissive IoT focused chain [16]. The solution is the voting by participants to govern cross chain FL in decentralized autonomous organizations. Smart contracts are implemented to automatically distribute tokens to the native currencies of participating chains. Standardization efforts may be implementing common formats to represent the model architectures and guarantee the privacy in blockchain [57]. The integrated FL environment needs to develop an environment which is comprised of models which can incorporate updates from cross platform blockchain preserving the network integrity. This shift is not easy; it represents the challenge technically and decentralized artificial intelligence systems are architected [58]. In future, decentralization must be balanced by managing the individual network limitations.

8.6.2 Regulatory and Ethical Implications

The complex regulatory and ethical challenges exist due to advancement of FL. In collaboration without moving the physical data is a legal grey area to provide clear compliance guidelines with the existing framework like Health Insurance Portability and Accountability Act and General Data Protection Regulation [27]. If any of the patient withdraw his or her consent for medical data usage in a FL environment, then technically all data will not be available.

The integrated FL blockchain network face challenge in multi directions spanning computer science, law and ethics. The emerging solutions equipped with specialized blockchain nodes and aggregation with ethics as per governable systems [49]. However, as FL penetrates highly regulated sectors like healthcare and finance, the lack of global consensus on decentralized artificial intelligence governance may spur regulatory arbitrage, with potentially harmful consequences for data sovereignty and algorithmic fairness.

8.6.3 Quantum-Resistant Blockchain for FL

The Quantum computing algorithm Shor's and Gover's is threat to integration of FL and blockchain. This is due to elliptic curve signature and hash based consensus mechanisms. For the safeguard model, post quantum cryptography can be integrated to FL and blockchain. The threat is most vulnerable to the sensitive industries like healthcare, finance and defence etc. Due to this Digital signature are replaced with Elliptic curve to Cryptographic Suite for Algebraic Lattices signature [50]. Now consensus algorithm proof of work must be replaced with post quantum cryptography alternatives. Scalable Transparent Argument of Knowledge enable Byzantine agreement with the post quantum signature which reduce FL aggregation latency. Zero-Knowledge proofs are used to preserve the sensitive information and communicate with the other participants. Hybrid transition architectures are being used to model to maintain the balance between security and practicality. The hybrid blockchain can be used with classical and post quantum signatures in parallel at the time of transition. The smart contract is used to change the credentials between prequantum and post quantum phases. The hardware modules will be also used like quantum key distribution to provide physical layer protection for high value model parameters [52].

Standardization efforts are also required to handle the abnormal situation inFL. To handle the standardization process, various techniques are implemented. National Institute of Standards and Technology (NIST) for the optimization of FL workflows, reduce the signature size for frequent model update transmissions [60]. Post Quantum Cryptography standards are adopted to manage incompatible standards.

The U.S. NIST estimates that critical FL blockchain systems must achieve quantum resistance by 2030 to mitigate harvest-now-decrypt-later attacks [61]. Pilot projects like IBM's Quantum-Safe FL for Healthcare are testing three-phase migration strategies: first is PQ signature adoption for new model updates, second is Retroactive re-encryption and Full consensus replacement with quantum-secure protocols [62].

This quantum threat vector demands immediate attention—unlike classical security patches, cryptographic transitions in decentralized FL systems require coordinated global action due to their inherent immutability and distributed trust models. The solution space will necessitate unprecedented collaboration between quantum physicists, cryptographers, and machine learning specialists to future-proof FL ecosystems.

8.7 CONCLUSION

The FL and blockchain together done the transformation to build decentralized, privacy preserving and secure artificial intelligence systems. In this chapter, the integration of both technologies is demonstrated. Blockchain addressed the challenges of centralized server. Blockchain FL integration also address the critical challenges i.e., trust, incentive calculation, security issues. It enhances the trust by keeping the data in local system. The machine learning model is train in the system where data is kept. Data will not be transferred to the centralized server. The trained model is transferred from the one system to another for the integration. Smart contracts contribute in the validation and verification process for the global model.

The incentive mechanism is strengthened with the integration of FL and blockchain. The contribution of multiple participants in the model training is recorded and incentive is calculated based on their participation. The participation of each participant is traceable with the help of blockchain technology. Various industries have their own data protection laws i.e. Health Insurance Portability and Accountability Act in the healthcare industry. Still there are challenges of scalability, communication overheads. In future lightweight blockchain designs need to explore with the help sharding and layer 2 solutions. There is need for interoperability among the various types of blockchain for the support of heterogeneous FL system. For the multiple party operation zero-knowledge proofs is used for adaptive security mechanism.

The fusion of FL and blockchain marks a significant leap enabling secure, transparent and collaborative intelligence without compromising data sovereignty. Still there are challenges in ongoing innovations in cryptographic techniques, consensus algorithms and decentralized governance. By addressing these research gaps, we can unlock the full potential of decentralized artificial intelligence, fostering a future where privacy and collaboration coexist seamlessly.

REFERENCES

[1] Abid, A. A. M. A., Hazar, M. J., Mabrouk, M., & Zrigui, M. (2023). Proposal of a modified hash algorithm to increase blockchain security. *Procedia Computer Science*, 225, 3265–3275.

[2] Arora, P., & Nagpal, R. (2022, May). Blockchain technology and its applications: A systematic review of the literature. In *Proceedings of the International Conference on Innovative Computing & Communication (ICICC)*.

[3] Attaran, M., & Gunasekaran, A. (2019). The evolution of blockchain. In *Applications of Blockchain Technology in Business: Challenges and Opportunities* (pp. 7–12). Cham: Springer International Publishing.

[4] Bonawitz, K., Eichner, H., Grieskamp, W., Huba, D., Ingerman, A., Ivanov, V., Kiddon, C. M., Konečný, J., Mazzocchi, S., McMahan, B., van Overveldt, T., Petrou, D., Ramage, D., & Roselander, J. (2019). *Towards federated learning at scale: System design*. SysML.

[5] Bhutta, M. N. M., Khwaja, A. A., Nadeem, A., Ahmad, H. F., Khan, M. K., et al. (2021). A survey on blockchain technology: Evolution, architecture and security. *IEEE Access*, 9, 61048–61073. https://doi.org/10.1109/ACCESS.2021.3072849.

[6] Cai, Z., Chen, J., Fan, Y., Zheng, Z., & Li, K. (2025). Blockchain-empowered federated learning: Benefits, challenges, and solutions. *IEEE Transactions on Big Data.*

[7] Chen, W., Xu, Z., Shi, S., Zhao, Y., & Zhao, J. (2018). A survey of blockchain applications in different domains. In *Proceedings of the 2018 International Conference on Blockchain Technology and Application* (pp. 17–21).

[8] Chen, Z., Wang, W., Yan, X., & Tian, J. (2018). *Cortex – AI on blockchain: The decentralized AI autonomous system*. Cortex White Paper.

[9] Dabbagh, M., Sookhak, M., & Safa, N. S. (2019). The evolution of blockchain: A bibliometric study. *IEEE Access*, 7, 19212–19221. https://doi.org/10.1109/ACCESS.2019.2895646.

[10] Damjan, M. (2018). The interface between blockchain and the real world. *Ragion Pratica*, 2, 379–406.

[11] Dubovitskaya, A., Xu, Z., Ryu, S., Schumacher, M., & Wang, F. (2017). Secure and trustable electronic medical records sharing using blockchain. *AMIA Annual Symposium Proceedings*, 2017, 650.

[12] Fu, J., Qiao, S., Huang, Y., Si, X., Li, B., & Yuan, C. (2020). A study on the optimization of blockchain hashing algorithm based on PRCA. *Security and Communication Networks, 2020*(1), 8876317.

[13] Gemeliarana, I. G. A. K., & Sari, R. F. (2018). Evaluation of proof of work (PoW) blockchains security network on selfish mining. In *2018 International Seminar on Research of Information Technology and Intelligent Systems (ISRITI)* (pp. 126–130). IEEE.

[14] Hussein, Z., Salama, M. A., & El-Rahman, S. A. (2023). Evolution of blockchain consensus algorithms: A review on the latest milestones of blockchain consensus algorithms. *Cybersecurity*, 6(1), 30.

[15] Jiang, Y., Sun, G., & Feng, T. (2022). Research on data transaction security based on blockchain. *Information*, 13(11), 532.

[16] Kayikci, S., & Khoshgoftaar, T. M. (2024). Blockchain meets machine learning: A survey. *Journal of Big Data*, 11, Article 9.

[17] Kitchenham, B. (2004). *Procedures for performing systematic reviews* (Technical Report No. 33). Keele University.

[18] Konečný, J., McMahan, B., & Ramage, D. (2015). *Federated optimization: Distributed optimization beyond the datacenter* (arXiv:1511.03575). arXiv. https://arxiv.org/abs/1511.03575.

[19] Konečný, J., McMahan, H. B., Ramage, D., & Richtárik, P. (2016). *Federated optimization: Distributed machine learning for on-device intelligence* (arXiv:1610.02527). arXiv. https://arxiv.org/abs/1610.02527.

[20] Konečný, J., McMahan, H. B., Yu, F. X., Richtárik, P., Suresh, A. T., & Bacon, D. (2016). *Federated learning: Strategies for improving communication efficiency* (arXiv:1610.05492). arXiv. https://arxiv.org/abs/1610.05492.

[21] Konečný, J., McMahan, H. B., Yu, F. X., Richtárik, P., Suresh, A. T., & Bacon, D. (2016). Federated learning: Strategies for improving communication efficiency. *arXiv preprint arXiv:1610.05492.*

[22] Kumar, L., Sharma, A., Sharma, H., & Sharma, S. (2023, May). Blockchain in Healthcare: Portal for Electronic Health Records. In *Proceedings of the KILBY 100 7th International Conference on Computing Sciences.*

[23] Lee, C. S., Baughman, D. M., & Lee, A. Y. (2017). Deep learning is effective for classifying normal versus age-related macular degeneration OCT images. *Ophthalmology Retina*, 1(4), 322–327. https://doi.org/10.1016/j.oret.2017.02.002.

[24] Levis, D., Fontana, F., & Ughetto, E. (2021). A look into the future of blockchain technology. *PLoS One*, 16(11), e0258995.

[25] Liu, D., Miller, T., Sayeed, R., & Mandl, K. D. (2018). *FADL: Federated-autonomous deep learning for distributed electronic health record* (arXiv:1811.11400). arXiv. https://arxiv.org/abs/1811.11400.

[26] Li, W., Deng, X., Liu, J., Yu, Z., & Lou, X. (2023). Delegated proof of stake consensus mechanism based on community discovery and credit incentive. *Entropy*, 25(9), 1320.

[27] López-Sorribes, S., Rius-Torrentó, J., & Solsona-Tehàs, F. (2023). A bibliometric review of the evolution of blockchain technologies. *Sensors*, 23, 3167. https://doi.org/10.3390/s23063167.

[28] Mani, S., Chen, Y., Elasy, T., Clayton, W., & Denny, J. (2012). Type 2 diabetes risk forecasting from EMR data using machine learning. *AMIA Annual Symposium Proceedings*, 2012, 606.

[29] McMahan, B., & Ramage, D. (2017). *Federated learning: Collaborative machine learning without centralized training data*. Google Research Blog.

[30] McMahan, H., Moore, E., Ramage, D., & Agüera y Arcas, B. (2017). *Federated learning of deep networks using model averaging* (arXiv:1602.05629). arXiv. https://arxiv.org/abs/1602.05629.

[31] Michalski, R., Dziubałtowska, D., & Macek, P. (2020). Revealing the character of nodes in a blockchain with supervised learning. *IEEE Access*, 8, 109639–109647.

[32] Miotto, R., Wang, F., Wang, S., Jiang, X., & Dudley, J. T. (2018). Deep learning for healthcare: Review, opportunities and challenges. *Briefings in Bioinformatics*, 19(6), 1236–1246. https://doi.org/10.1093/bib/bbx044.

[33] Namasudra, S., & Akkaya, K. (2023). Introduction to blockchain technology. In S. Namasudra & K. Akkaya (Eds.), *Blockchain and its applications in Industry 4.0* (Vol. 119, pp. 1–15). Springer. https://doi.org/10.1007/978-981-19-8730-4_1.

[34] Nguyen, C. T., Hoang, D. T., Nguyen, D. N., Niyato, D., Nguyen, H. T., & Dutkiewicz, E. (2019). Proof-of-stake consensus mechanisms for future blockchain networks: Fundamentals, applications and opportunities. *IEEE Access*, 7, 85727–85745.

[35] Orabi, M. M., Emam, O., & Fahmy, H. (2025). Adapting security and decentralized knowledge enhancement in federated learning using blockchain technology: literature review. *Journal of Big Data*, 12(1), 55.

[36] Panda, S. K., Jena, A. K., Swain, S. K., & Satapathy, S. C. (Eds.). (2021). *Blockchain technology: Applications and challenges*. Springer.

[37] Podichetty, V., & Penn, D. (2004). The progressive roles of electronic medicine: Benefits, concerns, and costs. *The American Journal of the Medical Sciences*, 328(2), 94–99. https://doi.org/10.1097/00000441-200408000-00003.

[38] Raj, J. S. (2021). Security enhanced blockchain based unmanned aerial vehicle health monitoring system. *Journal of IoT in Social, Mobile, Analytics, and Cloud*, 3(2), 121–131.

[39] Ramageri, B., & Arjunwadkar, M. V. (2020). Applications of blockchain technology in various sectors: A review. *International Journal of Future Generation Communication and Networking*, 13(2), 94–99.

[40] Sameera, K. M., Nicolazzo, S., Arazzi, M., Nocera, A., KA, R. R., Vinod, P., & Conti, M. (2024). Privacy-preserving in Blockchain-based Federated Learning systems. *Computer Communications*, 222, 38–67.

[41] Saraji, S. (2023). Introduction to blockchain. In *Sustainable oil and gas using blockchain* (Vol. 98, pp. 49–60). Springer. https://doi.org/10.1007/978-3-031-30697-6_3.

[42] Sarmah, S. S. (2018). Understanding blockchain technology. *Computer Science and Engineering*, 8(2), 23–29.

[43] Sharma, S., Tomar, V., Arora, S. (2025). Leveraging Federated Explainable AI with Blockchain for Secure Healthcare Data Analysis: A Promising Approach for Improved Patient Outcomes. In: Raj, G., Unhelker, B., Choudhary, A. (eds) *Advances in Artificial Intelligence and Machine Learning. ICAAAIML 2023*. Lecture Notes in Electrical Engineering, vol. 1264. Singapore: Springer. https://doi.org/10.1007/978-981-97-9507-9_1

[44] Simon, S. J. (2006). An examination of the financial feasibility of electronic medical records (EMRs): A case study of tangible and intangible benefits. *International Journal of Electronic Healthcare*, 2(2), 185–200.

[45] Singh, G., Garg, V., & Tiwari, P. (2021). Introduction to blockchain technology. In R. Agrawal & N. Gupta (Eds.), *Transforming cybersecurity solutions using blockchain* (pp. 1–18). Springer. https://doi.org/10.1007/978-981-33-6858-3_1.
[46] Singhal, B., Dhameja, G., & Panda, P. S. (2018). Introduction to blockchain. In *Beginning blockchain* (pp. 1–23). Apress. https://doi.org/10.1007/978-1-4842-3444-0_1.
[47] Taherdoost, H. (2023). Smart contracts in blockchain technology: A critical review. *Information*, 14(2), 117.
[48] Thomas, S. G., & Myakala, P. K. (2025). Beyond the cloud: Federated learning and edge AI for the next decade. *Journal of Computer and Communications*, 13(2), 37–50.
[49] Tierney, M. J., Pageler, N. M., Kahana, M., Pantaleoni, J. L., & Longhurst, C. A. (2013). Medical education in the electronic medical record (EMR) era: Benefits, challenges, and future directions. *Academic Medicine*, 88(6), 748–752.
[50] Tomar, V., Kumar, N., & Srivastava, A. R. (2023). Single sample face recognition using deep learning: A survey. *Artificial Intelligence Review*, 56(Suppl 1), 1063–1111. https://doi.org/10.1007/s10462-023-10551-y
[51] Tomov, Y. K. (2019). Bitcoin: Evolution of blockchain technology. In *2019 IEEE XXVIII International Scientific Conference Electronics (ET)* (pp. 1–4). IEEE. https://doi.org/10.1109/ET.2019.8878322.
[52] Tran, T., Nguyen, T. D., Phung, D., & Venkatesh, S. (2015). Learning vector representation of medical objects via EMR-driven nonnegative restricted Boltzmann machines (ENRBM). *Journal of Biomedical Informatics*, 54, 96–105. https://doi.org/10.1016/j.jbi.2015.01.006.
[53] Wang, C., Jiang, H., Zeng, J., Min, Y. U., Huang, Q., & Zuo, Z. (2021). A review of blockchain layered architecture and technology application research. *Wuhan University Journal of Natural Sciences*, 26(5), 14.
[54] Wang, C., & Zhao, J. (2023). Network approaches in blockchain-based systems: Applications, challenges, and future directions. *Computer Communications*, 212, 141–150.
[55] Wang, Z., & Hu, Q. (2021). *Blockchain-based federated learning: A comprehensive survey* (arXiv:2110.02182). arXiv. https://arxiv.org/abs/2110.02182.
[56] Wang, Z., Yan, B., & Dong, A. (2022). Blockchain empowered federated learning for data sharing incentive mechanism. *Procedia Computer Science,* 202, 348–353. https://doi.org/10.1016/j.procs.2022.03.046.
[57] Yadav, A. S., Singh, N., & Kushwaha, D. S. (2023). Evolution of blockchain and consensus mechanisms & its real-world applications. *Multimedia Tools and Applications*, 82, 34363–34408. https://doi.org/10.1007/s11042-023-14624-6.
[58] Yang, J. J., Li, J. Q., & Niu, Y. (2015). A hybrid solution for privacy preserving medical data sharing in the cloud environment. *Future Generation Computer Systems*, 43, 74–86. https://doi.org/10.1016/j.future.2014.07.001.
[59] Yang, K., Fan, T., Chen, T., Shi, Y., & Yang, Q. (2019). *A quasi-Newton method based vertical federated learning framework for logistic regression* (arXiv:1912.00513). arXiv. https://arxiv.org/abs/1912.00513.
[60] Yong, H., Lee, C., & Wang, D. (2017). *Artificial intelligence computing platform driven by blockchain.* Singapore: DeepBrain Chain.
[61] Zhou, S., Li, K., Xiao, L., Cai, J., Liang, W., & Castiglione, A. (2023). A systematic review of consensus mechanisms in blockchain. *Mathematics*, 11(10), 2248.
[62] Zheng, X., & Feng, W. (2021). Research on practical byzantine fault tolerant consensus algorithm based on blockchain. *Journal of Physics: Conference Series*, 1802(3), 032022.
[63] Zheng, Z., Xie, S., Dai, H., Chen, X., & Wang, H. (2017). An overview of blockchain technology: Architecture, consensus, and future trends. In *2017 IEEE International Congress on Big Data (BigData Congress)* (pp. 557–564). IEEE.
[64] Zuo, X., Wang, M., Zhu, T., Zhang, L., Yu, S., & Zhou, W. (2025). Federated learning with blockchain-enhanced machine unlearning: A trustworthy approach. *IEEE Transactions on Services Computing*, 1428–1444.

Chapter 9

Cyber resilience through adaptive federated learning

Neetha S. S., Shivangi Singh, and Deepa S.

9.1 INTRODUCTION TO CYBER RESILIENCE AND FEDERATED LEARNING (FL)

9.1.1 The evolving landscape of cyber threats and the imperative for resilience

Todays digital landscape is all about the unprecedented diversity and intensity of cyber-attacks, with the resulting all-encompassing disruptions in operations, massive data breaches, and substantial economic losses (Boyens, 2020; Rangapur et al., 2022). Although traditional centralized learning models have some significant merits, they are inherently vulnerable to severe flaws such as data leakage, excessive communication requirements, and the intrinsic risk of single points of failure (Pasquini et al., 2022). The growing dependence of critical services such as the round-the-clock availability of electricity, water, data, goods, and financial services on digital technology further accentuates the threat of cyber-attacks, rendering cyber resilience an issue of all-out priority, quite possibly even a matter of life and death (Müller et al., 2023).

The ever-changing nature of cyber threats necessitates a systematic reevaluation of cybersecurity strategies. Historically, the primary emphasis has been placed on hardening cyber systems against potential threats, with the goal of preventing breaches in the first place. While this preventionist strategy is still an indispensable component of any security framework, growing awareness has converged on the realization that cyber defense cannot always be absolutely prevented in a dynamically changing threat landscape. The focus has, therefore, been shifted towards ensuring that systems still operate, or recover quickly,even in the case of a security breach. This transition is a fundamental change of cybersecurity philosophy from an exclusively defensive, perimeter-based model to a more integrated, adaptive, and recovery-oriented model. Such a move entails not only preventing attacks but also the continuity of critical operations under hostile conditions. This change of thought necessitates the development of new architectural models and operation procedures that necessarily entail fault tolerance, flexibility, and rapid recovery capabilities, as opposed to purely static perimeter barriers (Gold, 2011; Trump et al., 2025). Such attainment of cyber resilience, therefore, is seen as an ongoing, iterative process that necessitates constant monitoring, analysis, and system upgrading, as opposed to a single, one-off installation. This very dynamism naturally aligns with the principles and capabilities offered by machine learning paradigms (Parisi & Kanan, 2019).

DOI: 10.1201/9781003660330-9

9.1.2 Foundational concepts of cyber resilience

Cyber resilience is a multidimensional and multifaceted concept, and a number of authoritative bodies provide definitions that are converging towards the idea of sustained functionality in hostile environments. Cyber resilience is the ability to anticipate, withstand, recover from, and adapt to adverse conditions, stresses, attacks, or compromises on systems that use or are enabled by cyber resources"(Bodeau, 2019; Ross, 2021), as defined by the National Institute of Standards and Technology (NIST). This broad definition can be applied to virtual and physical infrastructures alike. Other definitions support this idea, emphasizing the ability of an organization to continuously deliver the intended outcome, despite cyber attacks, or to protect electronic data and systems from cyberattacks, and quickly resume business operations in the case of a successful attack" (Björck et al., 2015).

NIST further offers four strategic principles to drive activities towards attaining cyber resilience:

- Anticipate: This credo involves deterrence, avoidance, and prevention measures. It involves proactive planning to neutralize potential attacks and continuous tweaking of a systems attack surface to render it challenging for exploit attempts on the part of attackers.
- Withstand: This is the practice of designing and building systems that are able to withstand damage, repair themselves, deflect danger, or continue to function at some level even after the removal or failure of some compromised parts.
- Recovery: These are the processes used after a security incident. They include returning to an earlier, untainted state, regaining critical functions through duplication, or modifying existing system elements to strengthen compromised areas. While detection can determine the choice of a recovery process, systems can also use these processes independently of real-time detection to alter the attack surface.
- Adapt: This principle focuses on the need for continuous improvement. It involves correcting known weaknesses or gaps by implementing new controls and restructuring system requirements, architecture, design, configuration, or processes as per lessons learned from previous experiences.

The adapt principle itself recognizes the need for continuous learning and the adaptation of systems to meet known vulnerabilities or changing conditions. It is at this point that machine learning, in the form of adaptive learning algorithms, comes into play. Machine learning algorithms can analyze trends around emerging threats, adjust real-time security controls, and improve their defense systems, essentially making the adapt principle actionable from a technological standpoint (Dini et al., 2023). It therefore stands to reason that machine learning, and adaptive federated learning (AFL) specifically, acts not simply as a threat detection tool; instead, it is a fundamental enabler of the adapt principle within the cyber resilience paradigm, allowing for dynamic adjustment of defense systems to a constantly changing threat environment.

9.1.3 Overview of FL: principles and paradigm

FL is an emerging machine learning paradigm in which the algorithms are learned in multiple independent sessions with individual decentralized data without requiring centralized data storage. Instead of sharing raw datasets, the mechanism is based on model-update sharing and aggregation precisely gradients, weights (Akhtarshenas et al., 2024; Li et al., 2020), or biases to cooperatively learn a global model. This new idea was beautifully described by Brendan McMahan in a landmark research paper in 2016. The central principle of FL is encapsulated by an iterative process through a chain of significant interactions among servers and clients, popularly termed as FL rounds as shown in the Figure 9.1.

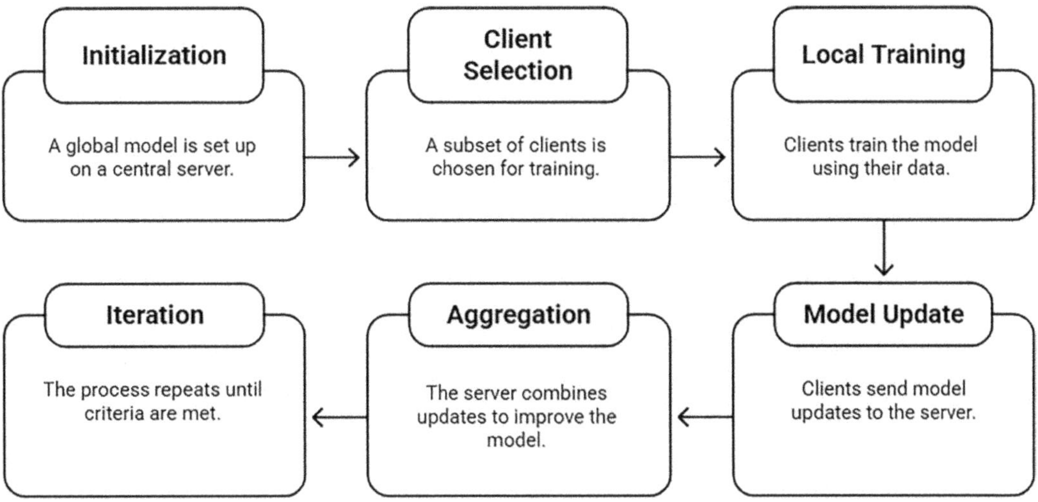

Figure 9.1 Federated learning process.

1. **Initialization:** A global machine learning model is first selected and set up on a central server.
2. **Client Selection:** For each round, some subset or fraction of local nodes (clients) are chosen to participate in the training process.
3. **Local Training:** Some of the customers download the state of the global model and train it locally on their own, on-device data.
4. **Model Update:** After the completion of decentralized training, the model updates, including updates or gradients of the parameters, are communicated from the clients to the central server, while the data is left as initially received.
5. **Aggregation:** The master server gathers and consolidates these model updates from all participating clients to generate an improved iteration of the global model.
6. **Iteration:** Steps 2-5 are iteratively repeated for several rounds until a pre-specified termination condition, for example, a specified maximum number of rounds or a specified model accuracy condition, is reached.

FL is naturally driven by fundamental concerns such as data privacy, data minimization principle, and data rights of access. Its natural advantages are strong data protection since original data is stored securely in local devices; reduced communication costs since only efficient model updates are exchanged; and facilitating decentralized training, which promotes collaboration without data centralization (Kaissis et al., 2020; Konečný et al., 2015, 2016). The inherent design choice of FL, under which raw data has to stay decentralized, is a critical design choice that actively addresses the issue of privacy from the very beginning, rather than considering privacy controls as a secondary discipline (Sheller et al., 2020). This feature makes FL a powerful instrument for privacy-preserving machine learning. Thus, FL is not merely a technical innovation but is a strategic preference for situations where data privacy and strict regulatory compliance, as in the case of GDPR and HIPAA, are simply of the highest absolute order of importance (Pati et al., 2024). This feature has a special value in sensitive areas like healthcare or finance, where regulatory or ethical constraints limit data aggregation, thus creating a privacy-by-design solution that effectively reduces the risk attached to data leakage.

9.1.4 The convergence: why adaptive FL for cyber resilience?

The decentralized characteristic of FL possesses the critical benefits with regard to privacy but also possesses a unique set of issues that impact its efficiency and robustness. Some of these issues include device heterogeneity, which is marked by different computing resources and network configurations of the clients; data heterogeneity, due to non-IID data among the clients; huge communication overhead; and a number of security attacks, including poisoning and inference attacks.

AFL is a sweeping progression of the FL paradigm, carefully crafted to overcome its intrinsic shortcomings. AFL achieves this by adaptively adjusting the FL process in various dimensions, including client selection processes, local learning rates, and aggregation processes. Such adaptability built into the design is critical in maintaining the optimal performance and robustness in real-world deployments, which generally fall below the threshold of dynamism, uncertainty, and increased vulnerability to adversarial attacks (Chen et al., 2023; Zheng et al., 2024).

Traditional FL gains greatly in terms of privacy but loses out to being susceptible to new attack types and potential performance loss from heterogeneity. Cyber resilience by nature requires that systems have the ability to withstand and learn from hostile environments effectively. AFL mechanisms like adaptive client selection, resilient aggregation processes, and adaptive learning rates are explicitly designed to address the vulnerabilities inherent in FL and support overall system performance in an adversarial environment (Chen et al., 2023; Wang et al., 2021). AFL should therefore not be viewed as an incremental enhancement of FL but as a major innovation that increases the value of FL to cyber resilience. This is achieved by greatly enhancing its resilience and enabling operational continuity despite a wide range of threats and complex system dynamics. To make FL an effective tool for cyber resilience, its adaptive mechanisms should be viewed as core requirements and not add-on features in real-world deployments.

9.1.5 Global cyber resilience landscape (2024 - 2025)

Critical Performance Indicators:

- 85% of IT executives admit that computing innovation expands exposure to cyber risk.
- 90% rise in publicly extorted ransomware victims during 2023.
- 68% of data breaches are caused by human factors.
- 18% increase in claims for transfer fraud (2024 vs. 14% in 2023).
- 98.34% hybrid quantum-enhanced FL models accuracy for cyber attack detection.

The comparative Performance of federated learning(FL) security metrics is illustrated in Figure 9.2.

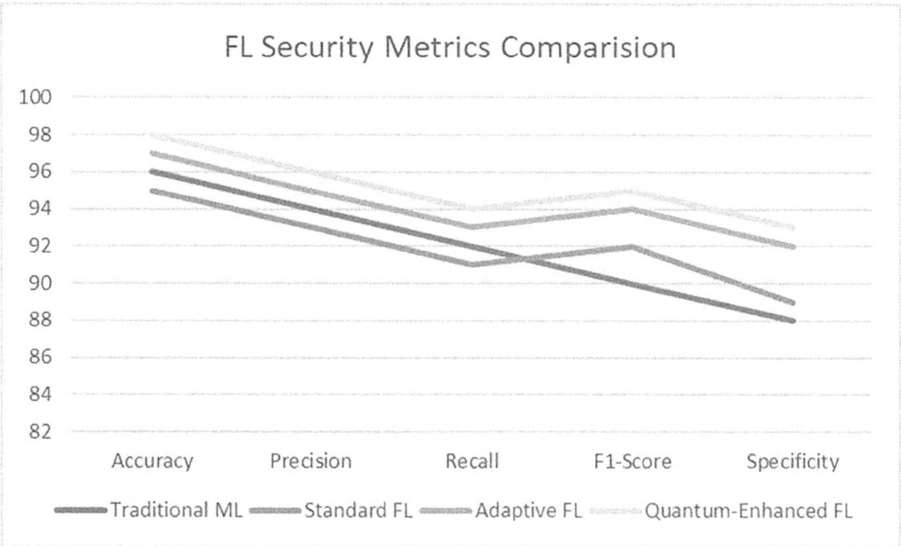

Figure 9.2 FL security metrics comparison.

9.1.5.1 FL security metrics comparison

The FL Security Metrics Comparison chart shows the comparative performance of four paradigms of machine learning Traditional Machine Learning, Standard Federated Learning (FL), Adaptive FL, and Quantum-Enhanced FL—on five most critical security metrics: Accuracy, Precision, Recall, F1-Score, and Specificity. Interestingly, Quantum-Enhanced FL leads in all the paradigms with values of over 98% on all the parameters, thus establishing its superior accuracy and reliability in identifying cyber threats. Coming in second place, Adaptive FL demonstrates significant improvements over Standard FL and Traditional ML, especially in recall and F1-Score, which indicates superior threat detection and balanced classification performance. Standard FL records overall improvement over Traditional ML, indicating the importance of decentralized learning in enhancing resilience. However, Traditional ML consistently records poor performance with specificity and recall values drooping down to around 89%, which is indicative of its lower robustness against cyber threats. The chart clearly shows a general performance enhancement from Traditional ML to Quantum-Enhanced FL, which indicates the advantage of incorporating adaptiveness and quantum computing into FL for effective cybersecurity defense.

9.2 CORE PRINCIPLES OF CYBER RESILIENCE

9.2.1 Definitional frameworks (NIST, ENISA, etc.)

Cyber resilience is theorized in terms of various definitional frameworks (Table 9.1), each emphasizing different features while maintaining in common a core focus on ongoing operational capability despite cyber adversity.

- **The National Institute of Standards and Technology** (**NIST**) provides a basic and widely used definition, according to which cyber resilience is the capacity to anticipate, withstand, recover from, and adapt to adverse conditions, stresses, attacks, or compromises on systems that use or are enabled by cyber resources (Neto et al., 2020; Stastny & Stoica, 2022).
- **The Pacific Northwest National Laboratory** (**PNNL**) explains cyber resilience as the ability to endure adverse events in a computer environment. The concept highlights that cyber resilience is a broader strategy than traditional cybersecurity, that is, the desire of systems to sustain operation and/or recover quickly in the case of a security breach (Björck et al., 2015; Ross et al., 2021).
- As per a complete definition **in Wikipedia,** cyber resilience is an entity's capability to always deliver the desired result, regardless of cyber-attacks.
- **European Central Bank** (**ECB**) defines cyber resilience as "the capacity to defend electronic systems and data against cyber attacks, and to restore business operations in a timely manner in the event of a successful attack." This particular definition particularly highlights the extremely high reliance of the financial system on digital technologies, and the borderless nature of cyber threats by definition (Freire & Padilla, 2019).

Through all these varied definitions, there is a thread of commonality: universal recognition of operational continuity. There can be variation in expression, but there is a thread common to all the definitions that they all emphasize guaranteeing operational continuity and enabling rapid recuperation against the backdrop of cyber-attacks. This perspective transcends prevention, for intrusions are an inevitable part of the modern digital world (Björck et al., 2015). The effort, therefore, shifts from prevention to mitigating the impact of such breaches and ensuring continued provision of critical services. This shared element points to the imperative need for adaptive and responsive mechanisms in any cybersecurity defense framework. Any system or framework, therefore, that aims to possess genuine cyber resilience has top priority not only for strengthening its defenses but also for the incorporation of end-to-end monitoring, detection, response, and adaptive learning capabilities to ensure the unbroken continuity of business processes or critical services (Björck et al., 2015).

Table 9.1 Comparative definitions of cyber resilience

Source	*Definition of Cyber Resilience*	*Key Emphasis*
NIST	"The ability to anticipate, withstand, recover from, and adapt to adverse conditions, stresses, attacks, or compromises on systems that use or are enabled by cyber resources"	Holistic, four-phase lifecycle (anticipate, withstand, recover, adapt)
PNNL	"The ability to weather adverse events in a computing environment." Broader than cybersecurity, emphasizing continued operation and quick recovery post-breach	Operational continuity, rapid bounce-back, broader scope than cybersecurity
Wikipedia	"An entity's ability to continuously deliver the intended outcome, despite cyber-attacks"	Continuous delivery, despite attacks
ECB	"The ability to protect electronic data and systems from cyberattacks, as well as to resume business operations quickly in case of a successful attack"	Protection and rapid business resumption, especially in financial systems

9.2.2 Strategic principles: anticipate, withstand, recover, adapt

Building on the basic definition made by NIST, efforts at achieving cyber resilience generally follow four strategic principles guiding the design and function of resilient systems:

- Anticipate: This concept includes prevention, avoidance, and deterrence measures. It entails proactively preparing against possible threats and continuously reconfiguring an attack surface of a system to render it harder for attackers to take advantage. It includes being alert to possible threats and vulnerabilities before they happen.
- Withstand: This means designing systems that are able to resist potential attacks even when they are not detected initially. This may include designing intolerance for some level of damage, enabling automatic repair processes, deflecting attacks by sending them away from critical targets, and removing attacked system components while still allowing processes to continue despite them.
- Recovery: In the case of a security disruption or attack, this principle focuses on restoring operations. Techniques include rolling back to a pre-determined, working configuration, recreating critical functions by replication, or modifying existing system components to enable impacted areas. Detection can inform selecting a recovery technique, but systems may also initiate such techniques independently, unnoticed, to alter the attack surface and facilitate a quicker return to normal operations (Bartock et al., 2016).
- Adapt: This principle focuses on learning from experience and ongoing improvement. It proposes strategies like redefinition, which involves modifications to the needs, structure, design, setup, or operating procedures of the system in response to lessons learned from negative incidents, and correction, which involves the removal or addition of controls to neutralize known exposures or vulnerabilities.

The adapt principle is most significant because it requires constant learning and adaptation of systems to known weaknesses or changing situations. Machine learning-adaptive learning algorithms, in other words—can be of tremendous value in this context. Machine learning algorithms can adapt to new patterns of attacks, update security policies in real time, and change their defenses, anthropomorphizing the adapt principle at the technical level. Machine learning, and AFL, as such, go beyond being a detection tool; it is an enablement of the adapt principle in the context of cyber resilience, enabling the dynamic adaptation of defense systems.

9.2.3 Cyber resilience vs. cybersecurity: A broader perspective

Cyber resilience is a broader and more holistic model than traditional cybersecurity. While cybersecurity is primarily concerned with hardening and protecting cyber systems against potential threats, cyber resilience builds on this effort by including the critical principle that systems must be able to continue to operate and/or recover rapidly upon security breach or disruption. The key Strategic principles of cyber resilience are illustrated in Figure 9.3.

Differentiation is critical in guaranteeing the functionality of critical services. Cyber resilience ensures that critical services—such as the uninterrupted supply of electricity, water, data, goods, and financial transactions—are resilient even during crisis situations. A truly cyber-resilient network is intentionally designed to ensure that its most critical elements continue to function, even though they have been compromised by an attack or disruptions. The critical capabilities required for guaranteeing cyber resilience include advanced cyber

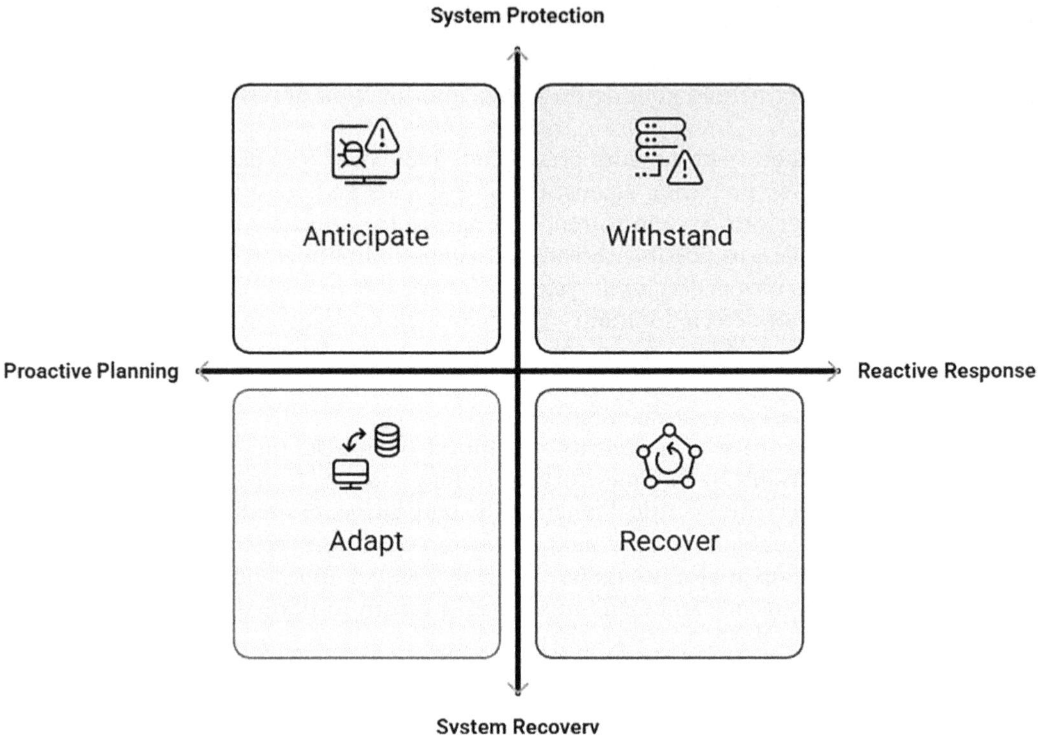

Figure 9.3 Strategic principles of cyber resilience.

analytics and situational awareness, robust system architecture, dependable automation for cyber systems, the ability to forecast the effect of cyber effects, and dynamic response mechanisms in real time.

The conceptual divide between cybersecurity and cyber resilience is a shift from a static defense strategy to one of ongoing operation. Cybersecurity is typically described as the establishment of a secure defensive perimeter, its primary aim being to be unassailable. Cyber resilience, however, recognizes the intrusiveness of security intrusion and works towards maintaining operational capability both during and post-attack. This mandates the development of systems with self-healing and self-adapting features, enabling them to dynamically reconfigure or reroute processes in an attempt to maintain critical services. The focus on real-time dynamic response and assured automation also lends credence to this perspective. Organizations must therefore invest in developing the capability to adapt responses and automated interventions, away from fixed security to more adaptive and intelligent defense mechanisms that enable continuous operation in the face of changing threats.

9.3 FL: MECHANISMS AND CHARACTERISTICS

9.3.1 Decentralized training and data privacy

FL refers to a decentralized machine learning procedure where models are trained on different devices or servers, and each one holds a local dataset, thereby precluding raw data collection centrally. Such structuring is particularly important in applications where privacy needs to be the central concern, and the data cannot be easily transferred with much convenience in terms of distances or organizational units for legal, ethical, or competitive reasons.

The most significant benefit of FL in the realm of cybersecurity is its inherent potential to augment data privacy without affecting the performance and accuracy of the model. By ensuring raw data is stored, FL significantly mitigates the risk of large-scale data breaches and facilitates adherence to stringent data protection regulations, including the General Data Protection Regulation (GDPR) and the Health Insurance Portability and Accountability Act (HIPAA). This technique is a direct countermeasure to the threats associated with data centralization. Traditional machine learning models rely heavily on centralized data repositories, which by nature constitute a single point of risk and are attractive, high-value targets for cyber-attacks. FLs decentralized nature directly addresses this vulnerability by disseminating both data and computational load, mitigating the honeypot effect of centralized data storage. This architectural approach is a thoughtful and intentional response to a serious cybersecurity risk. FL is therefore highly applicable in high-sensitivity applications in industries like healthcare, finance, or critical infrastructure, where legal or ethical limitations restrict data aggregation. It offers a privacy-by-design environment that actively mitigates threats of data leakage.

9.3.2 The FL process: From local training to global aggregation

The process of FL is an iterative client-server process consisting of a series of basic client-server communication, also known as FL rounds. A round is specifically designed for collaborative model enhancement with data-locality preservation:

1. Initialization: It begins with a preliminary choice and initialization of a machine learning model by a central server, which will serve as a global model.
2. Client Selection: In each subsequent round, some fraction of the potential local nodes (clients) is selected to participate in the process. It can be randomly selected or selected by more sophisticated criteria.
3. Configuration and Local Training: The chosen clients are given the global model state. The model is locally trained by the clients on their individual private local data. Local training is generally done by a stochastic learning algorithm, for example, stochastic gradient descent (SGD), on average.
4. Reporting and Model Update: Each of the chosen clients calculates and sends only its local model updates, that is, weights, biases, or gradients, to the central server for aggregation upon finishing their local training. Importantly, raw data never leave the client device.
5. Aggregation: The global server summarizes these model updates from all the clients that are taking part. It then combines these local models or updates received to create a new, enhanced global model. The element-wise weighted arithmetic mean is one of the most common aggregation strategies, used extensively in the FedAvg algorithm.
6. Termination: Iterations 2 to 5 are executed iteratively until a given termination condition is reached. This condition may be a maximum number of training iterations, reaching a satisfactory model accuracy level, or any other performance criteria.

The aggregation stage, in which local contributions are aggregated, is a vulnerable stage for model enhancement as well as for susceptibility to potential attacks. Though local data is not disclosed, malicious clients may insert altered data or tamper with their model updates at this stage, resulting in so-called poisoning attacks. The poisoning attacks can severely degrade the performance of the global model or inject nefarious backdoors. The integrity and strength of the aggregation process thus directly contribute to the overall robustness of the FL system. This necessitates that FL for cyber resilience research and development focus significantly on the design and deployment of robust and resilient aggregation methods to combat malicious inputs effectively and preserve the reliability and accuracy of the global model.

9.3.3 Types of FL (horizontal, vertical, transfer)

FL can be classically categorized into three broad categories, which are differentiated on the basis of the data distributional properties among the participating clients (Figure 9.4):

- Horizontal Federated Learning (HFL): Also known as sample-based FL, this type involves collaborative training of clients with the same feature space but different sample space in their datasets. Such a situation is common when clients share the same data structure (e.g., medical records with the same fields) but have different user bases or data instances (e.g., other hospitals).
- Vertical Federated Learning (VFL): Also known as feature-based FL, VFL centers on model construction from datasets that have a common sample space but distinct feature spaces. This happens when different organizations possess data on the same entities (for example, a bank and an e-commerce website possessing details on the same customers) but possess different features or attributes for the entities. An alignment process is normally employed to find common data samples among clients.
- Federated Transfer Learning: This method entails local fine-tuning of pre-trained models for unique tasks. It uses knowledge acquired from a generalized model, typically trained on a huge and heterogeneous dataset, and fine-tunes it with regard to the specific requirements and data patterns of individual clients.

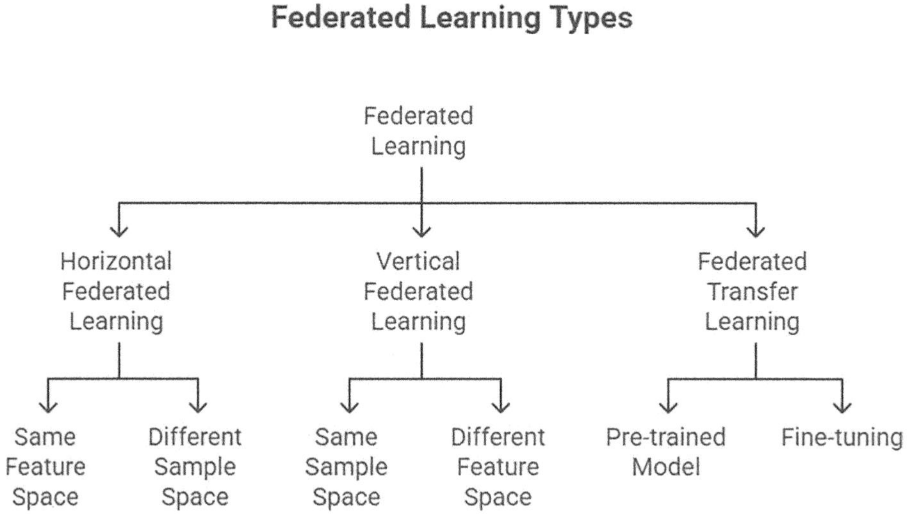

Figure 9.4 Federated learning types.

The different flavors of FL present different challenges in terms of data distribution, and the selection of flavors directly impacts the corresponding measures of resilience implemented. The case of HFL is pertinent in enabling collaborative threat detection among different organizations that may share common network logs but have different internal datasets. VFL, by contrast, is needed in merging heterogeneous security knowledge obtained from different departments of the same organization, for example, human resources, information technology, and finance, about the same users or assets. This means that efficient resilience measures require proper adaptation to the concrete FL structure and the concrete nature of the underlying data. Finally, this makes a one-size-fits-all cyber resilience measure in FL insufficient; solutions require good knowledge of the base data distribution, proper choice of the FL flavors, and the deployment of their respective adaptive approaches.

9.3.4 Inherent benefits and limitations of standard FL

Traditional FL offers a compelling model for decentralized machine learning with many significant advantages, particularly in situations where privacy is of the essence. However, its unique architecture also offers a series of challenges that must be overcome to achieve true cyber resiliency.

Advantages:

- Privacy Preservation: FL most notable strength lies in its capacity to retain raw data locally, addressing directly major privacy concerns and being able to accommodate rigorous regulatory frameworks.
- Lower Communication Costs: Through the transmission of merely compressed model updates and not cumbersome raw data, FL lowers communication overhead considerably, which proves effective for bandwidth-limited networks and big systems.
- Decentralized Training: FL allows for joint training of models without centralization of data, which naturally mitigates the risk of single points of failure and loads computation.
- Scalability: FL possesses the ability to scale very well to the vast number of participating devices varying from smartphones to IoT sensors and supports learning over vast, distributed datasets.

Restrictions:

- Communication Overhead (Residual): Despite the reduction in raw data transfer, model-update transmission remains communication overhead-intensive, especially in cases of multiple data transfers, frequent synchronizations, or low network reliability.
- Heterogeneity of Devices: Differences in computing capacities, network access, and power constraints among the participating clients can lead to stragglers (non-responding or slow devices), which can drastically affect training speed and fairness.
- Data Heterogeneity (Non-IID Data): Local datasets frequently exhibit significant variations in terms of quantity, quality, and diversity, characterized as a non-IID distribution. Such statistical heterogeneity may result in diminished performance, inadequate generalization of the global model, and prolonged convergence rates.
- Residual Privacy Issues: Even if raw data is not released, the model parameters being shared can similarly expose personal information via sophisticated inference or reconstruction attacks.

- Security Vulnerabilities: FL systems are exposed to special security threats like poisoning attacks (where attackers contaminate training data or manipulate model updates), backdoor attacks (where malicious actions are slipped in undetected), and Byzantine failures (where malicious actors disrupt global model convergence).
- Interpretability and Fairness: The decentralized aspect of FL can keep developers from seeing the entire training dataset, which can decrease the interpretability of the models choices. Furthermore, certain FL environments can enable bias against certain parties, such as against the devices supporting the most frequent kinds of models, and this can lead to fairness problems.

The inherent contradiction of decentralization is that it can create new vulnerabilities. Whereas FL has been shown to effectively solve the problem of data privacy in centralized systems, it brings forth a new range of problems of distributed systems. The decentralization process itself, as it enhances privacy, creates new potential attack surfaces (e.g., data poisoning and Byzantine failures) and operational challenges (e.g., heterogeneity and added communication overhead) that do not exist in conventional centralized methods. This is a vital trade-off that adaptive FL attempts to overcome. Therefore, the implementation of FL by itself does not necessarily constitute cyber resilience. It needs a deep understanding of its inherent limitations and the strategic utilization of adaptive mechanisms to deal with these new vulnerabilities so that the benefits of decentralized learning are more than the drawbacks.

9.4 ADAPTIVE FL FOR ENHANCING CYBER RESILIENCE

AFL is the dynamic adaptation of FL processes to achieve enhanced performance, efficiency, and adversarial robustness against a wide range of challenges, such as adversarial attacks and system/data heterogeneity. Mechanisms for adaptation are required to design genuinely cyber-resilient FL systems that can function in real-world complex environments.

9.4.1 Adaptive client selection strategies

Adaptive client selection is an essential process because it structures clients' participation in FL rounds according to different aspects influencing model performance, system constraints, as well as special attributes for each client. The approach can involve approximating utility metrics for all potential clients according to different considerations, for example, data quality and computational resources, and selecting the most beneficial and reliable clients for every training iteration systematically. The objective of this approach is to strike a balance between maximizing the overall model performance and maintaining diversity among involved clients.

The function of adaptive client selection towards augmenting cyber resilience is described by two main facets. By systematic client selection, the system realizes significant model accuracy gains, up to 7% as cited, as well as significant training time reductions, possibly up to 25%. This dimension facilitates global model convergence effectively and efficiently, even in heterogeneous data distribution settings. Besides this, systems implementing adaptive client selection typically possess strong fault tolerance schemes, for example, checkpointing, to enable effective recovery from client dropout and ensure continuity of the training process in real-world settings. When a client is lost or disconnects, the corresponding workload can be redistributed, or the saved state can be restored, thus ensuring continuity of the overall learning path. Crucially, while utility scores are used for client selection purposes, privacy protection is ensured by applying differential privacy to the model updates (gradients) instead of to the utility scores themselves, thus protecting sensitive client data during training while offering significant privacy assurances.

This strategic allocation of resources to resilience is a distinguishing feature. Random selection of clients creates inefficiencies and vulnerabilities, for example, taking in malicious or low-quality clients, or being saddled with stragglers that delay the process. Adaptive client selection makes this a strategic decision, optimizing for performance and resilience by preferring reliable and informative participants while handling resource constraints optimally. This directly enhances the withstand and recover themes of cyber resilience by offering efficient and reliable model updates. Thus, future FL deployments for cyber resilience must go beyond simple random sampling and form sophisticated adaptive client-selection algorithms capable of dynamically adapting to real-time network conditions, client reliability, and data utility.

9.4.2 Resilient and adaptive aggregation methods

Aggregation is a core process in the paradigm of FL, in which local updates provided by individual clients are combined to form an updated global model. Adaptive and robust aggregation methods play with the way these updates are assessed or selected and thus enhance the resilience of the global model to attacks launched by malicious or untrusted clients.

Several mechanisms exemplify this approach:

- AdaFed: This involves participants joining and exiting FL tasks and offering fault tolerance with little work on the aggregation programmer's end. AdaFed has exhibited very high efficiency with more than a 90% reduction in resource requirements and expenses with little effect on aggregation latency, as an adaptive and scalable architecture specifically for FL aggregation. It utilizes serverless or cloud functions to dynamically deploy aggregation processes, and elastically scale to handle.
- Resilient Estimation: This technique involves using an updated geometric mean aggregation of local model parameters. The method is designed to counteract the negative impacts with regard to imbalanced local model updates and thus improve global model convergence, robustness, and stability.
- Resilient Aggregation Methods: Techniques like Krum and Median-based aggregation are employed to filter out malicious or anomalous updates during the process of model aggregation, thereby making sure that only real and reliable updates are added to the global model. Yet it should be noted that these simple methods can turn out to be inadequate in the face of highly adaptive and sophisticated attackers.
- Weighted Aggregation: Weighted aggregation techniques are employed for systems like FedAV that are meant for collaborative driving automation. Weighted aggregation techniques assign larger weights to the inputs of vehicles with smaller training losses, hence assigning larger weights to more accurate and reliable local models while aggregating.

The contribution of adaptive aggregation methods to improving cyber resilience is invaluable. These methods are essential to attack prevention in the form of countering poisoning attacks and Byzantine failures by preventing or lessening the malicious contributions' impact, ensuring the integrity and correctness of the global model. Adaptive aggregation platforms like AdaFed also significantly enhance scalability and resource efficiency, enabling FL systems to accommodate an extensive number of heterogeneous participants without serving as performance bottlenecks. Through forecasting client participation dynamics (e.g., clients joining or leaving) and managing failures, these methods guarantee seamless operation of the aggregation process, directly facilitating the practices of withstand and recover in cyber resilience.

The establishment of these approaches illustrates a cyclical arms race over the strength of aggregation techniques. There is a strong tension in that, although powerful aggregation techniques such as Krum and Median exist, they tend to fail against adaptive attackers who can dynamically change their attack strategies. This suggests a perpetual arms race where defense mechanisms need to adapt continuously to counter more sophisticated and adaptive attacks. Thus, the requirement for adaptive aggregation transcends efficiency; it becomes a factor of survival against smart and adaptive attacks. Future research should emphasize the creation of aggregation mechanisms that are not only resilient but also naturally adaptive to the evolving strategies of attackers, potentially incorporating real-time anomaly detection and dynamic weighting through trust or behavioral analysis.

9.4.3 Adaptive regularization and optimization techniques

Adaptive optimization and regularization techniques are at the forefront of enhancing FL model stability, convergence, and robustness, particularly in adversarial-attack and data-heterogeneity environments (Fraboni et al., 2022).
Critical mechanisms are:

- Adaptive Regularization: This is done by adding a regularization term locally to the local objective function dynamically at the client-side training. The term limits local updates in an effort to remain closer to the original global model. This is especially effective in addressing the non-IID data challenges, prevalent in FL, and the global model convergence. The regularization coefficient can be adjusted dynamically upon observing the clients local and global performance diversification to achieve a more adaptive and efficient learning process.
- Adaptive Learning Rates (α-SGD): It enables all the clients to employ an individual step size adjusted to the local smoothness of the function to be optimized on the individual client's dataset. This technique in practice responds to the significantly heterogeneous nature of FL clients, as one, constant learning rate may fall short for many participants (Kim et al., 2023).
- Gradient Clipping: A lightweight privacy protection method, gradient clipping restricts the size of gradients during local training. The step prevents potential information leakage via gradient inference, reduces communication overheads, and preserves numerical stability, thus lowering the threat of model inversion attacks.
- MMPA Model for Tuning Parameters: The Modified Marine Predator Algorithm (MMPA) is an optimization algorithm specially designed to effectively tune the hyperparameters of ensemble models, such as the Gated Recurrent Unit (GRU), Temporal Convolutional Network (TCN), and Convolutional Autoencoder (CAE), for the use of cyber-attack detection systems (Luo et al., 2010). The algorithm's good global search capability is needed to identify the optimal configurations, thereby greatly improving the accuracy, stability, and efficiency of the detection system, particularly when dealing with complex, high-dimensional data.

- Adaptive Threshold Adjustment (ATMFF): In traffic forecasting tasks, ATMFF is used to adaptively adjust the decision threshold utilized for classification (Bohara, 2020). The adaptation is achieved using a confusion matrix rate-based screening-weighted ensemble of weak classifiers, which improves the accuracy in identifying adversarial instances and thus the reliability of the predictive model.

Adaptive regularization and optimization techniques are an essential driving force towards improved cyber resilience. These techniques enable higher convergence and stability in the global model, particularly when dealing with non-IID data, an inherent issue in FL. These developments directly contribute to the improvement of the withstand ability of cyber resilience by making the learning process more robust against changes in data distribution. Furthermore, techniques like gradient clipping and adaptive parameter tuning (e.g., MMPA) assist in enhancing the models resistance to adversarial interference, for example, poisoning and inference attacks, either by limiting malicious modifications or increasing the models ability to detect them. Moreover, lightweight mechanisms like gradient clipping also enable communication efficiency, thus making the deployment of FL on resource-constrained edge devices more viable (Chen et al., 2023).

The following adaptive techniques enable fine-grained control towards system-wide resilience. They go beyond mere far-reaching architectural changes, enabling targeted control at the individual client and model update levels. Through dynamic regulation of regularization terms, learning rates, and clipping thresholds, these techniques specifically target the internal dynamics of the learning process as being vulnerable to adversarial tampering or adversely affected by heterogeneity. Such micro-level controls are critical towards the establishment of macro-level cyber resilience. Efficient cyber resilience, therefore, not only necessitates resilient aggregation techniques but also the application of smart, adaptive optimization and regularization techniques at the local client level to ensure the quality and integrity of individual contributions as well as the aggregate model.

9.4.4 Mechanisms for fault tolerance and anomaly detection

Fault tolerance and anomaly detection mechanisms are crucial in constructing cyber-resilient FL systems to accommodate disruptions or malicious actions while keeping them operational and intact.
Chief mechanisms are:

- Anomaly Detection: This is the use of methods such as statistical analysis or machine learning to identify outliers in model updates or user activity. For instance, gradient distribution analysis can effectively identify updates whose deviation from the mean is extremely large, indicating the possibility of adversarial activity or system malfunction.
- Resilience in Modular FL Frameworks: In asynchronous FL methods, when a worker (client) pulls out its contribution midway through a training task, the task is automatically rescheduled to the next available worker based on the scheduling protocol, thereby ensuring that important computations get done eventually (Gupta et al., 2022). Synchronous methods, however, consider an epoch or global communication round to be done once a proportion (e.g., 50% of the chosen subpool) of workers are able to send their updates effectively. This ensures continued training despite the failure or disconnection of a minority of workers.

- Checkpointing: Robust mechanism through which clients checkpoint their model state in binary files at fixed intervals. In the event of failure, the system can recover the client state from the last checkpoint and resume training without the need to train from scratch. In the event of failure at aggregation, the global server can wait for recovery or offload the client's load to other active clients to continue training.
- Client Reputation Scoring: Combined with blockchain logging, this approach encourages accountability and enhances poisoning protection. The server first checks each client's contribution for poisoning or deviation from the predetermined learning process before it accepts any updates; the aggregation is merely on trusted updates submitted by weighted client reputation scores and consistency checks.

These mechanisms are at the heart of cyber resilience. They maintain operational continuity by ensuring that the FL learning process continues unabated even in the event of a client failure, disconnection, or presence of unreliable devices. This has a direct relation to the withstand and recover aspects of cyber resilience. Techniques for anomaly detection are important for attack detection and mitigation since they detect suspicious or malicious updates, enabling the system to eliminate the impact of poisoning attacks, adversarial manipulations, and Byzantine attacks. Detection and elimination of the impact of unreliable devices by these mechanisms are likely to enhance the reliability and trustworthiness of the FL process.

These processes not only render FL systems fault-tolerant but also proactive self-healing systems. Real-time anomaly detection enables real-time detection of anomalies, whether malicious or inadvertent, and fault tolerance processes enable automatic recovery or switching over to maintain operation. This brings FL close to the ideal notion of assured automation for cyber systems.Therefore, the creation of sophisticated real-time anomaly detection and automated fault recovery systems is of paramount significance in applying FL in high-risk, dynamic environments where unbroken operation is critical.

9.4.5 Integration of privacy-preserving technologies (differential privacy, homomorphic encryption, SMPC)

FL itself automatically offers privacy to some extent through localizing data in raw form, yet model update transmission remains vulnerable to possible privacy issues. In order to solve these current problems and further strengthen safeguards for shared updates and raw data, advanced privacy-protection technologies are integrated into FL frameworks.
These technologies involve:

- Differential Privacy (DP): This is a method that involves adding calibrated noise to model updates or gradients before aggregation. This mathematical approach provides formal guarantees that it remains statistically impossible to tell whether any individuals data was included in the training set or not. The amount of added noise is intentionally managed with a privacy parameter (epsilon, ε), where smaller values of epsilon provide stronger privacy guarantees, but potentially at the cost of some level of model accuracy.
- Homomorphic Encryption (HE): HE is a cryptographic method whereby computations can be performed directly over the encrypted data without their prior decryption. In FL, clients can encrypt their model updates before sending them to the server. The server sums up the encrypted updates, and only the final aggregated model is decrypted. This method keeps the updates of every client confidential in plaintext, even from the central server.

- Secure Multi-Party Computation (SMPC): SMPC allows several parties to jointly compute a function from their secret inputs without revealing the inputs to each other. In FL settings, SMPC is employed to securely aggregate model updates in a manner that no update is ever disclosed to single parties or to the central server at aggregation time.

The use of these privacy-enhancing technologies makes it a key building block of cyber resilience. The approaches significantly enhance privacy by protecting sensitive data from a range of attacks, including inference, reconstruction, and membership inference attacks, that are key FL vulnerabilities. Improved privacy stimulates trust among participants and establishes increased participation in collaborative learning activities. Further, by enabling continued operation of learning processes without raw data sharing, these approaches inherently enable data minimization principles, thereby reducing the overall attack surface. Their use also enables compliance with strict data protection regulations (e.g., GDPR, HIPAA), thereby making FL a feasible solution in highly sensitive applications.

In order for FL to be truly cyber resilient, and particularly in use scenarios where privacy is a requirement, these future-proof cryptographic and privacy-enhancing technologies are essential building blocks that need to be correctly combined and tuned to minimize performance trade-offs, e.g., between model accuracy and differential privacy noise, or computational expense.

9.4.6 Role of blockchain in securing FL

The explicit use of blockchain technology within FL systems has a strong potential to enhance their trustworthiness, transparency, and security (Table 9.2). This deployment is typically done through the use of blockchain logging to give an auditable and tamper-evident record of all model updates that are traded in the FL system. This produces an unalterable ledger record of all the transactions and model versions, hence giving a verifiable record of the learning process.

The importance of blockchain technology in supporting cyber resilience is considerable. It facilitates greater transparency and encourages participant trust by offering verifiable, tamper-evident logs of model exchange. The ability is particularly valuable in decentralized environments, in which the existence of a single, centrally trusted authority might be lacking or inappropriate. The inclusion of blockchain also ensures accountability and integrity. It defends against malicious tampering and fraudulent contribution, such as model poisoning, by verifying that all updates are audited. The method can be easily combined with mechanisms for scoring client reputation to encourage accountability and only utilize trusted contributions. The decentralized nature of blockchain by design reduces the risk of a single point of failure and therefore the overall resilience of the FL system.

Blockchain provides a decentralized trust model to decentralized learning. FL is decentralized, yet traditional FL relies on a central server for aggregation, which can become a de facto single point of failure or centralized point of trust in the process. Blockchain provides a decentralized trust model to this decentralized learning setting, and the system is more auditable and resilient. This is in directions of trustless solutions as a new research agenda, where one decreases dependency on centralized parties. Thus, the incorporation of blockchain can have a substantial positive impact on the integrity and trustworthiness of FL systems, especially in environments with multiple, perhaps untrusted, organizations or devices, thus enhancing their cyber resilience against internal and external attacks.

Table 9.2 Key adaptive mechanisms in federated learning for cyber resilience

Adaptive Mechanism	*Description*	*Contribution to Cyber Resilience*
Adaptive Client Selection	Dynamically adjusts client participation based on performance, system constraints, data quality, and computational capacity	Improves accuracy and efficiency, enhances fault tolerance (checkpointing), preserves privacy (with DP)
Resilient and Adaptive Aggregation	Dynamically adjusts how local model updates are weighed or selected (e.g., AdaFed, modified geometric mean, Krum, Median)	Mitigates poisoning/Byzantine attacks, improves scalability and resource utilization, ensures fault tolerance
Adaptive Regularization and Optimization	Dynamically adjusts regularization terms, learning rates (e.g., α-SGD), and gradient clipping thresholds	Improves convergence stability (non-IID data), enhances robustness against adversarial attacks, optimizes resource usage
Fault Tolerance and Anomaly Detection	Incorporates mechanisms like task reassignment, checkpointing, and statistical analysis of updates to detect and recover from failures or malicious behavior	Ensures operational continuity despite client failures/disconnections, detects and mitigates adversarial attacks
Privacy-Preserving Technologies	Integrates Differential Privacy (DP), Homomorphic Encryption (HE), and Secure Multi-Party Computation (SMPC) into the FL process	Enhances privacy guarantees, protects sensitive data from inference/reconstruction attacks, ensures regulatory compliance
Blockchain Integration	Uses blockchain for auditable and tamper-proof recording of model updates	Provides transparency, builds trust, ensures accountability, and enhances integrity against adversarial interference

9.5 PRACTICAL APPLICATIONS AND USE CASES

FL that is adaptive is becoming a state-of-the-art approach to enhancing cyber resilience across many important sectors by leveraging its privacy-protecting, decentralized, and adaptable nature in an effort to address complex security challenges.

9.5.1 Network anomaly and intrusion detection systems

In the context of network security, FL allows real-time monitoring and collaborative testing of network traffic and user behavior from a diverse range of sources without exposing underlying sensitive raw data. This adaptive mechanism allows for quick and accurate detection of anomalies and potential attacks that otherwise escape detection in partitioned systems. Adaptive client selection frameworks, for example, have been extended to applications in network anomaly detection. Such general-purpose frameworks dynamically adjust client participation while incorporating differential privacy and fault tolerance techniques, greatly enhancing detection accuracy while also reducing training time in parallel. This feature is especially crucial for anomaly detection in distributed and heterogeneous networks, e.g., those in Internet of Things (IoT) environments or complex automotive communication networks. Enhanced resilience is achieved through the development of proactive threat detection, drastic response time reduction, and enhanced accuracy in detecting aberrations characteristic of potential cyber threats, hence ultimately reducing the chances of successful cyberattacks.

9.5.2 Malware detection and classification in cooperation

AFL offers an excellent means of combating the constant danger of evolving malware. Multiple organizations can learn from various malware samples and share their experience without compromising data privacy. The shared experience enables the building of robust malware detectors that can evolve in real time, offering robust protection against changing cyber-attacks. Intrusion detection and malware classification are particular paradigms of FL that are normally employed with light methods that maintain the privacy of data, such as gradient clipping, differential privacy, and encrypted model aggregation. These approaches enable multiple clients to work together securely and effectively, even when dealing with highly sensitive malware data. The power of this approach lies in the capacity to maintain robust malware detection and ongoing updates that enable instant responses to new malware types and significantly prevent the spread of infections among connected systems.

9.5.3 Predictive analysis for proactive cyber defense

In addition to reactive detection, FL greatly improves predictive modeling from collective analysis of past data collected from varied sources. Aggregate intelligence affords the ability to forecast potential attack vectors and forthcoming threats. This proactive approach enables organizations to adjust their defense mechanisms and prevent cyber-attacks before they arise. To adapt to variations in computational power and network capabilities of different devices, which are common in large predictive maintenance systems, adaptive optimization algorithms are proposed. In addition, advanced techniques, such as reinforcement learning algorithms, can dynamically change security protocols in accordance with real-time network conditions and changing threats, thus outdoing static rule-based systems. This innovation converts cybersecurity from a reactive to a proactive system, enabling organizations to forecast and prevent threats before they arise, thus constructing the anticipate concept in the field of cyber resilience.

9.5.4 Resilient systems in critical infrastructures (e.g., IoT, smart cities, cooperative driving automation)

FL demonstrates tremendous potential in environments with limitations and dynamics, especially in mission-critical infrastructures, where traditional centralized learning approaches tend to struggle due to high latency and low bandwidth.

- Cooperative Driving Automation (CDA): FedAV is an example par excellence ofFL usage in simulating cyberattacks and anomaly detection in cooperative vehicle platooning systems. Its decentralized framework ensures each vehicle conducts autonomous learning, thus effectively defeating adversarial attacks, ensuring privacy of data, and reducing vehicular network communication overhead. The adaptive features are weighted aggregation methods that give greater weightage to lower training loss vehicles, thus selecting more precise local models for global updates.

- IoT and Smart Cities: FL has a significant role in improving security in smart city infrastructure by enabling local training of models on edge devices, thereby maintaining data privacy. Federated Adaptive Clustering (FedAC) algorithm, for instance, groups edge devices based on data similarity and computational resources available, maximizing local training while minimizing communication overhead. Its dynamic adaptation-based re-clustering ability allows the system to adapt to changing data distributions and available devices, maintaining high model performance and efficiency in dynamic urban environments.
- Underwater Drone Networks: A federated approach has been proposed that improves the resilience of zero-day attack detection in underwater drones with high data locality, thereby countering the unusual problems of high latency and low bandwidth (Table 9.3) in such networks.
- Smart Energy Grids and Financial Institutions: FL is used in financial institutions to train models on customer transaction information, and in energy grids for smart meter usage information, all with data confidentiality carefully under control.

FL enables distributed, mission-critical resilience. Critical infrastructures are inherently distributed, typically legacy systems with high uptime requirements. Centralized security for these systems is typically impractical or undesirable. FLs ability to decentralize learning, along with its privacy-preserving flavor and adaptive mechanisms, makes it well-suited

Table 9.3 Applications of adaptive federated learning in cyber resilience

Application Area	*Specific Use Case/ Example*	*Adaptive FL Contribution to Resilience*
Network Security	Anomaly and intrusion detection systems	Real-time, collaborative threat identification; adaptive client selection for efficiency and fault tolerance
Malware Defense	Malware detection and classification	Collective intelligence for robust, evolving malware classifiers without data sharing
Proactive Defense	Predictive analysis for cyber attacks	Collaborative analysis of historical data to anticipate attack vectors; dynamic policy adaptation
Critical Infrastructure	Cooperative Driving Automation (CDA)	Decentralized anomaly detection in vehicle platoons; adaptive aggregation for adversarial robustness
Critical Infrastructure	IoT and smart cities security	Adaptive clustering for efficient, privacy-preserving security; dynamic re-clustering for changing environments
Critical Infrastructure	Underwater drone networks	Improved zero-day threat detection with strict data locality
Financial Systems	Fraud detection and transaction monitoring	Collaborative training on sensitive financial data while preserving customer privacy
Energy Grids	Smart energy grid systems	Privacy-preserving model development for predictive energy management from smart meter data
Authentication	IoT device identification	Utilizing energy consumption patterns for adaptive, privacy-preserving authentication

to these environments. It transforms them into self-protecting, resilient networks rather than exposed, centralized targets. The Cooperative Driving Automation and Smart Cities examples graphically illustrate this shift from protecting individual devices to protecting a whole interdependent systems resilience. Adaptive FL is thus well-placed to become a cornerstone technology for the protection of the next generation of interconnected, mission-critical systems, spreading its influence from traditional IT security to operational technology (OT) and industrial control systems (ICS) environments.

9.6 CHALLENGES, LIMITATIONS, AND OPEN RESEARCH PROBLEMS

While it holds much promise to enhance cyber resilience, AFL poses many excellent challenges that are dynamic and critical research and development areas.

9.6.1 Handling variability in data and systems

The most dramatic challenge to FL is posed by the existence of statistical heterogeneity, or non-IID (non-independent and identically distributed) data. Local data of the client may have high variability owing to factors like geographical location, behavior of the user, usage patterns, or sensor settings. This variability may lead to drastic performance degradation, reduced global model generalization capabilities, and increased convergence times (Chen et al., 2024; Zheng et al., 2024). Various devices have varying capabilities, such as hardware strength, network quality, power supply, and storage. These variations can cause the stragglers problem, with devices taking longer to process or going offline occasionally. This can degrade the quality of training and render it unfair.

Nowadays, adaptive learning methods such as adaptive hierarchical learning, client clustering, and customized federated models assist in solving such issues. Adaptive client selection mechanisms and efficient resource allocation are utilized to solve system differences. The problem of developing more generalized and resilient adaptive methods that are effective at dealing with high degrees of differences without sacrificing much performance is one of the current challenges. Fairness between clients with significantly different data distributions and avoiding bias towards dominant patterns in the data is a primary and open issue.

The chronic problem of heterogeneity among participants is a main limitation of the expansion and success of operations. Most of the studies concentrate on these differences, demonstrating that they are not an outlier phenomenon but a ubiquitous issue that widely impacts the success, correctness, and actual deployment of FL at scale. If this issue is not adequately addressed, it can limit the advantages that FL can provide to enhance cyber resilience (Chen et al., 2024; Wang et al., 2023). Thus, studies must transcend theoretical demonstrations of success in idealized conditions and aim for practical solutions that perform well in very heterogeneous and real-world conditions.

9.6.2 Communication overhead and scalability issues

Although it is intended to minimize raw data transfer, FL also comes with a tremendous challenge in terms of communication overhead and scalability. Updating such models, particularly in communication between potentially millions of IoT devices, incurs communication costs and can be a massive source of latency. This is further exacerbated by the rate at which rounds of communication need to happen and by the challenge of synchronization in large-scale distributed settings.

Existing techniques to address these issues are techniques such as gradient clipping and parameter updates from Fisher information. These techniques serve to constrain the amount of updates transmitted, thereby reducing communication costs. Asynchronous updates are among the approaches that have been used to reduce latency by allowing clients to update the global model irrespective of other contributors preparedness. (Güler & Yener, 2021; Xu et al., 2020) Modular FL systems are also experimenting with various communication protocols, including Zenoh and MQTT, to optimize the efficiency of communication in various deployment scenarios. However, the yet-open challenge is how to achieve optimal communication efficiency with model accuracy and privacy preserved, particularly in large, dynamic environments that are plagued with intermittent connectivity.

The scalability issues and communication overhead reflect a multi-dimensional trilemma of scalability, efficiency, and privacy. With the evidence we have, it is a difficult optimization task to balance scalability, communication efficiency, and privacy at the same time. For instance, stronger privacy guarantees (such as those provided by more differential privacy noise) can impair model accuracy or require extra rounds of communication, and actually efficient communication protocols can have the side effect of compromising security. It is a difficult optimization task that requires an optimal trade-off between competing goals. Therefore, future work will have to revolve around designing new compression algorithms, smart scheduling strategies, and novel communication protocols that can efficiently balance such competing goals in order to enable truly scalable and secure FL systems.

9.6.3 Robustness against adaptive adversarial attacks (poisoning, byzantine, inference)

FL architectures, despite their privacy advantages, are susceptible to multiple sophisticated cyber-attacks, thus posing significant challenges in terms of their strength and overall cyber resilience. Some of these threats include:

- Poisoning Attacks: Attackers maliciously tamper with their training data or local model updates with the motive of lessening the global model's performance, adding biases, or embedding hidden backdoors.

Inference Attacks: Attackers utilize the updates of the shared model or the global model to make inferences on the sensitive information of some clients' private training data.

- Byzantine Failures: These include corrupted or malicious clients sending random or garbage updates, affecting the convergence of the global model and causing poor performance.
- Adaptive Adversaries: A highly consequential and novel threat concerns the lack of effective defense against attackers who adaptively alter their attack strategy; for example, drop out and then rejoin the system to continue their attacks. Existing base secure aggregation protocols, such as Krum and Trimmed Mean, have been proved ineffective in the context of such adaptive attacks.

Sophisticated defense techniques against such attacks are robust aggregation methods (e.g., Krum and median-based methods), gradient similarity-based anomaly detection methods, trust-based weighting models (e.g., FLTrust), and adaptive clipping methods (e.g., Adaptive Robust Clipping, ARC). Privacy-preserving techniques such as Differential Privacy (DP), Homomorphic Encryption (HE), and Secure Multi-Party Computation (SMPC) are also employed to counter the dangers of inference attacks (Abadi et al., 2016; Rajalaxmi & Natarajan, 2008). However, there is a major challenge in developing lightweight, scalable, and adaptive security protocols that can effectively counter sophisticated, dynamic, and stealthy adversarial attacks, especially those launched by adaptive adversaries. This is a significant obstacle to the mass use of FL in applications that require robust security.

The presence of adaptive adversaries necessitates that basic defense systems are not sufficient. FL systems will need to learn to anticipate and comprehend patterns of attacks and dynamically adjust their defense, as opposed to reacting to issues only after they have occurred. This follows the ideals of anticipate and adapt, which are fundamental components of being resilient against cyber-attacks (Aaron et al., 2024). Therefore, future research will need to employ sophisticated artificial intelligence techniques, such as reinforcement learning or game theory, to fine-tune the security configuration of FL. This will develop intelligent defense systems with a higher capability to outmaneuver adaptive adversaries and transcend basic reactive security.

9.6.4 Fairness, interpretability, and benchmarking complexities

In addition to performance and security, FL also presents challenges in terms of ethical concerns as well as usability.

- Equity: Optimization of the global model for every client can lead to suboptimality for users with specific or minority data distributions, and this poses serious fairness issues. It may produce an average-good, overall global model that performs poorly for some underrepresented client groups.
- Interpretability: The decentralized design of FL makes it challenging for developers to have access to the entire training dataset, which can reduce the interpretability of the models behavior considerably. Understanding why a model is producing specific predictions or decisions during debugging, building confidence, or ensuring regulatory compliance is vital, but it is challenging when raw data is distributed and personal.
- Benchmarking Complexities: There is no standardized benchmarking framework for evaluating FL algorithms yet. FL evaluation does not entail merely considering individual dimensions like in classic centralized machine learning but entails considering multiple dimensions simultaneously, including communication cost, training time, convergence rate, model accuracy, client fairness, and privacy guarantees. Such multidimensional evaluation makes direct comparisons between FL methods challenging and slows progress.

Existing solutions to tackle fairness and personalization involve localized fine-tuning, model interpolation, or multi-task learning in personalized FL settings. Activities such as LEAF and OARF are gaining pace to overcome the shortcomings of standardized benchmarking. Open problems are to develop fair and resilient means to impose fairness among highly diverse clients while preserving performance and privacy. Development of FL models with better interpretability without losing the inherent data privacy is a key area. Additionally, developing broadly accepted benchmarking standards is essential to enable comparative studies, speed up innovation, and enable safe real-world deployment of FL systems.

These difficulties then go beyond solely technical performance requirements to include ethical concerns and deployment practicalities. In order for FL to be widely accepted, particularly in high-stakes applications, it not only needs to be adequately technical but also transparent, fair, and verifiable. This requires interdisciplinarity with ethicists, lawyers, and system designers, alongside machine learning scientists, to tackle these intricate socio-technical problems and develop genuinely trustworthy FL systems.

9.7 FUTURE TRENDS AND EMERGING DIRECTIONS

The area of AFL in the context of cyber resilience is evolving at a breakneck pace, delineating various potential avenues of future research and development directed at surpassing existing limitations and revealing new functionalities.

9.7.1 Synergies with next-generation networks (e.g., 6G)

One of the major trends is the enhancement of FL for future networks, i.e., 6G, on the basis of intelligent resource scheduling, semantic communication, and intelligent edge-cloud coordination. The expected features of 6G networks are ultra-low latency, artificial intelligence-based network management, and greatly improved resilience. The new features of 6G are expected to enable a more resilient and more flexible platform for FL, thereby enabling better communication, real-time adaptation, and enhanced security for decentralized AI applications on CyberEdge networks. This relationship will be critical for FL-based cyber resilience techniques to be scaled to very large-scale IoT deployments and other highly interconnected systems.

This convergence means a more network-aware FL, where the learning process itself is optimally tailored to the prevailing network conditions, not merely imposed upon the infrastructure that exists. This may enable the creation of inherently self-optimizing systems that constantly respond to network conditions, mobility patterns, and changing security requirements. Future FL architectures will hence be co-designed with network protocols, leading to inherently more resilient and efficient systems from the outset.

9.7.2 Large language model (LLM) potential for resilient FL

Large Language Model (LLM) utilization in FL is an important trend, allowing for collaboration across multiple domains and silos under strong FL. LLMs create new opportunities for decentralized and privacy-conscious training on edge devices, particularly when integrated with model compression algorithms, tailored FL methods, and secure communication protocols.

The use of LLMs has the potential to transform threat intelligence sharing and natural language-based anomaly detection in FL environments. This would enable multiple organizations to collectively create advanced threat models from unstructured data sources, like text security reports or system logs, without revealing the raw, sensitive data itself. This would enable more advanced and adaptive threat responses beyond mere numerical pattern detection. Current FL is numerically biased. The integration of LLMs introduces semantic comprehension to the distributed learning. This would imply that FL systems would not only be capable of detecting numerical anomalies, but also analyze the intent and context of cyber threats from unstructured data, enabling more intelligent and adaptive defense. Thus, federated LLM research for cybersecurity has the potential to liberate new capabilities for understanding advanced attack stories and crafting more human-like, adaptive defense strategies.

9.7.3 Quantum-resistant cryptography and trustless architectures

As a preparation for future possible adversaries with quantum computing capabilities, one of the key trends is the exploration of integrating quantum-resilient techniques into FL designs. This upcoming move is a try at offering long-term confidentiality and integrity of FL systems against future possible attacks. There is an effort to develop trustless solutions that are decentralized and do not trust central authorities, thereby making FL systems more fault-tolerant and robust overall.

As quantum computing technology advances, existing methods of protecting information can be vulnerable and easily compromised. Quantum-resistant cryptography is a method that promises to render FL systems long-term secure and private against such an attack, making them more cyber-attack resilient (Peters et al., 2023). Trustless architectures potentially involving new forms of blockchain or other decentralized ledger technologies will also assist in reducing single points of trust and failure, distributing control, and making systems more cyber-resilient. The new approach uses the word anticipate in cyber resilience in looking ahead to problems that are not yet fully realized but are likely to occur. It is the creation of future-proof security protocols in FL. Therefore, quantum-resistant investment in FL is required early on to prevent an impending quantum-apocalypse for secure decentralized systems.

9.7.4 Towards interoperable and self-optimizing resilient FL systems

Future research paths are toward developing interoperable learning frameworks that allow easy cross-domain collaboration and preserve data privacy and regulatory compliance with great importance. This also includes the development of network-aware FL and federated reinforcement learning. These technologies will make it possible for self-optimizing systems to adapt in real time to changing network conditions, mobility patterns, and shifting security requirements.

These new concepts will result in highly independent and flexible FL systems that can adapt themselves, learn from the environment, and enhance their performance and security in real time. That is what we are looking for in cyber resilience, where systems can automatically anticipate, resist, rebound from, and adjust to attacks. The key objective of cyber resilience is to continue operating without interruption, preferably requiring little or no assistance from humans. Self-healing FL systems, driven by reinforcement learning and network awareness, achieve this autonomous ideal, wherein the system can adapt its defenses and operations as required. This implies that the future of cyber resilience will increasingly depend on smart, autonomous FL agents that can learn, adapt, and defend against threats in a decentralized and self-organizing world.

9.8 CONCLUSION

Employing AFL is a significant step towards having complete protection against cyber-attacks. It maintains data privacy through decentralized training and employs sophisticated techniques such as smart client selection, robust aggregation, adaptive optimization, and robust fault tolerance. Due to this, FL systems are becoming increasingly capable of predicting, resisting, recovering from, and adapting to evolving cyber threats. From enhancing network anomaly detection and group-based malware classification to protecting critical infrastructures such as cooperative driving automation and smart cities, AFL offers a promising paradigm for building resilient and trustworthy digital ecosystems.

In the face of obvious challenges, such as system and data heterogeneity, communication overhead, and the continuous threat posed by adaptive attackers, ongoing research into cooperations with future networks (e.g., 6G), paradigm-shattering potential of large language models, and visionary quantum-resistant cryptography design will likely further entrench FLs role as a pillar technology for forthcoming cyber-resilient systems. The path to truly autonomous and self-tuning resilient FL systems is already well set and stands poised to redefine the boundaries of cybersecurity in an increasingly interconnected and hostile world.

REFERENCES

Aaron, W. C., Irekponor, O., Aleke, N. T., Yeboah, L., & Joseph, J. (2024). Machine Learning Techniques for Enhancing Security in Financial Technology Systems. *International Journal of Science and Research Archive*, 13(1), 2805. https://doi.org/10.30574/ijsra.2024.13.1.1965

Abadi, M., Chu, A., Goodfellow, I., McMahan, H. B., Mironov, I., Talwar, K., & Zhang, L. (2016). Deep Learning with Differential Privacy. In *Proceedings of the 2022 ACM SIGSAC Conference on Computer and Communications Security*. https://doi.org/10.1145/2976749.2978318

Akhtarshenas, A., Vahedifar, M. A., Ayoobi, N., Maham, B., Alizadeh, T., Ebrahimi, S., & López-Pérez, D. (2024). Federated Learning: A Cutting-Edge Survey of the Latest Advancements and Applications. *Computer Communications*, 228, 107964. https://doi.org/10.1016/j.comcom.2024.107964

Bartock, M., Cichonski, J., Souppaya, M., Smith, M., Witte, G., & Scarfone, K. (2016). Guide for Cybersecurity Event Recovery. https://doi.org/10.6028/nist.sp.800-184

Björck, F., Henkel, M., Stirna, J., & Zdravković, J. (2015). Cyber Resilience – Fundamentals for a Definition. In *Advances in intelligent systems and computing* (p. 311). Springer Nature. https://doi.org/10.1007/978-3-319-16486-1_31

Bodeau, D. (2019). Cyber Resiliency Overview. *ACM SIGAda Ada Letters*, 38(2), 58. https://doi.org/10.1145/3375408.3375412

Bohara, B. (2020). Adaptive Threshold for Online Object Recognition and Re-identification Tasks. arXiv (Cornell University). https://doi.org/10.48550/arxiv.2012.14305

Boyens, J. M. (2020). Key Practices in Cyber Supply Chain Risk Management: Observations from Industry. https://doi.org/10.6028/nist.ir.8276-draft

Chen, C., Liao, T., Deng, X., Wu, Z., Huang, S., & Zheng, Z. (2024). Advances in Robust Federated Learning: Heterogeneity Considerations. arXiv (Cornell University). https://doi.org/10.48550/arXiv.2405.09839

Chen, H., Wang, H., Jin, D., & Li, Y. (2023). Advancements in Federated Learning: Models, Methods, and Privacy. arXiv (Cornell University). https://doi.org/10.48550/arXiv.2302.11466

Dini, P., Elhanashi, A., Begni, A., Saponara, S., Zheng, Q., & Gasmi, K. (2023). Overview on Intrusion Detection Systems Design Exploiting Machine Learning for Networking Cybersecurity. *Applied Sciences*, 13(13), 7507. https://doi.org/10.3390/app13137507

Fraboni, Y., Vidal, R., Kameni, L., & Lorenzi, M. (2022). A General Theory for Federated Optimization with Asynchronous and Heterogeneous Clients Updates. arXiv (Cornell University). https://doi.org/10.48550/arXiv.2206.10189

Freire, F. F., & Padilla, V. S. (2019). A Contingency Plan Framework for Cyber-Attacks. *Journal of Information Systems Engineering & Management*, 4(2). https://www.jisem-journal.com/download/a-contingency-plan-framework-for-cyber-attacks-5898.pdf

Gold, S. (2011). The Future of the Firewall. *Network Security*, 2011(2), 13. https://doi.org/10.1016/s1353-4858(11)70015-0

Güler, B., & Yener, A. (2021). Sustainable Federated Learning. arXiv (Cornell University). https://doi.org/10.48550/arXiv.2102.11274

Gupta, M., Goyal, P., Verma, R., Shorey, R., & Saran, H. (2022). FedFM: Towards a Robust Federated Learning Approach For Fault Mitigation at the Edge Nodes. 362. https://doi.org/10.1109/comsnets53615.2022.9668376

Kaissis, G., Makowski, M. R., Rückert, D., & Braren, R. (2020). Secure, Privacy-Preserving and Federated Machine Learning in Medical Imaging. *Nature Machine Intelligence*, 2(6), 305. https://doi.org/10.1038/s42256-020-0186-1

Kim, J. L., Toghani, M. T., Uribe, C. A., & Kyrillidis, A. (2023). Adaptive Federated Learning with Auto-Tuned Clients. arXiv (Cornell University). https://doi.org/10.48550/arXiv.2306.11201

Konečný, J., McMahan, H. B., & Ramage, D. (2015). Federated Optimization: Distributed Optimization Beyond the Datacenter. arXiv (Cornell University). https://doi.org/10.48550/arXiv.1511.03575

Konečný, J., McMahan, H. B., Ramage, D., & Richtárik, P. (2016). Federated Optimization: Distributed Machine Learning for On-Device Intelligence. arXiv (Cornell University). https://doi.org/10.48550/arXiv.1610.02527

Li, T., Sahu, A. K., Talwalkar, A., & Smith, V. (2020). Federated Learning: Challenges, Methods, and Future Directions. *IEEE Signal Processing Magazine*, 37(3), 50. https://doi.org/10.1109/msp.2020.2975749

Luo, Y., Szidarovszky, F., Al-Nashif, Y., & Hariri, S. (2010). Game Theory Based Network Security. *Journal of Information Security*, 1(1), 41. https://doi.org/10.4236/jis.2010.11005

Müller, N., Bao, K., Matthes, J., & Heussen, K. (2023). CyPhERS: A Cyber-Physical Event Reasoning System Providing Real-Time Situational Awareness for Attack and Fault Response. *Computers in Industry*, 151, 103982. https://doi.org/10.1016/j.compind.2023.103982

Neto, N. N., Madnick, S., Paula, A. M. G. de, & Borges, N. M. (2020). A Case Study of the Capital One Data Breach. *SSRN Electronic Journal*. https://doi.org/10.2139/ssrn.3542567

Parisi, G. I., & Kanan, C. (2019). Rethinking Continual Learning for Autonomous Agents and Robots. arXiv (Cornell University). https://doi.org/10.48550/arXiv.1907.01929

Pasquini, D., Raynal, M., & Troncoso, C. (2022). On the (In)security of Peer-to-Peer Decentralized Machine Learning. arXiv (Cornell University). https://doi.org/10.48550/arxiv.2205.08443

Pati, S., Kumar, S., Varma, A., Edwards, B., Lu, C., Qu, L., Wang, J. J., Lakshminarayanan, A., Wang, S., Sheller, M., Chang, K., Singh, P., Rubin, D. L., Kalpathy-Cramer, J., & Bakas, S. (2024). Privacy Preservation for Federated Learning in Health Care [Review of Privacy Preservation for Federated Learning in Health Care]. *Patterns*, 5(7), 100974. https://doi.org/10.1016/j.patter.2024.100974

Peters, N. A., Alshowkan, M., Chapman, J. C., Pooser, R. C., Rao, N. S. V., & Newell, R. (2023). Long-Term Cybersecurity Applications Enabled by Quantum Networks. arXiv (Cornell University). https://doi.org/10.48550/arXiv.2304.14479

Rajalaxmi, R. R., & Natarajan, A. M. (2008). An Effective Data Transformation Approach for Privacy Preserving Clustering. *Journal of Computer Science*, 4(4), 320. https://doi.org/10.3844/jcssp.2008.320.326

Rangapur, A., Kanakam, T., & Jubilson, A. (2022). DDoSDet: An Approach to Detect DDoS Attacks Using Neural Networks. arXiv (Cornell University). https://doi.org/10.48550/arXiv.2201.09514

Ross, R. (2021). Developing Cyber-Resilient Systems. https://nvlpubs.nist.gov/nistpubs/SpecialPublications/NIST.SP.800-160v2r1.pdf

Ross, R., Pillitteri, V., Graubart, R., Bodeau, D., & McQuaid, R. (2021). Developing Cyber-Resilient Systems. https://doi.org/10.6028/nist.sp.800-160v2r1

Sheller, M., Edwards, B., Reina, G. A., Martin, J., Pati, S., Kotrotsou, A., Milchenko, M., Xu, W., Marcus, D. C., Colen, R. R., & Bakas, S. (2020). Federated Learning in Medicine: Facilitating Multi-Institutional Collaborations Without Sharing Patient Data. *Scientific Reports*, 10(1). https://doi.org/10.1038/s41598-020-69250-1

Stastny, P., & Stoica, A. (2022). Protecting Aviation Safety Against Cybersecurity Threats. *IOP Conference Series Materials Science and Engineering*, 1226(1), 12025. https://doi.org/10.1088/1757-899x/1226/1/012025

Trump, B. D., Mitoulis, S. A., Argyroudis, S., Kiker, G. A., Palma-Oliveira, J. M., Horton, R. A., Pescaroli, G., Pinigina, E., Trump, J., & Linkov, I. (2025). Threat-Agnostic Resilience: Framing and Applications. *International Journal of Disaster Risk Reduction*, 124, 105535. https://doi.org/10.1016/j.ijdrr.2025.105535

Wang, J., Xu, Z., Garrett, Z., Charles, Z., Liu, L., & Joshi, G. (2021). Local Adaptivity in Federated Learning: Convergence and Consistency. arXiv (Cornell University). https://doi.org/10.48550/arxiv.2106.02305

Wang, T., Du, Y., Gong, Y., Choo, K. R., & Guo, Y. (2023). Applications of Federated Learning in Mobile Health: Scoping Review. *Journal of Medical Internet Research*, 25. https://doi.org/10.2196/43006

Xu, J., Glicksberg, B. S., Su, C., Walker, P., Bian, J., & Wang, F. (2020). Federated Learning for Healthcare Informatics. *Journal of Healthcare Informatics Research*, 5(1), 1. https://doi.org/10.1007/s41666-020-00082-4

Zheng, S., Yuan, W., Wang, X., & Duan, L. (2024). Adaptive Federated Learning via New Entropy Approach. *IEEE Transactions on Mobile Computing*, 23(12), 11920. https://doi.org/10.1109/tmc.2024.3402080

Chapter 10

Quantum threats and federated AI

Shyam R., Swetha C. V., and Jesupriya J.

10.1 INTRODUCTION

10.1.1 Federated learning (FL) in finance: The overview

FL is a nascent ML paradigm. FL facilitates collaboration between various financial institutions in model training and preserving confidentiality of raw data [1, 2, 3]. Each institution can preserve the integrity of data by processing locally and transmitting updates in relation to the model. Such capability is especially needed within the finance sector because of an imperative to keep sensitive data protected [4, 5]. FL facilitates organizations to share without violating stringent privacy regulations. For instance, banks can share to develop fraud detection models based on data included in a large variety of datasets without accessing customers' personal data. Such collaboration not only makes prediction models more efficient but allows new financial service concepts through sharing of knowledge [6, 7].

10.1.2 The importance of privacy and security

In the banking sector, data privacy and security integrity cannot be overstated. Banks deal with highly sensitive information, such as client information, transaction history, and proprietary market information. Decentralized FL architecture circumvents some of the privacy issues by retaining raw data in-house at each institution. Nevertheless, the architecture design of such a system exposes it to exploits. Hackers can try to retrieve original data from standard model updates or inject malicious data to destroy model integrity [8]. Consequently, the use of robust security measures such as differential privacy, HE technique and secured multi-party computation becomes inevitable. These strategies attempt to circumvent data leakage and unauthorized access and ensure collaborative benefits of FL are not at the expense of privacy and security.

10.1.3 Why quantum threat analysis?

A significant advancement in computing capability is the introduction of quantum computing and with it comes opportunity and danger for most sectors, including the financial industry. Quantum computing is promising a lot, but also poses danger to existing security

DOI: 10.1201/9781003660330-10

measures protecting data in FL systems. Shor's and Grover's algorithms can potentially break into data that is encrypted using conventional encryption techniques, rendering existing security measures ineffective. Having seen this impending danger, organizations such as Europol have urged the financial industry to prepare against the dangers of quantum computing. The Quantum Safe Financial Forum, a coalition of central bank and large financial institution members, emphasizes the need to identify weak encryption standards and switch to alternatives that are quantum-resistant. This is a proactive measure to make FL systems resistant to new technology and new cyber threats.

10.2 BACKGROUND STUDIES

10.2.1 Principles of FL

Decentralized ML system called FL allows user, such as financial institutions to be jointly trained without sharing their sensitive data to create a global model. Any local client retains local data to itself and sends only model updates, i.e., gradients, to a global server, and the global model is updated from the local data aggregated. It is especially beneficial to the financial sector, where data privacy protection and compliance with regulations are relevant, as it enables institutions to jointly learn without disclosing data [9].

10.2.2 Modern cryptographic techniques used in FL

Various cryptographic methods are used to provide security and preserve privacy of information in FL:

- **SMPC:** Without revealing the input of multiple parties the SMPC helps multiple users to compute functions jointly over a computer Note: SMPC – Secure Multi-Party Computation.
- **HE:** Once the data is encrypted, computations can be performed by applyingHE. Upon decryption data will be obtained as the result of operations performed on the original plain text.
- **Differential Privacy:** Adds statistical noise to data or alters model parameters to avoid identification of individual data points.

These techniques together enhance overall security and privacy of FL systems by safeguarding data during training and aggregation procedures.

10.2.3 Fundamental principles of quantum computing

Information manipulation using the concept of quantum physics is made possible by quantum computing, which is not possible with the transitional computers. The quantum computation bit equivalent is the qubit, which, unlike a classical bit to store a 0 or a 1, can be in a superposition of both at the same time. Qubits also possess the ability to exhibit entanglement, where the state of one qubit is inextricably connected with the other regardless of distance. In some situations, these features allow quantum computers to outperform traditional computers in complex computations. Security related quantum algorithms [10], [23].

10.2.3.1 Case study: Leveraging quantum principles for cryptographic challenges

10.2.3.1.1 Background

As data volumes grow and security threats become more sophisticated, the limitations of classical computing in solving certain complex problems become apparent. Quantum computing, grounded in the fundamental principles of superposition and entanglement, offers a paradigm shift in computation with significant implications for both cryptanalysis and cryptographic design.

10.2.3.1.2 Quantum fundamentals in action

- Superposition: A bit in classic computer candy in either 0 or 1format. A qubit exist in a superposition of states in quantum computing, which enables a quantum processor to represent and evaluate several state at once. For some algorithm to achieve quantum speedups this parallelism is essential [23].
- Entanglement: Regardless of their physical separation qubits may exchange state thanks to the quantum entanglement which enables one state two immediately affect another. There is a more intricate link data manipulations made possible by this feature, which is essential for quantum information protocols like teleportation and Quantum Key distribution [23].

10.2.3.1.3 Real-world application: Cryptographic breakthroughs via quantum algorithms

- Shor's method: This method uses entanglement and super positioning to factor big number tenfold quicker than traditional algorithms. A quantum computer could potentially factor a 2048-bit integer in minutes, whereas a conventional computer may take years to do so. RSA and other public key systems are at risk because of this [23].
- Grover's Algorithms: This algorithm shows a quadratic speedup for brute force key searches and other unstructured database searches. Although it is less by lengthening the key example AES256. This has a direct effect on symmetric encryption methods like AES.

10.2.3.1.4 Implications in cybersecurity strategy

A major financial services firm conducted internal tests simulating future quantum capabilities by using emulated quantum circuits to assess their cryptographic infrastructure. They discovered that over 90% of their encryption mechanisms relied on RSA or ECC-based protocols—both vulnerable to quantum attacks. The organization began migrating to hybrid models combining classical and post-quantum algorithms, while also investing in quantum education for security personnel to better understand the computational principles and emerging threats.

Two quantum algorithms pose significant implications for cryptographic security:

10.2.4 Shor's Algorithm: was in 1994, Peter Shor created the Shor's algorithm, which effectively factors big number and calculate discreet logarithms. Public key cryptosystem like RSA which depends on difficulty of factorization, are often employed but the security of source technique is threatened by its ability factor integers in polynomial time [11]

Algorithm 1: ShorFactorization(N)
Input: Integer N to be factorized
Output: Non-trivial factors (p, q) of N

1: Choose a random integer a, where 1 < a < N
2: If gcd(a, N) ≠ 1, then return gcd(a, N) as a factor
3: Use Quantum Order Finding to compute r = order(a mod N)
4: If r is odd OR a^(r/2) ≡ -1 (mod N), repeat from step 1
5: Compute p = gcd(a^(r/2) - 1, N)
6: Compute q = gcd(a^(r/2) + 1, N)
7: If p and q are non-trivial factors of N, return (p, q)
8: Else, repeat the process [24]

Subroutine: $\boldsymbol{Quantum\ Period\ Finding}(\boldsymbol{a}, \boldsymbol{N})$
(Abstracted - performs the core quantum computation)
Input: a, N where $gcd(a,\ N) = 1$.
Output: Period r of $f(x) = a^x\ modN$, or NULL on failure.
Determine n such that $\boldsymbol{N^2 < 2 = Q < 2N^2}$.
Initialize state: $|\grave{\boldsymbol{E}}_o\rangle \leftarrow (1/\sqrt{\boldsymbol{Q}})\,\boldsymbol{£} < 0x < \boldsymbol{Q}|\boldsymbol{x}\rangle|\boldsymbol{0}\rangle$.
Apply modular exponentiation

$$\boldsymbol{U\_f} : |\psi_1\rangle \leftarrow U\_f|\psi_0\rangle = (1/\sqrt{\boldsymbol{Q}})\,\boldsymbol{£} < \boldsymbol{0x} < \boldsymbol{Q}|\boldsymbol{x}\rangle|\boldsymbol{a^x\ modN}\rangle.$$

Measure the second register (result $\boldsymbol{k}$). State collapses for the first register.

Apply QFT to the first register: $|\psi_2\rangle \leftarrow \boldsymbol{QFT}|\psi_1\boldsymbol{\_collapsed}\rangle$.

Measure the first register and obtain outcome y.
Use Continued Fractions Algorithm on $\boldsymbol{y / Q}$ to find the best estimate $\boldsymbol{c' / r'}$.
Verify candidate r': Check if $\boldsymbol{a}\,^\wedge(\boldsymbol{r'}) \equiv 1(\boldsymbol{mod\ N})$.
IF verification succeeds THEN RETURN r' ELSE RETURN NULL.

10.2.4.1 Explanation of key equations/logic

Period Finding Goal: Find smallest $\boldsymbol{r}>0$ such that $\boldsymbol{a}^r \equiv 1(\boldsymbol{mod\ N})$.

Factoring Logic (Step 2e):
If r is even and $\boldsymbol{a}\,^\wedge(\boldsymbol{r}/2)\langle binary\,data, 1bytes\rangle\langle binary\,data, 1bytes\rangle - 1(mod\,N)$, then:

$$a^r - 1 \equiv 0(\text{mod}\,N)$$

$$(\boldsymbol{a}\,^\wedge(\boldsymbol{r}/2) - 1)(\boldsymbol{a}\,^\wedge(\boldsymbol{r}/2) + 1) \equiv 0(\boldsymbol{mod\ N})$$

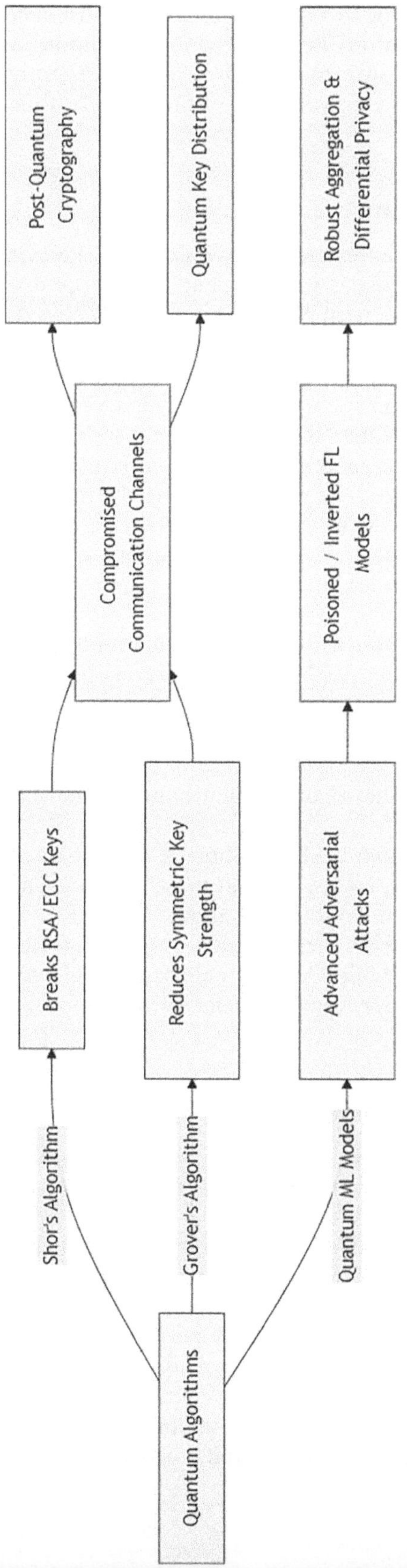

Figure 10.1 Shor's algorithm.

Since neither term is $0(\boldsymbol{mod}\ N)$, $\boldsymbol{GCD}(\boldsymbol{a}^{\wedge}(\boldsymbol{r}/2)\pm1,\boldsymbol{N})$ must yield non-trivial factors of N.

Quantum Core: The Quantum Period Finding subroutine uses quantum parallelism and the Quantum Fourier Transform (QFT) to find r efficiently, which is the classically hard part. Figure 10.1 shows the workflow of Shor's algorithm used for quantum-based integer factorization.

10.2.5 Grover's algorithm

Inventor and Year: As per the statement, it was invented by Lov Grover at Bell Labs in 1996.

Purpose: The primary purpose is to solve the "unstructured search problem." Suppose one has a large list or database with N entries, and one wishes to locate a specific item (or perhaps a small number of specific items) that satisfies some given criterion. Importantly, the database is "unstructured" in the sense that there is no helpful organization or indexing scheme (e.g., alphabetical ordering in a telephone directory). Any prior knowledge about the likely location of the target item is zero.

Classical Method: Within the context of a basic computer, the only certain way of locating a target item on an unstructured list is by inspecting the individual items individually one by one until the intended item is found. In the worst-case scenario, one will have to look through all the N items. Normally, it is expected that one will search about N/2 items. This provides time complexity of order N, since the time required increases linearly with the size of the database [13].

Quantum Method: Grover's algorithm employs quantum mechanics principles (superposition and interference/amplitude amplification) to accomplish this search in much less time.

Quadratic Speedup: O(N) to O(√N)

The Speedup: Grover's algorithm does not make the search instantaneous, nor does it give an exponential speedup like Shor's algorithm does for factoring. It gives a quadratic speedup. This implies that rather than taking around N steps, it takes around √N (square root of N) steps.

The implications are shocking: In the example of a database with 1 million (1,000,000) entries, a traditional computer would make at most 1 million checks. But a quantum computer using Grover's algorithm would make about √1,000,000 = 1,000 calls (oracle calls). In the example of a database with 1 trillion entries (10^12), traditional computation would take at most 10^12 checks, while Grover's approach would take about √10^12 = 10^6 (1 million) operations. The improvement in efficiency gets more and more dramatic as the variable N gets larger.

10.2.6 How it works (Conceptual)

Superposition: It starts by placing a quantum state in a configuration that represents a superposition of every possible element of the database at the same time, with each element having an equal probability amplitude.

Oracle: A quantum "oracle" or "black box" operation is specified. Such an oracle can differentiate the target item(s). When applied, it properly "marks" the target item(s) by changing the sign (phase) of their probability amplitude, but leaving others unaffected [13].

Amplitude Amplification is the core iterative operation in the algorithm. After the oracle marks the target(s), another operation, often called the "Grover diffusion operator," is performed. This operation cleverly increases the amplitude and, as a result, the probability of measurement of the found item(s), while simultaneously reducing the amplitudes of the unmarked items. It successfully flips all amplitudes with respect to the average amplitude [14].

Iteration: The use of the Oracle and the Diffusion operator is done approximately O(√N) times. With each iteration, the possibility of the target object being found increases.

Measurement: Once the optimal number of iterations is attained, the quantum state is measured. Because of the process of amplification, there is a highly likely chance that the result of measurement will be the target item being sought. Implications for Symmetric Key Cryptography:

Symmetric Cryptography: Encryption methods that employ a common secret key for both encryption and decryption, such as Advanced Encryption Standard and Data Encryption Standard or ChaCha20, etc. Keeping this crucial information hidden is the only way to ensure security [13], [14].

Brute-Force Attack: The most basic attack against symmetric cryptography is a brute-force search. An attacker tries every possible key until they find the one that correctly decrypts a known piece of ciphertext or produces meaningful plaintext. If a key has k bits, there are N = 2^k possible keys. Classically, finding the key takes $O(N) = O(2^k)$ attempts in the worst case.

Grover's Impact: A brute-force key search perfectly fits the description of an unstructured search problem. The "database" is the set of all possible $N = 2^k$ keys, and the "target item" is the correct secret key. The "oracle" is a function that checks if a given key correctly decrypts a small piece of known ciphertext. Grover's algorithm can perform this search in $O(\sqrt{N}) = O(\sqrt{2^k}) = O(2^{k/2})$ quantum operations.

Halving Effective Key Length: This quadratic speedup effectively halves the security strength provided by the key length. A k-bit key under a Grover attack provides roughly the equal standard of security as a k/2-bit key under a classical brute-force attack. For example:

AES-128 (128-bit key) has a classical security strength of 128 bits ($O(2^{128})$ operations to break).

Against Grover's algorithm, its effective quantum security strength is reduced to about 64 bits ($O(2^{64})$ quantum operations).

Necessitating Longer Keys: Because 64-bit security is generally considered breakable (though still computationally intensive), the standard recommendation to maintain security against potential future quantum computers is to double the key size. This is why algorithms like AES-256 (with 256-bit keys) are recommended for long-term security, as they offer approximately 128 bits of security (O(2^128) quantum operations) against Grover's algorithm, which is currently considered secure. Figure 10.2 illustrates the working principle of Grover's algorithm for accelerated unstructured search.

10.2.6.1 Evaluating cryptographic resilience

The existence of algorithm such as Grover's against symmetric encryption And Shor's against asymmetric or a public key cryptography like RSA Indicates that the quantum computing might be a serious threat to current cryptographic infrastructure.

Gaining an understanding of substantial quantum algorithm is crucial to the global movement to create an institutionalized post quantum cryptographic PQC—new cryptographic techniques (both symmetric and asymmetric) that are envisioned to remain secure against attacks by both for classical and quantum computer platforms.

Risk Assessment: By examining the impact of algorithms such as Grover's on current standards (such as AES), cryptographers and security experts can evaluate the risks, establish migration schedules, and make strategic decisions regarding the implementation of new PQC standards to maintain future data security [25].

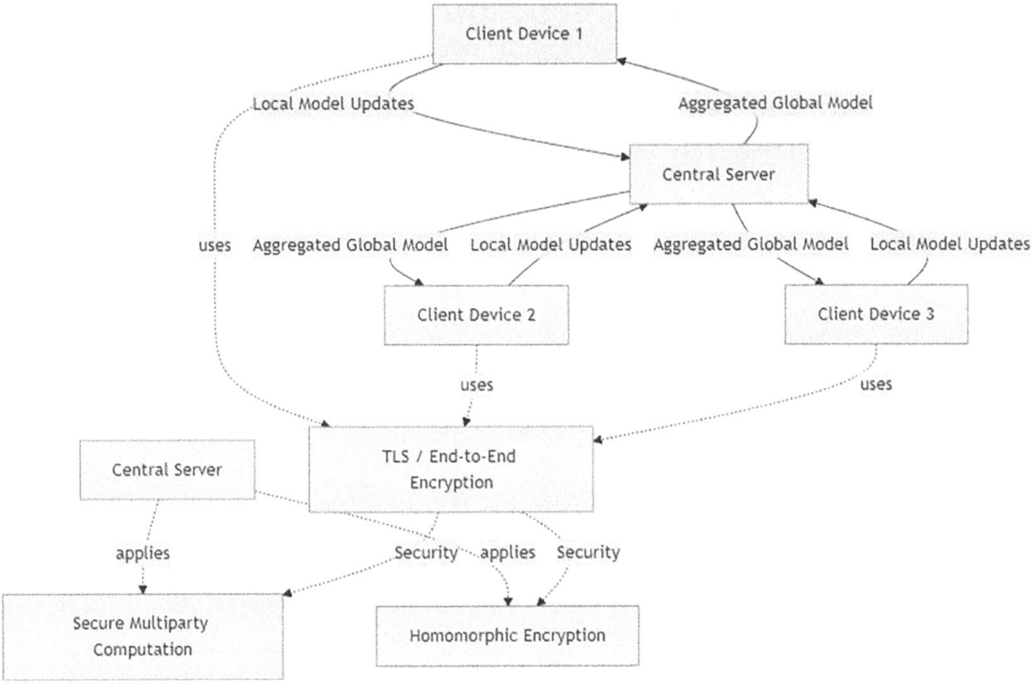

Figure 10.2 Grover's algorithm.

10.2.6.2 Case study: Quantum-resilient federated fraud-detection workflow using kyber-encrypted gradients

10.2.6.2.1 Overview

Financial institutions like banks often need to collaborate to detect fraud patterns across multiple organizations. However, sharing raw customer data violates privacy laws (e.g., GDPR, PCI-DSS) and exposes institutions to cybersecurity risks.

How FL Helps.

- Banks train a shared fraud-detection model without moving sensitive transaction data.
- Each bank trains locally on its own dataset and shares only model gradients, not raw data.

Why Quantum-Resilient Security is Needed.

- Current encryption (RSA, ECC) may become vulnerable to Shor's algorithm on future quantum computers.
- Using Kyber-encrypted gradients ensures post-quantum security, protecting communications even against future quantum adversaries.

Workflow Steps.

1. Model Initialization: A central aggregator initializes a fraud-detection model (e.g., deep neural network).

2. Local Training: Each participating bank trains the model locally on its private transaction data.
3. Secure Updates: Model gradients are encrypted using Kyber before being sent to the aggregator.
4. Secure Aggregation: The aggregator combines encrypted updates (optionally using secure multi-party computation).
5. Global Model Sharing: The updated model is redistributed to all banks for the next round.
6. Fraud Prediction: The final trained model can detect suspicious transactions without exposing sensitive customer data.

10.2.6.3 Case study: Evaluating cryptographic resilience in the era of quantum

10.2.6.3.1 Background

With the rapid advancement of quantum computing, traditional cryptographic systems face an unprecedented challenge. Modern digital infrastructure relies heavily on cryptographic protocols—both asymmetric (e.g., RSA, ECC) and symmetric (e.g., AES)—that are foundational to data security, online privacy, and global communication systems. However, quantum algorithms like Shor's and Grover's threaten to undermine these security guarantees.

10.2.6.3.2 Quantum threat analysis

Search algorithm public key cryptography like RSA, DSA and ECC Are directly threatened by Shor's algorithm, Which is made to factor huge number and compute discrete logarithmic in polynomial time. The security of these systems is based on a higher factor number but efficiently solvable by quantum ones. For instance, RSA-2048, currently considered secure, would be rendered vulnerable to decryption if a large-enough quantum computer (estimated at ~4,000 logical qubits) becomes practical.

Grover's Algorithm: While symmetric cryptographic systems like AES are less vulnerable, Grover's algorithm provides a quadratic speed-up for brute-force key search. For example, Grover's algorithm can reduce the complexity of cracking AES-128 from 2^{128} to 2^{64}, effectively halving the security level [12]. This does not entirely break symmetric systems but necessitates longer key lengths (e.g., AES-256) for post-quantum resilience.

10.2.6.3.3 Post-quantum cryptography (PQC) and strategic response

Understanding these quantum algorithms is essential for developing PQC solutions. PQC focuses on creating cryptographic systems—particularly for the key exchange and digital signatures and also public-key encryption—that are secure against both classical and quantum attacks. Algorithms such as lattice-based cryptography (e.g., NTRU, Kyber), are codebase cryptography, and Hash algorithm based signatures are leading candidates under evaluation by NIST's PQC standardization process.

10.2.6.3.4 Risk assessment and migration planning

Organizations and governments are now conducting quantum risk assessments to evaluate the impact of these threats on existing infrastructure. For example:

- Symmetric Systems: Gradual migration to longer key lengths and hybrid cryptographic approaches.
- Asymmetric Systems: More urgent migration paths involving hybrid certificates, dual-algorithm protocols, and future-ready cryptographic stacks.

The U.S. National Institute of Standards and Technology (NIST) has recommended preparing for a quantum-safe future by 2030, urging stakeholders to begin cryptographic inventory and establish migration strategies.

10.3 QUANTUM THREAT LANDSCAPE

The quantum threat landscape is a paradigm shift in the cybersecurity landscape, especially for FL systems. As quantum computing advances, serious threats are being posed to the cryptographic foundations that are at the core of secure communication and data protection. It is crucial to learn about these vulnerabilities to build robust defense against new quantum threats. One of the challenges under the quantum threat landscape is related to the vulnerability of current FL systems to quantum-based attacks. FL encompasses, the process of training a ML model across several dispersed servers or devices that stores a local data samples without requiring them to be shared. It heavily depends on the cryptographic techniques to guarantee the security of the data present inside. The strength of money currently used cryptographic models is being undermined by the emergence of quantum computing. The majority of the public key cryptosystem includes RSA and elliptical curb cryptography which can factor large number effectively and solve discrete algorithms issues, data that has been encrypted using these algorithms might be decrypted by a powerful quantum computer, thereby compromising the confidentiality and integrity of the information [15].

Cryptographic primitives that are under possible attack include RSA, ECC, and even symmetric-key primitives like AES, though to a lesser extent. The increased vulnerability of RSA and ECC is due to their reliance on the difficulty of certain mathematical problems that are solvable by quantum computers with vastly greater efficiency. For example, the security of RSA is based on the challenge of factoring integers, whereas the security of ECC depends on the elliptic curve discrete logarithm issue. The above problems are computable in polynomial time by Shor's algorithm and thus make such cryptographic primitives insecure against quantum attacks. While symmetric-key primitives like AES are not immediately susceptible to Shor's algorithm, they are vulnerable if their keys are managed through a public-key infrastructure which is inherently vulnerable.

Quantum attacks involve advanced cryptographic methods used in FL, such as Secure Aggregation and HE. Secure Aggregation is a method to ensure that aggregated model updates of different contributors to an FL system do not violate confidentiality. The method involves encryption of updates and aggregation thereof in a manner that individual inputs cannot be traced. In case, however, cryptographic building blocks supporting them are vulnerable to quantum attacks, the security of Secure Aggregation would be violated. Likewise, HE allows for performing calculations on encrypted data without needing to decrypt it, thus preserving the confidentiality of the data. Quantum attacks on the cryptographic building blocks used in HE would in turn have the potential to open the encrypted data, thereby violating privacy. Apart from these imminent threats, the quantum threat environment comprises other indirect threats. For example, utilization of quantum key distribution (QKD) would enhance the security of FL systems using theoretically unbreakable encryption keys. The utilization of QKD is, however, still in its nascent stages and is susceptible to practical issues like the need for special infrastructure and the limited reach of quantum communication channels. Even if QKD is successfully implemented, it leaves the vulnerabilities of the underlying cryptographic primitives utilized in FL systems exposed [16].

To counter these quantum threats, one needs to design and deploy post-quantum cryptographic algorithms. They are quantum-resistant and can offer long-term security to FL systems. A few examples of these are lattice-based cryptography, hash-based signatures, and multivariate polynomial cryptography. It will take a lot of work, i.e., standardization, implementation, and deployment, to shift to PQC. But it is something that needs to be done to secure FL systems for the quantum computing age.

The quantum threat environment is a multifaceted challenge to the security of F L systems. Existing cryptographic primitives under threat, the susceptibility of advanced cryptographic techniques, and the need for post-quantum substitutes highlight the necessity to counter the threats. With an understanding of the distinct threats and the design of robust countermeasures, the cybersecurity community can protect FL systems against the dynamic quantum threat environment.

10.4 POTENTIAL ATTACK VECTORS IN FL

10.4.1 Quantum-powered model inversion and data reconstruction

Model inversion attacks are a critical and pressing privacy integrity threat to FL systems since they aim to recover the original input data from the accessible outputs or the model updates generated during the learning process. FL is specifically designed with the aim of evading the direct sharing of raw data among the various participants and the aggregators in the middle; however, it must be noted that the gradients or model parameters, which are exchanged during training, can inadvertently leak sensitive user data that would compromise user privacy. In more traditional settings, these kinds of attacks depend on what is known as gradient leakage, which involves exploiting the subtle patterns that exist in the weight updates or the predictions generated by the model to infer certain attributes of individual data points, such as personal information like age, income, or categories of transactions made.

The arrival of quantum computing represents a radical enhancement of the competence and effectiveness of such attacks, as it eliminates some computational hurdles that have long rendered model inversion an unrealistic endeavor in traditional computing paradigms. Quantum algorithms, including Grover's algorithm, have an unparalleled ability to speedup the search process in complex and high-dimensional feature spaces. Such functionality enables attackers to quickly find and identify data representations related to their targets among a large number of candidate options. The quadratic speedup provided by such quantum techniques makes quantum-aided inversion not only significantly more accurate but also much shorter in time to conduct. Moreover, the use of quantum machine learning (QML) techniques—e.g., quantum kernel techniques and variational quantum classifiers—has the ability to further enhance the effectiveness of the inference process. This technological development enables reversing rich data profiles from model update aggregates. When assessed in financial FL scenarios, this capability can enable the reconstruction of complete transaction histories, individual credit assessments, or complex risk determinations inferred from gradient data. Such advancements present a serious risk to the existing regulatory and ethical controls deployed to preserve privacy protection.

10.4.2 More powerful adversarial and poisoning attacks based on quantum capabilities

Aside from the vulnerability to inversion attacks, FL systems are also vulnerable to significant adversarial attacks from poisoning and adversarial attacks. In such cases, malicious users intentionally input tainted or malicious data, as well as deceptive updates, intended to bias the learning process of the global model. Two primary forms of such adversarial techniques can be recognized: The first is data poisoning, in which incorrect or deceptive training data is intentionally given to the local model and thus disables the local model's capability to learn. The second form is model poisoning, in which adversaries design specially tailored adversarial gradient updates intended to manipulate the convergence of the model to a correct model of the data. Both forms of attacks have the potential to severely degrade the performance of the model or even cause strategic biases that compromise the integrity of the learning process. Quantum computing introduces new avenues for such attacks, with optimization powers beyond classical capabilities. Quantum annealing and variational quantum algorithms, for example, can effectively traverse the adversarial perturbation space and find configurations that are highly effective and difficult to identify. These quantum-based techniques reduce the time and computational cost for creating optimal attack vectors, allowing adversaries to more effectively compromise models. The effect of such attacks is particularly devastating in financial systems. Malicious model updates can quietly poison credit scoring systems, introduce systematic bias in loan approval systems, or invalidate fraud detection models—leading to unfair treatment of clients, regulatory noncompliance, or even financial instability. The stealth and accuracy provided by quantum-assisted adversarial approaches significantly increase the risk profile of FL in finance and highlight the pressing need for quantum-resilient defenses.

10.4.3 Threats to differential privacy mechanism

Differential Privacy (DP) is applied widely in FL to avoid reverse-engineering single points of data even from aggregated shared statistical results. It achieves this by incorporating calibrated noise into model updates or query submissions.

But quantum computing threatens DP with two types of threats:

1. Noise filtering: Quantum algorithms such as quantum Fourier transforms may be employed by attackers to filter out or invert injected noise, particularly when it is bounded or structured, thus exposing original model updates.
2. Improved query capability: Quantum computing can enable faster and more capable query mechanisms—basically making more inferences per unit of noise, and possibly breaking the privacy guarantees that DP typically provides. Breach of DP practices using quantum means can reveal concealed traits or transactions in financial situations where individual-level data is sensitive and well-protected, breaking compliance regulations such as CCPA 5 and GDPR [18].

10.5 POST-QUANTUM CRYPTOGRAPHY (PQC)

10.5.1 Post-quantum cryptography and the NIST standardization initiative

Current cybersecurity techniques are actually at risk because of the rapid advancement of quantum computing. The issue at hand is that trusted classical encryption systems such as ECC, Diffie-Hellman, and RSA are vulnerable to quantum computing. These conventional techniques rely on discrete logarithms, which would easily be compromised through quantum computing algorithms such as Shor's algorithm that factor large numbers efficiently with tremendous speed. Because of this, extremely advanced quantum computers might render some of the existing cryptographic techniques useless, and it will become more probable that criminals will be able to exploit secured information, digital signatures, and secret messages.

The NIST launched a comprehensive and internationally coordinated standardization project in 2016 with the goal of discovering cryptographic algorithms that are resistant to quantum computing. The initiative, known as the PQC Standardization project, was to review a wide set of potential algorithms that were proposed by researchers across the globe. Criteria that were taken into consideration during evaluation included portability across platforms, computation performance, ease of implementation, bandwidth usage, and resistance to quantum and classical attacks.

After years of intense testing, assessment, and public review, NIST released a collection of four basic algorithms that are most likely to be the basis of future quantum-resistant cryptographic systems:

- CRYSTALS: Kyber is a lattice-based key encapsulation scheme (KEM) with a specific focus on public-key cryptography. It is useful across a wide range of contexts such as secure communication and data encryption in decentralized networks due to its ability to find a good and efficient tradeoff between security and performance.
- CRYSTALS-Dilithium: A digital signature framework grounded in lattice cryptography, Dilithium is characterized by its strong security assurances, high performance, and side-channel resistance. The scheme performs optimally in use cases where identity authentication and protection of data integrity are critical, such as in software update systems and digital identity authentication.
- FALCON: FALCON is another lattice-based signature scheme, and it is distinguished by having compact key and signature sizes, this makes it particularly appropriate for environments with limited resources, such as embedded systems and Internet of Things (IoT) devices. Its mathematics are more complex than Dilithium's mathematics, but it provides the same security with better data compactness.
- SPHINCS+: SPHINCS+ is yet another hash-based digital signature that is not number-theoretic assumption-based, unlike the other three schemes. It is considered to be very conservative and robust, particularly when long-term security is categorically necessary. However, it is slower in performance and generates bigger signatures compared to its lattice-based equivalents.

These decisions mark an important stride toward quantum-proofing global digital infrastructure. By staying ahead of quantum attacks and establishing post-quantum cryptographic tools through standardization, NIST is creating a foundation for a safer digital future—especially in high-stakes domains like finance, healthcare, and national defense. Governments and institutions are now encouraged to begin deploying these post-quantum algorithms in their systems ahead of the "quantum advantage" era, when quantum computing power could turn into an in-the-wild threat to data security.

10.5.2 Lattice-based and hash-based and multivariate cryptosystems

Lattice-Based Cryptography: It depends on the complexity of lattice problems like the Learning With Errors (LWE) problem which is assumed to be quantum-attack resistant.

CRYSTALS-Kyber and CRYSTALS-Dilithium are fine examples of this category, having solid security foundations and reasonable performance.

Hash-Based Cryptography: Relying on the security of cryptographic hash functions, hash-based protocols like SPHINCS+ provide quantum-resistant digital signatures. These protocols leverage one-time signatures combined with Merkle tree topologies to enable multiple secure signings. Even though they guarantee strong security benefits, the considerations include bigger signature sizes and the need for effective implementation techniques.

Multivariate Cryptography: Multivariate cryptosystems are among the most promising post-quantum contenders in relation to the challenges associated with solving multivariate polynomial systems within finite fields. Schemes like Rainbow have been proposed, with potential signature size and computational efficiency advantages. Challenges remain in proving their security against novel attack paradigms and in optimizing their performance for real-world applications.

10.5.3 Integrating PQC into FL pipelines

The process of integrating PQC within the FL protocols is a multi-party and intricate procedure involving numerous disparate computational and communicational, and structural, constituents. At the very least the PQC schemes are categorically unavoidable if we are to uphold the security of FL systems on our journey to the quantum age, there must be the concession that their integration is with huge trade-offs to be obeyed.

10.5.4 Computational overhead

One of the most basic challenges that we face is in the field of PQC originates from native computational intricacy of PQC algorithms. In stark contrast to conventional cryptographic designs like RSA or ECC, which have been painstakingly optimized to maximize their performance, some of the PQC contenders—particularly those built on lattice schemes and error-correcting codes—have a tendency to consume much more computational power for critical operations like key generation, encryption, decryption, and signature verification. This extent of intricacy proves to be extremely problematic in FL deployments where edge devices, which comprise many types of technology like smartphones, Internet of Things (IoT) sensors, or embedded systems, have limited computational capabilities. When PQC operations are made a part of these systems without proper consideration, they have a tendency to greatly impact the efficiency of model training as well as data aggregation operations, which leads to higher latency and increased power consumption. Such an impact can be extremely detrimental, particularly in large-scale deployments where resources are limited and efficiency is of prime importance.

Cost of Communication: Besides computational need, most of the PQC algorithms also consume much larger ciphertexts and key sizes. As an example, public key size in lattice schemes like NTRU or Kyber can be a few kilobytes in comparison to the few hundred bytes of ECC. In FL with the constant movement of model update and encrypted parameter between clients and the central node, this increases communication overhead. Bandwidth utilization and latency could become prohibitive, particularly under limited connectivity in decentralized networks or in real-time responsive applications.

10.5.5 Standardization and compatibility

One of the most pressing challenges for contemporary technology is the constantly changing environment of PQC standards. The NIST is the central focus of the process to finalize recommendations about PQC. This kind of strategy implies that certain algorithms must be revised or potentially could become obsolete in the future, meaning that FL pipelines must constantly adapt to keep up with future breakthroughs. For long-term system design, these kinds of variations in standards cause serious problems since existing implementations would have to be altered to conform to newer standards or to effectively counter unknown vulnerabilities that could be found in the future.

Furthermore, incorporating PQC into current FL infrastructures is no easy task; it requires compatibility with a range of additional security protocols, heterogeneous data formats, and a range of privacy mechanisms.

General Data Protection Regulation (GDPR), Health Insurance Portability and Accountability Act (HIPAA), and Payment Card Industry Data Security Standard (PCI-DSS) are some of the regulatory standards that have to be followed while conducting these operations. It is therefore critical that cryptographers, systems engineers, and ML researchers come together to address the integration challenges that come with it. Managing to find a balance between security and efficiency requires the creation of robust middleware solutions, adaptive compression schemes, hybrid cryptographic constructions, and improved PQC primitives that are specific to federated environments. The only thing that can protect FL systems from the quantum threat is by promoting multi-disciplinary innovation.

10.6 MITIGATION STRATEGIES

10.6.1 Advances in quantum computing, FL systems

FL system needs to evolve as well to be safe from new vulnerabilities using advanced quantum computing, the main approach is consisting quantum resilient FL architecture which are engineered to maintain the data confidentiality and model integrity and technique of against advisory quantum capability processing. In such architecture incorporating the post quantum cryptographic (PQC) true call across the FL Pipeline to facilitate and secure communication, here the model aggregation the main component of such architecture includes quantum safe encryption replacing the traditional encryption like RSA and ECC with the help of Post Quantum Cryptography Putin and such as CRYSTALS-Kyber the noise augmented privacy methods, which finds the DP through the injection of the dynamic noise against quantum de-anonymization. The architecture will further make use of quantum information threat models which takes into account of the impact of parallel quantum attacks such as brute force decryption. At the highest significance the study demonstrates the feasibility of the practical implementation of lightweight latency based cryptographic algorithm in its ways FL with the potential for improved quantum resilience vs. computational efficiency trade off [21].

10.6.2 Secure multi-party computation (SMPC)

Parallel integrating secured multi-party computation SMPC with the post quantum computing PQC will serve as a highly effective safeguard. SMPC will allow multiple parties to collaboratively compute a function using private input while keeping those input confidential. This conventional SMPC protocol are not quantum resistance. By combining PQC primitives most notably latency based cryptographic methods into SMPC schemes a wide range of security improvements can be obtained. This will also include quantum resistant secret searching process encrypted aggregations of model updates to hybrid solutions that combines SMPC with HE to offer layered security a study in 2022 introduced a hybrid PQC and SMPC model that optimized low latency distributed learning capability while also providing a strong resistance to quantum attack thereby exhibiting high applicability in the real world application [22]. Secondly a visible option is the use of a block chain based FL system that ensures a design which is resistant to quantum interfaces. Block chain technology provides an immunity and decentralized ledger which suits for securing strong models update and providing a transparency in collaborative learning environment. But conventional block chain protocols used elliptical curve cryptography and hashing algorithm both of which are susceptible for quantum attacks. To counter this vulnerabilities quantum resilient block chain FL system is considered as a substitute for classical digital signature such as ECDSA with the post quantum cryptography equivalent like SPHINCS + which includes tamper proof audit trails to identify and correct miscellaneous contributions and header concise mechanism, for example a study in 2023 introduced a PQC enabled block chain framework that uses a quantum safe authentication and distribution ledger to provide data integrity and traceability in FL environments.

10.7 FUTURE DIRECTIONS

10.7.1 Quantum FL: Advantages and challenges

Quantum Federated Learning (QFL) is an innovative interdisciplinary fusion of FL and quantum computing with tremendous potential for breakthroughs in privacy-preserving distributed artificial intelligence. The general aim of QFL is to enhance scalability and efficiency in distributed ML systems, all while preserving privacy through the peculiar features of quantum physics, including superposition, quantum parallelism, and entanglement. Perhaps its greatest advantage can be the remarkable speedup in model training that it can achieve. Especially in situations where high dimensionality or resource constraints dominate, quantum computers will most likely offer faster FL convergence due to their intrinsic capability to address optimization problems. Furthermore, QFL offers scalability by handling large-scale datasets and intricate models distributed in decentralized nodes efficiently.

Security is an exciting direction, especially in adversarial environments, since quantum cryptographic primitives enable data security during model communication and aggregation. In mission-critical financial use cases like fraud detection, portfolio optimization, and anomaly detection, QML can bring novel learning paradigms that can surpass traditional models [17]. However, extreme challenges are associated with the deployment of QFL. Quantum hardware is still in its infancy due to limitations like a finite number of qubits and high error rates. Technical challenges also arise in the integration of quantum components with traditional FL infrastructure; this hybrid architecture is still in the development and largely experimental stage.

Ambient noise and decoherence affect quantum computations and make the training results less reliable and accurate. The quantum analog of classical financial information also requires adherence to data privacy laws like the CCPA and GDPR, which is an additional problem. Despite these challenges, QFL is an engaging research and imaginative area. Ongoing improvements in quantum hardware, better algorithms, and synchronized laws will allow for its full capabilities and make FL for finance safe, scalable, and efficient.

10.7.2 Quantum-enhanced privacy-preserving AI

The area of privacy-preserving artificial intelligence (PPAI) is being revolutionized by quantum computing, which raises new challenges and opportunities. Apart from upending the basic principles of traditional cryptography methods, quantum computing also presents how to improve AI's privacy features. One major advancement in this direction is Quantum Homomorphic Encryption (QHE). It allows us to perform calculations on encrypted quantum data without revealing the original information and enables us to use classical HE in the quantum realm. The innovation greatly improves data privacy through enabling very secure cloud inference and AI training. Researchers are also targeting Quantum Differential Privacy (QDP), which further obscures sensitive data in AI systems using statistical techniques and quantum noise. The breakthroughs aim to make it more difficult to reconstruct individual data elements, even in adversarial systems that are quantum-computing enabled. By enhancing the resistance to collision and reducing the communication overhead interception during distributed training theory quantum secure multi-party computation. Another quantum leap fuses quantum mechanism to enhance the conventional secure multi-party computation protocol the sensitive data in banking sector such as quantum innovations have clear applications. Quantum enhanced privacy for instance can enable cooperative credit scoring models which will allow the banks to train predictive models together without disclosing the clients identities or confidential information about the bank. Similarly while safeguarding individual transactions detail of fraud detection techniques allows the enterprises to share the threat knowledge however the real world implementation continues to be hindered by the lack of a matured quantum algorithm that can maintain the privacy in artificial intelligence. The software and debugging the environment is necessary for quantum privacy methods which are still in development and existing prototypes of quantum homomorphic encryption (QHE) and quantum digital signature (QDS), requires a computational power for the fault tolerance quantum computers that are yet to be materialized [20]. The recent development in quantum AI technology involves mechanism that are infiltrated into financial infrastructure to maintain and safeguard the privacy of compliances with regulatory requirement while realizing the next generation performance in data driven financial services.

10.7.3 Finance standardization projects and regulatory pressures

The intersection of FL and the quantum technology with a highly sophisticated artificial intelligence has highlighted the necessity for updating the standards and regulatory guidelines. In a financial market where sensitive data and compliances are essential conventional security protocols are inadequate against the quantum informed attacks from empowered attacks. The effort is thus underweight to make the FL system resilience and stronger than before. The National Institute of Standard Technology (NIST) and The World Bank innovation in this area through its PQC standardization is pursuing an exhaustive testing process wherein NIST has chosen quantum resistant encryption and signing algorithms CRYSTALS-Kyber and SPHINCS+, respectively to serve as replacement protocol for insecure RSA and ECC protocol adopted by F L Communication Networks. These standards are likely to serve as the building blocks for FL data exchange protocols that are quantum-attack resistant. Parallel to these, global bodies such as ISO/IEC are establishing technical standards for block chain, AI security, and post-quantum protocols, while the IEEE Quantum Initiative pushes the boundaries of error correction best practice, hardware interoperability, and ethical quantum-AI integration [19]. Standardization is crucial to instill consistent, auditable, and interoperable security habits in quantum-era FL. Regulatorily, the shift toward quantum-aware technologies has knotty implications. Existing data protection regulations will have to be adapted to determine what constitutes "adequate security" when facing quantum attacks. Banks will need to redefine their infrastructure and install certified PQC algorithms to remain compliant. Legal problems also exist in regard to quantum-induced vulnerabilities on increasingly decentralized FL networks in terms of liability. Cross-border cooperation on data also has new challenges, as differences in quantum preparedness between jurisdictions can create asymmetries in managing risk and regulating enforcement. Shifting to quantum-resistant federated AI systems will have to be complemented by concerted policy-making to enable innovation without compromising accountability as well as protections for sensitive financial data.

10.8 CONCLUSION

This chapter discusses the intersection of FL and quantum computing, especially in the financial sector where data security is the top priority. FL provides model training in a decentralized setting without compromising the users' privacy; nevertheless, the emergence of quantum computing introduces new weaknesses to its security foundations. Specifically, quantum algorithms such as Shor's and Grover's weaken the security of traditional cryptographic structures like RSA, ECC, and symmetric encryption, consequently exposing available FL frameworks to potential data loss and breaches of confidentiality. Further, attackers with quantum capabilities access may enhance the efficacy of attacks on model inversion, poisoning, and DP breaches, thus undermining the confidence that is at the heart of FL frameworks. To mitigate these issues, PQC) algorithms like CRYSTALS-Kyber, Dilithium, and SPHINCS+ have been proposed as suitable remedies. However, the use of these algorithms in FL is still marred by resource limitations and deployment issues in distributed systems. Countermeasures like the employment of SMPC, block chain-based openness, and PQC-inspired security architectures provide promising defense strategies but also provide scaling and interoperability challenges. For the future, QFL is a promising direction by harnessing the capabilities of quantum technology to improve the effectiveness and precision of training; however, this progress is still marred by current limitations on hardware development as well as breakthroughs in algorithm developments.

Following these observations, it is necessary to design quantum-conscious FL protocols natively secure, infrastructure-compatible, and ensuring secure communication and consensus in the presence of a quantum threat environment. Such platforms should be hardware-agnostic and should be able to seamlessly run on classical and quantum-advanced technology. Governments, banks, and AI research must collaborate and devise visionary frameworks that can foresee quantum threats rather than react to them.

Despite recent progress, significant research gaps remain. Some of them include the absence of efficient hybrid quantum-classical FL algorithms, limited research on quantum-friendly privacy techniques, and insufficient strong adversarial defense techniques against quantum attacks. System-level challenges, including how to incorporate PQC into low-latency environments and how to migrate existing FL frameworks, remain as well. Scalability issues and security vs. energy efficiency trade-offs remain yet to be fully understood. Finally, legal and ethical concerns—most importantly those regarding data ownership, auditability, and compliance—are to be addressed so that FL systems are not compromised on trustworthiness and security during the quantum era.

REFERENCES

[1] Qi, P., Chiaro, D., Guzzo, A., Ianni, M., Fortino, G., & Piccialli, F. (2024). Model Aggregation Techniques in Federated Learning: A Comprehensive Survey. *Future Generation Computer Systems*, *150*, 272–293.

[2] Dutta, S., Karanth, P. P., Xavier, P. M., de Freitas, I. L., Innan, N., Yahia, S. B., ... & Neira, D. E. B. (2024). Federated Learning with Quantum Computing and Fully Homomorphic Encryption: A Novel Computing Paradigm Shift in Privacy-Preserving ML. *arXiv preprint arXiv:2409.11430.*

[3] Bhatia, A. S., & Neira, D. E. B. (2024). Federated Learning with Tensor Networks: A Quantum AI Framework for Healthcare. *Machine Learning: Science and Technology*, *5*(4), 045035.

[4] Qiu, D., Luo, L., & Xiao, L. (2024). Distributed Grover's algorithm. *Theoretical Computer Science*, *993*, 114461.

[5] Mohammed, A. (2025). *Cyber Security Implications of Quantum Computing: Shor's Algorithm and Beyond.* https://doi.org/10.6084/m9.figshare.28328492.v1

[6] Mamatha, G. S., Dimri, N., & Sinha, R. (2024). Post-Quantum Cryptography: Securing Digital Communication in the Quantum Era. *arXiv.* https://arxiv.org/abs/2403.11741

[7] Hassan, W., & Mohamed, H. (2024). Applications of Federated Learning in AI, IoT, Healthcare, Finance, Banking, and Cross-Domain Learning. In Elngar, A.A., Oliva, D., & Balas, V.E. (Eds.). *Artificial Intelligence Using Federated Learning* (pp. 175–195). CRC Press. https://doi.org/10.1201/9781003482000

[8] Beltrán, E. T. M., Gómez, Á. L. P., Feng, C., Sánchez, P. M. S., Bernal, S. L., Bovet, G., ... & Celdrán, A. H. (2024). Fedstellar: A Platform for Decentralized Federated Learning. *Expert Systems with Applications*, *242*, 122861.

[9] Muthalakshmi, M., Jeyapal, K., Vinoth, M., PS, D., Murugan, N. S., & Sheela, K. S. (2024, August). Federated Learning for Secure and Privacy-Preserving Medical Image Analysis in Decentralized Healthcare Systems. In *2024 5th International Conference on Electronics and Sustainable Communication Systems (ICESC)* (pp. 1442–1447). IEEE.

[10] Khang, A., Rath, K. C., Panda, N., & Kumar, A. (2024). Quantum Mechanics Primer: Fundamentals and Quantum Computing. In A. Khang (Ed.), *Applications and Principles of Quantum Computing* (pp. 1–24). IGI Global Scientific Publishing. https://doi.org/10.4018/979-8-3693-1168-4.ch001

[11] Huguenin-Dumittan, L. E. (2024). *Secure and Efficient Cryptographic Algorithms in a Quantum World* (No. 10522). EPFL.

[12] Nadeem, M., Sarkar, A. K., & Ishrat, M. (2024). Securing Information Systems Through Quantum Computing: Grover's Algorithm Approach. In *Computational Intelligence Applications in Cyber Security* (pp. 299–306). CRC Press. https://doi.org/10.1201/9781003514312-18

[13] Joshi, M., Mishra, M. K., & Karthikeyan, S. (2024). Leveraging Grover's Algorithm for Quantum Searchable Encryption in Cloud Infrastructure and its Application in AES Resource Estimation. *International Journal of Theoretical Physics*, *63*(8), 209.

[14] Sarah, D., & Peter, C. (2024, March). On the Practical Cost of Grover for AES Key Recovery. In *Presentation at the 5th NIST PQC Standardization Conference.*

[15] Baseri, Y., Chouhan, V., & Ghorbani, A. (2024). Cybersecurity in the Quantum Era: Assessing the Impact of Quantum Computing on Infrastructure. *arXiv preprint arXiv:2404.10659.*

[16] Singh, S., & Sakk, E. (2024). Implementation and Analysis of Shor's Algorithm to Break RSA Cryptosystem Security. *Authorea Preprints.*

[17] Javeed, D., Saeed, M. S., Ahmad, I., Adil, M., Kumar, P., & Islam, A. N. (2024). Quantum-Empowered Federated Learning and 6G Wireless Networks for IoT Security: Concept, Challenges and Future Directions. *Future Generation Computer Systems.* Advance online publication.

[18] Olabim, M., Greenfield, A., & Barlow, A. (2024). A Differential Privacy-Based Approach for Mitigating Data Theft in Ransomware Attacks. *Authorea Preprints.*

[19] Shamo, S. A. (2024). Bridging the Quantum Divide: A Comprehensive Analysis of NIST and ISO Standards for Post-Quantum Cryptography and Strategies for Global Harmonization. *Available at SSRN 4864519.*

[20] Liu, F., Zheng, Z., Gong, Z., Tian, K., Zhang, Y., Hu, Z., ... & Xu, Q. (2024). A Survey on Lattice-Based Digital Signature. *Cybersecurity*, 7(1), 7.

[21] Thomas, S. G., & Myakala, P. K. (2025). Beyond the Cloud: Federated Learning and Edge AI for the Next Decade. *Journal of Computer and Communications*, *13*(2), 37–50.

[22] Daniel, J. (2025). Secure Multi-Party Computation for Healthcare Big Data Queries. *Journal of Cybersecurity and Privacy*, 6(1), 2. https://doi.org/10.3390/jcp6010002

[23] FasterCapital. (n.d.). *Classical algorithms*. LearnHub – FasterCapital. Retrieved August 20, 2025, from https://fastercapital.com/keyword/classical-algorithms.html

[24] Placentia-Yorba Linda Unified School District. (n.d.). *Home*. Retrieved August 20, 2025, from www.pylusd.org

[25] Mansoor, K., Afzal, M., Iqbal, W. et al. (2025). Securing the Future: Exploring Post-Quantum Cryptography for Authentication and User Privacy in IoT Devices. *Cluster Computing, 28*, 93. https://doi.org/10.1007/s10586-024-04799-4

Chapter 11

Next-gen and autonomous federated systems

Divya K. S. and Soumya K.

11.1 INTRODUCTION

Federated learning (FL) has developed over the last ten years into an innovative approach that facilitates collaborative model creation while maintaining data privacy protection. Although traditional federated systems work well, they have significant difficulties conducting large-scale operations, adjusting to new surroundings, and making judgments in complicated financial circumstances without human intervention. The financial services sector must create new federated systems because it requires intelligent, safe, real-time data analysis for networks that are decentralized. The chapter examines autonomous federated systems by outlining their technological elements, key advances, and applications in the financial industry. The research proposes a future direction that builds self-optimizing federated networks that preserve operational effectiveness and trust by fusing AI coordinating systems with quantum-resistant security mechanisms and continuous learning systems.

11.1.1 Overview of federated systems evolution

Over the years, federated systems have grown from simple distributed computing models to intricate networks able to supply a variety of distinct services. Federated systems enabled regulated access to data in their early days, even though they were first positioned by connecting distinct databases or applications across institutions. These systems used static policies that were not intelligent or flexible, so they required manual configuration. Although having been distributed geographically, these systems' centralization in design often caused governance issues and performance hitches [1].

The need for privacy, decentralized intelligence, and real-time collaboration constantly pushed for the addition of modern technology in order to increase the efficacy of federated computing. The most well-known of these are edge computing, secure multi-party computation (SMPC), and lightweight consensus-establishing methods. A major turning point in this process was the discovery of FL, which enables several nodes to train their machine learning models locally without sharing raw data. By doing this, bandwidth is saved and privacy issues are resolved.

Federated systems didn't start out nearly as polished as they sound today. In the early days, they were more or less a practical fix—ways to let a few different databases or applications talk to each other without giving away too much control. Universities, for instance, often used them so researchers could peek into one another's archives without actually handing over the raw data. It worked, but only just. Everything had to be manually configured up and wired together back then. Once policies had been created, they were then discarded unchanged even when circumstances changed. Surprisingly, the control felt

DOI: 10.1201/9781003660330-11

centralized regardless of the geographical dispersion of these systems. And that centralization caused headaches: bottlenecks when too many requests piled up, arguments over who was really in charge, and little room for the systems to adapt on their own [2].

As people pushed for faster collaboration and stronger privacy protections, these federated setups started borrowing ideas from newer technologies—things like SMPC, edge processing, even lighter consensus models that wouldn't slow everything down. Then came what felt like a real turning point: the ability for different nodes to train models on their own data without actually passing that data around. Instead of shipping raw patient records or financial logs across a network, only the insights traveled. That shift not only saved bandwidth but also calmed a lot of nerves about leaks and surveillance. Because of that, federated systems suddenly made sense in places where secrecy isn't optional—think hospitals safeguarding medical histories, banks bound by regulatory firewalls, or defense agencies where even a small slip could be disastrous. Of course, the appeal doesn't mean every problem is solved. These systems can still be messy to manage, and not every organization is ready to trust them fully. But compared to their earlier forms, the leap is striking.

Over the past couple of years, federated systems have picked up some new abilities—things like smarter ways of adapting on the fly and tools that can watch over processes in real time. They don't feel like those old, stiff data-sharing networks anymore. Instead, they behave more like flexible environments that can bend and reshape themselves when resources change or when people suddenly ask more of them. The bigger push now, though, is toward making these systems less dependent on constant human oversight. The idea is to get them to set themselves up, repair small issues without waiting on engineers, and even fine-tune how they run as conditions shift. Whether that's realistic in every case is debatable—autonomy often introduces its own risks—but the direction is clear. And it's really the blending of several things at once—machine intelligence, edge-level processing, and new decentralized rules—that makes this vision seem within reach rather than just a neat theory.

In recent years, the addition of AI-based coordination and real-time decision-making has improved the scope and power of federated systems. These federated systems incorporated with AI coordination operate dynamically and are able to share database infrastructure dynamically. The trend is now moving towards intelligent systems that are also autonomous, enabling them to self-configure and optimize operations without manual intervention. The merge of AI, edge computing, and decentralized protocols has resulted in a demanding next-generation systems practically.

11.1.2 The need for next-gen and autonomous approaches in finance

Regulation and risk have a big influence on the banking sector. Every decision has consequences, and even some outages in service. They can damage customer trust and cause large losses in revenue. So that speed and flexibility are not just desirable qualities; they can give banks a competitive advantage. Still, many organizations are using outdated software and fragmented systems. These systems can't effectively communicate with each other. Additionally, cyberthreats are becoming more serious every year; in fact, they are becoming more incisive and intentional. The rise of cryptocurrencies and other digital assets adds another level of complexity.

In banking, where the margin for error is slim, the ability to keep data local while still learning from it on a broader scale matters a great deal. Federated systems make that possible. They allow institutions to train models that can spot fraud, assess risk, or even refine credit scoring, all without sending sensitive transaction data across borders. That's a big win for compliance with rules like General Data Protection Regulation (GDPR), but it doesn't shut the door on innovation—the analytics can still move forward. This approach can also do identity verifications easier and speed up international transactions. It leads to faster settlements, fewer issues, and lower costs.

Federated systems stand out because they can manage themselves. In banking systems, even a millisecond's delay can affect profits, so automation is a critical thing. These systems can identify problems, share and transfer workloads, and reroute traffic instantly, all while obeying compliance rules. They also add automated governance. That means the system can adjust to new regulations or market changes without waiting for manual updates, giving banks both stability and flexibility.

The future of finance will rely on systems that are secure, decentralized, and flexible enough to handle constant change. Federated models move in that direction. They combine distributed design with smart decision-making, giving a framework that can manage both growth and risk. As banking and payments become more digital and global, these systems won't remain on the sidelines. They will move to the center, building trust, keeping operations stable, and helping firms meet strict regulations.

11.1.3 Scope and structure of the chapter

This chapter looks closely at federated systems—where they started, how they've evolved, and where they may be going next. The focus is on their growing role in finance and other fields where reliability is critical. The concept starts with the early days of basic data sharing and then traces the key developments that molded the platforms we see today. Over time, issues like privacy, scalability, and autonomy come to the main picture and become the central concerns of the technology. The focus then turns to the finance sector, exploring why newer federated approaches have gained so much importance nowadays. Real-world examples show how they perform in challenging areas: they ensure data privacy, comply with regulations, defend against cyberattacks, and have fast decision-making ability. Consider all these advantages—by combining automation with decentralized control, we can build systems that are both smarter and more self-reliant.

In the later sections, the chapter turns to the pieces of architecture that make autonomy in federated systems possible. It touches on decentralized orchestration, intelligent agents, blockchain, and the protocols that let systems adapt as conditions change. Alongside these ideas come some stubborn problems—model drift, uneven resources, and the challenge of building trust.

11.2 DEFINING NEXT-GENERATION FEDERATED SYSTEMS

Next-generation federated systems—well, they're a bit of a step into the unknown compared to the old-school versions. Sounds great, right? But, honestly, it's not foolproof. You still need smart design and some human oversight, especially when you're dealing with sensitive stuff like bank transactions or patient records.

It's not just about moving tasks from one node to another. These systems juggle them. Imagine a bunch of banks processing cross-border payments. One server lags, another picks up the slack. Clever, but it can go wrong if the data's messy or incomplete. They lean on AI, edge computing, blockchain, and even 5G. All fancy tools, sure—but the real test is keeping it reliable when things aren't neat. At the end of the day, the aim is… well, it's messy to define exactly, but roughly: handle data safely, make decisions without babysitting, and keep the whole thing humming. And even then, there are trade-offs. Nothing's perfect.

Old federated systems—they needed a ton of manual setup and struggled whenever the infrastructure was mixed or the workload spiked. The new ones, though, are a different story. They can adjust on the fly, route tasks intelligently, work together across multiple agents, and follow rules without someone micromanaging every step. Over time, they even learn a bit from what's happened before, tweaking how they perform based on experience and the context they're in.

These features aren't just tech fluff—they really matter in places like hospitals, banks, smart cities, or defense networks. Real-time responses, strict compliance, and scalability aren't optional there. Decentralization is a further significant concept. Trust has been distributed across the network, facilitated by cryptography and consensus, as compared to relying on a single central authority [3]. What this really means is that people can work together safely without having to give away personal information. That's the main reason these technologies appeal to industries where confidentiality isn't negotiable. Their strength lies in the mix—they can scale up, stay flexible, and adapt quickly in real time. Put together, those qualities make them stand out and allow them to keep working even in today's unpredictable online world.

11.2.1 Characteristics of next-gen systems

11.2.1.1 Scalability

Scalability is one of the biggest concerns for modern federated systems. Consider a network where data just keep generating and sharing. The older versions of federated systems struggled in these scenarios. Their regulations and dependence on central servers often turned into bottlenecks. The newer designs are built to handle this more smoothly. They let you spin nodes up or shut them down as needed, depending on how much work there is or what resources are free. In addition, they employ strategies like asynchronous update transmission, model encoding, and job scheduling that maintains an eye on edge devices. The idea is to keep the system fast and accurate, even when it's running at full tilt with tons of nodes.

11.2.1.2 Interoperability

Another big deal for next-gen federated systems is interoperability—basically, getting different platforms, devices, and data types to actually talk to each other. In real life, that means organizations with totally different setups can join the same network without tearing their own systems apart. Pulling that off isn't simple. You need open standards, modular designs, and middleware that can sort out all the mismatched data formats and communication quirks. Think about healthcare. A federated system there has to handle info from hospital databases, wearable devices, and insurance platforms. All of them speak slightly different "languages," but interoperability lets the system make sense of it without forcing anyone to rebuild everything from scratch [5].

11.2.1.3 Real-time adaptability

What really makes next-gen systems stand out is their ability to adjust on the fly. Seriously, anything can happen—network hiccups, data shifting in weird ways, or parts of the system just failing. These systems have to notice all that and react immediately, without waiting for a central boss to tell them what to do. They achieve this through the use of event-driven logic, network monitoring, and feedback learning. In essence, the system adjusts itself as it goes along via detecting what is and is not working. And it's only after you imagine self-driving vehicles or stock trading that you realize how important this is.

11.2.2 Integration of AI and edge computing

What's really interesting about next-generation federated systems is how they mix AI and edge computing—two things that, on paper, seem obvious together, but in practice are pretty tricky to pull off. AI is basically the brain here. It identifies errors, modifies models, predicts outcomes, and is even able to perform decisions on its own. On the other side, edge computing is similar to placing the processing on a sensor, smartphone, or local server, which are the same locations in which the data is stored. That is crucial since returning all the data to a central server might be very slow, consume a lot of bandwidth, and present privacy issues. With this setup, data can be processed and models trained close to home. The system might aggregate updates every so often, using something like federated averaging, so the bigger picture is still learned without moving raw data around. For the most part, it respects privacy and is more rapid and effective. It's not perfect, of course. Improper synchronization can lead to local devices possessing limited power, sporadic connectivity, and disorganized aggregating models [6]. Nevertheless, when it functions, it's very incredible: a system that can operate worldwide, think locally, and hide crucial details.

Another cool thing about this AI-and-edge combo is what you might call context-aware intelligence. Basically, the AI running at the edge can learn the quirks of its own environment and react quickly. Take a smart city's traffic system, for example.

But it doesn't stop there. AI can also help orchestrate the whole network. Imagine intelligent agents quietly keeping an eye on resource use, spreading out computational loads, and even spotting potential failures before they happen. Pair that with edge computing, and you get a system that's fast, efficient, and a bit proactive—it tries to fix problems before you even notice them. Of course, it's not perfect. Devices can be underpowered, connections can fail, and sometimes the local models disagree in ways that are tricky to reconcile. Still, as more devices and data sources come online, this partnership between AI and edge computing is basically what makes next-gen federated systems scalable and mostly self-managing.

11.2.3 Role of blockchain in autonomous collaboration

Blockchain is really handy when it comes to building trust in next-gen federated systems. Think about it: in these networks, you've got multiple organizations—or sometimes even competitors—working together without giving up full control or sensitive data [7]. That's tricky. Blockchain helps through keeping a decentralized ledger whereby every interaction or transaction is recorded in a manner that makes it difficult for tampering. You don't need a central authority to dictate to you because everyone sees the same past. It's not magic, of course—blockchain can at times be sluggish or costly—but it's a clever method for improving the openness and reliability of collaboration.

Blockchain really shines when you're trying to get autonomous collaboration to work. The smart contracts it supports are, well... basically little agreements that execute themselves when certain conditions happen. In a federated system, that could mean checking models, deciding who can use what resources, doling out incentives, or making sure policies are followed. Imagine a bunch of banks in different countries. Instead of someone manually reconciling accounts or checking compliance, the contracts do it automatically. Saves time. Cuts costs.

But that's not the only thing blockchain does. Federated systems pull in data from all over—local devices, sensors, different organizations. That said, it's not perfect. Updating all the nodes can be slow, and it can eat up resources. Still, having that verifiable chain of events gives you a level of trust you just can't fake.

Blockchain also helps with reputation management in federated systems. Basically, it can keep track of how participants behave—things like the quality of the models they contribute or whether they follow the rules. Over time, this builds a dynamic trust profile. The idea behind it is easy to understand: if you work hard, your reputation will increase; if you try to cheat, it will show. This is especially useful in open federated networks where people or organizations may not be acquainted with one another [8]. By making accountability decentralized, blockchain helps create a system that can basically govern itself. Now, if you look at Figure 11.1, it shows a typical centralized FL setup. Multiple clients—Client 1 through Client N—train models locally on their own private data. They don't share the data itself, just the updates to their models. A central server collects those updates and combines them into a global model. After that, the clients acquire an updated global model for the next training sessions. This cycle—local training, update, global aggregation—keeps repeating. The neat part? Everyone's data stays private, but the shared model keeps getting smarter.

Table 11.1 explains traditional federated systems. They typically rely on a centralized client-server architecture, where clients send their locally trained model updates to a central server for aggregation. Communication is one-way—from clients to the server—and model aggregation takes place solely at that central point. This structure leads to low fault tolerance and scalability challenges due to server dependency [9]. Privacy is maintained through basic techniques like differential privacy (DP), but these systems often struggle with non-IID (non-identical and independent) data and heterogeneous devices. Their application is mostly limited to basic use cases like mobile keyboards or predictive text systems.

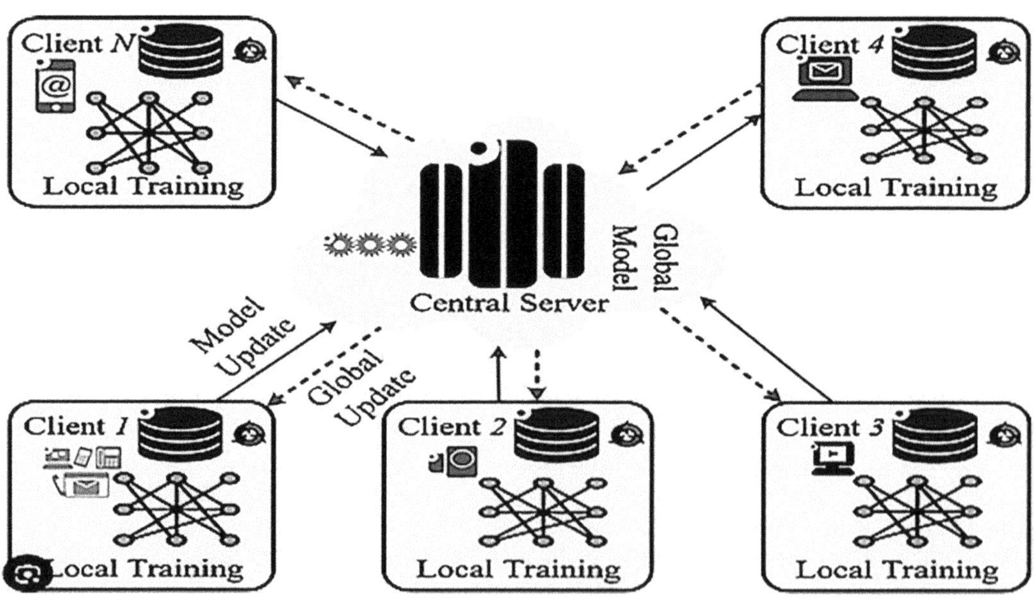

Figure 11.1 Evolution of federated learning architectures.

Table 11.1 Comparative table of traditional vs next-gen federated systems

Aspect	*Traditional Federated Systems*	*Next-Gen Federated Systems*
Architecture	Centralized (client-server)	Decentralized/hierarchical/peer-to-peer
Communication Pattern	One-to-many (clients to central server)	Many-to-many (clients coordinate directly or in hierarchy)
Model Aggregation	Performed at central server	Distributed or multi-tier aggregation
Fault Tolerance	Low – dependent on central server	High – resilient to single-point failures
Scalability	Limited due to server bottlenecks	High – supports large-scale client networks
Privacy Mechanisms	Basic DP and secure aggregation	Advanced techniques (homomorphic encryption, secure multi-party computation)
Data and System Heterogeneity	Poor handling of non-IID data and device variability	Designed for heterogeneity and personalization
Use Case Maturity	Used in pilot-stage industry applications (e.g., mobile keyboard)	Emerging in finance, healthcare, edge AI, autonomous vehicles
Latency and Efficiency	Higher due to sequential updates	Improved with asynchronous and edge-computing optimizations
Governance and Control	Centralized control	Decentralized governance and collaborative policies

In contrast, next-generation federated systems embrace decentralized, hierarchical, or peer-to-peer architectures, allowing clients to communicate directly or via structured tiers. Aggregation is distributed, improving scalability and resilience to server failures.

11.3 AUTONOMY IN FL

Federated Learning, or FL, is really changing the game in collaborative machine learning. Instead of moving all the data to a central place, the models get trained across lots of distributed clients—think smartphones, edge sensors, or local servers. In the older setups, there was usually a central orchestrator calling the shots. Nowadays, people are starting to talk more about autonomy in FL systems.

11.3.1 Levels of autonomy in federated systems

FL autonomy can be seen as a spectrum, with the system operating almost totally on its own at one extreme and everything being manually controlled at the other. The simplest description of manual FL is that all of the tedious tasks, such as assigning models, selecting which clients obtain training, preprocessing data, and scheduling aggregations, are performed by people or a central server. Every little detail, from fixing errors to tweaking hyperparameters, needs explicit human supervision. Sure, this gives you maximum control, but it's a nightmare at scale. It's slow, expensive, and can't keep up when the network conditions start changing unexpectedly [10].

As FL has grown up a bit, semi-autonomous systems have started showing up. They're kind of a middle ground—some things run on their own, but humans still keep an eye on the big picture. For example, the system might pick which clients to include or tweak the learning rate based on preset rules or feedback. Humans usually step in for the tricky stuff, or when things don't go as planned. These systems often follow heuristic policies and can adapt a little on their own. The big win? Scaling becomes way easier, and daily operational headaches drop. You see this a lot in enterprise setups, where rules and compliance can't be ignored—but honestly, it's not a perfect solution; there's always some tension between automation and control.

At the very top level, fully autonomous FL systems are pretty wild—they basically run themselves from start to finish. They handle everything: setup, configuration, model updates, retraining, even optimization. They can pick which clients to include based on things like available resources, data quality, or network hiccups. No humans needed to nudge them. In addition, they are capable of recognizing and dealing with abnormalities in real time, such as slow nodes or attempts to manipulate the data [12]. When AI agents are in charge, the system adjusts its strategy based on prior behavior.

11.3.2 Self-healing and self-optimizing models

Beyond making decisions on their own, federated systems are now being built to repair and improve themselves. A self-configuring system can identify failures and weak points, slowdowns, or even security threats. They can fix them without people's instructions. For instance, if some clients send in bad status—whether from a cyberattack or a hardware glitch—the system can end the communication, roll back changes, and adjust its process to keep the overall model safe. This kind of resilience comes from tools like anomaly detection, trust scoring, and designs that use redundancy [13]. Each client can be given a trust score based on past behavior, and the system can lower or block input from suspicious ones. Techniques such as ensemble learning or blockchain-based audit trails also help the system recover from mismatched versions, data errors, or syncing problems.

Self-optimizing federated systems take things a step further. They are enabled to learn themselves over time to improve their performance. Instead of performing the same task again and again, they change their own settings to boost accuracy, efficiency, or even energy use. They integrate concepts like meta-learning and online learning to fine-tune training on the fly. In scenarios a model can adjust its own hyperparameters, pick the best aggregation method, or switch between synchronous and asynchronous modes depending on what the clients and network conditions demand at that moment. This flexibility really matters in messy, and challenging real world environments. Imagine a mobile network where bandwidth is tight—the system might automatically switch to compressed or sparse updates to save resources. Or imagine an application where speed is critical; the model could lean on low-latency, high-power to get results faster than a client can ever think of.

Figure 11.2 shows how banking data moves across three main layers—input, preprocessing, and application. Each bank trains a model locally using its own private data, and instead of sharing that raw data, only the trained model is sent to the cloud. There, the models are combined to create a stronger global model [14]. This global model produces predictions, which are processed through an explainable AI (XAI) layer to improve interpretability. Based on the learning rate and explanation, the model may be refined or stored in cloud data storage. Real-time banking data is also continuously analyzed for fraud detection; if a transaction is flagged as fraudulent, it is securely handled. The entire process

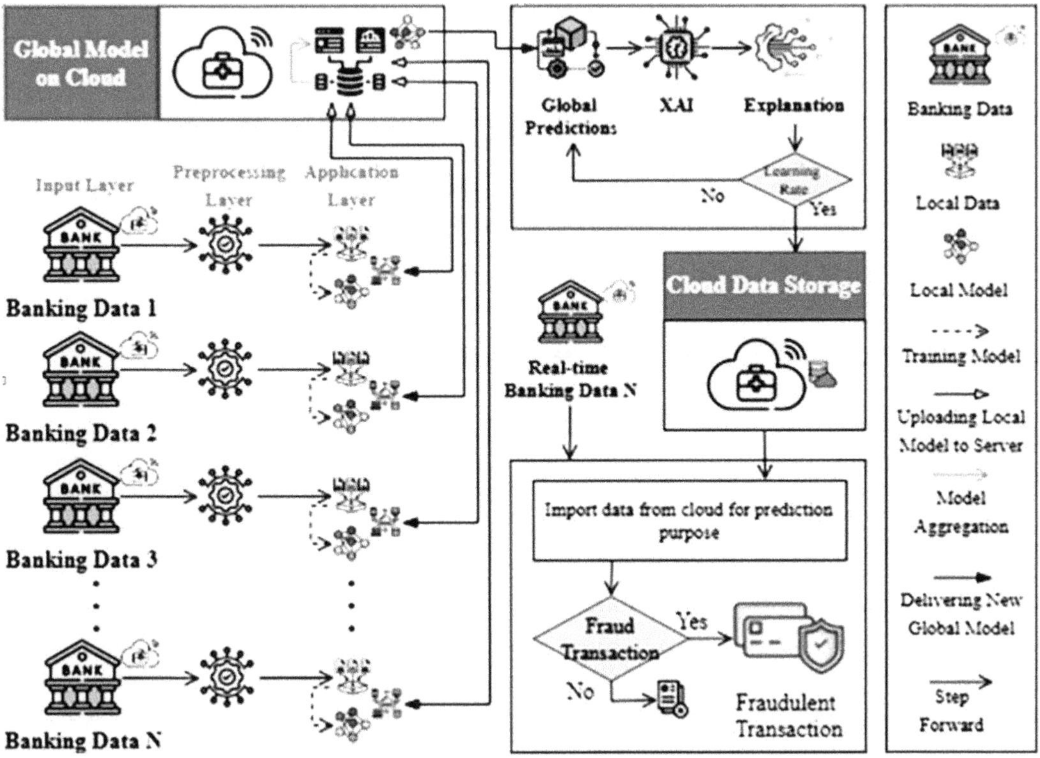

Figure 11.2 Architecture of an autonomous federated financial fraud detection system.

supports privacy, decentralization, and intelligent decision-making in federated financial systems.

Table 11.2 presents a taxonomy of federated systems based on autonomy levels, progressing from manual to fully autonomous capabilities. At **Level 0**, all coordination is manual, with no automation. **Level 1** introduces basic rule-based automation, followed by **Level 2**, which enables reactive responses to issues like client dropout or data imbalance. **Level 3** brings adaptive intelligence with dynamic task allocation and resource management. At **Level 4**, systems demonstrate collaborative intelligence, where multiple agents negotiate and cooperate using policy-driven logic. Finally, **Level 5** represents fully autonomous federated intelligence, capable of self-management, explainability, trust-building, and secure operations without human intervention [15].

11.4 AI-DRIVEN COORDINATION AND RRCHESTRATION

As FL expands into fields like banking and healthcare, the systems that support it are growing more complicated. They bring together many different participants, wide-ranging datasets, and networks that do not always perform consistently. Running such systems cannot rely only on fixed settings or continuous manual supervision, since both approaches quickly reach their limits. Instead, more intelligent methods of organizing the components' connections are required. In actuality, this entails putting in place mechanisms that enable devices

Table 11.2 Taxonomy of autonomy in federated systems (based on capability)

Level	*Autonomy Capability*	*Key Features*	*Examples*
Level 0	Manual Coordination	Human-led orchestration, static scheduling, no automation	Basic FL testbeds, manual model updates
Level 1	Rule-based automation	Basic rules for training cycles, pre-defined triggers for model aggregation	Early industrial FL pilots
Level 2	Reactive autonomy	Responds to events (e.g., dropout, data skew), supports limited self-healing	Federated optimization with retry logic
Level 3	Adaptive autonomy	Dynamic task assignment, adaptive learning rate, smart resource allocation	Context-aware FL systems
Level 4	Collaborative intelligence	Multi-agent collaboration, policy-driven negotiation among clients	Decentralized FL with game-theory support
Level 5	Fully autonomous federated intelligence	Self-managing, self-healing, explainable, trust-aware, and security-adaptive	Autonomous banking FL, healthcare AI grids

or organizations to efficiently share updates, divide their responsibilities, and maintain the process as a whole even when circumstances change. Researchers are considering a variety of concepts to achieve this, such as collaboratively self-sufficient agents, contract-like norms that restrict participation, impartial negotiation procedures, and optimization strategies that adapt system performance. When combined, these strategies offer up the possibility to federated networks that are more resilient and flexible.

11.4.1 Multi-Agent Systems (MAS) for Federated Coordination

Under a framework termed a multi-agent system (MAS), several autonomous agents work together to deal with issues that would be too complex for one unit to manage. In FL, MAS provides an ideal solution for organizing and overseeing scattered consumers. Each agent may represent a hospital, bank, edge device, or another actor with data. Agents can make choices based on their immediate surroundings while still pursuing a common goal if they have their own local intelligence [16]. This implies that in practice, agents can organize training cycles, synchronize update schedules, analyze hardware or network limitations, and react to system alterations as they happen. Another distinctive feature of MAS designs is resilience; if one agent quits or is compromised, the other agents can change their structure to keep on learning.

The behavior of agents in a multi-agent system could be greatly enhanced by artificial intelligence. Agents can efficiently handle resources, choose when to train, and save energy by improving their skills through learning through reinforcement. Another layer is added by game theory, which supports agents in resolving disputes in a way that encourages cooperation while preserving their autonomy. The main advantages of MAS are its flexibility and scalability, which enable the inclusion of new agents or the deletion of existing ones without endangering the system as a whole. They are especially well-suited for federated networks in sectors like banking, where user bases and members are constantly shifting, because they are flexible.

11.4.2 Smart contract-based node behavior management

Blockchain-based smart contracts can be utilized in FL systems to manage members without the need for a central authority. These contracts are helpful for tasks like assigning incentives and consequences, verifying contributions, and deciding who gets to take part in a training round because they only carry out the rules that have been included in them. Incorporating machine learning models into this process allows the contracts to adapt to context rather than just following predefined rules [17]. If a node delivers reliable updates, it might be rewarded more. Since there is no need for a central referee, good behavior is rewarded and bad behavior is punished, thereby preserving the integrity of the link.

Smart contracts might enhance transparency and accountability in FL systems. Whether it's sending out prizes or modifying the model, every action is forever documented in the blockchain record. This allows one to verify that the rules have been correctly followed by examining each node's prior conduct. Such an open and permanent log is very helpful in financial environments where regulatory compliance and trust are crucial. These contracts offer a reliable basis for communication between parties that might not otherwise trust one another since they function in an autonomous way and might be difficult to change once executed.

11.4.3 Nodes dealing in trustless negotiation

Participants in FL applications in the financial sector are typically rival businesses, such as banks, insurance providers, or payment service providers. Of course obviously, none of them wants to give up raw data or naively believe what the others have to offer. "Trustless" negotiating becomes crucial for this reason. The premise is that various organizations can nevertheless collaborate and train common models without depending on a central authority or on individual trust. AI gives agents the ability to assess risks, examine proposals, and decide based on predetermined criteria. Techniques like SMPC and homomorphic encryption (HE) can be incorporated into the federated averaging process. In this manner, it is possible to safely mix and negotiate model updates without releasing sensitive data or proprietary parameters [18].

An AI agent that assists in decision-making can represent each financial institution in an FL environment. To determine how updates are weighted, how frequently training should take place, and which aggregation approach makes the most sense, these agents assess privacy constraints, data diversity, and system speed. Negotiations frequently make use of smart contracts, also referred to as automatically executing digital agreements. For instance, a bank might wish to hold off on releasing updates until the finished model exhibits equity across various customer groups or reaches a specific accuracy level. The agents can keep an eye on these indicators as the system functions and adjust their strategy as needed.

Table 11.3 compares key operational aspects of human- and AI-coordinated federated systems.

Human-coordinated systems rely on manual decision-making, which limits scalability, slows response times, and often requires administrator intervention for tasks like model aggregation or resource allocation. In contrast, AI-coordinated systems use intelligent agents to autonomously manage these tasks in real time, enabling faster, more scalable, and adaptive operations. They also enhance fault tolerance, optimize learning dynamically, and enforce security through smart contracts and automated monitoring [5]. As a result, AI-coordinated systems are better suited for complex, large-scale, and evolving environments, while human-coordinated models are typically limited to smaller, more static use cases.

Table 11.3 Human-coordinated vs. AI-coordinated federated systems

Feature	*Human-Coordinated Federated Systems*	*AI-Coordinated Federated Systems*
Coordination Method	Manual configuration and human decision-making	Autonomous orchestration via AI agents
Scalability	Limited; coordination becomes complex with more nodes	High; scalable to large, dynamic environments
Response Time	Slow; relies on human intervention	Fast; real-time adaptive responses
Fault Tolerance	Low; human delay may affect continuity	High; self-healing mechanisms respond automatically
Model Aggregation	Scheduled or manually triggered	Dynamically triggered based on data flow and learning metrics
Resource Allocation	Static or administrator-defined	Adaptive and optimized via intelligent agents
Decision-Making	Based on predefined rules or admin expertise	Driven by context-aware algorithms and feedback loops
Security and Compliance	Enforced manually	Enforced using smart contracts, AI monitoring, and anomaly detection
Learning Optimization	Rarely updated unless manually revised	Continuously improved using reinforcement learning or meta-learning
Use Case Readiness	Suitable for small-scale or regulated deployments	Ideal for large-scale, decentralized, and mission-critical applications

11.4.4 Energy and cost optimization using AI algorithms

As FL scales to include thousands or even millions of edge devices and institutional nodes, the cumulative computational and energy costs become a significant concern. AI-based energy and cost optimization techniques are crucial for making large-scale federated deployments sustainable and economically viable. AI algorithms can be applied to monitor and predict resource consumption patterns across the network. Machine learning models can analyze client behavior, network conditions, and power usage to create profiles that help in optimizing client selection. Not every device in a federated network has the same capacity. Some are fast, with strong processors and steady internet, while others might be slow, with limited battery or weaker connectivity. In practice, this means the system shouldn't treat all clients equally. For instance, powerful devices may be used more frequently, while weaker or smaller devices might contribute less frequently without slowing down processes. Even here, reinforcement learning may assist in identifying practical ways to conserve energy, such as reducing the number of training steps, transmitting updates less frequently, and compressing data before distributing it. These modifications minimize the use of resources yet preserve the overall accuracy of the model. Another useful trick is grouping similar clients together. Devices can train in smaller clusters at first, then incorporate their results into the global model if they feature identical hardware, data, or network conditions. As a result, there is a fewer need for regular interaction with the main computer. Stated differently, the entire procedure becomes lighter and more effective. This is particularly helpful for edge devices, where data usage and battery life are constant concerns. By making these changes, gadgets continue to improve significantly and remain active for longer periods of time. The same logic applies on the cloud side. Running federated systems at scale can be expensive, so AI tools are often used to manage resources. They can predict when activity will go up, add more computing power only when needed, and scale things down again

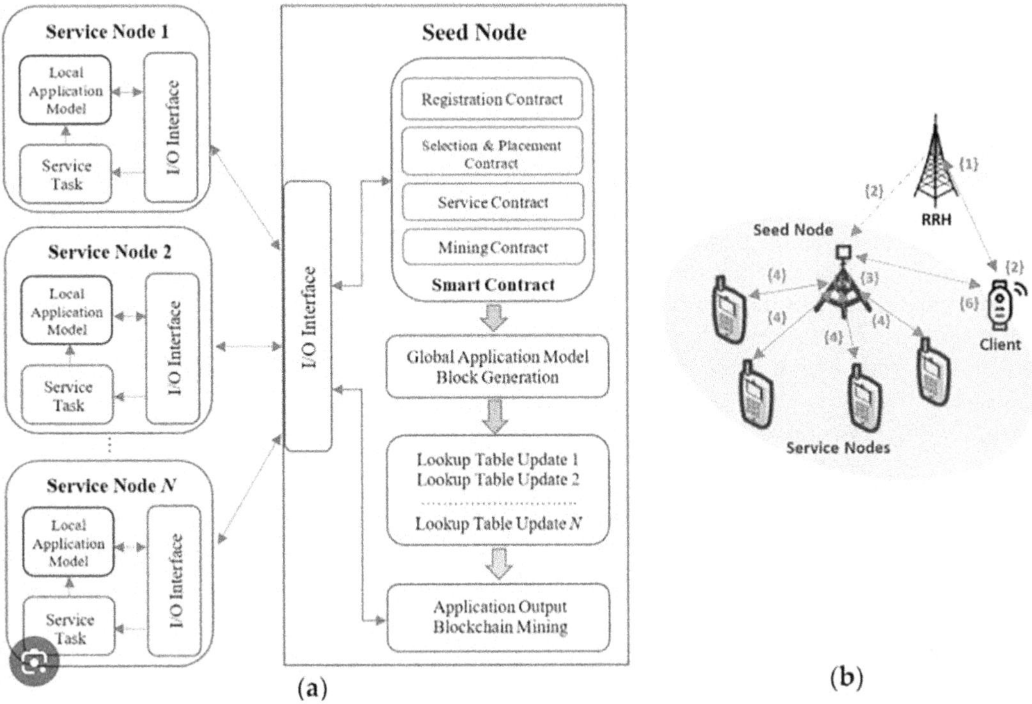

Figure 11.3(a) Workflow of smart contract execution and service coordination in the federated network.
Figure 11.3(b) Communication scenario between seed node, service nodes, and client devices.

to avoid waste. This kind of cost management is particularly important in finance, where systems process huge numbers of transactions and speed really matters. By combining performance with efficiency, AI makes it possible to run FL at a large scale without running into unsustainable costs.

The diagram in Figure 11.3 illustrates a smart contract–driven federated service architecture involving **service nodes**, a **seed node**, and a **client**. In part (a), each service node maintains a local application model and executes service tasks through an I/O interface. These nodes interact with a seed node that hosts multiple smart contracts (e.g., registration, placement, mining) to coordinate model updates and manage tasks. The seed node aggregates local outputs, generates a global application model, and mines blockchain blocks containing the results. Part (b) shows the communication flow: the client transmits data via RRH to the seed node, which then coordinates with multiple service nodes [19]. The seed node facilitates model coordination (steps 3–5), and final outputs are sent back to the client, completing a secure and autonomous federated loop.

11.5 PRIVACY AND SECURITY TECHNIQUES OF NEXT-GEN AND AUTONOMOUS FEDERATED SYSTEMS

11.5.1 Enhanced DP techniques

DP has long been a cornerstone in privacy-preserving machine learning, offering mathematical guarantees that the inclusion or exclusion of a single individual's data does not significantly affect the output of an algorithm. By introducing calibrated noise to the gradients or model updates, DP is normally employed in FL to safeguard the privacy of each unique client. Standard DP sometimes involves a challenging trade-off: the poorer the model, the stronger the privacy. The issue is apparent when the data is high- dimensional or the client distributions are different. A recent study has attempted to reduce this stress by using more flexible methods.

One technique is local DP with customization. In other words, each customer is free to select the degree of privacy they want for their data, depending on sensitivity or policy. During training, systems powered by AI may even monitor accuracy and modify noise levels. Privacy is safeguarded in this way without substantially harming performance.

There are also tricks like gradient clipping (basically limiting the size of updates) and pairing it with smarter noise calibration. Gaussian or Laplacian noise can be tuned depending on context, rather than being fixed. Another idea is privacy amplification by subsampling. Instead of involving every client in every round, only a random subset takes part, which naturally improves privacy.

11.5.2 Homomorphic encryption and Secure multi-party computation (SMPC)

SMPC and HE, which both allow computing on encrypted data without revealing its underlying content, are frequently used in FL to accomplish privacy-preserving computation. This implies that clients can give the server encrypted model updates, and the server can aggregate them without ever observing the raw numbers [20]. After aggregation, the resulting encrypted global model can be decrypted only by authorized parties. This property is particularly valuable in FL scenarios where the central aggregator must not access individual client information, as seen in collaborative environments among banks or healthcare institutions.

Modern implementations use partially or fully HE schemes, with trade-offs between performance and functionality. Libraries like Microsoft SEAL and IBM HELib offer frameworks to implement HE in practical FL systems. Despite its computational overhead, recent research focuses on approximate HE and packing techniques to reduce latency and memory requirements, making real-time encrypted model aggregation increasingly feasible. SMPC, on the other hand, splits data or computation tasks across multiple parties such that no single party can reconstruct the input, yet they can jointly compute a function over the distributed inputs. SMPC protocols like secret sharing and garbled circuits are now being used in FL settings where clients collaboratively compute global model parameters without disclosing individual updates to any party, including the server.

By combining HE and SMPC, hybrid systems can offer stronger security guarantees. For example, SMPC may handle model update aggregation while HE secures intermediate computations. These techniques together eliminate single points of failure, resist collusion, and provide high assurance even in untrusted or adversarial environments.

11.5.3 Next-level privacy techniques using swarm intelligence

An emerging area of privacy research in FL lies in the application of swarm intelligence, inspired by decentralized biological systems such as ant colonies, bee swarms, and bird flocks. Swarm-based techniques emphasize distributed decision-making, redundancy, and adaptability—properties that align well with the principles of federated systems. The actions and reactions of the swarm-based FL system are similar to those of natural swarms. Instead of waiting for a central authority to govern the process, each node makes decisions locally based on its observations and any signals it receives from peers in the vicinity. Patterns of global coordination start to appear quite naturally once enough nodes accomplish this. One immediate advantage is that privacy tends to improve as no one party ever collects or controls everything. Another instance is particle-swarm optimization (PSO)-powered federated optimization [21].

Swarms have the capacity to organize themselves, raising isolation from clients who seem dubious or reinforcing bonds amongst those who seem reliable. Because of their flexibility, they are more resilient than encryption-heavy methods, which can be readily breached by an attack. Furthermore, rigorous synchronization isn't necessarily necessary for swarms [17]. They can continue to function asynchronously instead of waiting for everyone to queue up at the same checkpoint, which frequently feels more natural in untidy real-world networks.

11.5.4 Quantum-resilient security for federated systems

People working on FL are starting to look nervously at the rise of quantum computing. The worry is pretty simple: once quantum machines become strong enough, many of the encryption methods we rely on today—RSA (Rivest–Shamir–Adleman), ECC (Elliptic Curve Cryptography), and so on—may no longer be safe. Shor's algorithm, for example, is already well known for breaking RSA in theory, and Grover's shows that even symmetric ciphers aren't immune. That puts a lot of pressure on researchers to rethink how "secure" communication in these systems should actually be defined. This is where post-quantum cryptography comes into play. Instead of depending on number-theory problems that quantum computers excel at, it leans on alternative mathematical puzzles that appear resistant even to quantum attacks. Lattice-based approaches, in particular, are attracting interest because they can support things like HE, which lets institutions share updates without exposing raw data [23]. Even though none of these is a general solution, research is also being done on additional families, such as code-based, hash-based, and multivariate polynomial systems [18]. Whether they have to do with speed, complexity of implementation, or scalability, each has its own set of trade-offs. But the underlying trend is evident: if FL is to be trusted in the quantum era, it must be built on these new foundations rather than the ones we have been using for decades.

Some people argue that post-quantum tools aren't enough on their own, and they've started looking at quantum key distribution, or QKD, as another line of defense in federated systems. The basic idea is appealing: if someone tries to eavesdrop on the key exchange, the intrusion can be detected because of the way quantum states collapse. That makes it much harder to steal the keys silently. The downside is obvious, though. QKD still needs very specialized hardware and reliable optical links, which means it's far from easy to use outside of research labs or high-budget environments. A few areas—think central banks or defense systems—might see value in testing it earlier than others. In the short run, hybrid approaches are more realistic. You keep the existing classical encryption, but pair it with algorithms that are expected to be resistant to quantum attacks. That way, older systems don't break, and newer ones slowly become harder to crack. But preparing FL for the quantum age isn't just about swapping encryption libraries. It most likely calls for rethinking how trust is distributed among nodes, what kind of infrastructure is most cost-effective, and how much performance we are prepared to give up in favor of more robust security. To phrase it differently, the decisions we make now are both technical and strategic.

A privacy-preserving FL workflow with multiple learners and a central server that is unstable with raw data is shown in Figure 11.4. In this arrangement, each participant uses the latest version of the shared global model to do local training on its own device. A local update is the result of this training, and it is encrypted before being sent to the server.

The server's role is limited to combining these encrypted updates without ever accessing the underlying data. Once the aggregation is completed, the combined result is securely decrypted to obtain the overall update. This updated global model is then redistributed back to all participants, allowing the learning process to continue in a secure and collaborative loop.

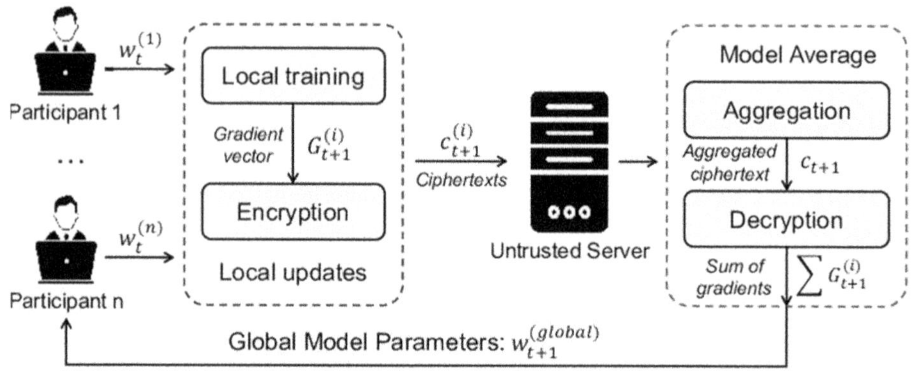

Figure 11.4 Next-gen privacy stack for federated financial systems.

Table 11.4 Security protocols comparison – current vs future models

Security Aspect	*Current Models*	*Future Models*
Data Privacy	DP, Basic encryption	Homomorphic encryption, federated differential privacy
Communication Security	TLS/SSL encryption	Blockchain-secured messaging, quantum-safe encryption
Aggregation Security	Trusted aggregator, secure aggregation	Multi-party computation (MPC), Secure hardware enclaves (SGX)
Authentication	Password or token-based	Biometric or behavior-based authentication
Client Trust	Assumed trust or simple validation	Trust scoring, dynamic reputation systems
Attack Resistance	Partial defense against poisoning or inference attacks	AI-driven anomaly detection, Byzantine-resilient aggregation
Smart Contract Integration	Rare or none	Full integration with AI-governed smart contracts
Auditability and Transparency	Centralized logs or admin-controlled	Decentralized, immutable audit trails (e.g., blockchain)
Model Integrity	Verified manually or post hoc	On-chain model fingerprinting and auto-verification
Regulatory Compliance	Manually monitored	Self-updating compliance rules based on AI and smart contracts

Current and future security protocols in FL systems are compared in Table 11.4. Existing models, which frequently presume client trust and manual oversight, rely on basic approaches like DP, TLS encryption, and trusted aggregators. Future models, contrary to expectations, aim to enhance security by utilizing cutting-edge technology such as multi-party computation, blockchain-secured communication, and HE [22]. They also introduce AI-driven anomaly detection, smart contract integration, and decentralized audit trails for enhanced transparency and resilience. More intelligent, scalable, and resilient security frameworks will be provided by future systems with dynamic trust mechanisms and automated compliance.

11.6 SELF-EVOLVING FL MODELS

Distributed systems are getting more complex and, at the same time, more independent. Because of this, FL can no longer rely only on the old approach of training models in fixed sessions with rigid settings. Those traditional setups often end after a few predefined rounds and don't account for long-term growth, memory, or the ability to adapt to new situations. In practice, though, areas like finance, healthcare, smart cities, and edge devices don't work that way. They generate new patterns all the time, and the systems behind them need to respond on the spot while also getting better as they go. The concept of self-evolving federated models is introduced here. With regard to these models, learning cannot be something that happens once but rather an ongoing, adaptive process that develops with experience. As opposed to focusing on one task at a time, they apply their knowledge to several projects, platforms, and situations. They also use constant input to improve their choices. In short, this direction in FL research points toward systems that learn the way people do—gradually, cumulatively, and with the ability to adapt when the environment shifts. In the next section, we will look more closely at four key aspects of this shift: lifelong learning, meta-learning, cross-platform transfer, and reinforcement-driven policy optimization.

11.6.1 Lifelong learning in distributed nodes

Continuous learning, commonly referred to as lifelong learning, is typically used to describe a system that continues after training. Rather, it continues to build on its prior understanding. In FL, that is crucial since things change quickly. For instance, a hospital could discover themselves faced with a hitherto unheard-of disease. Conversely, your phone is silently gathering fresh data every day, such as how often you use wallets or how you utilize apps. The model would have missed all of this if it had remained frozen on day one. Therefore, the goal of continual learning is straightforward: to adapt to life's changes while maintaining mindfulness of the lessons gained thus far. In distributed settings, lifelong learning enables each node to train its local model on sequential tasks without needing to restart the learning process. This leads to personalized yet cumulative learning trajectories. However, achieving lifelong learning in FL is challenging due to the catastrophic forgetting problem, where learning new tasks can overwrite knowledge from previous tasks. To mitigate this, techniques such as elastic weight consolidation, experience replay, and task-specific regularization have been adapted to decentralized environments [23].

Moreover, federated lifelong learning systems must also incorporate mechanisms for knowledge sharing across nodes. A node encountering a novel situation could benefit from another node's prior experience with a similar context. This form of cross-node transfer learning, however, must be executed under strict privacy constraints, making it a non-trivial problem. Hence, decentralized memory architectures, model distillation, and collaborative curriculum learning are being explored to build knowledge bases that evolve continuously while respecting client autonomy and privacy.

11.6.2 Meta-learning for federated environments

Meta-learning, often described as "learning to learn," is a powerful approach to improving adaptability across tasks by training models that can generalize quickly with limited data. In FL, where tasks may vary across clients (e.g., different hospitals diagnosing similar diseases, or different users with unique behavioral patterns), meta-learning allows the system to rapidly adapt to new client distributions without extensive retraining. One of the most popular meta-learning strategies is Model-Agnostic Meta-Learning (MAML), which seeks a global model initialization that can be quickly fine-tuned to new tasks using only a few local updates. In federated contexts, MAML can be extended by treating each client's task as part of a meta-task distribution. The central server aggregates updates not to train a single global model, but to find an initialization point that works well across diverse client-specific problems.

More recent adaptations like FedMeta and Per-FedAvg explore personalized meta-learning in FL, where each client uses the shared meta-model as a base for local fine-tuning. These approaches reduce communication costs while improving convergence rates on heterogeneous datasets [24]. Meta-learning in FL environments addresses core challenges such as task variability, limited local data, and fast adaptation requirements, making it an essential building block for self-evolving federated systems that must operate under volatile and personalized conditions.

11.6.3 Cross-platform learning and model transferability

FL systems often span heterogeneous environments, involving mobile devices, IoT sensors, edge servers, and cloud data centers. Each platform presents unique constraints in terms of computational power, communication bandwidth, and data modalities. Cross-platform learning refers to the ability of federated models to function effectively across these diverse systems, while model transferability focuses on transferring learned knowledge from one domain or client group to another. When federated models are expected to run across very different platforms, one size rarely fits all. A model built for a high-end server cannot be deployed unchanged on a lightweight mobile or IoT device. In practice, engineers deal with this by making the architecture platform-aware—reducing complexity where necessary, or applying compression and quantization so that smaller devices can still contribute [25]. Sometimes, lighter clients learn indirectly through methods like federated distillation, where they absorb useful patterns from the larger, more powerful models without handling the full workload themselves.

Transferability is another challenge. It's not enough for a model to work well on its original task; it should also adapt when the setting shifts. Think of a fraud detection system trained in one country. Institutions can simply retrain the decision layers and transfer the deeper feature representations instead of beginning from scratch in a different region. This is made achievable by methods like domain adaptation, zero-shot learning, or representation disentanglement, which guarantee that information persists while reducing the strain of retraining. The advantages are twofold: a greater range of devices and companies can participate, and FL becomes scalable and economical. Transferability also speeds up deployment into new environments, which is important in sectors like finance where risks, data patterns, and rules change frequently.

11.6.4 Reinforcement learning for policy optimization

Reinforcement learning (RL) is essentially about teaching an agent to make better decisions over time by experimenting, getting feedback, and adjusting its strategy based on rewards. For instance, it can help decide which clients should participate in a given training round, when to adjust the learning rate, or even how often updates should be communicated back to the server.

One of the most promising uses is adaptive client selection. An RL-driven controller can consider variables such as the quality of the local data, the real computing power of a device, or even the device's dependability in prior rounds, rather than blindly including every client. The result is a system that reduces energy and bandwidth waste, two of the largest obstacles in real-world deployments, while also achieving faster convergence.

One of the more challenging aspects of FL is that you can't simply adjust the knobs (such as learning rate, update frequency, or batch size) and expect them to function properly everywhere. Every client has different conditions. Reinforcement learning gives a way out of that rigidity. Every client has different conditions. Reinforcement learning gives a way out of that rigidity. Instead of relying on someone to tune these hyperparameters by hand, an RL agent can adjust them on the fly, depending on how the local training is going and how the global model responds. That tends to make the system more stable, and also more personalized, especially when the data is uneven or messy across different clients.

Aggregation is another headache. Averaging updates sounds simple, but in practice it often fails because some clients are noisy, or their data is just very different from the rest. RL can help here too, by learning policies that decide how much weight to give each client. Maybe you trust recent updates more, or maybe you give higher weight to a client with richer, cleaner data. The point is, the weighting isn't fixed—it's learned.

There's also this emerging idea of federated reinforcement learning, where the clients don't just train models—they act like RL agents themselves. Instead of isolated learning, they coordinate policies for bigger, system-wide goals. Picture delivery companies across a city collectively figuring out routes without handing over their private data, or banks fine-tuning transaction flows while still keeping customer information local. The exciting part is that it blends local learning with global cooperation, so the system adapts intelligently as conditions shift [24].

11.7 CASE STUDIES IN FINANCE

Finance is one of the clearest testing grounds for FL. The sector is overloaded with sensitive data, strict regulations, and an ongoing demand to share insights without breaking privacy laws. The majority of the personal and transactional data that banks, insurers, fintech companies, and even credit bureaus hold is legally restricted from leaving the organization that gathered it. Centralized data pooling is almost difficult due to regulations such as the GDPR in Europe, Payment Card Industry Data Security Standard (PCI-DSS) for payments, and national banking specifics. FL offers a solution to this bottleneck by allowing models to be trained locally, at the source, without transferring raw data anywhere. That shift is not just theoretical—it opens up the chance for genuine collaboration across institutions that normally compete or are barred from sharing information.

In the following section, I look at both practical deployments and conceptual case studies where FL has already been applied, or at least seriously considered, in finance. The focus is on three areas where the stakes are high and the benefits tangible: fraud detection, credit scoring, and regulatory compliance.

11.7.1 Autonomous fraud detection across banks

One of the biggest problems facing the global banking system is fraudulent transactions. They can take many different forms, including insider trading, money laundering, identity theft, account takeover, and synthetic fraud. Conventional models for detecting fraud depend on centralized databases that compile transactional data in order to spot unusual trends. However, such centralization introduces risks of data leakage, legal non-compliance, and significant infrastructure overhead. Moreover, fraudsters continuously adapt their tactics, making it imperative for detection systems to evolve autonomously. In this context, FL enables autonomous and collaborative fraud detection across multiple banks. Each financial institution trains a local model using its own private customer transaction data [25]. These local models learn the behavioral patterns of legitimate and illegitimate transactions, including time-of-day variations, merchant categories, transaction frequencies, device fingerprints, and geolocation trails. Periodically, only the model parameters—not the raw data—are sent to a central server or a decentralized blockchain layer for secure aggregation.

One successful deployment architecture involves using reinforcement learning and continual learning to enable self-evolving fraud detectors. Each participating bank trains an agent that adapts to changing fraud patterns, and through secure parameter aggregation, these agents benefit from collective intelligence. A suspicious behavior flagged in one bank—such as sudden cross-border fund transfers or unusual IP address logins—can help other banks preemptively flag similar risks, even if they have never encountered such patterns before.

To further enhance the robustness of these models, some institutions incorporate adversarial training and anomaly-aware aggregation functions. This approach filters out poisoned updates (from potentially compromised clients) and protects against drift caused by rare but legitimate behavior. The decentralized and adaptive nature of the FL framework makes it extremely difficult for fraudsters to reverse-engineer or manipulate the global model. Overall, FL enables banks to collaborate on fraud intelligence without ever sharing customer data, creating a scalable, privacy-preserving defense mechanism that is continuously evolving and inherently more secure than traditional centralized models.

11.7.2 Self-adaptive credit risk assessment

When banks or lenders talk about credit risk, they're really asking a simple question: will this person be able to pay the money back, and how likely is it to happen on time? The majority of credit rating tools continue to rely significantly on outdated, static databases. As a result, they frequently miss crucial indicators that could provide a more accurate picture of risk, such as abrupt alterations in people's spending patterns, changes in their transaction activity, or other signals that appear only in real time.

The issue is even sharper for newer lending services. Peer-to-peer platforms and small digital micro-finance apps usually don't have deep credit histories to work with. Without that background, the gaps in traditional scoring models become harder to ignore. In these cases, depending only on conventional models leaves big blind spots. What's really needed is a setup where multiple institutions can work together to build stronger risk models, but in a way that still protects customer privacy and respects the rules around data use.

FL opens up a new way to approach credit risk assessment. Instead of each bank or fintech working in isolation, they can train models together while keeping customer records private. In practice, this means that different institutions update a shared model using their own local data—whether that's repayment patterns, changes in income, app usage, online purchases, utility bills, or even social indicators. The raw information never leaves the source, but the collective updates help produce a scoring system that adjusts in real time and reflects a wider set of behaviors.

Federated models can be thought of as "self-adaptive" because they don't just sit on a static set of features. They shift as conditions shift. Credit risk, after all, isn't frozen in time—it changes with behavior, with economic signals, even with local events. If a borrower who usually pays on time suddenly skips a series of digital wallet top-ups, or stops logging into financial apps as often, that drop-off becomes a useful clue. The model can pick up on those small movements and re-weight its assessment accordingly, instead of waiting for the credit report to catch up months later. In practice, many systems use a two-tier setup. There's a global backbone that captures the broader lending patterns across institutions, and then local "heads" that are tuned to the customer base of each bank or fintech. A cooperative bank serving rural traders might put more emphasis on informal repayment markers, while an urban credit platform might lean heavily on e-commerce or salary deposit data. That mix—global patterns plus local nuance—is what makes these federated models better suited to real-world lending, where borrowers don't all look the same on paper.

Credit models built on FL are starting to borrow from meta-learning and transfer learning, which means that newer or smaller lenders don't have to start from scratch. They can plug into models that have already been trained by larger, more established institutions and then adapt them to their own context. This partially balances the playing field by offering community banks and microlenders with access to resources that were formerly restricted to large companies. Additionally, it can lessen the inbuilt discrimination that results from depending solely on traditional credit footprints, which is especially important in areas where a large number of borrowers lack any formal credit history.

Of course, regulators will still want to see how these systems reach their conclusions. That's where transparency layers come in. Techniques like federated SHAP or LIME can be used to pull apart a decision and explain why a certain applicant was flagged as high- or low-risk, without exposing raw data. It's not perfect yet, but it offers a path to meeting accountability standards in finance law while keeping data decentralized.

In short, FL doesn't just make credit scoring more private—it makes it more flexible and, potentially, more fair. Models can evolve as borrower behavior changes, while institutions retain sovereignty over their data.

11.7.3 Real-time regulatory compliance through FL agents

A complex collection of regulations that are always changing governs the banking industry. From Know Your Customer (KYC) procedures and anti-money laundering (AML) checks to transaction reporting, cybersecurity safeguards, and audit requirements that vary by nation, banks have a number of rules to balance. Typically, this has meant creating large, centralized compliance systems with rule-based engines and monitoring centers that process massive amounts of data. Despite their usefulness, these frameworks usually struggle to adapt swiftly to new threats or changes in the legislation.

Using tiny, intelligent agents dispersed throughout financial networks, FL offers a completely new approach to managing regulatory compliance. Consider these agents as little modules that are integrated into devices such as cloud cores, trading platforms, mobile banking apps, and ATMs.

Each agent operates locally, capturing transactions, user activity, and system changes in real time, learning from them, and sharing only encrypted model updates rather than transmitting raw data back to a central conformance center. Instead of being added afterward, privacy and compliance with regulations are integrated into the architecture of this design.

Instead of residing outside the system, regulations can be directly implemented into how these agents learn. One way to do this is through reinforcement learning, where the rules dictate the system's advantages and disadvantages. Over time, the agent figures out how to recognize suspicious activity, pick up on unusual KYC records, or check whether AML thresholds are being crossed. The setup can be extended further with smart contracts. For example, a contract could say that if a specific pattern appears, the system ought to terminate the transaction, give out an alert, or request the user for another form of authentication. It's essential that these precautions are associated with regulations that officials have already approved in lieu of becoming ad hoc since this allows the system to react promptly without violating the law.

Federated systems don't have to follow a single global rulebook; they can be tuned to the legal environment they operate in. A bank in Europe, for example, would train its models with GDPR rules at the center, while an American bank might give more weight to Foreign Account Tax Compliance Act (FATCA) or Financial Crimes Enforcement Network (FINCEN) requirements. The basic framework continues to allow all of the organizations to collaborate on information without exposing confidential data, even when their rules are different.

One of the most practical benefits of FL that is compliant is the capacity to do audits in real time. Instead of hiding its decision-making process, each compliance agent can record the actions it took and produce a trail that auditors can examine without ever viewing the actual transactions. That degree of openness not only reduces audit expenses but also boosts confidence between regulators and the banks they oversee. In today's contexts, these agents are frequently linked to risk scoring systems, cybersecurity checks, and reporting dashboards to provide managers with a cohesive view of the organization's regulatory compliance. As a result, compliance is moving away from a slow, reactive approach and toward one that is more flexible and forward-thinking, lowering costs, lowering legal risk, and enabling institutions to keep up with a rapidly changing regulatory environment.

11.8 CHALLENGES AND FUTURE TRENDS

One of the most discussed distributed AI techniques lately is FL. Despite its enormous potential, especially in industries like finance where data sharing is difficult, its actual application is far from simple. Scaling FL involves managing variable infrastructure, competing standards, and regulations that haven't fully caught up. Fairness, accountability, and control concerns are all recurrent problems; the issue is not limited to security vulnerabilities and delays in communication. Although the path to a completely autonomous federated system is convoluted and far from certain, the concept is attractive. However, the trajectory of hardware development—imagine brain-like neuromorphic devices or quantum processors—suggests that FL will develop in conjunction with these technologies rather than independently.

11.8.1 Challenges in deployment and standardization

It is not as easy as scaling up a lab prototype to implement FL in the real world. There are several obstacles to overcome, particularly in the areas of infrastructure, security, and interoperability. FL must operate across a diverse range of clients, from a smartphone with a little battery to an industrial server with massive storage, in contrast to centralized AI, which operates in a controlled environment. Naturally, these devices' capacities differ with regard to memory, bandwidth, processing power, and even energy limitations.

One of the hardest problems is heterogeneity, both in the data and in the systems themselves. The data often isn't IID; in practice it's messy, unbalanced, or skewed toward whatever each client happens to see. That makes it difficult to build models that can generalize well across the whole network without losing the personalization that FL promises. On top of this, communication is a bottleneck. It is costly to coordinate updates for thousands or millions of users, and latency increases as the number of participants increases. Although some methods, such as federated averaging, compression, and selective updates, can help, none of them fully resolve the issue, and their efficacy frequently varies greatly depending on the application.

Security is another pressure point. FL opens the door to model poisoning, backdoor attacks, and even data leakage through clever inference on model parameters. Malicious clients don't need to hack the system; they can simply submit bad updates. Right now, there's no universally accepted defense protocol, which leaves a lot of room for vulnerabilities.

Lastly, a significant obstacle is interoperability, or more specifically, its absence. With unique data formats, privacy safeguards, and aggregation criteria, various organizations typically create their own FL systems. This makes it more difficult to obtain regulatory permission and cross-sector collaboration. Although encouraging, initiatives like the IEEE P7002 standard on algorithmic transparency and many open-source FL libraries are still in their infancy and have, at best, been unevenly adopted.

11.8.2 Ethical and regulatory implications

One of the big appeals of FL is that the data never has to leave its original source, which gives it a natural edge in protecting privacy. That part is fairly straightforward. The harder part comes when you start looking at the bigger picture. Keeping information local doesn't erase the messy questions around ethics or regulation—it just reshapes them. Issues like who takes responsibility, how fairness is measured, whether proper consent is really being respected, and how governance should work only get more tangled when the system is spread across different organizations. A big sticking point is transparency. Even though FL protects sensitive data, the models it produces can still be biased or difficult to interpret—especially if the underlying training data carries the usual traces of inequality. Put such models into finance, say for credit scoring or loan approvals, and the risk is that existing discrimination quietly gets reinforced rather than reduced. Trying to make FL fair isn't straightforward. In centralized systems you can at least pull all the data together and run a bias check, but here the data stays scattered, so that option disappears.

On top of that, there's the legal side. Laws such as GDPR, Health Insurance Portability and Accountability Act (HIPAA), or California Consumer Privacy Act (CCPA) don't just care about data staying private. They expect proof that consent was given, that you can actually track how the data has been used, and that the decisions the model makes can be explained in plain language. Doing all of this inside a federated setup, where the information never actually leaves local machines or institutions, is still a pretty big unsolved challenge. That means federated systems need tools to trace data lineage and show compliance—even if the data itself never technically leaves the device. And then there's the thorny issue of responsibility. If a federated model makes a bad call—denies a loan unfairly or mislabels a transaction.

11.8.3 Roadmap to fully autonomous federated ecosystems

When people visualize the future of FL, they often think of intelligent, adaptive systems that are mostly devoid of normal human control. Naturally, maintaining that level of autonomy won't rely on a single technology. Layered progress will be required, including architecture modifications, learning theory innovations, enhanced communication protocols, and a decentralized governance system that can survive complexity.

In this regard, the concept of autonomous orchestration engines is a useful step. While the name may sound vague, its purpose is rather obvious: AI controllers and multi-agent systems quietly manage a variety of tasks in the background, including who trains when, how resources are shared, how errors are handled, and even how much traffic on the network there is.

Orchestration systems may get more advanced and efficient at detecting context over time. They may alter their tactics in reaction to real-time data or sudden changes in situations rather than sticking to set procedures. Consider a network of edge devices; some of that are suddenly overloaded with new data, some are losing connections, and some are running short on energy. Almost instantly, the system would arrange things to keep everything functioning. Naturally, there are risks associated with that level of autonomy. Hidden weaknesses in complex federated systems may go unnoticed until a problem arises, and when it occurs, the repercussions may be costly.

The development of learning models with the ability to continuously improve themselves is a further important factor in this history. When circumstances change, these systems adapt rather than remain unchanged. This means adapting to changing goals, reacting to fresh environmental information, and protecting against detrimental inputs. Once included into the structure of FL, methods like meta-learning, ongoing learning, and learning through reinforcement may enable models to continuously reorganize themselves, update their hyperparameters, and even evaluate their aggregation techniques.

Concurrently, there is a push toward blockchain-based and smart contract-based trustless federated systems. The appeal is clear: they create decentralized trust and safe incentive structures that allow clients to collaborate on model development even when they don't know or trust each other completely. Furthermore, these solutions may lessen some of the regulatory complications that occasionally come with large data sharing. These solutions include provenance monitoring, automatic compliance checks, and reliable audit trails.

As federated systems grow more independent, the regulations controlling them cannot just stay the same. Governance has to stretch to cover things we usually talk about in ethics—fairness, accountability, transparency—but in a way that's built right into the design of the models themselves. That might mean checking for bias while the system is actually learning, making sure the decisions it spits out aren't a total black box, and keeping the whole thing tuned to both user goals and broader social expectations. The bigger picture—at least the way it's often imagined—ends with something like a federation of AI societies: a loose but global network of agents and data holders, all working together on problems too big for any single group to solve. You could picture finance, healthcare, and scientific research each plugging into this kind of ecosystem. The hope is that it preserves privacy and autonomy while still pushing intelligence forward. Whether it really holds to those ethical promises once scaled up, though—that's the part still open to question.

11.8.4 The role of quantum AI and neuromorphic chips

As FL keeps scaling up, it's starting to run into limits. The usual hardware setups and algorithmic tricks that have carried it this far may simply not be enough to handle the sheer computational load or the need for near-instant responses. That's where some rather exotic technologies—Quantum AI and Neuromorphic Computing—are beginning to look less like sci-fi buzzwords and more like necessary tools.

Take quantum computing. Because qubits can juggle many states at once, a quantum machine can chew through massive combinatorial problems that would make a classical processor sweat. This isn't just abstract speed; it means faster model optimization, more efficient kernel calculations, and even stronger cryptographic guarantees. Imagine running a federated system where model updates are encrypted not just with standard protocols, but with quantum key distribution—suddenly the prospect of eavesdropping, even on hostile networks, becomes far less worrying.

There's also quantum machine learning creeping into the picture. Clients can avoid slaving away at resource-intensive pattern recognition or anomaly detection by using a QML-enhanced node to detect strange transaction patterns or modify reinforcement rules almost instantly. Obviously, because of the expensive price tag, specialized nature, and scarce supply of quantum computers, the technology isn't quite plug-and-play. The benefits of reducing such barriers, however, will be immense: federated systems that can handle richer and more complex models without having to make the difficult decision to compromise security and performance.

However, a different path is becoming available with neurological chips, which are pieces of hardware that are loosely based on the functioning of the brain. They perform differently from the processors we were used to. Instead of using brute-force computation of numbers, they use spiking neural networks and event-driven processing, which allows them to function with extremely low power consumption and quick reaction times. For small, resource-constrained devices like gadgets, home detectors, or even medical implants that need to adapt instantly but can't waste energy, they are therefore ideal for FL.

Directly executing federated models on this type of hardware allows to achieve local learning and near real-time response without using a lot of battery power. The situation becomes even more interesting when you start wondering about what might occur if quantum methods and neuromorphic systems truly converge. Theoretically, federated systems would diffuse such intelligence across connections in a hitherto unheard-of manner in addition to learning more quickly.

We're just getting started. The idealized hybrid design, in which neuronal efficiency and quantum strength complement one another, is still more promising than the actual one. However, if it materializes, it has the potential to advance FL beyond a mere technological advancement and toward something that truly transforms how distributed, autonomous intelligence works in society.

11.9 CONCLUSION

FL rapidly alters the entire paradigm for developing, implementing, and regulating data-powered intelligence in most privacy-sensitive businesses, especially banking. The main ideas discussed in the text are linked in this chapter according to their impact on the financial sector. In order to fully achieve the potential of federated ecosystems, it also emphasizes the importance for various types of cooperation.

11.9.1 Summary of key concepts

This chapter explored the basic concepts and developing designs of FL systems, especially those designed for autonomous and intelligent financial applications. We began by examining the layered autonomy in FL—from manually coordinated systems to semi- and fully autonomous learning environments. These stages reflect a gradual but critical progression toward decentralized decision-making and self-governed learning infrastructures. The integration of reinforcement learning agents, self-supervised models, and self-healing mechanisms was highlighted as a pathway toward building adaptive, resilient, and intelligent FL nodes. We also examined how AI-driven orchestration—through multi-agent systems and smart contracts—enables decentralized negotiation, behavior regulation, and energy-efficient collaboration among distributed financial entities [26].

A deep dive into next-generation privacy and communication techniques, such as enhanced DP, HE, and swarm-based methods, showcased how security remains central to federated deployments. Quantum-resilient protocols were introduced as the future of cryptographic robustness in distributed learning [27]. Further, we explored self-evolving models that adapt over time via lifelong learning, meta-learning, and cross-platform transfer. Real-world financial case studies—including fraud detection, adaptive credit risk modeling, and compliance management—demonstrated how FL can be practically implemented while preserving privacy and delivering intelligence across institutions.

11.9.2 Implications for the financial industry

FL is a tectonic shift in finance. It was simply not possible through siloed practices, and the only way forward is through collaborative and secure AI. This would make it possible for institutions to collaboratively develop intelligence in privacy across age-old silos while breaking through age-old silos that limited the sharing of information, innovation, and fraud detection. For banks, it enables real-time fraud detection across networks even in cases where individual institutions have limited data. Credit agencies and fintech firms may join forces to upgrade credit scoring and attain wider financial inclusion, especially for those who have practically no credit history. Simultaneously, regulators could rely on federated systems to track systemic risks without encroaching on institutional boundaries.

FL will decrease financial organizations' infrastructure costs, enhance personalization, and ease the strain of security and compliance. The banking sector has profited greatly from continuous learning models that can adjust to changing macroeconomic trends, user behavior, and emergent threats thanks to the formation of intelligent agents. Above all, FL has the potential to yield a financially secure and transparent system in which fairness, inclusivity, and data protection are at the very core, rather than on the periphery.

11.9.3 Call for interdisciplinary innovation

To create self-sufficient federated ecosystems, computer science expertise is insufficient on its own. Hardware engineers, behavioral scientists, economists, regulators, cryptographers, and AI researchers must all work together in a multidisciplinary manner. Every discipline is essential to finishing the overall image. Standards of accountability for decentralized AI systems must be formulated by legal professionals. Ethicists are in charge of correcting bias and making sure model results are fair. Low-power processors that are tailored for FL systems must be produced by hardware designers. Models that represent financial patterns unique to various contexts must be created by economists and subject matter experts.

It is incumbent on academic institutions, industries, and government agencies to take a very active role in building worldwide standards, interoperable protocols, and open-source tools—not only to assure trust but also to promote broader diffusion. It is then imperative for universities to mainstream FL as a core skill in their curricula so that graduates—and eventually professionals—will pursue careers as data scientists, financial analysts, and similar professionals. FL is more than just technical progress; it really represents a critical milestone on the way to privacy-preserving collaboration. Walking such paths fosters the need for a more proactive approach to ethical AI governance, decentralized intelligence systems, and international collaboration. With huge volumes of data resources and established trust frameworks globally, the financial sector takes a lead on this challenge. It needs, however, to move with emerging technologies, retain high ethical standards, and equally move with emerging technologies.

REFRENCES

1. Gurung, D., & Pokhrel, S. R. (2025). Chained continuous quantum federated learning framework. *Future Generation Computer Systems*, *169*, 107800.
2. Ye, C. Q., Li, H. J., Li, J., & Chen, X. Y. (2025). A feasible quantum walk-enabled blockchain with quantum delegated proof-of-stake consensus. *arXiv e-prints*, arXiv-2510.
3. Gurung, D., & Pokhrel, S. R. (2025). Communication efficient adaptive model-driven quantum federated learning. *arXiv preprint arXiv:2506.04548*.
4. Brakerski, Z., Gentry, C., & Vaikuntanathan, V. (2014). (Leveled) fully homomorphic encryption without bootstrapping. *ACM Transactions on Computation Theory (TOCT)*, *6*(3), 1–36.
5. Zhang, X., Deng, H., Wu, R., Ren, J., & Ren, Y. (2024). PQSF: Post-quantum secure privacy-preserving federated learning. *Scientific Reports*, 14, 23553.
6. Sünkel, L., Altmann, P., Kölle, M., & Gabor, T. (2024). Quantum federated learning for image classification. In *ICAART 2024*.
7. Li, P., Chen, T., & Liu, J. (2024, October). Enhancing quantum security over federated learning via post-quantum cryptography. In *2024 IEEE 6th International Conference on Trust, Privacy and Security in Intelligent Systems, and Applications (TPS-ISA)* (pp. 499-505). IEEE.
8. Scarpellini, et al. (2024). Efficient post-quantum cross-silo federated learning based on key-homomorphic PRF. *Mathematics MDPI*, 13(9), 1404.
9. Zhang, Y., Behnia, R., Yavuz, A. A., Ebrahimi, R., & Bertino, E. (2025). Efficient full-stack private federated deep learning with post-quantum security. *IEEE Transactions on Dependable and Secure Computing*.
10. Zhou, B. L., Lv, N., Guo, Y., & Li, Y. (2023, January). Recent advances on federated learning: A systematic survey. *arXiv preprint arXiv:2301.00000*.
11. Wen, J., Zhang, Z., Lan, Y., Cui, Z., & Zhang, W. (2023, November). A survey on federated learning: Challenges and applications. *International Journal of Machine Learning and Cybernetics*.
12. Soltani, B., Zhou, Y., Haghighi, V., & Lui, J. (2023). A survey of federated evaluation in federated learning. *arXiv preprint arXiv:2305.08070*.
13. Liu, W., Ye, M., Shi, Z., Wan, G., Li, H., Du, B., & Yang, Q. (2023). Federated learning for generalization, robustness, fairness: A survey and benchmark. *arXiv*.
14. Fan, B., Jiang, S., Su, X., Tarkoma, S., & Hui, P. (2024, December). A survey on model-heterogeneous federated learning: Problems, methods, and prospects. In *2024 IEEE International Conference on Big Data (BigData)* (pp. 7725-7734). IEEE.
15. Chhetri, B., Gopali, S., Olapojoye, R., Dehbash, S., & Siami Namin, A. (2023, June). A survey on blockchain-based federated learning and data privacy. *arXiv*.
16. Dhruvitkumar, V. Talati (2021). Decentralized AI: The role of edge intelligence in next-gen computing. *International Journal of Science and Research Archive*, 2(1), 216–232.
17. Figetakis, E., & Refaey, A. (2023, December). Autonomous MEC selection in federated next-gen networks via deep reinforcement learning. In *GLOBECOM 2023–2023 IEEE Global Communications Conference* (pp. 2045–2050). IEEE.

18. Anbalagan, S., Alhakami, W., Bhooma, M. J., Marimuthu, V. S., Dev, K., & Raja, G. (2024, June). Next-gen security: Enhanced DDoS attack detection for autonomous vehicles in 6G networks. In *2024 IEEE 99th Vehicular Technology Conference (VTC2024-Spring)* (pp. 1–5). IEEE.
19. Mohapatra, S., Mishra, A., & Mohanty, S. (2024, October). Next-gen healthcare: Blockchain-fuelled federated learning for IoMT security. In *2024 4th International Conference on Artificial Intelligence and Signal Processing (AISP)* (pp. 1–5). IEEE.
20. Gao, H., & Xu, Y. (2025). Guest editorial: Next-gen cloud-edge collaboration: Software, networking, and human-aware intelligence. *Mobile Networks and Applications*, 1–2.
21. Chen, M., Luo, K., Wang, P., Xiao, W., Liu, Z., Liu, A., ... & Chen, M. (2025). Federated deep reinforcement learning for combating cyber-threats specific to EV charging in next-gen WPT infrastructure. *IEEE Transactions on Intelligent Transportation Systems.*
22. Mohammad, M. F., Elmedany, W., & Sharif, M. S. (2025, August). Hybrid AI-Driven Intrusion Detection Systems. In *Joint International Conference on AI, Big Data and Blockchain* (pp. 178-194). Springer Nature Switzerland.
23. Hammad, E., Nag, A. K., Chennamaneni, A., Aghashahi, M., & Dogdu, E. (2021, October). A deep-defense approach for next-gen cyber-resilient inter-dependent critical infrastructure systems. In *2021 Resilience Week (RWS)* (pp. 1–7). IEEE.
24. Xianjia, Y., Queralta, J. P., Heikkonen, J., & Westerlund, T. (2021). Federated learning in robotic and autonomous systems. *Procedia Computer Science*, 191, 135–142.
25. Sheth, A. P., & Larson, J. A. (1990). Federated database systems for managing distributed, heterogeneous, and autonomous databases. *ACM Computing Surveys (CSUR)*, 22(3), 183–236.
26. Li, Y., Tao, X., Zhang, X., Liu, J., & Xu, J. (2021). Privacy-preserved federated learning for autonomous driving. *IEEE Transactions on Intelligent Transportation Systems*, 23(7), 8423–8434.
27. Pokhrel, S. R., & Choi, J. (2020). Federated learning with blockchain for autonomous vehicles: Analysis and design challenges. *IEEE Transactions on Communications*, 68(8), 4734–4746.

Chapter 12

A roadmap for federated learning adoption

Shashank Semwal, Chandra Prakash, and Bijesh Dhyani

12.1 INTRODUCTION

The field of federated learning (FL) is undergoing swift changes, particularly marked by a notable increase in academic articles since 2020 (Uddin et al., 2024). As data continues to grow at an exponential rate, centralizing data at the model's location will soon become impractical due to the substantial infrastructure and expenses required. Additional issues such as data privacy, computational expenses, communication overhead, scalability, and fairness mean that maintaining a single centralized model for all clients in a multi-client environment will prove unfeasible.

12.1.1 Current FL research landscape

The landscape of FL research is increasingly shaped by practical industry needs, with developments concentrating on four key domains: (1) Algorithms designed to address heterogeneity, such as clustered FL (IFCA) and adaptive aggregation (FedOpt) (Uddin et al., 2024), are being deployed in the financial sector (e.g., J.P. Morgan's federated risk modeling) and healthcare (e.g., Owkin's cancer research collaborations) to manage diverse, non-IID data among institutions while preserving data sovereignty; (2) Techniques aimed at privacy preservation, including secure aggregation (SecAgg+) and differential privacy (DP-FL), are now essential in regulated industries such as banking (e.g., SWIFT's fraud detection) and telecommunications (e.g., Google's Gboard next-word prediction), facilitating compliance with GDPR and HIPAA; (3) Optimization of efficiency, achieved through approaches such as gradient quantization (e.g., utilized in NVIDIA's Clara FL for medical imaging) and edge-tier architectures (exemplified by Amazon's Alexa voice model updates), enhances operational cost-effectiveness for IoT and mobile applications; and (4) Cross-domain FL frameworks are enabling collaborative model training among industry consortia, as exemplified by the MELLODDY project in the pharmaceutical sector, to improve drug discovery across competing entities. Moreover, IBM's evidence industrial adoption federated Watsonx.ai platforms and Intel's OpenFL toolkit for enterprise applications.

Emerging challenges include the adaptation to dynamic environments (e.g., Tesla's federated autonomous vehicle training adjusting to regional driving patterns) and the alleviation of energy constraints (for instance, Samsung's on-device FL for smartphones). While foundational contributions such as FedAvg and FedProx are integral to these systems, recent partnerships between industry and academia (Microsoft Research's FLaaS and Meta's PyTorch Federated) are fostering modular solutions to improve scalability and interoperability, thus reducing the gap between research and product.

DOI: 10.1201/9781003660330-12

12.2 EXISTING FOUNDATIONAL MODELS AND LIMITATIONS

There is improvement and enhancement done on existing base-line model coupled with new techniques and networks and architecture optimization. No model is perfect and ticks all the boxed for each use-case, with different implementation and scenario, base-line models need fine-tuning and customization.

12.2.1 Improvement and enhancement in foundational models and development

12.2.1.1 Federated proximal (FedProx)

The article (Li et al., 2020) presents FedProx, a refined version of FedAvg aimed at tackling the challenges of statistical (non-IID data) and system diversity (straggler devices) in FL. This framework enhances the local objective function by adding a proximal term, ensuring that client updates do not significantly stray from the global model, which helps prevent client drift. Moreover, FedProx supports partial client involvement, enabling devices with limited resources to submit incomplete updates without disrupting the training process. Empirical tests conducted on heterogeneous datasets—including synthetic non-IID divisions (MNIST, FEMNIST) and actual healthcare records (eICU)—highlight the superior performance of FedProx. For example, in highly non-IID conditions, FedProx reaches an accuracy of 98% on MNIST, whereas FedAvg only achieves 89%, and it also enhances AUC for mortality prediction tasks in eICU (medical record) by 15%. Additionally, in situations with stragglers (where half of the clients complete only 10% of the local epochs), FedProx converges twice as quickly as FedAvg while demonstrating a 30% reduction in accuracy variance among clients. The paper also provides theoretical convergence guarantees for non-convex objectives across heterogeneous data distributions, marking a significant improvement over FedAvg, which does not offer such assurances. While FedProx has notable benefits, it incurs a slight computational overhead of about 5% for each epoch because of the regularization introduced by the proximal term. Subsequent research (e.g., SCAFFOLD) has built on the foundations of FedProx by incorporating variance reduction strategies, enhancing overall robustness. This paper continues to be a pivotal reference in FL research, especially for situations that necessitate adaptability in data heterogeneity, such as cross-device FL or applications in healthcare and finance.

Limitation: FedProx incorporates a proximal term to address client drift, thereby theoretically guaranteeing convergence in the presence of statistical heterogeneity. Nonetheless, it neglects to confront system-induced biases that stem from variations in τ_k (local steps). While the proximal term penalizes deviations from the global model, it does not normalize updates with respect to τ_k, thereby failing to address the issue of objective inconsistency. Furthermore, the FedProx algorithm introduces a computational overhead of 5–10% per client because of the proximal term's regularization, which may prove to be a significant constraint for edge devices characterized by finite energy resources. The approach further neglects considerations of fairness, clients possessing smaller datasets or limited resources (thus contributing less frequently) may continue to encounter diminished performance. Notably, FedProx's resilience to non-IID data does not encompass cross-silo environments that feature institutional data silos (e.g., hospitals with significantly varied patient demographics), which necessitate more advanced personalization techniques such as pFedMe.

12.2.1.2 Stochastic controlled averaging for FL aka SCAFFOLD technique

(Karimireddy et al., 2020) It is an advanced network structure aimed at eliminating a major problem in FL based on data heterogeneity (non-IID distributions) and non-uniform local updates, known as client drift. Unlike FedProx, which uses a proximal term to limit updates, SCAFFOLD uses control variates (correction terms on both the server and client), reducing variance in local stochastic gradients.

This method explicitly rectifies client-specific biases, thereby facilitating alignment between local and global optimization paths. Empirical findings illustrate the resilience of SCAFFOLD across varied non-IID environments. In synthetic non-IID partitions of CIFAR-10, SCAFFOLD attains approximately 75% accuracy, surpassing the performance of FedAvg (~60%) and FedProx (~68%), especially under conditions of high heterogeneity. The authors theoretically demonstrate linear convergence rates for strongly convex objectives and offer assurances for non-convex scenarios, even when only a proportion of clients engage per round—representing considerable improvement over existing research. Importantly, the convergence of SCAFFOLD does not depend on assumptions of bounded gradient dissimilarity, thereby rendering it applicable to a wider range of more realistic FL scenarios.

Nevertheless, SCAFFOLD introduces increased communication overhead (client-server transmission of control variates) and exhibits sensitivity to hyperparameter settings (e.g., learning rates). Subsequent research, such as FedDyn (Acar et al., 2021), enhances its contributions by employing dynamic adjustments to regularization terms. SCAFFOLD continues to be a considerable influence in FL research, particularly in scenarios necessitating accurate gradient alignment, such as cross-silo FL or applications demanding high-fidelity convergence (e.g., financial modeling or healthcare).

Limitation: The application of control variables by SCAFFOLD effectively mitigates client drift; however, it also introduces a significant level of complexity. Each client is required to uphold and synchronize state variables (control variates), which results in an approximate increase of 30–50% in memory consumption and communication expenses. This makes SCAFFOLD unsuitable in large-scale cross-device FL like the ones between millions of mobile phones wherein lightweight protocols are of importance. The algorithm also assumes constant involvement with the clients, which is a paradigm that poses a challenge in dynamic environments where clients can drop dead without notice. The empirical assessments reveal that the behavior of SCAFFOLD is unpredictable when the participation of clients comes in a sporadic fashion because old control variables bring noise in the general update. Theoretically complex, the lack of straggler resilience and scalability limitation limits the application of SCAFFOLD to practical systems.

12.2.1.3 Model-contrastive FL

(Q. Li et al., 2021) MOON is a novel FL framework based on model-level contrastive learning to alleviate the problem of client data heterogeneity. Unlike other more standard approaches to FL to parameter averaging (like FedAvg) or equivalent gradient correction (like SCAFFOLD), the MOON framework leverages a contrastive loss to align local model representations to the global model, limiting divergence that can appear due to non-IID data distributions. The process enhances the uniformity of qualities throughout the clients by keeping the performance that is adjusted to the tasks.

Empirical evaluations were performed on standard benchmark data (CIFAR-10, CIFAR-100 and Tiny-ImageNet) to demonstrate the superiority of MOON over modern federate learning methods. MOON obtains an increase of 5.3% test accuracy compared to FedAvg and 3.1% compared to SCAFFOLD in highly non-IID environments. Moreover, MOON has increased rate of convergence, with lesser communication rounds required by 30% to reach stipulated performance grades.

The authors further substantiate the resilience of MOON in cross-silo FL contexts, demonstrating sustained improvements in medical imaging applications (e.g., a 7.8% increase in AUC for pneumonia detection within heterogeneous chest X-ray datasets).

MOON's contrastive mechanism maintains the geometric alignment of local updates with the global model, thereby alleviating the issue of catastrophic forgetting prevalent in conventional FL. Nevertheless, the approach introduces supplementary computational overhead because of the contrastive loss calculation (a 15% increase in per-epoch training time), which may constrain its implementation on resource-limited edge devices. Subsequent investigations (FedGKD) (Yao et al., 2021) enhance MOON by incorporating knowledge distillation, further augmenting its efficiency.

As a seminal contribution to representation-aware FL, MOON establishes a framework for subsequent research in federated self-supervised learning and cross-modal federated alignment, exemplified by vision-language models. Its relevance extends to fields necessitating strong feature generalization, such as healthcare and autonomous systems.

12.2.2 Personalization models

Personalization in FL is customized with global models to individual client data distributions while maintaining collaborative learning. Key approaches include: (1) Local Fine-Tuning, where end clients adapt the global model to their data via a few additional training steps (e.g., FedAvg + local epochs) (2) Multi-Task Learning, which jointly optimizes shared and client-specific parameters (e.g., pFedMe) (3) Model Interpolation, blending global and local models (e.g., FedPer) and (4) Meta-Learning, leveraging MAML-style updates for rapid client adaptation (e.g., Per-FedAvg). Privacy is preserved by avoiding raw data sharing, though challenges like catastrophic forgetting and bias amplification persist. Recent advances have explored hypernetwork-based architecture (e.g., FedRep) and clustered personalization for non-IID settings.

12.2.2.1 Personalized FL with moreau envelopes (pFedMe)

T. Dinh et al., (2020) presents pFedMe, an innovative framework for personalized federated learning (PFL) that distinguishes the optimization of personalized models from global aggregation. The primary innovation involves the reformulation of the local objective using the Moreau envelope, which serves as a proximal approximation to decouple the training of personalized models from updates to the global model. This two-tiered optimization strategy enables clients to adapt models to their specific local data distributions while simultaneously leveraging the advantages of collaborative federation. Empirical assessments conducted on standard benchmark datasets (MNIST, CIFAR-10, and synthetic non-independent and identically distributed (non-IID) environments) reveal that pFedMe exhibits enhanced performance relative to conventional FL approaches. For example, in the context of heterogeneous data partitions, pFedMe attains an accuracy of 92.3% on the CIFAR-10 dataset, surpassing the performance of FedAvg (85.1%) and Per-FedAvg (88.7%). Furthermore, pFedMe demonstrates accelerated convergence (as much as 40% reduction in communication rounds) compared to rival PFL techniques, including FedProx and APFL, while preserving robustness against statistical heterogeneity. The authors also offer theoretical convergence assurances for non-convex objectives, illustrating that pFedMe achieves a stationary solution under conventional assumptions, which represents a notable advancement over heuristic personalization strategies. A constraint of pFedMe is its significant computational overhead resulting from the nested optimization framework; however, this is partially alleviated through parallelizable updates. Subsequent research, such as that presented by (Q. Li et al., 2021), enhances pFedMe by integrating fairness constraints. This paper serves as a fundamental contribution to the field of personalized FL , especially in applications requiring client-specific adaptations, such as healthcare diagnostics or user-centric recommendation systems.

Limitation: The bi-level optimization framework of pFedMe separates personalization from global aggregation, resulting in state-of-the-art performance in non-IID environments. However, nested loop of optimization makes it cost increment by 20%–30% and thus inappropriate on resource constrained devices. There is also the risk of over-personalization in this strategy: Unusual data distributions on clients can end up forcing personalization of localized information resulting in loss of collaborative value of federation. Moreover, pFedMe neglects the heterogeneity of the systems assumed by its model equal capabilities of clients and does not offer facilities to counteract laggards. Privacy is another issue which is possible to present because personalized models can reveal some details about clients unless proper measures of precaution are provided (such as the use ofDP). The trade-offs experienced with pFedMe are extremely critical to balance in such contexts as federated healthcare where personalization and privacy are a top priority.

12.2.2.2 Federated batch normalization (FebBN)

FebBN presents a new method of addressing a severe problem of shifting feature distribution in systems of FL (X. Li et al., 2021). It has noted that conventional FL procedures such as FedAvg have had subpar performance when faced with non-independent and identically distributed (non-IID) distribution of attributes among clients, a frequently occurring instance in realistic deployments and medical imaging drawn by a variety of healthcare centers or sensor data collected from various environments. The main innovation of FedBN consists in an unusual way of managing the BN layers when aggregating a model. Although the analogous FL methods combine all the model parameters, FedBN shows a more subtle approach, where it keeps the local BN statistics, i.e., the mean and the variance, per client and globally aggregates on the rest of the model parameters. This design smartly preserves domain specific qualities of client-specific BN layers and at the same time allows them to simultaneously learn using shared features representations, thus giving a sensible balance amid personalization and generalization of learning in federated systems. Large-scale empirical evaluations leaving numerous benchmarks depict the superior performance of FedBN. FedBN reaches 5%–8% accuracy improvement compared with FedAvg in the setting of medical imaging (PathMNIST, TissueMNIST) especially when the degree of feature shift is high. Regarding the analysis of the time-series data (Digits dataset), the technique shows a significant 12 % increase in the classification effectiveness. Importantly, FedBN could reach the same amount of accuracy as centralized training protocols with half the number of communication rounds as contemporary approaches, e.g., FedProx, therefore, resulting in a significant increase in the efficiency of communications.

The theoretical backbones of FedBN explain their effectiveness in addressing highly crucial issues in the field of FL. The method systematically reduces the gap between distributions of features in clients and preserves necessary domain-specific characteristics through local BN maintenance. This two-pronged approach ensures that the different attributes of the data (local features) of the clients is preserved and that the full features of the global aspects are developed through the parameter aggregation. Notably, FedBN realizes the above improvements without incurring any significant computational cost compared to existing FL systems, which makes it particularly attractive to be deployed in the real world. Despite the significant benefits it offers, the paper does not disregard certain limitations linked with the FedBN methodology. The principal assessments emphasize medium-sized models (e.g., ResNet-18), thereby leaving inquiries regarding scalability to more extensive architectures unanswered. The advantages are less significant for datasets exhibiting minimal feature shift, and the approach necessitates client-specific BN storage within cross-device FL contexts. Notwithstanding these constraints, FedBN has significantly impacted subsequent investigations in domain-adaptiveFL, motivating extensions that utilize analogous principles for alternative normalization methods, such as LayerNorm in transformer architectures.

Federated BN continues to be especially significant for applications marked by intrinsic variations in feature distributions, including multi-institutional medical imaging analysis, heterogeneous IoT sensor networks, and multi-modal FL systems. The primary contribution of the paper resides in its refined and effective approach to addressing feature shift via selective parameter aggregation, resulting in considerable performance enhancements without incurring additional computational overhead. This progression signifies a crucial achievement in the evolution of pragmatic, efficient FL systems adept at managing data heterogeneity encountered in real-world scenarios.

12.3 EMERGING INNOVATIONS IN FL

12.3.1 Data augmentation

Data augmentation enhances FL performance by artificially expanding local datasets through techniques like image transformations (rotation, flipping), synthetic sample generation (GANs, diffusion models), or text paraphrasing. In FL, augmentation mitigates statistical heterogeneity (non-IID data) by creating more balanced local distributions, improving model generalization. Privacy-preserving methods—such as federated augmentation (clients share augmentation policies, not raw data) or DP (Di & Yu, 2023) noised synthetic samples—address confidentiality concerns. Challenges include computational overhead on edge devices and ensuring augmentation consistency across clients. Recent work (Liu et al., 2021) explores federated generative models to create globally useful synthetic data while preserving privacy.

12.3.1.1 FedMix

Su et al. (2025) presents an innovative data augmentation framework intended to tackle statistical heterogeneity in FL by modifying the Mixup technique for decentralized environments. FedMix functions within the mean-field approximation, generating synthetic samples through the interpolation of local data distributions among clients, thereby alleviating issues associated with non-IID data partitions. The fundamental innovation resides in its two-stage methodology: (1) Local Mixup augmentation, wherein clients create interpolated samples from their individual private datasets, and (2) global aggregation, through which the server estimates a combined Mixup distribution without requiring direct data transmission.

This approach maintains privacy while improving model generalization through the implicit alignment of feature representations across diverse clients.

Empirical assessment using standard benchmark datasets (CIFAR-10, FEMNIST, and Shakespeare) illustrates the enhanced performance of FedMix compared to traditional FL methods. For example, in severely non-IID conditions, FedMix attains an accuracy of 83.5% on the CIFAR-10 dataset, surpassing FedAvg (76.2%) and FedProx (79.8%). Remarkably, FedMix decreases client-level accuracy variance by 35%, signifying consistent performance across varied data distributions. The study additionally emphasizes FedMix's alignment with DP, demonstrating only a negligible performance reduction (~2%) upon the introduction of DP noise, in contrast to the more significant degradation observed in baseline methodologies. Moreover author also conducted a theoretical examination of FedMix model through the approach of mean-field theory, proposing that the algorithm converges to a stationary solution under moderate assumptions w.r.t client data distributions.

Notwithstanding its advantages, FedMix introduces computational overhead during the generation of local Mixup, especially for resource-limited edge devices. The study also recognizes constraints in high-dimensional data spaces (such as ImageNet), where interpolation may result in less meaningful synthetic samples. FedMix falls short of promoting future work which specifies that feature-level mixup be combined with it to eliminate this shortcoming, FedFM (Li et al., 2020) as an example. FedMix contributions are vital to privacy-preserving FL, especially on tasks where data heterogeneity is a major issue, e.g., medical imaging or cross-device personalization. The fact that this framework emphasizes implicit data harmonization, accomplished without involvement of raw data, corresponds with the high regulatory standards (i.e., GDPR), which make it a realistic candidate to be employed in field implementations.

12.3.2 Model-agnostic meta-learning (MAML)

The Meta-Learning frameworks such as Model-Agnostic Meta-Learning (MAML) and its extensions (e.g., Per-FedAvg, FedMeta) allow federated models to quickly adapt to new clients when little local data which is important property of non-IID case. Such approaches pre-train a universal meta-model on a variety of client tasks and improve rapid adaptation through use of few-shot fine-tuning at inference time. In FL, recent new and current MAML-class models get around this need by learning initialization parameters that can quickly attain high performance once they have undergone client-specific gradient updates to make communication less frequent. Difficulties are computational overhead of meta-training and catastrophic forgetting in dynamic environments. ETs in recent years such as personalized MAML (pMAML) and Bayesian Meta-FL enhance the robustness, but still, it retains a certain level of privacy using gradient masking.

12.3.2.1 Per-FedAvg

Per-FedAvg is an innovative framework that combines FL with meta-learning to address issues like statistical heterogeneity among clients (Fallah et al., 2020). The researchers frame individualized FL as a MAML challenge, wherein the global model acts as an initial state from which clients can effectively adjust to their local data distributions through a limited number of gradient iterations. This methodology diverges from traditional FL techniques (such as FedAvg) by specifically targeting the optimization of rapid client-specific adaptation instead of relying on a singular global model. Per-FedAvg theoretically ensures convergence for both convex and non-convex loss functions, illustrating that the algorithm achieves a stationary solution under conventional assumptions. The argument relies on the relationship between MAML and bi-level optimization, demonstrating that the global meta-update inherently considers the generalization of performance of models tailored to specific clients. Empirically, Per-FedAvg is assessed using image classification tasks (MNIST, CIFAR-10) and synthetic non-IID datasets, demonstrating a 12–15% improvement in accuracy over FedAvg under conditions of severe data heterogeneity. Significantly, the approach facilitates personalization using limited local data (e.g., 5 samples per client), emphasizing its applicability to resource-constrained environments. A significant innovation is the "meta-update" rule, which calculates global gradients according to the post-adaptation performance of clients, thereby facilitating the global model's suitability for rapid fine-tuning. Nevertheless, Per-FedAvg entails increased communication expenses compared to FedAvg, owing to the necessity of second-order gradient approximations; however, the authors introduce a first-order variant (Per-FedAvg-FO) to address this issue. Comparative experiments indicate that Per-FedAvg-FO preserves 90% of the advantages of the complete algorithm while diminishing computational overhead.

The significance of the paper resides in its theoretical robustness and pragmatic adaptability, shaping future research in personalized FL (FL) (e.g., pFedMe, Ditto). Its constraints encompass a susceptibility to hyperparameters (e.g., adaptation step size) and presuppositions regarding client similarity. Nonetheless, Per-FedAvg continues to serve as a fundamental reference for meta-learning-driven FL, especially in areas such as personalized healthcare or edge artificial intelligence, where swift adaptation to varied data is essential.

12.3.2.2 FedNova

The study (J. Wang et al., 2020) presents FedNova, an innovative federated optimization algorithm developed to mitigate the significant challenge of objective inconsistency inherent in FedAvg. The authors establish that the standard FedAvg is inherently prone to an optimization bias when different clients perform varying amounts of local computation (due to unequal numbers of computational resources or size of data they receive) causing skewed global updates to be executed and sub-optimal convergence. To solve this problem FedNova normalizes local updates based on the true number of local steps performed by individual clients, enabling consistent global optimization regardless of the differences in the local participation patterns. Theoretically, FedNova outlines an approach which decouples variability in training akin to local, global optimization, exhibits convergence guarantees on both convex and non-convex functions in terms of common assumptions. This indicates significant better performance compared to FedAvg, which does not have a similar theoretical soundness in heterogeneous settings.

The normalization technique demonstrates an independence from the selection of local solvers, rendering FedNova compatible with a diverse array of client-level optimizers (e.g., SGD, momentum-based approaches). Empirical validation using various benchmarks (CIFAR-10, EMNIST, and a synthetic logistic regression task) illustrates the enhanced performance of FedNova. In contexts characterized by significant system heterogeneity (in which clients execute varying numbers of local epochs), FedNova attains: Up to 15% improved test accuracy in comparison to FedAvg on CIFAR-10 under conditions of severe heterogeneity. Accelerated convergence rates, resulting in a 30–40% decrease in the number of communication rounds required to achieve specified accuracy thresholds. Enhanced fairness, characterized by a reduced accuracy variance (up to 50% decrease) across clients in comparison to FedAvg and FedProx. Importantly, FedNova sustains these benefits without incurring additional computational burden on clients, since normalization is executed server-side. The paper emphasizes the adaptability of FedNova, noting that it can be integrated with various advancements in FL, such as DP or gradient compression, without causing algorithmic conflicts.

Nevertheless, the authors observe that FedNova does not explicitly tackle statistical heterogeneity (non-IID data), although it enhances techniques such as FedProx or SCAFFOLD. Other studies have examined such hybrid techniques, and FedNova is an important building block of any federated optimization. This paper is particularly important in large-scale cross-device FL usages, where system-heterogeneity is inevitable (such as mobile devices with varying computational abilities). Its low complexity, theoretical rigor, and empirical performance makes FedNova a common baseline algorithm in the literature on federated optimization.

Limitations: The normalization of local updates that is offered by FedNova addresses the problem of objective inconsistency, but it has nothing to deal with statistical heterogeneity. Even though it allows fair aggregation to go over variable τ_k, it must be combined with other techniques (such as FedProx) to process non-IID data hybrid approach, which is not easy to integrate. Furthermore, FedNova introduces privacy concerns by potentially revealing client-specific computational patterns, such as inferring device capabilities. The methodology assumes static τ_k values, which may prove inadequate in dynamic environments where client resources vary (e.g., mobile networks with fluctuating bandwidth). In applications vital to fairness (e.g., loan approval), FedNova's absence of bias-mitigation mechanisms may exacerbate disparities among clients.

12.4 FUTURE DIRECTIONS FOR FL RESEARCH AND ADOPTION INCLUDE

The future of FL will focus on overcoming key challenges to enable widespread adoption. Research must advance scalable algorithms for massive, dynamic networks, integrating efficient communication protocols (e.g., sparse updates, adaptive compression) to reduce overhead. Theoretical foundations need strengthening to guarantee convergence in non-IID and asynchronous settings, while privacy-utility trade-offs require novel solutions like hybrid DP and secure multi-party computation. Personalization techniques, such as hypernetworks and meta-learning, will be critical for heterogeneous data environments. Industry adoption hinges on standardized frameworks for interoperability, regulatory-compliant tools, and energy-efficient FL for edge devices. Emerging areas include cross-modal FL (e.g., vision-language models), federated reinforcement learning, and AI governance for ethical FL deployments. Bridging these gaps will unlock FL's potential in healthcare, finance, and smart cities while preserving data sovereignty.

12.4.1 Continued optimization

Focus on improving communication efficiency, model robustness against attacks, and developing adaptive FL models that can manage dynamic participation.

12.4.2 Advanced personalization

Leveraging personalization techniques (e.g., client-specific models while using global knowledge) to improve accuracy in heterogeneous environments.

12.4.3 Integration with emerging technologies

Enhancing transparency, accountability, and security in FL systems.

12.4.4 Federated reinforcement learning

Broadening FL's applicability to dynamic, autonomous decision-making systems.

12.4.5 Scientific machine learning (SciML)

Designing FL to predict physical systems governed by equations, ensuring model predictions conform to physical laws, particularly for high-dimensional data and complex models.

12.4.6 Standardization and frameworks

The need for standardized benchmarks and evaluation protocols to facilitate fair comparisons and accelerate development. Frameworks like EdgeFL are emerging to offer simplified implementation, combined with enhanced customization and fault tolerance (Zhang et al., 2025).

12.4.7 Ethical considerations

Ongoing efforts to address fairness, bias, transparency, and accountability in FL systems, including auditing data sources, ensuring diverse participation, and providing clear user documentation.

12.4.8 Mass adoption

The global FL market is projected to grow significantly, reaching "$2.3 billion by 2032, growing at a remarkable CAGR of 35.4%" (Vertu, 2025). This growth underscores its transformative potential across diverse industries.

There are several areas in which FL requires improvement; one of the key areas is data heterogeneity. Data heterogeneity in FL pertains to the issue where various participants in a joint machine learning model training procedure possess differing data distributions, complicating the development of a universally effective model. Such variation may stem from disparities in data volume, feature space, label distribution, and other statistical characteristics among the devices or clients involved.

12.5 RESEARCH FOCUS

Data heterogeneity can appear in multiple forms, such as non-independent and identically distributed (non-IID) data. A primary concern is that data among clients frequently lacks in non-Independence and Identical Distribution (non-IID), indicating substantial differences in data distributions. This variability can cause client drift, where local models deviate from one another, leading to sub-optimal global model performance and inequities in model training. Data heterogeneity can arise due to several factors, including different sample size, feature distribution not found similar across clients, label skews, statistical heterogeneity. There are different techniques discovered for tackling data heterogeneity, we will discuss few over here.

12.5.1 Data shift

Data shift refers to the phenomenon where the statistical properties of data (e.g., feature distributions, label frequencies, or input-output relationships) vary across clients or over time. InFL , data shift is a critical challenge because it violates the Independent and identically Distributed (IID) assumption, leading to degraded model performance. There are three primary types of data shift:

12.5.1.1 Co-variate shift

Input distribution shift (H. Wang et al., 2020) occurs when the distribution of input features P(x) differs across clients, but the conditional distribution P(y|x) remains the same, for example, different hospitals use varying medical imaging devices, altering image resolutions (input shift), but the diagnostic criteria (labeling function) stay consistent.

12.5.1.2 Label shift

Prior probability shift (Ye et al., 2025) occurs when the label distribution P(y) changes, but the feature distribution given a label P(x|y) remains stable, for example; In credit scoring, one bank (Client A) serves mostly low-risk borrowers $P(y=0) \approx 0.8$, while another (Client B) serves high-risk borrowers $P(y=1) \approx 0.7$, but the features for each risk class (income, credit history and other demographic) follow similar patterns.

12.5.1.3 Concept shift

Conditional distribution shift (Badar et al., 2023) occurs when the relationship between inputs and outputs P(y|x) changes across clients or over time, for example, in fraud detection, a transaction pattern x, that was once labeled fraudulent y=1 may no longer be suspicious due to evolving attack methods.

12.5.2 How data shift affects FL

Data Shift severely affects the FL learning process, though.

Biased global model Standard FL algorithms FedAvg, compute a weighted average of client updates, assuming data distributions are similar, if one client's data dominates (due to larger n_k or extreme shifts), the global model becomes biased toward that client, harming performance on others. Even in case of FedProx as it penalizes the drift and reduces the impact, but what if the shift is indication of change in underlying behavior of the data for example, due to certain change in occupation or climatic condition, Client A samples started showing larger number of cases with cancer occurrence, FedProx will penalize since there is a drift in underlying model.

The global model

$$\omega, P_{global}(x,y)=\sum_{k}\frac{n_k}{k}P_k(x,y) \tag{5.1}$$

may not represent the true distribution.

Client Drift, in non-IID settings, local models diverge from the global model because they overfit their local data distribution. Example: A client with mostly "cat" images trains a model that performs poorly on "dog" images from other clients.

Convergence Issues FL algorithms (FedAvg's convergence) often assume IID data. Under the data shift. The global model may oscillate or stagnate instead of converging. Gradient updates from conflicting distributions create noise in optimization.

12.6 FUTURE ROADMAP OF FL AND DIRECTION OF IMPROVEMENT

FL faces significant challenges in handling data heterogeneity, where clients possess non-IID data, leading to biased or unstable model convergence. A promising approach to mitigate this issue involves preserving local metadata—statistical summaries of client data distributions, such as class frequencies, feature means/variances, or gradient similarities—while maintaining strict privacy guarantees. By securely aggregating and comparing this metadata, FL systems can quantify heterogeneity, detect outlier clients, and dynamically adapt training strategies without accessing raw data. Techniques such SecAgg and DP ensure metadata confidentiality, and techniques that use methods such as clustered FL to group clients whose distributions are similar together to perform specialized model training. Also, metadata-driven personalization techniques, which enable models to initialize, or get context-traded on better fairness and convergence. As an example, rare classes in client algorithms can have the option of increasing importance when aggregated (upweighting), or learning rates can be adapted to local data complexity using adaptive optimizers. Nevertheless, the issues that still must be addressed include the problem of achieving the balance between metadata utility and privacy, reducing communication overhead, and the problem of managing dynamic environments where data distributions change. New paradigms, such as federated meta-learning, synthetic metadata generation, and the use of lightweight similarity metrics should also be studied to achieve context-aware FL without sacrificing the desired scalability or security. Such paradigm shift to metadata-enhanced training may allow more robust, efficient, and fair FL systems in practical use including in healthcare, finance, and IoT.

Current research roadmap in FL focuses on addressing four main challenges namely: Statistical heterogeneity, system heterogeneity, technical balances of privacy and security, and the challenge of scaling. To overcome statistical heterogeneity, also called non-IID data distributions among clients, researchers propose the use of adaptive algorithms, such as clustered FL or meta-learning approaches, which can discover how data distributions differ, auto adaptive the model personalization strategies according to the requirements. The recent advances demonstrate dynamic clustering methods that can evolve with time fluctuations in the distributions of data. Regarding system heterogeneity, there is also some progress on two fronts: The improving communication using more powerful compression algorithm (e.g. adaptive gradient quantization, etc.) or designing the computation-sensitive systems that are capable of dynamically varying local computation needs based on real-time evaluation of device capabilities. Privacy-security innovations that have appeared in three important areas: (1) Hybrid differentially private approaches that allocate privacy budgets per-instance; (2) secure-aggregate techniques that reduces the communication overhead; and (3) adversarial training strategies that obtain high robustness and low privacy-violating cases. Research into how to increase scalability is being conducted by producing hierarchical models employing aggregation nodes (on the edge), edge-level aggregation updates and asynchronous update, coupled with intelligent or staleness-aware edge-level aggregations.

An active research direction combines foundational models with FL infrastructure, being concerned with parameter-efficient fine-tuning and layer-wise personalization algorithms to enable training on large models in a distributed way.

The field is also establishing comprehensive bench-marking frameworks to evaluate various aspects—accuracy, fairness, and resource use—under realistic non-IID and system constraints. Recent initiatives in cross-modal FL are addressing the challenges of federated training with diverse data types, such as integrating medical imaging with electronic health records, leveraging modality-specific encoders and fusion techniques. The roadmap emphasizes the need for theoretical models that can simultaneously evaluate convergence, generalization, and privacy guarantees within realistic FL configurations, moving away from the current approach of examining these factors separately. Practical implementation considerations are driving research into automated FL configuration systems capable of dynamically adjusting hyper-parameters, client selection strategies, and aggregation rules based on real-time system and data inputs. The community is also working on standardized evaluation frameworks and metrics that effectively capture the multiple goals of FL systems, including innovative fairness indicators for heterogeneous client groups and energy efficiency standards for edge implementations. A growing recognition of the need for specialized hardware-FL co-design is leading to investigations into FL-optimized chipsets and accelerator architectures that can accommodate the distinct computational requirements of federated training. As new challenges emerge from real-world applications, particularly in areas such as continual or lifelong FL and federated reinforcement learning systems, the roadmap is set to evolve further.

12.7 PRESERVING LOCAL METADATA AND CONTEXT-AWARE TRAINING IN FL

The idea of retaining and comparing local data context (metadata) across clients presents an alternative approach to enhancing FL in handling statistical and system heterogeneity. This approach involves extracting and analyzing data distribution characteristics, feature correlations, or dataset statistics from clients without violating privacy, then using this metadata to adapt the FL training process dynamically.

12.7.1 What is "Local data context" in FL

Local data context refers to metadata that describes the statistical properties of a client's dataset without exposing raw data. Examples include:

- Class distribution (label frequencies in classification tasks).
- Feature means/variances (for regression or deep learning).
- Covariance matrices (to understand feature correlations).
- Data scarcity indicators (e.g., few-shot learning scenarios).
- Concept drift measures (how data changes over time).

12.7.2 How metadata comparison helps manage heterogeneity

By comparing metadata across clients, FL systems can detect and quantify Heterogeneity by measuring non-IIDness (using KL divergence between label distributions), identifying outlier clients with extremely different data distributions, and clustering similar clients for grouped personalization (e.g., clustered FL).

It can also adapt training strategies by dynamic client weighting: Assign higher importance to underrepresented clients, personalized model initialization; Use metadata to guide local fine-tuning, adaptive aggregation; Adjust global model updates based on data skew, and resource-aware training; Allocate more computation to clients with complex distributions. Adding context-aware technique can improve Fairness and Robustness by mitigating bias by ensuring minority classes contribute meaningfully. Detect adversarial clients via abnormal metadata patterns and balance convergence speed by prioritizing difficult clients.

12.7.2.1 Secure aggregation (SecAgg) in FL

SecAgg ensures that the server cannot inspect individual client updates during model aggregation, preserving privacy while allowing global model updates (K. H. Li et al., 2021).

12.7.2.2 Working rinciples

- Masking with Cryptographic Techniques: Clients encrypt their model updates (gradients) using secret sharing or homomorphic encryption before sending them to the server. Only the sum of updates can be decrypted, not individual contributions.
- Multi-Party Computation (MPC): Clients collaborate to generate cryptographic keys (e.g., via Shamir's Secret Sharing). The server aggregates the masked updates and reconstructs only the combined result.
- Dropout Resilience: SecAgg protocols (Nazemi et al., 2024) handle client dropouts without leaking data.

12.7.2.3 Technical approaches for metadata-aware FL

Metadata-aware FL leverages statistical summaries of local data distributions—such as class frequencies, gradient similarities, or feature correlations—to improve model performance in heterogeneous settings while preserving privacy. Key technical approaches include:

- Federated Metadata Extraction: Secure computation of client-level statistics (e.g., mean/variance) via SecAgg or DP to prevent raw data leakage, as proposed in Jin et al., (2023).
- Clustered FL: Grouping clients with similar metadata (e.g., label distributions) to train specialized models, as seen in IFCA, where cluster-specific models reduce negative interference from non-IID data.
- Adaptive Aggregation (Lai et al., 2021): Dynamically weighting client updates based on metadata to balance contributions, as in FedBalancer (Keating, 2022), which prioritizes underrepresented clients.
- Privacy-Preserving Similarity Measures (Ballandies et al., 2023): Comparing metadata embedding (e.g., gradient directions) using cosine similarity or federated k-means with DP noise.

These methods enable context-aware personalization and fairness while addressing scalability and privacy trade-offs. Future work aims to integrate federated meta-learning and synthetic metadata generation for broader applicability.

12.8 CONCLUSION

The future of FL hinges on overcoming non-IID data and heterogeneity challenges to enable robust real-world adoption. Key directions include: (1) Advanced personalization techniques like dynamic clustering and meta-learning to tailor models to diverse client distributions without compromising collaboration; (2) Synthetic data and augmentation to harmonize disparities across clients while preserving privacy through generative models (e.g., GANs) and federated DP; (3) Theoretical breakthroughs in convergence guarantees for extreme heterogeneity, ensuring stability in decentralized environments; and (4) Cross-modal FL frameworks to unify disparate data types (e.g., images, text) under a cohesive training paradigm. Research in new lightweight, adaptive algorithms and hardware-FL build together will further enhance reach and scalability for edge devices. As FL matures, standardized benchmark tools and regulatory-compliant framework will bridge the gap between research and industry deployment, leading to fairness, efficiency, and privacy in industry applications ranging from healthcare, smart cities, finance etc.
Key Challenges: Catastrophic forgetting, bias propagation, and energy-efficient training.
Vision: A federated ecosystem where heterogeneous data fuels collaborative intelligence without sacrificing performance or privacy.

ABBREVIATION

AUC	Area Under Curve
BN	batch normalization
CAGR	Compound Annual Growth Rate
CIFAR-10	Canadian Institute for Advanced Research
CV	Computer Vision
CVF	Computer Vision Foundation
CVPR	Computer Vision and Pattern Recognition
DP	differential privacy
DP-FL	differential privacy-Federate Learning
eICU	electronic Intensive Care Unit
EMNIST	Electronic Modified National Institute of Standards and Technology database
FebBN	Federated Batch Normalization
FedAvg	Federated Averaging
FedBN	Federated Batch Normalization
FedBS	Federated Batch Specific
FedDG	Federated Domain Generalization

FedDyn	Federated Dynamic Regularization
FedFM	Federated Feature Matching
FedGKD	Federated General Knowledge Distillation
FedNova	Federated Normalize Average
FedOpt	Federated Optimized
FedPer	Federated Personalization
FedProx	Federated Proximal
FEMNIST	Federated Extended MNIST
FL	Federated Learning
FLaaS	Federated Learning as a Service
GANs	Generative Adversarial Networks
GDPR	General Data Protection Regulation
HIPAA	Health Insurance Portability and Accountability Act
IBM	International Business Machine
ICIS	Independent Commodity Intelligence Services
IEEE	Institute of Electrical and Electronics Engineers
IFCA	Iterative Federated Clustering Algorithm
IID	Independent and identically Distributed.
IoT	Internet of Things
LWA-HAND	lightweight attention hand
MAML	Model-Agnostic Meta-Learning
MELLODDY	Machine Learning Ledger Orchestration for Drug DiscoverY
MNIST	Modified National Institute of Standards and Technology
MOON	Model-contrastive Federated Learning
MPC	Multi-Party Computation
PFL	personalized federated learning.
pMAML	personalized MAML
ResNet-18	Residual Neural Network
SCAFFOLD	Stochastic Controlled Averaging for Federated Learning
SciML	Scientific Machine Learning
SecAgg	secure aggregation
SGD	Stochastic Gradient Descent
SWIFT	The Society for Worldwide Interbank Financial Telecommunications

REFERENCES

Acar, D. A. E., Zhao, Y., Navarro, R. M., Mattina, M., Whatmough, P. N., & Saligrama, V. J. (2021). Federated learning based on dynamic regularization. arXiv [Cs.LG]. Retrieved from http://arxiv.org/abs/2111.04263

Badar, M., Nejdl, W., & Fisichella, M. (2023). FAC-fed: Federated adaptation for fairness and concept drift aware stream classification. *Machine Learning*, *112*(8), 2761–2786. doi:10.1007/s10994-023-06360-7

Ballandies, M. C., Holzwarth, V., Sunderland, B., Pournaras, E., & vom Brocke, J. (2023). Constructing effective customer feedback systems -- A design science study leveraging blockchain technology. *arXiv [cs.SE]*.

Di, X., & Yu, P. (2023). *LWA-HAND: Lightweight Attention Hand for Interacting Hand Reconstruction*. Cham: ACM.

Dinh, C. T., Tran, N., & Nguyen, J. (2020). *Personalized Federated Learning with Moreau Envelopes*. Paper Presented at the Advances in Neural Information Processing Systems. https://proceedings.neurips.cc/paper_files/paper/2020/file/f4f1f13c8289ac1b1ee0ff176b56fc60-Paper.pdf

Fallah, A., Mokhtari, A., & Ozdaglar, A. (2020). Personalized federated learning: A meta-learning approach. *arXiv [cs.LG]*.

Jin, T., Pan, S., Li, X., & Chen, S. (2023). Metadata and image features co-aware personalized federated learning for smart healthcare. *IEEE Journal of Biomedical and Health Informatics, 27*(8), 4110–4119. doi:10.1109/JBHI.2023.3279096

Karimireddy, S. P., Kale, S., Mohri, M., Reddi, S., Stich, S., & Suresh, A. T. (2020). *SCAFFOLD: Stochastic Controlled Averaging for Federated Learning*. Paper Presented at the Proceedings of the 37th International Conference on Machine Learning, Proceedings of Machine Learning Research. https://proceedings.mlr.press/v119/karimireddy20a.html

Keating, J. P. (2022). Hierarchical structure in the trace formula*. *Journal of Physics A: Mathematical and Theoretical, 55*(36), 364001. doi:10.1088/1751-8121/ac82d6

Lai, F., Zhu, X., Madhyastha, H. V., & Chowdhury, M. (2021). Oort: Efficient federated learning via guided participant selection. *arXiv [cs.LG]*.

Li, K. H., de Gusmão, P. P. B., Beutel, D. J., & Lane, N. D. (2021). *Secure Aggregation for Federated Learning in Flower*. Paper Presented at the Proceedings of the 2nd ACM International Workshop on Distributed Machine Learning.

Li, Q., He, B., & Song, D. (2021). *Model-Contrastive Federated Learning*. Paper Presented at the Proceedings of the IEEE/CVF Conference on Computer Vision and Pattern Recognition (CVPR).

Li, T., Sahu, A. K., Zaheer, M., Sanjabi, M., Talwalkar, A., & Smith, V. (2020). *Federated Optimization in Heterogeneous Networks*. arXiv [Cs.LG]. Retrieved from http://arxiv.org/abs/1812.06127

Li, X., Jiang, M., Zhang, X., Kamp, M., & Dou, Q. (2021). FedBN: Federated learning on non-IID features via local batch normalization. *arXiv [cs.LG]*.

Liu, Q., Chen, C., Qin, J., Dou, Q., & Heng, P.-A. (2021). FedDG: Federated domain generalization on medical image segmentation via episodic learning in continuous frequency space. *arXiv [cs.CV]*.

Nazemi, N., Tavallaie, O., Chen, S., Mandalari, A. M., Thilakarathna, K., Holz, R., ... Zomaya, A. Y. (2024). ACCESS-FL: Agile communication and computation for efficient secure aggregation in stable federated learning networks. *arXiv [cs.CR]*.

Su, C., Wu, J., Zhang, R., Kang, Z., Xia, H., & Zhang, C. (2025). FedBS: Solving data heterogeneity issue in federated learning using balanced subtasks. *High-Confidence Computing*, 100322. https://doi.org/10.1016/j.hcc.2025.100322

Uddin, M. R., Shankar, G., Mukta, M. S. H., Kumar, P., & Islam, N. (2024). *Evolving Topics in Federated Learning: Trends, and Emerging Directions for IS Research*. Paper Presented at the ICIS 2024, Bankok, Thailand.

Vertu (2025). How ai federated learning is transforming industries in 2025 [online], 2025. *VERTU® Official Site*. Available from: https://vertu.com/ai-tools/ai-federated-learning-transforming-industries-2025/?srsltid=AfmBOopsxalnJOoQ0NMFWTmebRNA06IMGQlRXoE7kB7DdsHKL63Ww0bF [Accessed 19 Dec 2025].

Wang, H., Yurochkin, M., Sun, Y., Papailiopoulos, D., & Khazaeni, Y. (2020). Federated learning with matched averaging. *arXiv [cs.LG]*.

Wang, J., Liu, Q., Liang, H., Joshi, G., & Poor, H. V. (2020). Tackling the objective inconsistency problem in heterogeneous federated optimization. *Advances in Neural Information Processing Systems*, *33*, 7611–7623.

Yao, D., Pan, W., Dai, Y., Wan, Y., Ding, X., Jin, H., ... Sun, L. J. (2021). Local-global knowledge distillation in heterogeneous federated learning with non-iid data. arXiv [Cs.LG]. Retrieved from http://arxiv.org/abs/2107.00051

Ye, M., Huang, W., Shi, Z., Li, H., & Du, B. (2025). Revisiting federated learning with label skew: An over-confidence perspective. *Science China Information Sciences, 68*(9), 192102. doi:10.1007/s11432-023-4202-1

Zhang, H., Bosch, J., & Olsson, H. H. (2025). Enabling efficient and low-effort decentralized federated learning with the EdgeFL framework. *Information and Software Technology, 178*, 107600. https://doi.org/10.1016/j.infsof.2024.107600

Chapter 13

Cyber resilience in sports organisations

Federal learning for financial, fan, and athlete data security

Amitava Pal and Kavita Mathad

13.1 INTRODUCTION

Gone are the days when professional sports organisations were just about playing the games and delivering performance and entertainment—in the digital age, they have evolved into diverse, complex, data-driven ecosystems. These organisations control vast quantities of sensitive information—including biometric data, performance analytics, digital ticketing, company details, and worldwide sponsorships. Although this digital transformation encourages innovation and business prospects, it also greatly enlarges the attack surface for cybersecurity [1, 2].

Aside from actual attacks on physical resources, football clubs, Olympic bodies, and esports entities have been targeted by attacks that sought to extract financial data and personal data of athletes and fans or to manipulate competitive outcomes or disrupt live events [3]. At the same time, regulations such as the General Data Protection Regulation (GDPR) and corresponding national laws have increased pressure on organisations to govern the use of data by imposing strict data protection, accountability, and transparency requirements.

The decentralised, dynamic nature of modern sports data infrastructures is making traditional cybersecurity approaches—predominantly reactive and based on centralised, perimeter-based defense—increasingly insufficient. In such scenarios, cyber resilience comes into play. This relates to an organisation's ability not only to prevent, but also to quickly identify, isolate, and recover from cyberattacks. Resilience requires a trade-off between data utility, privacy, and collaboration between teams, leagues, healthcare providers, sponsors, and technology partners [4].

FL, the subject of this chapter, could be a prospective solution in such a framework evolution. FL is a promising approach that enables the decentralised training of machine learning models across multiple participants, without requiring raw data to be transmitted off-device. FL focuses on sharing only encrypted or privacy-preserving model updates [5], while maintaining data locality and avoiding centralisation of information—it is at high risk of breach due to centralising sensitive data. Such a distributed learning paradigm will be highly suitable for the sports industry, as privacy, compliance, and data ownership are key concerns.

DOI: 10.1201/9781003660330-13

Viewing through this lens, this chapter explores how FL can enhance cyber resilience in three key areas within sports organisations:

- Security of financial data—especially in the fight against fraud, and the security of payment systems;
- Managing digital engagement and personalised services; Fan data privacy;
- Athlete Data Privacy—Biometric, Health and Performance Data.

The chapter presents real-life examples and realistic frameworks to show how FL can enable a proactive and cooperative cybersecurity approach in the sports industry. It further explores the technical, legal, and ethical hurdles to implementing such systems, outlining a roadmap for future-proof data protection in an increasingly interconnected and vulnerable sector.

13.2 CYBER THREAT LANDSCAPE IN SPORTS

Sports organisations are becoming increasingly attractive targets for cybercriminals as they become more digitised, with operations shifting to the digital space, including performance tracking, fan engagement, and financial management. The massive quantities of sensitive information held by these organisations, combined with the prominence of athletes and the passion of millions of fans worldwide, create a digital environment that can be exploited more than most [6, 7].

Cyber threats to sporting organisations are becoming the norm, and the threats are becoming more complicated. The cascading impact of incidents like this on trust, reputation, and legal liabilities is demonstrated in major breaches, such as the case involving Football Australia where player contracts and fan details were leaked [8]. Additionally, the warnings to the sector against various instances of coordinated phishing attacks reinforces that social engineering campaigns are a real threat [9]. This leads us to consider the geopolitical nature of threats from cyber to sport, with a strong example being Operation Shady RAT where many organisations across the world including Olympic Committees were breached [10]. In this article, we focus on some important cyber threats that are present in the sport industry, demonstrating the examples with real-life cases.

13.2.1 Phishing attacks targeting employees and gamers

Threat Overview: Phishing is a form of social engineering in which an attacker sends an email that looks like it is coming from someone they are familiar with, attempting to persuade the user to provide their sensitive information or download some malicious application. This method is common within the sports sector using impersonation as an agent, sponsor or internal staff to target athletes, coaches and administrative personnel.

Extended Sample: A high profile football club preparing for an international event. A coaching staff receives an email that looks like it came from the club travel office requesting scanned copies of passports to assist with visa processing. The link directs users to a page that looks like a real government portal, however if you click it the user gets infected with malware. Malware that breaks into internal systems, ripping these files with Player Performances and Contracts. This leads to strategic disruption, reputational harm, and an increased risk of identity theft for athletes.

Why It Matters: Phishing relies on human stupidity above all other obstacles, which can lead to a significant bypass of technical defenses. Any one attack could be costly, exposing terabytes of data and potentially putting an entire organisation or even entire industries at risk of reputational damage or severe fines.

13.2.2 Violations of athlete genetic and medical data

13.2.2.1 Threat explanation

Athlete tracking technologies collect fine-grained biometric and health data—from wearables to injury tracking systems. Should this data be leaked, it could be utilised by betting syndicates, rival teams, or to assist with influencing contract negotiations [11].

13.2.2.2 Expanded scenario

Wearable sensors are used to encapsulate instantaneous physiological data during training at a national sports science lab. In the case of a misconfigured cloud server, the report was publicly available for weeks, running and allowing live data feeds. They get discovered by the media, sponsors withdraw sponsorship, and the organisation gets sued by athletes who have been affected.

13.2.2.3 Why it matters

This means that biometric and other health data are not just personal data; they are premium personal data. Their leaks represent a major ethical, legal, and commercial problem due to regulations such as HIPAA and GDPR.

13.2.3 Lorenze fan personal and payment data theft

13.2.3.1 Threat explanation

Due to the sheer volume of data that sports organisations handle from mobile apps, loyalty programs, and ticketing platforms, they are a prime target for financial fraud and identity theft [12].

13.2.3.2 Expanded scenario

Third-party payment plugin vulnerability breached a Football Club's Fan Engagement App. For weeks on end, attackers will amass thousands of payment records and personal details. Users only discover the breach when they notice unfamiliar charges on their credit cards. The club is hit by regulatory scrutiny, and the app is taken offline.

13.2.3.3 Why it matters

Data breaches are a deliberate act by a bad actor, meaning the brand's reputation and trust are compromised. Standards such as PCI DSS must be adhered to in order to prevent financial loss or disruption to operations.

13.2.4 Match-fixing through data leaks

13.2.4.1 Threat rxplanation

Thus, real-time sports data such as fitness conditions, match tactics, and team compositions could be exploited by malicious agents to manipulate not only match results but also betting markets [13].

13.2.4.2 Expanded scenario

Hackers access Coach's Cloud Account days ahead of Tennis Grand Slam, publish documents on Ace Player's Injury. The betting syndicate then bets against the player with inside knowledge, causing him to perform poorly. Investigators are tasked with identifying the foreign IP address from which the breach originated.

13.2.4.3 Why it matters

The integrity of matches is at the core of what makes sport credible. Leaks of the kind that change outcomes or odds for betting lead to a collapse of public trust, not to mention regulatory compliance.

13.2.5 Regulatory environment

With a relentless rise in cyber threats, the variety of data protection laws with which sports organisations need to comply is only increasing:

GDPR: Regulates the processing of data related to EU citizens, emphasising transparency, consent, and effective notification in the event of a breach.

Example(you as a club role): A football club uses non-anonymised ticket sales data for marketing purposes, with the consequence that the GDPR investigation and fine comes to their door.

HIPAA: The Health Insurance Portability and Accountability Act of 1996 (HIPAA) is a U.S. law that protects the privacy of personal health information.

Sample case: A journalist receives a tip about a player's injury report from an athletics department, creating potential legal issues.

PCI DSS: Payment card application security

Scenario: A breach of a club's merchandise store containing unencrypted payment data, resulting in fines for compliance violations.

Today, sports organisations operate at the intersection of entertainment, technology, and data. As more threats target everything from health records to match outcomes, the need for cyber resilience has never been greater. However, it is not just prevention, but detection, response, and recovery. FL, as further discussed in the next section, is also a practical framework for expanding cybersecurity while maintaining data privacy and the operational status quo.

13.2.5.1 Example: Hacked the official website of FC Barcelona to conduct fraud

13.2.5.1.1 Background

A cybersecurity firm named AdEx found a suspicious redirect hosted under what seemed to be the official website of FC Barcelona on November 16, 2022. The link directs users to an online gambling website instead of genuine club content—likely targeting the Indonesian market [14]. The attack was able to use an actual subdomain of the real FC Barcelona domain, not a spoof—this helped lend legitimacy to the approach.

13.2.5.1.2 The incident

FC Barcelona initially hosted its main website on Amazon Web Services (AWS). However, the rogue subdomain's Domain Name System (DNS) had been misconfigured to go through Google Cloud DNS, which enabled the redirection to work outside of the club's usual oversight processes—due to the little amounts of traffic and the fact that the subdomain was not indexed by search engines, conventional monitoring tools that could have traced it down, never detected it [15].

13.2.5.1.3 Security and data risk

While not officially reported as a breach of personal or financial data, the risks were high. Visitors could have thought they were on an official page and entered sensitive details. The attack could have phishing, credential theft, or malicious downloads using the trusted brand of the club. The subdomain did not appear significant enough for the club's internal systems to flag the issue.

This incident illustrates how an attacker can exploit passive infrastructure misconfigurations—without requiring direct access to core systems—to execute a malicious campaign [16].

13.2.5.1.4 How it happened

This was most likely due to a dysfunction in subdomain governance. Attackers hijacked or created a long-forgotten subdomain within the DNS hierarchy of FC Barcelona. Since it was hosted separately and independently from the rest of the site, the subdomain was outside the location of standard monitoring and update cycles. This enabled malicious actors to disguise traffic needs undetected for an unknown period.

13.2.5.1.5 Impact

Fan Interactions with a Fake Site—Fans visiting the fraudulent website may associate the gambling scam with the club, potentially leading to brand erosion.

Lack of Operational Blind Spot: The club's DNS policies and infrastructure governance were ineffective.

Regulatory Risk: If something goes awry with the informatics/analytics, even in the absence of a direct data breach, misuse of digital assets could have GDPR or PCI DSS implications if there was any European user interaction or payment processing.

13.2.5.1.6 Lessons learned

It is essential to Govern Subdomains: All subdomains, including unused ones, should be inventoried and monitored to identify potential security risks.

Enforce DNS Consistency: There should be an immediate red flag when the hosting provider and DNS providers do not match.

No More One-Time Scans: The tool must run regular scans for DNS and domain assets to find signs of configuration drift or misuse.

Internal breaches are not the only source of threat: External attack surfaces can be built using misconfigurations, which can be exploited before conventional security protocols can detect them.

13.3 KEY ASSETS IN SPORTS CYBERSECURITY

In today's sports industry, cybersecurity extends far beyond traditional IT protection. It involves defending a broad range of high-value digital assets critical to how sports organisations perform, engage with fans, and generate revenue. As clubs and leagues increasingly rely on digital platforms, attackers exploit these assets for financial gain, competitive sabotage, and reputational damage [17]. This section outlines four major asset categories that must be prioritised in any robust cyber resilience strategy.

13.3.1 Financial data

Financial data lies at the heart of sports operations—from digital ticketing and online merchandise to sponsorship payments and player transfer contracts. Cybercriminals increasingly target these financial systems to steal funds or extort organisations through ransomware. For example, *Legends International*, a global venue management firm, suffered a significant breach that compromised payment and tax data, also revealing the financial exposure of third-party vendors [18].

Attackers may manipulate payment gateways, inject malware into e-commerce platforms, or compromise vendor credentials. Beyond direct financial losses, these breaches can sever trust with sponsors and commercial partners. As digital transactions become central to sports operations, securing them through encryption, access controls, and PCI DSS compliance is essential.

13.3.2 Fan data

Fan data—collected through ticket sales, mobile apps, loyalty programs, and CRM systems—includes names, emails, contact details, preferences, and often payment information. This makes it a prime target for identity theft, phishing campaigns, or resale on the dark web [19]. Breaches affecting fan data have been reported across leagues, including unauthorised access to email and marketing systems during major events.

For example, attackers compromised fan engagement platforms associated with major clubs to harvest login credentials and payment records, thereby damaging the brand's reputation. Under regulations like GDPR, mishandling personally identifiable information (PII) can result in legal penalties and a loss of fan trust. Sports organisations must ensure that they have proper consent mechanisms, encryption, and role-based access control.

13.3.3 Athlete data

Athlete data—ranging from biometric sensor outputs to drug testing records and injury reports—is among the most sensitive information in sports. It has both medical and strategic value. A recent breach involving Australian Football League (AFL) players resulted in the leak of confidential drug test results, raising concerns about both privacy and competitive integrity.

If leaked, such data can be exploited by rival teams, betting syndicates, or the media to manipulate match outcomes or influence contract negotiations. Given the legal protections around medical information (e.g., HIPAA in the U.S.), securing athlete data requires end-to-end encryption, audit trails, and strict data minimisation practices [20].

13.3.4 Interconnected platforms

The digital sports environment is becoming increasingly interconnected, encompassing apps, wearables, stadium Wi-Fi, IoT sensors, and cloud-based analytics. A weakness in any component can jeopardise the entire system. For instance, an unpatched third-party app plugin could create a backdoor into a club's broader network.

During live events, attackers can exploit open WiFi networks to launch man-in-the-middle attacks or gain access to backend systems. Wearables may leak real-time biometric data if misconfigured. Effective cybersecurity requires continuous monitoring, patch management, and network segmentation, along with thorough vendor risk assessments and evaluations.

13.4 CHALLENGES IN SECURING SPORTS DATA

Despite growing awareness, sports organisations face a unique mix of cybersecurity challenges rooted in their complex operational environment. Unlike traditional enterprises, sports ecosystems involve multiple stakeholders, operate across fragmented infrastructure, and manage high-value targets [21].

13.4.1 Diverse stakeholders

The sports ecosystem includes teams, leagues, medical providers, broadcasters, sponsors, and tech partners—each with its own infrastructure and cybersecurity practices. Disparities in protection levels across this network create systemic vulnerabilities (SecureWorld, 2023).

For example, a broadcaster using outdated cloud configurations or a medical partner storing unencrypted athlete data could compromise the entire supply chain. Attackers often exploit the weakest link, as seen in multiple Olympic cyberattacks where entry points were found in loosely protected third-party systems (Wired, 2022).

13.4.2 Decentralised infrastructure

Sports organisations typically operate in highly decentralised environments, collecting and transmitting data from stadiums, training facilities, and athlete residences. This leads to inconsistent security coverage across cloud platforms, mobile apps, and IoT devices (Infront, 2023; Villanova University, 2021).

A football club might manage ticketing via one cloud vendor, athlete data through another, and merchandise systems via a third. Lack of visibility across this fragmented infrastructure increases the likelihood of misconfigurations and delayed breach detection. Coordinating consistent security policies becomes operationally complex.

13.4.3 High-value targets

The nature of sports data—encompassing real-time analytics, injury reports, and personal information of celebrity-level—makes it exceptionally attractive to attackers (ESET, 2022). Threats range from identity theft to ransomware campaigns timed around high-profile events, such as the World Cup or Olympics (Wired, 2022).

For example, the 2018 Winter Olympics cyberattack, known as "Olympic Destroyer," disrupted event systems and targeted logistics and broadcast services (Wired, 2022). High-profile athletes are frequent targets for social engineering, hacking attempts, and reputational sabotage.

Securing sports data requires more than firewalls and antivirus software—it demands a multi-stakeholder, cross-disciplinary strategy grounded in operational realities. As threats evolve, FL offers a forward-thinking solution: Enabling collaborative threat detection and risk modeling across clubs, leagues, and vendors, without exposing sensitive data. In a sector where reputation, performance, and revenue are deeply intertwined with digital trust, the need for coordinated, privacy-preserving cybersecurity has never been greater.

13.5 FL IN SPORTS

The sports industry is undergoing a digital transformation, relying heavily on data-driven strategies to enhance athlete performance, fan engagement, and financial operations. However, with the increasing collection of data comes heightened privacy risks and regulatory challenges. FL has emerged as a privacy-preserving machine learning paradigm, allowing multiple stakeholders—such as clubs, leagues, and vendors—to collaboratively train AI models without exposing raw data [22, 23].

In FL, the model is sent to each participant's local environment, where it is trained on-site. Only model updates (e.g., gradients or parameters), not the actual data, are shared with a central aggregator [24]. For instance, rather than centralising athlete performance data from several football clubs, each club can train the model locally and contribute to a shared model that benefits from broad data representation while maintaining confidentiality.

13.5.1 Benefits for sports organisations

Data Privacy and Compliance: FL ensures compliance with data protection laws, such as the GDPR and HIPAA, by keeping sensitive data—such as medical records or personally identifiable information—within the organisation [25, 26].

Reduced Centralised Risk: By decentralising data storage, FL reduces the likelihood of mass breaches from a single point of failure [27]. Even if one participant is compromised, the rest of the system remains intact.

Cross-Organisational Collaboration: FL facilitates model training across competitive organisations without requiring data sharing, supporting joint projects in fan analytics, injury prevention, or anti-fraud initiatives, without compromising proprietary data [28].

13.6 FL FOR FINANCIAL DATA SECURITY

13.6.1 Fraud detection without sharing financial records

The professional sports industry handles vast amounts of financial data—ranging from ticket sales and merchandise to media rights. Centralised storage of such data exposes it to significant cyber risk. FL enables distributed training of fraud detection models, allowing stakeholders to detect irregular transactions (e.g., credit card fraud or ticket scalping) without exposing transaction-level data.

13.6.2 Collaborative anomaly detection

Fraudsters often exploit silos between clubs or platforms. FL mitigates this by enabling decentralised stakeholders to identify coordinated attacks. For example, clubs can detect bulk fake ticket purchases when model insights are aggregated, even if individual data sets appear benign [29]. This collaborative defense aligns with both regulatory mandates for data minimisation and strategic cybersecurity goals [30].

13.6.3 Learnings from other industries

Banking, telecommunications, and healthcare have already implemented FL to detect fraud and anomalies across institutions [31]. In finance, multi-party FL deployments have shown improved fraud detection accuracy without compromising data sovereignty [32]. Sports leagues, such as the Premier League, could adopt similar approaches to detect systemic threats across franchises—improving security without compromising trust.

13.7 FL FOR FAN DATA PROTECTION

13.7.1 Personalised marketing without exposing fan data

Fan engagement platforms collect significant PII—such as emails, payment data, and interaction histories. FL can help clubs train AI models that personalise content or offers without centralising user data. Each team can use its own CRM and mobile app logs to train models locally and send only encrypted updates to a shared server, preserving fan anonymity and competitiveness.

13.7.2 Ensuring GDPR compliance

FL aligns with key GDPR principles such as *data minimisation* and *privacy by design* [33]. Since no raw data leaves the source, the legal obligations around consent and cross-border transfers are reduced. This structure also aids in auditing and compliance, as organisations maintain control over the handling of personal data.

13.7.3 Parallel: Google's Gboard

Google introduced FL for Gboard in 2017, using local device training to improve autocorrect and suggestions without collecting raw keystroke data [34]. A similar architecture could apply to fan engagement in sports: Clubs collaboratively improve predictions for fan behaviour without sharing CRM records or personal details.

13.8 FL FOR ATHLETE DATA PRIVACY

13.8.1 Injury prediction models across teams

High-performance sports rely on sensitive health and performance data. FL enables cross-team collaboration on models for injury prediction or fatigue detection using local athlete data such as HRV, workloads, and medical scans. This avoids data pooling and protects athlete confidentiality.

13.8.2 Protecting biometric and health data

Athlete data is subject to strict protections under laws like HIPAA and GDPR. FL supports data minimisation by ensuring personal health data stays on local systems and is not aggregated in vulnerable data lakes. Access control and logging further enforce compliance and traceability.

13.8.3 Fictional case study: AIS injury prediction collaboration

Consider a fictional project led by the Australian Institute of Sport, involving teams from netball, rugby, and soccer. Each team trains a model on their own athletes' data to predict injuries. The AIS centrally aggregates only encrypted model updates, producing a generalised, privacy-preserving tool that helps reduce injuries across teams without compromising confidentiality.

13.9 TECHNICAL IMPLEMENTATION OF FL IN SPORTS

13.9.1 Infrastructure and secure aggregation

Each sports entity must host local servers or edge devices (e.g., team CRMs, athlete wearables) capable of training models. Frameworks like TensorFlow Federated, PySyft, or Flower support secure aggregation of updates, often protected by differential privacy or homomorphic encryption.

13.9.2 Secure communication

FL requires encrypted communication channels using TLS/SSL, with protocols like gRPC or RESTful APIs. In high-latency use cases, such as real-time monitoring, 5G infrastructure enhances update speed. Techniques like Secure Multiparty Computation (SMPC) defend against gradient leakage and data poisoning.

13.9.3 Blockchain for traceability

Blockchain can complement FL by recording immutable logs of training events, contributor identities, and model updates. This is crucial when models inform key decisions (e.g., athlete recovery), offering auditable transparency and access control through distributed ledgers [35].

13.9.4 Governance and access control

FL success depends on governance policies that define data ownership, permissions, and compliance. Systems like Role-Based Access Control (RBAC) and Attribute-Based Access Control (ABAC) restrict access based on roles and contexts. Tools like explainable AI dashboards and consent management APIs further align FL workflows with GDPR/HIPAA mandates.

13.10 CYBER RESILIENCE STRATEGY FOR SPORTS ORGANISATIONS

To protect the increasingly complex digital ecosystems within sports, a modern cyber resilience strategy must blend cutting-edge techniques such as FL with zero-trust architecture, continuous threat monitoring, and adaptive recovery frameworks. These strategies aim to reduce vulnerabilities, ensure compliance, and safeguard data integrity across distributed networks.

13.10.1 Combining FL with zero-trust architecture

While FL decentralises model training to preserve data privacy, pairing it with zero-trust architecture (ZTA) significantly enhances system resilience. ZTA operates on the principle of continuous verification, enforcing strict identity authentication, device validation, and least-privilege access, regardless of network location. In the context of sports organisations, handling biometric, financial, and fan data, ZTA prevents lateral movement across systems in the event of a breach. When federated nodes are fortified with zero-trust controls, they reduce exposure to internal and external threats while ensuring model training remains secure.

13.10.2 Continuous monitoring and threat intelligence sharing

The sports industry's threat landscape is dynamic, encompassing ransomware, phishing, and insider risks. FL supports collaborative anomaly detection across teams and venues by training local models on logs and telemetry data, sharing only updates and not raw data [36]. This enhances detection accuracy without compromising privacy.

Additionally, threat intelligence sharing—via sector-specific platforms or ISACs—enables early identification of attack vectors and coordinated response. Federated approaches ensure such collaboration occurs without exposing sensitive internal data, strengthening the sector's collective cyber defense.

13.10.3 Disaster recovery and incident response

Despite preventative measures, cyber incidents may still occur. A resilient recovery strategy must include real-time backup of model states, secure model checkpointing, and integrity verification protocols specific to FL environments. Sports organisations must develop playbooks addressing FL-specific threats, such as model poisoning or adversarial updates [37].

Simulated response drills involving legal, IT, communications, and athletic staff can enhance readiness. These cross-functional rehearsals help organisations maintain trust and operational continuity following a breach, minimising both reputational and competitive impacts.

13.11 ETHICAL AND LEGAL CONSIDERATIONS

The application of FL in sports analytics and fan engagement raises significant ethical and legal concerns. These include transparency, fairness, regulatory compliance, and the informed use of sensitive personal data.

13.11.1 Consent management for athlete and fan data

Transparent consent management is essential when collecting and processing athlete and fan data, particularly under regulations such as GDPR, CCPA, and LGPD. Sports organisations must ensure that individuals are informed of data usage, FL participation, and withdrawal options. Tools such as consent dashboards and auditable logs help meet these standards.

Heightened protections are especially vital for biometric and health data, requiring explicit consent and possibly oversight from ethics boards, particularly in elite sports settings where power imbalances may exist.

13.11.2 Ensuring fairness and transparency in FL models

Bias in FL models can stem from unbalanced or non-IID datasets—especially across different clubs, regions, or sports. Regular fairness audits, bias detection algorithms, and demographic-specific testing can help mitigate disproportionate impact [38]. Tools such as SHAP or LIME may provide transparency, helping stakeholders understand model outputs.

To institutionalise responsible AI use, governance boards should be formed to oversee FL development, data stewardship, and model validation, aligning with the European Commission's AI ethical guidelines and IEEE standards.

13.11.3 Navigating global data protection laws

FL facilitates compliance with cross-border data laws by keeping raw data local, reducing the need for risky international transfers. However, legal complexities remain. For example, a team in the EU working with a partner in Brazil must comply with both GDPR and LGPD, requiring joint data agreements, local storage provisions, and DPIAs.

Legal and technical teams must work together to integrate privacy-by-design principles into every stage of FL deployment. Standardising data mapping and access protocols further supports lawful data practices in multi-jurisdictional operations.

13.12 FUTURE OUTLOOK

The integration of FL in sports continues to evolve, offering promising opportunities for innovation, regulatory adaptation, and cross-sport collaboration.

13.12.1 FL combined with synthetic data for safer AI model testing

Combining FL with synthetic data is a promising direction. Synthetic datasets—produced through GANs or other generators—allow testing of AI models without exposing real data, making them ideal for model debugging and bias detection [39]. In sports, this could mean validating injury prediction algorithms or engagement models without using actual athlete or fan data, promoting safety and privacy in innovation pipelines.

13.12.2 Cross-sport federated ecosystems

Future sports analytics will likely involve cross-disciplinary federated networks—where basketball, football, and rugby organisations collaborate to train models that benefit from diverse datasets. Applications include generalised injury prevention, fraud detection, and behavioural analysis. These ecosystems encourage broad innovation while maintaining local autonomy and competitive secrecy.

With proper governance and access control (e.g., RBAC or ABAC), such ecosystems may enable shared advancement without risking regulatory non-compliance or data leakage.

13.12.3 Role of government and international sports bodies

Global regulators and sports federations—such as the IOC, FIFA, or WADA—must establish standards and auditing protocols for FL systems used in sports. Their role includes incentivising federated privacy-preserving technologies, mandating ethics reviews, and facilitating cross-border model cooperation.

Public-sector support for FL infrastructure, combined with compliance frameworks, will accelerate the adoption of FL. Governments may also promote certification schemes for AI systems that use FL responsibly, aligning innovation with ethical mandates and public trust [40].

REFERENCES

[1] Ahmad, I., Awan, I., Bakhshi, A., & Aziz, B. (2024). Federated learning and cyber resilience: A systematic review. *Journal of Cloud Computing, 13*(1), Article 23. https://doi.org/10.1186/s13677-024-00671-3

[2] National Institute of Standards and Technology. (2023, March 7). Privacy attacks in federated learning. *Cybersecurity Insights Blog*. www.nist.gov/blogs/cybersecurity-insights/privacy-attacks-federated-learning

[3] Ali, M., Anwar, A., & Zhang, K. (2020). Privacy threats in machine learning: The case of federated learning. *arXiv preprint*. https://arxiv.org/abs/2012.06810

[4] Khan, H., Abbas, A., Khan, W., & Amin, R. (2023). Federated learning with differential privacy and secure aggregation. *arXiv preprint*. https://arxiv.org/abs/2306.17338

[5] Abdel-Basset, M., Manogaran, G., Mohamed, R., & Abd Elatif, M. (2022). A privacy-preserving framework using federated learning for healthcare systems. *Journal of Healthcare Engineering, 2022*, 1–14. https://doi.org/10.1155/2022/6131971

[6] ESET. (2022, March 28). Cybercriminals play dirty: 10 cyber hits on the sporting world. *WeLiveSecurity*. www.welivesecurity.com/en/cybercrime/cybercriminals-play-dirty-10-cyber-hits-sporting-world/

[7] Reuters. (2024, May 15). Cyber threat outlook for the sports industry. *Reuters Legal*. www.reuters.com/legal/legalindustry/cyber-threat-outlook-sports-industry-2024-05-15

[8] The Guardian. (2024, May 14). AFL players' private data leaked in sports drug testing scandal. www.theguardian.com/sport/article/2024/may/14/afl-players-data-protection-leak-breach-drug-test-results

[9] SpamTitan. (2024, February 8). Phishing warning issued to sports industry following spate of attacks. *SpamTitan Blog*. www.spamtitan.com/blog/phishing-warning-issued-to-sports-industry-following-spate-of-attacks/

[10] Wikipedia. (n.d.). Operation Shady RAT. *Wikipedia*. Retrieved July 27, 2025, from https://en.wikipedia.org/wiki/Operation_Shady_RAT

[11] Zadeh, A., Taylor, D., Bertsos, M., Tillman, T., Nosoudi, N., & Bruce, S. (2021). Predicting sports injuries with wearable technology and data analysis. *Information Systems Frontiers, 23*(4), 1023–1037. https://doi.org/10.1007/s10796-020-10018-3

[12] United Nations Office of Counter-Terrorism. (2021, October 6). Guide on the security of major sporting events: Promoting sustainable security and legacies [PDF]. United Nations. https://unicri.org/Publication/Major-Events-Security-Sport-Violent-Extremism-Prevention

[13] Funt, D. (2025, October 28). The Sports-Betting disaster. *The New Yorker*. www.newyorker.com/news/the-lede/the-sports-betting-disaster

[14] Petkauskas, V. (2022, November 25). *FC Barcelona's official website exploited for fraud*. Cybernews. https://cybernews.com/news/fc-barcelona-official-website-fraud/

[15] Neagu, C. (2022, November 28). FC Barcelona's website used by scammers for fraud. *Heimdal Security Blog*. https://heimdalsecurity.com/blog/fc-barcelonas-website-used-by-scammers-for-fraud/

[16] CyberFlow. (2022). The FC Barcelona domain was exploited in a redirect attack to a gambling site. *CyberFlow Threat Brief*.

[17] Infront. (2023, November 10). Cybersecurity in sports: The silent threat to digital stadiums and athletes. www.infront.sport/blog/sports-technology/cybersecurity-sports

[18] TechRadar. (2024, May 8). Entertainment venue management giant Legends International reveals major data breach. www.techradar.com/pro/security/entertainment-venue-management-giant-legends-international-reveals-major-data-breach

[19] SecureWorld. (2023, October 18). Cyber threat to sports: Why leagues and teams are under siege. www.secureworld.io/industry-news/cyber-threat-to-sports/

[20] Villanova University. (2021, May 3). The need for digital defense in the sports industry. *Villanova Sports Law Blog*. www1.villanova.edu/villanova/law/academics/sportslaw/commentary/mslj_blog/2021/TheNeedforDigitalDefense.html

[21] Wired. (2022, February 13). The untold story of the 2018 Olympics cyberattack and the hackers behind it. www.wired.com/story/untold-story-2018-olympics-destroyer-cyberattack/

[22] Liu, P., Li, X., Zang, B., & Diao, G. (2024). Privacy-preserving sports data fusion and prediction with smart devices in distributed environment. *Journal of Cloud Computing Advances Systems and Applications*, *13*(1), 2. https://doi.org/10.1186/s13677-024-00671-3

[23] Nasr, M., Shokri, R., & Houmansadr, A. (2021). Adversary instantiation and modeling in federated learning. *arXiv preprint*. https://arxiv.org/abs/2302.03654

[24] Kairouz, P., McMahan, B., Avent, B., Bellet, A., Bennis, M., Bhagoji, A. N., ... & Zhao, S. (2021). Advances and open problems in federated learning. *Foundations and Trends® in Machine Learning, 14*(1–2), 1–210. https://arxiv.org/abs/2011.05411

[25] Brisimi, T. S., Chen, R., Mela, T., Olshevsky, A., Paschalidis, I. C., & Shi, W. (2018). Federated learning of predictive models from federated electronic health records. *International Journal of Medical Informatics, 112*, 59–67. https://pubmed.ncbi.nlm.nih.gov/35571697/

[26] KM, S., Nicolazzo, S., Arazzi, M., Nocera, A., KA, R. R., P, V., & Conti, M. (2024). Privacy-preserving in Blockchain-based Federated Learning systems. *Computer Communications*, 222, 38–67. https://doi.org/10.1016/j.comcom.2024.04.024

[27] Jere, M., Aamir, M., & Andersson, K. (2023). A survey on federated learning in cyber-physical systems. *arXiv preprint*. https://arxiv.org/abs/2310.04546

[28] Das, D., Kalra, A., & Dutta, K. (2023). A survey on federated learning in edge computing: Research challenges and applications. *Neural Computing and Applications, 35*(12), 8253–8281. https://link.springer.com/article/10.1007/s00521-023-09410-2

[29] Zhang, S., Li, M., Liu, J., & Zhang, C. (2024). Privacy-preserving federated learning: A blockchain-based framework. *International Journal of Distributed Ledger Technologies, 8*(1). https://link.springer.com/article/10.1007/s44227-024-00022-3

[30] Upadrista, V., & Settel, J. (2025). Fraud detection in the airline industry: Tackling financial losses through transfer learning and federated learning. *COJ Robotics & Artificial Intelligence*. https://crimsonpublishers.com/cojra/fulltext/COJRA.000583.php

[31] Archer, B. (2025, March 20). How federated learning strengthens fraud detection in 2025. *UK Finance*. www.ukfinance.org.uk/news-and-insight/blog/how-federated-learning-strengthens-fraud-detection-in-2025

[32] Arora, S., Beams, A., Chatzigiannis, P., Meiser, S., Patel, K., Raghuraman, S., Rindal, P., Shah, H., Wang, Y., Wu, Y., Yang, H., & Zamani, M. (2023, October 6). Privacy-preserving financial anomaly detection via federated learning & multi-party computation (arXiv preprint arXiv:2310.04546). arXiv. https://doi.org/10.48550/arXiv.2310.04546

[33] MusKeteer. (2021). Benefits and challenges of federated learning under the GDPR. *Medium.* https://h2020musketeer.medium.com/benefits-and-challenges-of-federated-learning-under-the-gdpr-15c89ff76d9c

[34] McMahan, B., & Thakurta, A. (2022, February 28). Federated learning with formal differential privacy guarantees. *Google Research Blog.* https://research.google/blog/federated-learning-with-formal-differential-privacy-guarantees

[35] Qammar, A., Karim, A., Ning, H., & Ding, J. (2023). Securing federated learning with blockchain: A systematic literature review. *Artificial Intelligence Review*, 56(5), 3951–3985. https://doi.org/10.1007/s10462-022-10271-9

[36] Rieke, N., Hancox, J., Li, W., Milletarì, F., Roth, H. R., Albarqouni, S., ... & Cardoso, M. J. (2020). The future of digital health with federated learning. *NPJ Digital Medicine, 3*(1), 1–7. https://arxiv.org/abs/1907.09173

[37] Bagdasaryan, E., Veit, A., Hua, Y., Estrin, D., & Shmatikov, V. (2020). How to backdoor federated learning. *arXiv preprint.* https://arxiv.org/abs/1807.00459

[38] Bonawitz, K., Eichner, H., Grieskamp, W., Huba, D., Ingerman, A., & Ivanov, V. (2019). Towards federated learning at scale: System design. *arXiv preprint.* https://arxiv.org/abs/1902.01046

[39] Duddu, V. R., Karuppiah, M., Sivasankaran, S., & Kotecha, K. (2023). Synthetic data generation for federated learning using GANs. *Applied Sciences, 14*(11), 4788. www.mdpi.com/2076-3417/14/11/4788

[40] FinTech Curated. (2023). Federated learning: Enhancing fraud detection while protecting privacy. https://fintechcurated.com/regulatory-and-compliance/federated-learning-enhancing-fraud-detection-while-protecting-privacy/

Chapter 14

Ethical AI in federated financial systems

Balancing privacy, utility, and fairness in a decentralized era

Md Aminul Islam, Md Mizanur Rahman, Muhammad Fahad Saleem, Mahi Monjina, Aimee E. Mirto, Sonjoy Ranjon Das, and Divya Saleela

14.1 INTRODUCTION: FEDERATED LEARNING (FL)

In the financial sector, Artificial Intelligence (AI) is transforming the world more than ever. AI is used by banks, insurance corporations, and other financial institutions to accomplish significant tasks such as detecting fraud in real-time, assessing the credit worthiness of people, anticipating what they may require, and ensuring that they abide by laws in order to prevent money laundering. Through the analysis of large volumes of transaction data and other data, AI identifies patterns that may be overlooked by people and assists in identifying abnormal behaviour, mitigating lending risks, and decision-making regarding financial matters more efficiently.

Nevertheless, with the increase in the number of financial companies depending on AI, new ethical and legal issues arise. The conventional AI solutions will tend to gather and keep all customer information at a single location. This increases chances of the data being abused or stolen. It may also render companies more difficult to comply with stringent privacy regulations such as the General Data Protection Regulation (GDPR) in Europe or the California Consumer Privacy Act (CCPA). Since financial companies are highly sensitive on the information that they possess, they are under pressure by regulators and the general population to ensure privacy, prevent discrimination, and ensure that AI decisions can be explained and trusted.

FL is one of the new methods that can resolve such issues. Under FL, various financial institutions or banks can collaborate to train potent AI models without having to exchange raw customer data. Banks store all their data on their respective systems and only provide minor updates to the global model of the AI (such as numbers that enhance the model). Such updates are synthesized in a safe manner. This implies that privacy is set as default within the system to assist the companies to meet the regulations of privacy that govern the extent of information they are allowed to share. FL can be used in various cases like banks can work together to detect fraud across multiple companies, small lenders can learn from data of big financial institutions to make transparent credit decisions, and insurance companies can improve risks management without revealing private information. Because of these benefits, FL became an important and trustworthy step towards building AI systems. Using FL means financial companies must find a balance between protecting privacy, keeping their AI models accurate, making sure the models are fair to everyone, and those are unbiased. Moreover, adding extensive privacy protections can decrease accuracy. Or, different banks might have data of different quality, which can create bias that affects certain groups unfairly. Also, it can be unclear who is responsible when multiple companies work together on the same AI system.

DOI: 10.1201/9781003660330-14

This chapter will look at these important questions: Why is FL becoming so popular in finance? How does it help with privacy and data rules? What ethical problems does it raise? And how can financial companies find the right balance between privacy, accuracy, and fairness in this new, decentralised way of working?

14.2 THE RISE OF FL IN FINANCE

Why FL? Privacy, compliance, and decentralization

Financial institutions represent the registered agents who can be trusted to hold huge quantities of very sensitive and personally identifiable information in the modern digital economy. This encompasses all the transaction histories, account balance, biometric information, and behavioural information. All such data is tightly restricted by international privacy standards [27], such as the GDPR within the European Union, CCPA in the United States, and sectoral requirements under Basel III and national banking secrecy regulations [49].

Conventional centralised Machine Learning (ML) suffers an inherent privacy challenge since the training processes usually treat all raw data as a set available in a central location. This exposes sensitive information of the customers to breaches, incidents threats, and misuse [1]. This is not only a technical problem in an industry where the integrity of information and trust are critical; it is also a reputation and regulatory risk.

These challenges offer a good solution for FL. In structure, FL is an off-centric learning framework that enables various financial entities to enjoy a collective education of a joint ML model, but without raw and sensitive data being moved beyond restricted silos [22, 33]. Rather, every institution locally trains the model on its own data and transmits only encrypted or masked updates to the model (e.g., gradient or weight parameters) to an aggregation server that can securely combine and aggregate the model updates. The summed model is then reopened, and this enhances the precision of the global model in each iteration while maintaining privacy. Such a treatment is directly in line with data minimisation, local control, and privacy-by-design that modern privacy regulations entail (Art. 5 GDPR). Data sovereignty is sensitive in the case of global banks and cross-border data transfer, where data residency local provisions must be honoured.

14.2.1 Expanding the use cases: Real-world scenarios

FL is not only an academic concept; it is operationally useful in a variety of high-impact financial applications:

14.2.1.1 Inter-institutional fraud detection

When the relationship between two institutions has a loophole, fraudsters are likely to use it to commit cross-banking fraud. In the case of FL, multiple banks can unite to create powerful defence designs about fraud grounded on the patterns across the silo of multiple establishments without necessarily sharing raw transaction histories and guarding their competitive secrets [53]. As an example, one can consider that Bank A recognizes a recurring micropayment, and bank B recognizes a recurring chargeback to the same IP address: FL can safely learn such global fraud cues.

14.2.1.2 Credit scoring co-op credit of underserved markets

Smaller community banks and credit unions cannot afford more expensive and various sets of data by which they can train decent credit scoring models. With FL, such institutions can exchange the knowledge they gather with their larger counterparts which will help them to devise more reasonable and reliable credit ratings to borrowers with thin credit histories without infringing information protection safeguards at home [6]. This opens opportunities of financial inclusion in low-financed regions. These situations explain why FL is no longer a mere theoretical construct but a working requirement within present financial systems that should not only address competitive but also compliance requirements as well.

14.2.1.3 Protection against money laundering (AML) and suspicious activity monitoring

According to the AML regulations, the institutions should maintain a close monitor on the suspicious patterns that cut across borders in terms of international borders and accounts. Raw transactional data however is generally prohibited to be shared due to the existence of stringent secrecy legislation. On the one hand, FL will enable a shared layer of learning in terms of pattern recognition, and this will imply that banks, payment processors and even regulators will be better placed to determine intricate laundering schemes without going over the legal boundaries [52].

14.2.1.4 Personalized financial services, no data centralization

Personal risk scoring and loan offering, and insurance quoting are also included under new applications. By means of FL, the institutions can localize models to the local customer segments and, consequently, achieve improvements on the global model. This also ensures there is the equilibrium between compliance and personalisation.

What is significant about this now is that the children stand a chance to bring out the kind of change that will make a difference in their lives. The rate of AI adoption and more rigid rules and regulations allow being easier to assume that FL almost instantly transitioned to the hypothetical level to the operational space. Its greater importance is reflected in larger projects including the FATE (Federated AI Technology Enabler) project of the Linux Foundation, integration of FL into the Gboard predictive text of Google, and combined pilots with the European Central Bank [22, 37]. FL does not only influence financial institutions to enhance their AI benefits but also creates trust and by keeping up with the new legal and ethical climate.

14.3 ETHICAL CHALLENGES IN FL FOR FINANCE

The trilemma: Privacy vs. utility vs. fairness

FL does not automatically solve the ethical and governance challenges that arise when AI is deployed in sensitive financial contexts. Instead, it surfaces a fundamental **ethical trilemma**—the inherent tension among **Privacy, Utility**, and **Fairness**. These three dimensions are each vital for building trustworthy, regulation-aligned AI systems, yet they often conflict in practice.

Privacy

The defining advantage of FL is its decentralized, privacy-preserving techniques. By design, client data never leaves local silos; only model updates—potentially protected with techniques like Differential Privacy (DP), Secure Aggregation (SecAgg), or Homomorphic Encryption (HE)—are shared [22]. These techniques significantly reduce the risk of raw data exposure and align with strict privacy laws such as the GDPR. However, ensuring robust privacy often means adding statistical noise to the data or performing computations on encrypted values, which can reduce model accuracy if not carefully calibrated [1, 17].

Utility

For FL to deliver real business value, the collaboratively trained global model must maintain high utility—in other words, it must be sufficiently accurate and reliable for tasks such as fraud detection, credit scoring, and anti-money laundering (AML). Yet achieving high utility in a decentralized setup is technically challenging. Financial institutions often operate with highly heterogeneous data silos that vary in size, quality, and feature representation. Skewed or non-IID (non-independent and identically distributed) data can create convergence problems or introduce bias if larger institutions dominate the training process [22, 33].

Fairness

Even when privacy is protected and utility is high; fairness remains a significant ethical concern in FL systems. If the underlying data contains structural biases—for example, underrepresentation of minority or disadvantaged groups—these can persist or even amplify in the global model [19]. Moreover, the decentralized nature of FL complicates fairness auditing: raw data is never centralised, so direct inspection of sensitive attributes across all institutions is not always feasible. This means that fairness must be built into both local training objectives and the aggregation process, often requiring sophisticated bias mitigation strategies like fairness-aware federated optimization or adversarial debiasing [6, 21].

14.3.1 A persistent balancing act

These tensions make the **privacy–utility–fairness trilemma** unavoidable. Strengthening privacy safeguards, such as adding more noise for DP or adopting stronger encryption, can degrade model performance and limit utility. Optimising purely for accuracy and business outcomes can lead to discrimination or systemic bias if fairness constraints are not enforced. Enhancing fairness—for example, by reweighting updates or introducing post-hoc bias corrections—can sometimes reduce performance or conflict with strict privacy guarantees that limit the observability of sensitive group attributes.

As Kairouz et al. [22] emphasise, these trade-offs are not theoretical. They must be actively managed in practical deployments, documented in risk registers, and made transparent to regulators and stakeholders alike. Ultimately, there is no "one-size-fits-all" solution—responsible governance in FL for finance requires a thoughtful, context-specific approach that considers data distribution, model use cases, local privacy laws, and the needs of vulnerable groups.

14.3.2 Navigating regulatory landscapes: GDPR, CCPA, Basel III

Adding to the technical and ethical complexity of FL in finance is the **constantly evolving regulatory landscape**, which sets out clear obligations for how sensitive customer data must be collected, processed, stored, and shared. Frameworks such as the **GDPR** in the European Union and the **CCPA** in the United States both establish strong data subject rights and place significant constraints on the free movement of personal information across borders [49].

Under the GDPR, for example, financial institutions must adhere to **data minimisation** (Article 5) and purpose limitation principles, which require that only the minimum amount of data necessary for a specific task is processed. They must also implement **privacy by design and by default** (Article 25), which is directly supported by the architecture of FL, as raw data never leaves institutional silos [22]. Additionally, Article 22 grants individuals the right not to be subject to solely automated decision-making that has significant effects, such as the rejection of a loan or a negative credit rating, without appropriate safeguards. This provision creates a strong incentive for explainability and auditability in AI systems [18].

Likewise, the **CCPA** provides consumers with the right to know what personal data is being collected, to request deletion of that data, and to opt out of its sale to third parties—all of which must be operationalised in any AI system that processes personal data. Although the CCPA lacks a specific right to explanation near to that of the GDPR, its emphasis on transparency and data minimisation is very close to the design of FL systems.

Meanwhile, industry-specific models, like Basel III, also strengthen the governance standards of implementing advanced analytics and AI in banking. Basel III focuses on effective risk management, validation of the model, and independent control to guarantee that the AI model does not create systemic risks unknown to the whole financial system [7]. This implies that the institutions shall have to prove that their federated models are not merely technically strong, but also fair, explicable and there exists strict continuous monitoring.

The existing overlaps in the frameworks, indicating that FL cannot be only a technical cure, but as a component of a regulatory strategy. With privacy-preserving differentiations (including DP, HE, or Secure Multi-Party Computation) and fairness-sensitive ones (including bias auditing and bias mitigation), financial institutions can enhance their compliance, as well as retain the trust of their customers, business partners, and even regulators [6, 19].

Over the next few years, with regulators in the global community shifting to explicit AI regulation regimes, like the upcoming EU AI Act, the role of showing ethical governance and accountability in federated financial systems will continue to increase [49]. Finally, FL is more than a technological breakthrough, but it is a useful facilitator of responsible AI within the framework of real-life laws.

A clear Venn diagram or triangle shows the three intersecting areas—Privacy, Utility, and Fairness—highlights key trade-offs and tensions faced by practitioners. Figure 14.1 serves as an anchor for the entire chapter, reminding readers that responsible AI in finance is not about optimising a single objective, but about managing competing priorities.

14.3.2.1 Moving forward

By unpacking why FL is rapidly emerging as a foundational strategy for collaborative, privacy-preserving, and regulation-friendly AI in the financial sector—and by acknowledging the complex ethical trade-offs at its core—this introduction sets the stage for the detailed theoretical frameworks, technical building blocks, and practical use cases [55] explored in the sections that follow.

In doing so, this analysis demonstrates that while FL can address pressing challenges around data privacy, compliance, and inter-institutional collaboration, it does not eliminate

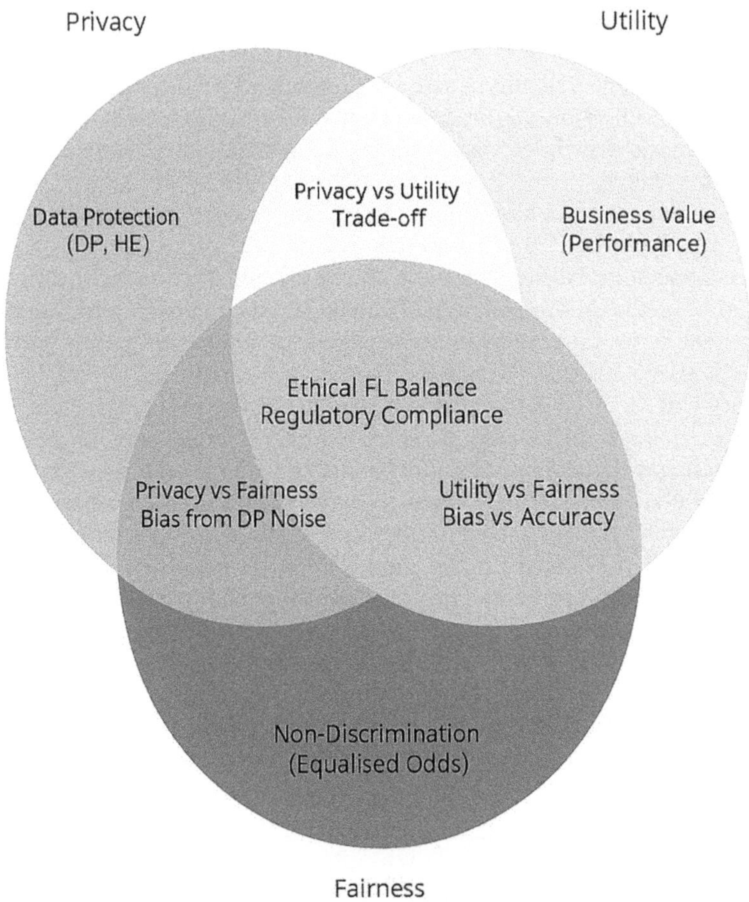

Figure 14.1 Federated learning ethical trilemma in finance.

the need for active, context-aware governance. Instead, it highlights the essential balancing act between protecting sensitive information, maintaining high model performance, and ensuring that AI-driven decisions are fair, explainable, and accountable to the people and communities they affect.

Taken together, these insights invite financial practitioners, policymakers, and AI researchers alike to envision a future in which decentralized AI does more than just deliver competitive advantage—it also upholds the fundamental principles of **data protection, fairness, transparency, and trust.** By embedding ethical safeguards directly into the design, deployment, and oversight of federated financial systems, stakeholders can help ensure that the next generation of AI-enabled finance is not only more resilient and innovative but also more equitable and socially responsible.

14.3 THEORETICAL FOUNDATIONS

The theoretical foundation of FL in finance refers to the core concept of FL, and mathematical, algorithmic and systematic or system level principles of the learning to justify the use of FL techniques in financial applications. The core architecture of FL defines how clients or data holders communicate and share the global ML model's updates, and how model's tasks are managed across financial institutions such as banks, credit bureaus, credit reference agencies and insurers. The mathematical principle of the FL refers to the optimisation problem to data centralisation, algorithmic principles refer to how efficiently the model is trained, and systematic principles ensure the model is scalable, secure and efficient in real-world distributed systems.

In FL, clients or data holders have their own private datasets and they want to train a ML model collaboratively without sharing their raw data [22]. Clients could be local, national or regional banks such as HSBC, NatWest, Barclays, and Nationwide, different branches of the same bank, credit unions, financial institutions such as insurance companies, credit unions, investment firms, and credit reference agencies such as Experian and Equifax, and regulatory participants such as Financial Conduct Authority (FCA) and Prudential regulation Authority (PRA). Each client trains a model locally on its own data and sends the updated parameters back to the central server for aggregating into the global model. The central server manages the global ML model across all clients on a real-time basis to detect if any biases take place and mitigate them to avoid biases or bring fairness to the model. The central server first creates a base model and sends it to all clients or to a subset of clients when required. Clients train the model by their individual local data collaboratively and send algorithm-specific updates (e.g., FedAvg, FedProx or FedOpt) to the central server without sharing their data with others. The central server aggregates the updates and shares the new global model again with all clients for next round if needed. The central server keeps track of all versions, uses validation techniques to ensure model performance and compliance, and deploys the model to client sites. Typically, in a FL architecture, any number of clients can be connected through a loosely coupled, distributed system, as illustrated in Figure 14.2.

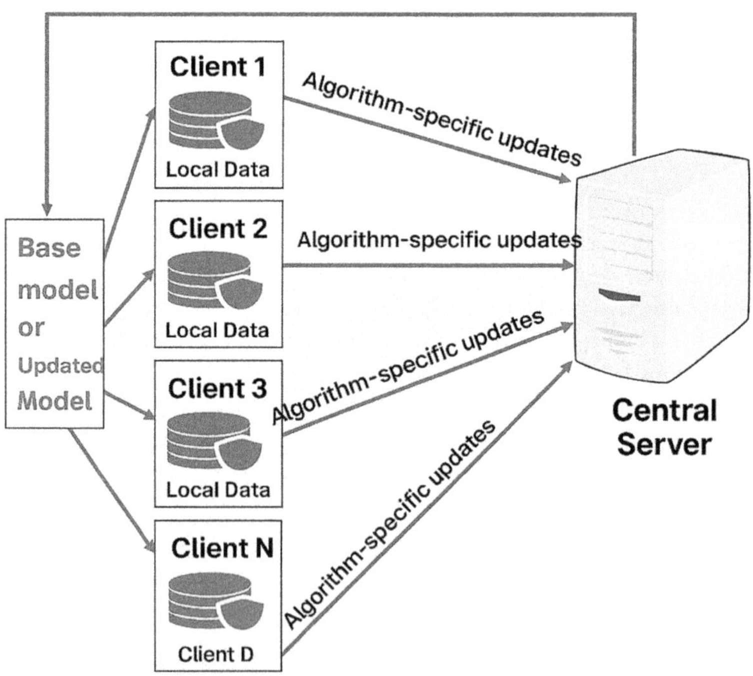

Figure 14.2 FL architecture.

In FL, issues of unfairness and bias may take place while some clients train the model with millions of transactions related data and some other clients train the model with only a few hundreds or thousands of data. The FL is based on the following mathematical principle to minimise a global loss across all clients without centralising data, and it is used behind all FL optimisation algorithms to preserve privacy [33]:

$$\min F(w) = \sum_{k=1}^{K} p_k F(w)$$

where:

$\text{K}: \text{Number of clients}(\text{e.g., banks})$

$p_{k=\frac{n_k}{n}}: \textit{Weight of client k based on local data volume}$

$F_k(\omega): \textit{Local loss function at client k}$

$\omega: \textit{Shared model parameters}$

$$\text{Each } F_k(\omega) = \frac{1}{n_k} \sum_{i=1}^{n_k} l\left(\omega; x_i^{(k)}, y_i^{(k)}\right)$$

where :

$l: \textit{loss function}(\textit{e.g., cross} - \textit{entropy})$

$\left(x_i^{(k)}, y_i^{(k)}\right): \textit{Local data sample at client k}$

F_k may vary significantly across clients and n_k is not equal across clients.

The FL employs an optimisation algorithm tailored to the model's requirements to efficiently train a ML model in distributed, privacy-preserving, and resource-constrained settings. FL typically operates in a non-IID system, where different clients may have varying data distributions. For example, one client or bank may collect one set of customer features, while another client may collect a different set of customer data with different features. Steps are as followed:

Steps:

1. Server sends global model w_t to clients
2. Each client does local training for E epochs on its data
3. Clients send updated weights w_t^k to the server
4. Server aggregates:

$$w_{t+1} = \sum_{k=1}^{K} p_k w_t^k$$

The FL reduces communication between clients and the central server but introduces convergence challenges such as instability or slower learning when data is non-IID. When the client data is non-IID, such as having skewed labels or features, the local model tends to diverge, which cause the global model to converge more slowly, become less stable, and

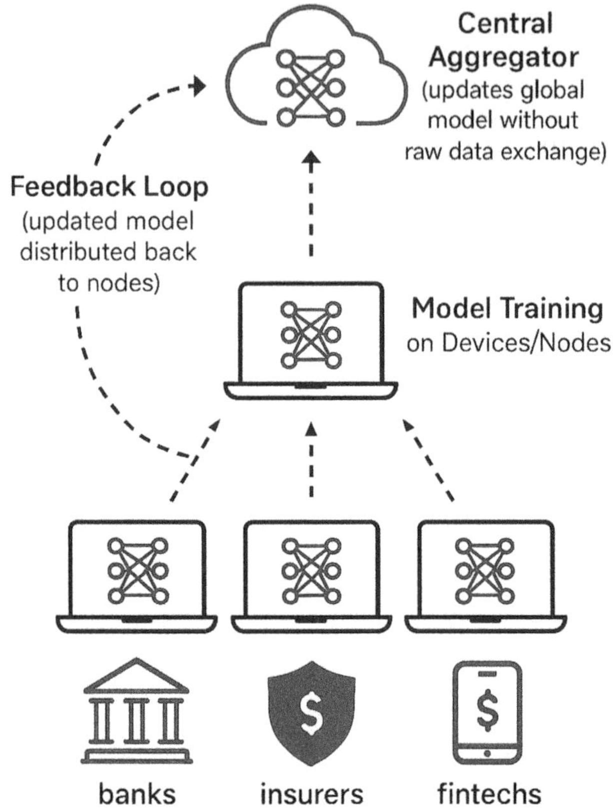

Figure 14.3 FL workflow in finance.

produce sub-optimal results. For resolving this issue many researchers have proposed different optimisation algorithms such as FedAvg and FedSGD by McMahan et al. [33], FedProx by Li et al. [26], FedNova by Wang et al. [51] and FedOpt by Reddi et al. [39] (Figure 14.3).

The Systematic principles ensure the global model is scalable, secure, efficient, and work in real-world distributed systems. For this, a subset of clients can be selected randomly or manually in each round to update the global model. The communication between clients and the central server may be expensive. To mitigate this, techniques such as reducing the number of communication rounds, applying model compression (e.g., quantization and pruning), using normalised updates or deltas (i.e., sending only the difference between the old and new models) and transmitting sparse updates (only large changes) can be employed depending on the model's requirements. The central server can use some privacy-preserving mechanisms, such as DP to add noise to local model updates and mask individual clients, SecAgg to aggregate updates without revealing their contents, HE to enable computation on encrypted updates and Trusted Execution Environments (TEEs) to secure hardware enclaves for aggregation.

14.3.1 FL: A technical primer

Traditional centralised learning faces significant challenges related to privacy, data ownership and regulatory compliance. For overcoming these issues, FL provides a decentralised learning approach where model training occurs locally at a client or on a local device without sharing raw data. A brief technical primer on FL is provided below to help readers to understand its core concepts, terminology, and underlying techniques.

14.3.1.1 Horizontal vs. vertical FL

There are two typical types of FL—Horizontal FL (HFL) and Vertical FL (VFL). They are also called modes of FL. In HFL, data is partitioned by rows, and it is also called sample-based FL. For example, in this FL, two clients or banks may have the same features such as Customer ID, Age, Account No, Sort Code, Type of Account, Balance, Credit Score, and Income but different customers (e.g., Bank A has customers 1 to 1000 and Bank B has customers1001 to 2000). Each client collaborates and trains a model locally without sharing their customers' information with anyone else (privacy-by-design), and shares model updates through the central server [22].

In VFL, data is partitioned by columns or features, and it is also called feature-based FL. For example, in this FL, two clients or banks share the same customers with different features. Bank A and B both have customers 1 to 2000 but Bank A has Customer ID, Age, Account No, Sort Code, and Balance features but Bank B has Customer ID, Type of Account, Credit Score, and Income features. Each client collaborates and trains a model without sharing their customers information with anyone else (privacy-by-design) and shares model updates through the central server [22].

14.3.1.2 Privacy-preserving techniques

In FL, different privacy-preserving techniques are used to preserve clients' privacy when sending updates to the central server. These techniques are crucial for ensuring robust data protection and regulatory compliance. Table 14.1 summarises aspects of privacy-preserving techniques.

SecAgg – With this technique, the central server cannot see individual client's single updates. The technique can be considered as 'Secret Santa' style of masking. The client masks their gradient/weight updates using one-time pads [10]. The central server only learns the sum or average of the client updates after the masks are cancelled during aggregation and must never see any individual updates. This technique protects clients' data through masking and cryptographic techniques.

Secure Multi-Party Computation (SMPC) – This technique enhances confidentiality and trust where multiple parties can collaboratively compute a function over their private data without disclosing the data itself, which is highly valuable in FL systems [11]. For example, three banks want to find out the average income of their customers without revealing individual income data to one another. The technique calculates the average of their customers' incomes and shares the results only. Each client encrypts its local model updates by using SMPC and the updates are securely aggregated at the central server. SMPC is a broader cryptographic framework that supports secure evaluation of any complex function beyond aggregation, including collaborative tasks such as joint training or secure inference, without revealing inputs. However, the technique incurs high overhead as the number of parties increases for complex computations.

DP – DP adds calibrated or controlled noise (usually Laplace or Gaussian) to the local model updates before they are sent to the central server. The technique makes it statistically difficult to infer individual data points used to train the model without revealing specific transactions [1]. For example, before sending the model updates to the central server, a little "blur" is added to each customer's data, ensuring that no other client can

Table 14.1 Aspects of privacy-preserving techniques

Feature/Aspect	*SecAgg*	*SMPC*	*DP*	*HE*
Privacy Guarantee	Hides individual model updates during aggregation	Hides inputs and intermediate computations	Prevents leakage through noise addition	Enables computation on encrypted data
Data Encryption	Partial (during aggregation only)	Yes (secret sharing among parties)	No (adds noise instead of encryption)	Full encryption (typically using public-key)
Accuracy Trade-off	Minimal	Minimal to moderate	High (due to noise)	None (ideal), but high computational cost
Computation Overhead	Low to moderate	High (especially with increasing parties)	Low	Very high (especially for complex models)
Communication Overhead	Moderate	High (frequent interactions between parties)	Minimal	High
Scalability	High (designed for federated settings)	Moderate (requires synchronous, coordinated steps)	High	Low to moderate
Common Use Cases	Federated Learning, IoT	Collaborative ML, joint computations	Public release of statistical data, ML with privacy	Secure data outsourcing, encrypted inference
Security Model	Honest-but-curious server assumption	Malicious/ Byzantine or semi-honest parties	Statistical adversary model	Passive adversary (can't decrypt ciphertext)
Main Limitation	Cannot protect against client collusion	Communication complexity, performance bottlenecks	Reduced model utility	Extremely slow, not practical for real-time use
Maturity in Practice	High (used in Google's FL deployments)	Moderate (used in academic and some industry cases)	High (backed by theoretical guarantees, e.g., DP-SGD)	Low (limited by hardware & algorithm efficiency)

determine the original data. It guarantees strong privacy for clients, but it may reduce the system performance or accuracy.

HE – This technique ensures that clients' data remains encrypted throughout the training process. The central server just receives the clients' updates in encrypted form and aggregates their weights into the global model without ever decrypting them (Gentry, 2009). It offers strong data security throughout the training process; however, due to heavy or complex operations, the system performance may drop down. To cut down the computational time or cost, only clients' sensitive data is encrypted.

14.3.1.3 Federated optimisation algorithms

In a large distributed system, clients' communication with the central server may be time-consuming and inefficient. A FL system uses optimisation algorithms for optimising the global model across all clients. Some popular optimisation algorithms are discussed below, highlighting their main features in Table 14.2.

14.3.1.3.1 FedAvg (2017)

The Federated Averaging or FedAvg algorithm, introduced by McMahan et al. [33], is one of the most popular optimisation algorithms for preserving data privacy. In FL, each client trains their own model using their local data, calculating their weights for multiple epochs and sends the full set of updated weights to the central server. The central server averages their clients model weights to build the global model [33]. This is one of the most widely used algorithms and improves communication efficiency between clients and servers due to fewer communication rounds. For example, 3 banks are working on online fraud detections by analysing customers' transactions. Banks 1, 2, and 3 train their models using their own customers' transactions related to 700, 1000, and 500 records. After training locally for some time, each of the three banks sends its version of the model to the central server. The central server then averages the parameters from all three models (perhaps giving more weights to Banks 2, 1, and 3 due to the size of their datasets) and builds a global model. The global model is then sent back to all banks for the next round, if needed.
The algorithm operates based on a weighted voting system.

Let's say we have a global model of linear expression, $y = \omega \cdot x + 1$ with input feature x, initial global weight $\omega = 1.0$, Learning rate $\eta = 0.1$ and two clients A with $x = 1$ and $y = 3$, and B with $x = 2$ and $y = 6.5$ data at their own sites.

Client A calculations:

- Local prediction: $y^A = 1.0 \cdot 1 + 1 = 1 + 1 = 2$
- Error: $e = y - y^A = 3 - 2 = 1$
- Gradient: $\nabla\omega = -e \cdot x \cdot (y - y^A) = -(1) \cdot 1 \cdot (3 - 2) = -1$
- Local weight update: $\omega^A = y^A - \eta \cdot \nabla\omega = 2 - 0.1 \cdot (-1) = 2 + 0.1 = 2.1$

Client B calculations:

- Local prediction: $y^B = 1.0 \cdot 2 + 1 = 2 + 1 = 3$
- Error: $e = y - y^B = 6.5 - 3 = 3.5$
- Gradient: $\nabla\omega = -e \cdot x \cdot (y - y^B) = -(3.5) \cdot 2 \cdot (6.5 - 3) = -3.5 \cdot 2 \cdot 3.5 = -22.4$
- Local weight update: $\omega^B = y^B - \eta \cdot \nabla\omega = 3 - 0.1 \cdot (-22.4) = 3 + 2.24 = 5.24$

The Client A and B send update weights $\omega^A = 2.1$ and $\omega^B = 5.24$ respectively to the server. Then the server performs a weighted average of the updated weights, $\omega_{t+1} = \frac{1}{2}(2.1 + 5.24) = \frac{7.34}{2} = 3.67$ and the final global weight after FedAvg is 3.67.

14.3.1.3.2 FedSGD (2017)

The Stochastic Gradient Descent (SGD) or FedSGD algorithm, introduced by McMahan et al. [33], aims to enhance privacy and reduce communication overhead. The algorithm is used to train a ML model across multiple clients where each client computes gradients of the loss based on its local data and then sends gradients to the central server for the aggregation of the global model [33]. Using this algorithm, only gradients are shared instead of raw data.

Using the same FedAvg example for Clients A and B, each client calculates their local gradient, $\nabla\omega = -1$ for Client A and $\nabla\omega = -22.4$ for Client B. These gradients are then sent to the central server. The server computes the average gradient:

$$g = \frac{1}{2}\left(-1 + (-22.4)\right) = \frac{-23.4}{2} = -11.7$$

The global model weight is then updated as follows:

$$\omega = 1.0 - \eta \cdot g = 1.0 - 0.1 \cdot (-11.7) = 1.0 + 1.17 = 2.17$$

Thus, after the first round, the global model weight is updated to 2.17.

14.3.1.3.3 FedProx (2020)

The FedProx algorithm, introduced by Li et al. [26], extends FedAvg by adding a proximal regularisation term to improve performance on heterogeneous or non-IID data. In the FL system, clients compute their updated weights same as FedAvg on local data using a proximal term to reduce clients' drift and send full weight to the server for aggregation. Due to adding a proximal term to the local objective, the algorithm cannot go too far from the global model and can handle heterogeneous or non-IID data better [26]. The algorithm gently pulls the central model and coordinates with it to prevent them from going off too far from the intended global model.

14.3.1.3.4 FedNova (2020)

The FedNova or Federated Normalised Averaging algorithm, introduced by Wang et al. [51], is considered a fair contribution algorithm because each client's contribution is weighted fairly, regardless of how much computational work they perform. In the FL system, after receiving clients' models, the central server adjusts their impacts on the global model based on their contributions instead of blindly combining their individual models. The algorithm normalises each client's update by its number of local SGD steps, eliminating objective inconsistency when clients do unequal work. According to Wang et al. [51], the algorithm sends normalised updates or deltas, the difference between the new and old model, divided by steps taken or number of local SGD steps to mitigate unequal work. The algorithm provides more stable and accurate results over heterogeneous or non-IID data, solving objective inconsistency problems; clients that do more work do not dominate global model update [51].

14.3.1.3.5 FedOpt (2020–2021)

The Adaptive Server Optimisers or FedOpt algorithm, introduced by Reddi et al. [39], uses adaptive server-side optimisers instead of simple averaging for global model aggregation.

The algorithm helps the central server to improve its performance using smarter strategies or adaptive optimisers (e.g., FedAdam, FedYogi, FedAdagrad) and sends updated model weighting just like FedAvg [39]. After receiving model updates from clients, the central server does not just average all clients' models, keeps track of which clients send improved model updates and weights them more for building the global model. The model learns faster but the system may need a better or more intelligent central server. According to Reddi et al. [39], by using smart optimisers, the algorithm helps the model learn faster and takes half the time of FedAvg.

14.3.1.3.6 Personalised FL

The Personalised FL, based on Model-Agnostic Meta-Learning (MAML) to personalise models using a global initialisation, was introduced by Fallah et al. [15]. Instead of using a shared model for everyone, each client gets a customised model based on their own data. For example, based on a client's updates, preferences, or computational patterns, the central server recommends three personalised items to a client instead of a general list of items. This algorithm allows custom adjustments of the model for each client and makes applications like wealth management that need tailored predictions for different client groups [15].

14.3.1.3.7 SCAFFOLD algorithm

The SCAFFOLD algorithm was introduced by Karimireddy et al. [24] to fix client drift over heterogeneous or non-IID data, maintaining a local control variate vector and stopping the local model to move in different directions. The client receives global model and server control variate, and after training the model, it sends updated model weights including both model and control signal corrections just like in FedAvg to the server.

14.3.1.3.8 MOON algorithm

The MOON algorithm, a personalised FL algorithm introduced by Li et al. [25], addresses the challenge of heterogeneous or non-IID data by using contrastive learning techniques. The algorithm improves local model quality, stability and accuracy significantly though it has high computational overhead from contrastive loss. After training the model with this algorithm, the client sends model weights along with the supervised loss or cross-entropy and contrastive loss to the server for aggregation, like the traditional FedAvg algorithm.

14.3.1.3.9 RedDistill algorithm

The RedDistill algorithm, based on Federated Knowledge Distillation, introduced by Seo et al. [43], is a popular algorithm to reduce communication costs and improve privacy. After local training the model with this algorithm, the client sends soft predictions or logits on a public or proxy dataset to the server. The server aggregates these logits from clients to mimic the ensemble of client outputs using distillation loss (e.g., Kullback-Leibler divergence).

14.3.2 Ethical frameworks for AI in finance

AI is one of the most popular and usable tools nowadays in many fields, including Finance. However, it raises ethical concerns over fairness, transparency, and accountability. To

Table 14.2 Comparison of optimisation algorithms

Algorithm	*Year (Intro)*	*Core Idea*	*Local Compute per Round*	*Cost*	*Non-IID Robustness*	*Typical Finance Use-case*	*Key Pros*	*Key Cons*
FedAvg	2017	Clients run several local SGD epochs, server averages weights	*e* local epochs	**Low** – fewer uploads	Medium	Mobile-payment fraud, AML alerts	Cuts traffic 10-100× vs. FedSGD; simple to implement	Can diverge on highly skewed data
FedSGD	2017	Each client computes **one** mini-batch gradient then sends it	1 mini-batch	**High** – every step syncs	Low	Real-time credit-risk updates where latency ≈ 0	Easier theory; fast model freshness	Heavy bandwidth; slow wall-clock training
FedProx	2020	Adds a **proximal term** to keep local models from drifting far from global	*e* local epochs + prox-reg	Low	**High** – designed for heterogeneity	Joint bank–fintech scoring where data / compute vary	Stabilises training on unbalanced clients	Extra hyper-parameter μ; slight speed drop
FedOpt	2020–21	Uses **adaptive server optimisers** instead of plain SGD	Any (flexible)	Low	High	Large-scale card-fraud FL needing fast convergence	Fewer rounds, better final AUC on skewed data	Tuning server LR/ momentum is tricky
Personalised FL	2019–24	Split the model: **shared trunk + client-specific head** (or contrastive/ reg-based personalisation)	Similar to FedAvg	Low-Medium	**Very High** – tailors to each client	Wealth-manager robo-advisers needing bank-specific insights	Best local accuracy; mitigates client drift	Larger on-device model; complex evaluation
SCAFOLD	2020	Uses control variates to reduce client drift in non-IID settings	*e* local epochs + control updates	Medium	Very High	Decentralised customer churn models across branches	Fast convergence; reduces variance due to data heterogeneity	More communication due to control variates

MOON	2021	Contrastive learning to align local and global models	*e* local epochs + contrastive loss	Medium	Very High	Behavioural fraud detection with skewed features	Strong personalization; enhances representation learning	Requires extra memory and tuning contrastive loss
RedDistill	2020	Uses knowledge distillation; clients send logits instead of weights	Local inference + distillation	Very Low	High	Cross-institutional learning with strict privacy (e.g., private banks)	Drastically reduces communication; model-agnostic	Slightly lower accuracy; needs public data or proxy model

overcome these issues, a strong ethical framework is required to measure and mitigate bias and ensure fairness, privacy and transparency, and accountability. Ethical frameworks make it easier to incorporate AI into day-to-day practices in Finance.

The ethical framework includes the following three items:

- Algorithm fairness metrics to measure and mitigate bias across the FL model and see if the model is unfair
- Bias Mitigation to address unfairness and ensure the model is fair across all clients
- Trade-off logs to demonstrate to regulators, clients, and customers that a balanced approach has been undertaken.

14.3.2.1 Algorithmic fairness metrics—disparate impact and equalized odds

These metrics ensure that individual clients and groups of clients are treated fairly and equitably. A model is unfair if decisions are made more favourable for a client or to a group of clients than for another, which is called disparate impact. An equalised odds metric ensures the similar accuracy and error rates across all groups of clients, requiring equal true-positive and false-positive rates across all groups [19].

14.3.2.2 Bias mitigation in federated systems

The global model is monitored in relation to bias sources in FL, such as skewed client data (e.g., one bank has most transactions), noise from DP (e.g., added noise can increase error gaps) and VFL feature gaps (e.g., hidden proxies or post-code leak bias) [6, 26]. For mitigating these biases, appropriate toolboxes or techniques should be used, such as fairness-aware client selection, clipping gradients by group before adding noise and post-hoc constraints on EO after aggregation.

14.3.2.3 Ethical trade-offs in FL

The global model ties theory with practice and balances the interests of all parties in FL to ensure data security, accuracy, and fairness. However, small financial companies may need additional resources to join into the FL systems or fraud detection models, and without such resources, their customers may not be well protected. If they can afford the investment, they can gain significant benefits over such global models.

14.4 DETECTING BIAS IN HETEROGENEOUS DATA SILOS

With the introduction of ML systems in especially essential areas, the issue of algorithmic fairness has become more prominently discussed. The challenge of auditing such systems is especially hard where the data is stored in a wide, geographically distributed silo, like that in a bank, hospital, or regional office. This is a socio-technical problem and even though the use of ML is on the rise, there is a lack of well-developed governance frameworks to facilitate the assurance of fairness [47]. The privacy, legal or organisational constraints that may surround the actions of centralising data also tend to make this impossible. FL proposes a model training method whereby no raw data are exchanged. Nevertheless, fairness auditing in FL is a fresh and little-discovered area. In this section, an in-depth examination of gender bias will be presented by discussing the major techniques of Fairness Auditing (FA).

Contemporary ML and AI applications are based on fairness and collaboration. With high-performing models being implemented in socially important fields such as finance, healthcare, and criminal justice, it is necessary to guarantee equitable results. Fairness is a key ingredient to the more general purpose of AI to social good, which seeks to disseminate brought-about technological advantages among many peoples. In most real-world applications, the data is decentralised across organisations, and therefore, the conventional centralised fairness audit is no longer viable [38]. FL simplifies the collaborative model development and maintains data privacy, though it brings in problems because of the local data distributions.

There are many instances that have undermined the popular faith in algorithms because the results were biased towards certain groups of people [5]. Cooper [14] points out that algorithmic decision-making in human resources may result in gender discrimination, a factor that is reflected by the academic research. Indicatively, there are research that have investigated ethnic-based biased predictions on recidivism. The algorithm applied to give A-level grades in the COVID-19 pandemic was highly criticised in the United Kingdom due to its demographic bias [29]. The advent of large language models (LLM) such as ChatGPT-3.0 and GPT-4.0, as well as generative adversarial networks (GANs), has increased the need to audit and allow for customization of ML systems in consumer applications.

The evaluation of algorithmic fairness is essential to preserving trust and reliability in automated decision-making systems [32], AI-driven ones in particular [46]. To measure discrimination in the results of the ML, researchers have suggested several fairness measures. Independent verification of fairness claims is very vital as these systems have more influence in making high stakes decisions. Although other measures like personal and group fairness are available, none of the measures can be assumed to be universal, and there can be a conflict between definitions. The practices within industry usually are based on self-declared standards of fairness that are not externally proven. Thus, reliable ML systems should deliver fairness computation as well as third-party auditability to reinforce fairness claims.

14.4.1 Case study: Gender bias in credit scoring

It is not a secret that ML has been proved to be effective in assessing the creditworthiness of loan applicants. Nonetheless, it is feared that using automated decision-making processes can lead to disparity treatment of groups or individuals, which can be discriminatory.

Table 14.3 Comparison of privacy-preserving techniques in finance

Technique	*Strengths*	*Weaknesses*	*Use Case in Finance*
DiP	Strong privacy guarantees	Reduced model accuracy	Credit scoring, fraud detection
HE	Secure computation on encrypted data	High computational overhead	Secure financial transactions
SMPC	No data sharing, collaborative work	Communication overhead	Risk modelling across banks
FL	Data remains decentralized	Vulnerable to poisoning/ gradient attacks	Anti-money laundering (AML)

The paper [53] aims to discuss this concern by evaluating the efficiency of 12 top-rated bias mitigation strategies in 5 fairness measures, in addition to determining how accurate and potentially profitable they are to financial institutions. In the process of analysis, the authors have determined the issues that surround attainment of fairness and retention of accuracy and profitability, as well as the most effective and least effective mitigating measures (Table 14.3).

14.4.1.1 The challenge of fairness in automated credit scoring

The study commences by admitting that there is a growing dependency on ML) to automate. financial industry credit scoring. The benefits that this shift is likely to hold are many, including the reduced costs of operation, better loan issuance, and increased scalability. However, it simultaneously raises essential ethical and regulatory issues with fairness. Algorithmic decision-making can unintentionally replicate or exacerbate social inequalities, particularly when biased or non-representative training data include correlations between sensitive attributes (such as age, gender, or socio-economic status) and creditworthiness. Regulators and stakeholders are particularly concerned about the opacity of ML models and their implications for fairness, accountability, and explainability, especially in high-stakes domains such as consumer finance.

14.4.1.2 Bias metrics and mitigation methodologies

To explore and address the problem of algorithmic bias systematically, the author evaluates twelve widely known bias mitigation methods based on five well-defined measures of fairness: Statistical Parity Difference (SPD), Equal Opportunity Difference (EOD), Disparate Impact (DI), Average Odds Difference (AOD), and the Theil index. Such numbers measure group and individual fairness. The strategies can be divided into three categories, namely, pre-processing (e.g., reweighing, disparate impact remover), in-processing (e.g., adversarial debiasing, Gerry Fair, exponentiated gradient), and post-processing (e.g., reject option classification, calibrated equalised odds). All approaches are aimed at biasing at a certain point in the ML process. As the analysis shows, fairness measures are in many cases incompatible, that is, the enhancement of one may harm another, and it is impossible to have universal solutions.

14.4.1.3 Experimental design and trade-off analysis

With the use of these two datasets a standard benchmark dataset (German credit data) and a proprietary consumer loan dataset from a Romanian bank. The author benchmarked the selected methods under real-world conditions. The consumer dataset presented additional challenges due to its size, feature complexity, and class imbalance (e.g., only 5.7% of loans were defaulted). The experiments followed a rigorous pipeline involving data cleaning, feature encoding, fairness metric computation, and model evaluation based on both fairness and business utility. The results revealed that several mitigation methods, such as Learning Fair Representations and Exponentiated Gradient Reduction, successfully improved multiple fairness metrics simultaneously. However, these improvements often came with noticeable reductions in classification performance or profitability, underscoring the inherent trade-off between fairness and financial objectives in real-world applications.

14.4.1.4 *Practical implications, limitations, and future research*

The findings indicate that while many methods can help reduce bias, none offer a universally superior solution. Practitioners must select bias mitigation strategies based on their specific fairness goals, regulatory context, and performance thresholds. The study also reveals that many ML fairness solutions are difficult to scale or adapt to noisy, unbalanced, or high-dimensional data often found in industrial applications. Furthermore, in-processing methods tend to be more complex to tune and less adaptable than pre- or post-processing methods. The authors recommend a practitioner-centric approach: Testing multiple strategies and selecting one that offers a practical balance between fairness, interpretability, and business viability [50]. They also call for additional qualitative research into the socio-contextual causes of unfairness and propose future work to explore fairness in cost-sensitive and energy-efficient AI systems.

14.4.2 Adversarial debiasing in FL

FL is a distributed ML framework that is communication-efficient and preserves the privacy of users by keeping raw training data local. A major challenge in this setting arises from user heterogeneity differences in local data distributions. Which can result in biased and unfair models, particularly disadvantaged minority groups. While adversarial learning is a well-established method for mitigating bias in centralised settings, its application in FL poses unique difficulties. These include the need for sensitive group information and increased computational demands, which may compromise user privacy and device capabilities. To address these issues, this work introduces Federated Adversarial Debiasing (FADE), a novel framework that enforces fairness without requiring users to disclose protected attributes. FADE allows individual participants to opt out of the adversarial component based on privacy preferences or resource limitations. The academic narrative illustrates that under ideal conditions; FADE achieves comparable global optimality to centralised algorithms. Furthermore, they analyse convergence limitations and propose an effective solution. The proposed method is validated through extensive empirical studies in settings such as unsupervised domain [16] adaptation and fairness-aware FL.

A fundamental challenge in FL arises from the heterogeneity among users' differences in data distributions, task objectives, or sampling conditions. This can lead to *negative transfer*, where knowledge sharing across users degrades rather than improves performance. As mentioned by Hong et al. [21], this heterogeneity undermines the generalisability of the global model. One strategy to mitigate this issue involves finding a consensus among users, often through *knowledge distillation*, as demonstrated in prior works. In contrast, the present work explores a novel and more efficient alternative: Applying adversarial debiasing to align users from different groups, thereby reducing group-based bias while preserving user privacy and model utility.

Moreover, Adversarial learning has proven to be a powerful technique for mitigating bias in centralised ML. It operates by formulating an adversarial objective in which an encoder is trained to minimise the extent to which sensitive information can be inferred by a discriminator [21]. This approach has been successfully employed to disentangle task-specific features that may contribute to negative transfer to facilitate unsupervised domain adaptation and, more recently, to promote fair learning [48]. However, significant barriers arise when attempting to apply adversarial methods within the FL context. Most existing approaches rely on a top-down paradigm, whereby the server orchestrates the construction of an adversarial loss based on access to sensitive group attributes (e.g., gender or ethnicity).

Again, Hong et al. [21] argue this requirement conflicts with one of the core tenets of FL preserving data privacy since it necessitates the exposure of protected attributes that users may be unwilling or unable to share.

14.4.3 Risk analysis

The broad adoption of ML systems into highly stakes and socially relevant domains has increased the need to be fair, transparent, and accountable. However, detecting and countering bias is especially difficult in the situations where data is distributed among decentralised and heterogeneous sources like in banking and healthcare. FL provides a practical alternative since it allows developing the model collaboratively, without having to centralise the sensitive information. Nevertheless, their very heterogeneity of such distributed systems creates significant fairness issues, particularly to minorities and marginalised groups. The lack of standardised auditing frameworks and the inclusion of metrics of dissimilar fairness also makes it more difficult to achieve fairness in the results of diverse users and partitions of data.

Both the technical innovation and development of the practice of governance are required to achieve fairness in federated environments. Statistical Parity Difference, Equal Opportunity Difference, and Disparate Impact are fairness metrics that can be used to quantitatively measure algorithm bias. However, as it is empirically shown, maximisation of one measure can result in unintended performance declines in another, arguing in favour of context-sensitive, multi-metric assessment measures. A case study on gender bias in credit scoring, which shows what trade-offs of predictive ability and ethical responsibility. Although there are a few bias mitigation strategies, such as pre-processing adjustments, in-processing adversarial approaches, and post-processing corrections, none of them can be viewed as a complete solution to all the issues of fairness.

FADE (Fairness-Aware Decentralised Evaluation) represents a notable improvement in the area of solving the problem of fairness peculiar to FL. FADE allows the participants to selectively participate in the enforcement of fairness without compromising privacy by revealing the attributes under protection. Experiments have shown that FADE is able to deliver fairness results as good as those of centralised models, but with the benefits of a decentralised architecture. Moreover, the framework is geared to fit practical limitations like user heterogeneity and low computational power and is thus a scalable and privacy-aware approach to fairness auditing in federated systems.

Ultimately, ensuring fairness in federated and siloed learning environments is not merely a technical problem but a socio-technical imperative. Future work must integrate insights from law, ethics, and social science to complement algorithmic interventions. As large-scale AI systems like LLMs and generative adversarial networks increasingly operate in public domains, the need for independent auditing, external verifiability, and dynamic fairness adaptation becomes even more urgent. Without such safeguards, the risk of perpetuating systemic biases through seemingly objective algorithms will persist, threatening both public trust and the equitable promise of AI for social good.

14.5 LAB TUTORIAL: IMPLEMENTING ETHICAL FL FOR FINANCE

Demanding computational resources and good-quality datasets, the progress of ethical AI in Federated Financial (FL) systems will entail the implementation of privacy and fairness as well as the compliance with regulations. FL will allow the financial institutions to train

Table 14.4 Ethical challenges and mitigation strategies in FL for finance

Challenge	*Example Impact*	*Mitigation Strategy*
Privacy vs Utility	Reduced prediction accuracy	Optimized DP parameters, hybrid methods
Fairness vs Accuracy	Biased loan approvals	Fairness-aware FL algorithms
Regulatory Compliance	Violation of GDPR/financial rules	Auditability, explainable FL
Security Threats	Model poisoning, data leakage	Robust aggregation, anomaly detection

the ML models in a collaborative way but without having to share the raw data, and this made it one of the most suitable for fraud detection, credit scoring, and risk management [22]. Nonetheless, FL is prone to success only in case there are some representative datasets at hand and frameworks that facilitate secure, privacy-preserving computations. This paragraph gives a detailed explanation of three important datasets a PaySim (fraud detection), German Credit (fair credit scoring), and LEAF (federated benchmarks) and correspondingly associated code repositories and ethical AI tools to apply FL in finance so that the learner will be aware and expert of real-world scenarios (Table 14.4).

14.5.1 Federated financial AI sample datasets

14.5.1.1 Australian census of population and housing (Fraud detection)

PaySim is a synthetic data generating simulation of mobile money transactions, both fraudulent and legitimate [28]. It reproduces Facebook-like financial transaction patterns, and as such it is a useful source of training data to learn a fraud detection model under a federated regimen.
Features:

- has 6 million+ transactions with labels (fraud/legitimate)
- has features such as transaction amount, sender/receiver IDs and timestamps.
- constructed them to resemble realistic cases of financial crimes (e.g. money laundering, phishing schemes).

Lab exercise 1: Federated fraud detection with DP

Without sharing transaction details, banks can jointly train a fraud-detecting model. Privacy is guaranteed using DP techniques (e.g. adding Laplace noise to gradients) [1].

Download and Practice: https://github.com/AminRana/Datasets-and-Tools-for-Ethical-AI-in-Federated-Financial-Systems/blob/main/Practice%20Code

14.5.1.2 German credit dataset (Fair credit scoring)

The German Credit dataset found on University of California, Irvine (UCI) ML Repository is a benchmark to be used to evaluate fairness in credit risk models. It involves such attributes as age, gender, loan history, and credit risk category (good/bad).
Features:

- A database of 1,000 entries, 20 attributes (categorical and numerical).
- Applied in measuring algorithmic inclination (e.g. gender/age discrimination in loan approvals).

Lab Exercise 2: Fairness-Aware FL of Credit Scoring

Financial institutions can train models with the mitigation of bias and techniques such as reweighting or adversarial debiasing. Federated equality measures (e.g. disparate impact ratio) may be cross applied on decentral data silos.

Download and Practice: https://github.com/AminRana/Datasets-and-Tools-for-Ethical-AI-in-Federated-Financial-Systems/blob/main/Practice%20Code

14.5.1.3 LEAF framework datasets (Synthetic FL benchmarks)

The framework, LEAF (LEArning on Federated Datasets), offers pre-processed data to be used in FL research [12]. It includes:

- FEMINIST (handwritten characters recognition).
- Shakespeare (predicting next-word in text).
- Artificial monetary divisions of simulated decentralized banking data.

Features:

- Non-IID data splits to resemble the real world of FL.
- Facilitates cross-silo (institutional) and cross-device (user-level) FL experimentations.
- Use Case in 'Decentralized Financial Data Partitions simulation': By splitting credit risk data, banks can use their Algorithms based on FL without breaching privacy. It is valuable when testing benchmarks of SecAgg [11].

More: https://github.com/AminRana/leaf

14.5.2 Ethical AI tools and code repositories

14.5.2.1 Privacy-preserving FL in TensorFlow federated (TFF)

The TFF initiative by Google is an open-source framework to train FL with DP and SecAgg suggested by Google Research (2022).
Features:

- Features DP-FedAvg (injecting noise into model updates).
- Keras/TensorFlow models compatible.
- Model Code (DP Federated Averaging):

Practice: https://github.com/AminRana/tensorflow-federated

14.5.2.2 Bias mitigation AI fairness 360 (IBM)

A fully featured system to find and address bias in ML models [8].
Features:

- Introduces disparate impact remover, adversarial debiasing.
- Operates federated models receiving analysis of local updates.
- FL Example Code: https://github.com/AminRana/AIF360

14.5.2.3 Production-grade FL FATE

It is an open-source FL system capable of HE and multi-party computation (MPC).
Important Characteristics:

- Applied to practice in real banking use (e.g. cross-institutional risk modelling).
- Supports PyTorch and Scikit-learn.

GitHub: https://github.com/FederatedAI/FATE
Reflection for Hands-on Lab Exercises of Ethical FL in Finance.

Lab Exercise 1: Federated fraud detection with DP
Goal: To train an FL model on PaySim information under privacy.
Steps:

1. Normalize the amount of transactions in Preprocess PaySim (encode categorical features).
2. Apply limited gradient exposure implementation of DP-FedAvg.
3. Measure the effectiveness of a model (precision-recall of the fraud detection).

Lab Exercise 2: Fair Credit Scoring with Adversarial Debiasing
Goal: Decrease the bias of gender/age in German Credit data.
Steps:

1. Such Disparate Impact Remover should be applied prior to federated training.
2. Replicate FL aggregation giving adversarial debiasing.
3. Statistical parity difference (metrics of fairness).

Lab Exercise 3: HE based SecAgg
Goal: Evaluate HE-secured FL on the LEAF financial partitions.
Steps:

1. Update models in an encrypted fashion with PySyfts Paillier scheme.
2. Summations are unreconstructable.
3. They compare the difference between the run time and plaintext FL.

This section indicates key datasets (PaySim, German Credit, LEAF) and tools (TFF, AIF360, FATE) to run ethical FL in finance. Integrating privacy-conscious technologies (DP, HE) with fairness-sensitive algorithms, financial institutions will develop the Ang that meets the regulatory requirements (GDPR, CCPA) [18] and can be less biased. Investigation of quantum-resistant FL and real-time federated fraud detection should be done in the future.

14.6 EMERGING CHALLENGES AND FUTURE DIRECTIONS

FL is an operation configuration that is rapidly developing to form a core of developing AI-based solutions in decentralized networks, especially in the financial context. However, several new challenges limit the full capabilities of FL, so it needs to evolve more such domains as quantum security, explanation of models, real-time decision-making [41]. In this section, three important future directions will be discussed include the resort to quantum security in FL, explainability in federated models [54] and the realization of autonomy to aid real-time applications.

14.6.1 Quantum-secure FL: Post-quantum cryptography (Lattice-based HE)

The cryptographic protocols which are the main component of FL systems, can be affected by attacks as a result of the further evolution of quantum computing. Most of the widely used cryptography algorithms based on problems which are hard to solve (factoring or discrete logarithm) can be cracked with quantum computers, including RSA and ECC (Elliptic Curve Cryptography) [4, 35]. This becomes a serious challenge to both confidentiality and security of the FL systems in the quantum era.

Post-Quantum Cryptography (PQC) is an attempt to develop cryptographic schemes that cannot be cracked by the power of quantum algorithms. According to Malygina et al. [30], Lattice-based HE is an effective algorithm, enabling the execution of computations, on ciphered information, without decryption. In FL, it may include confidentiality and security of intra-model updates issued by various nodes without the sensitivity of a financial system or confidentiality of information [36]. Lattice-based HE uses advanced mathematical objects (lattices) to protect against quantum attacks, so that the FL system will not suffer because quantum computing becomes common.

The incorporation of PQC in FL systems will mean finding trade-offs between performance and security. Although the security provided by lattice-based HE is high, it is computationally expensive, and that may slow down the model training process [3]. One of the most important challenges is to devise PQC schemes that are scalable and computationally viable to real-time financial uses.

Future Outlook

Financial industry has to take the initiative to shift rapidly to the quantum-resilient FL infrastructures and communicate with cryptographic specialists and regulating bodies. The interim solution should be a dual-stack security model (classical and post-quantum) [40]. The spending in the quantum-safe hardware accelerator and optimization of encrypted models should be indispensable.

14.6.2 Explainability in federated models: Federated SHAP values

Explainability is a critical aspect in trust, compliances, and making ethical choices in ML models, particularly models used in sensitive sectors such as the financial sphere. One problem of FL is that interpretable models that are decentral to each other must be trained in the various nodes [2]. SHAP (Shapley Additive Explanations) values and other commonly used methods to explain are not simple to apply to FL: a distributed environment and privacy restrictions do not allow applying them directly (Figure 14.4).

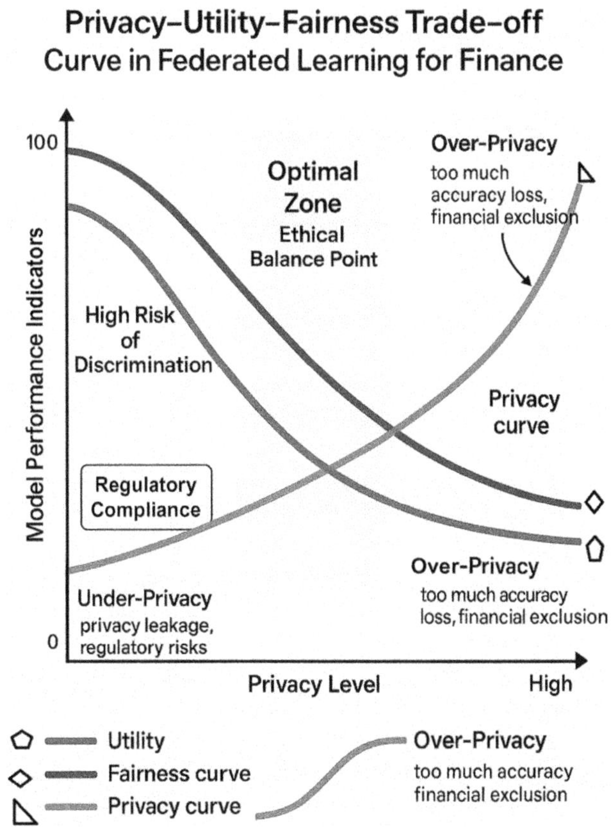

Figure 14.4 FL trade-offs in finance.

As the study of Teixeira et al. (2023) indicates, federated SHAP values are a novel way out of this issue. The value of each feature to MLmodel prediction is presented in SHAP values, a concept based on game theory. Another essential condition in the context of FL would be the presentation of algorithms that can compute SHAP values in a form of predictive privacy friendliness that sensitive data will not be disclosed, and the model should be interpretable [9].

To achieve this federated SHAP values are founded on safe aggregation procedures, by which the contribution of the individual feature can be calculated, though the specific data points [20] are not divulged. The issue is to ensure that the explainability techniques do not undermine privacy guarantees of the model [23]. As the FL can be explained, financial institutions would have the possibility to not only enhance transparency but also automatize decisions more profitable regarding regulatory compliance since the reasoning of deciding does not require any understanding of company secrets.

Future Outlook:

FL models need to consider the explainability as a key design criterion. New studies in federated interpretability toolkits and auditable AI should drive the need to push accountability and trust among the users. In addition, one of the aspects that regulators may soon demand as one of the AI regulation frameworks in the financial sector should be model transparency.

14.6.3 Autonomous FL for real-time decision making

Financial sector is a robust industry where decision making is vital in real time. FL and Federated systems able to make instant, data-driven decisions on decentralized nodes, is self-evident [31]. Autonomous FL enables models to work without constant human monitoring and update themselves using the latest obtained information, whether it is in the form of recognizing fraudulent transactions or increasing the credit score [13].

Real-time decision-making in FL is, nevertheless, challenging due to several reasons:

Data heterogeneity: The FL systems are likely to operate on various machines or disparate institutions with divergent data distribution [34]. These heterogeneous data will require being fastened quickly within a real time environment without affecting the model accuracy.

Adaptive Learning: The other aspect of complexity is the ability of the federated models to restructure with the rapid changing financial circumstances e.g. in the market or when the customer patterns change unexpectedly. Adaptive learning techniques must be incorporated into Real-time decision making (RTDM) and AGI to refresh their decision-making mechanisms with new information on an ongoing basis e.g. online learning or reinforcement learning [45]. It involves coming up with models that are tolerant to concept drift without necessarily going through the low performance and low privacy.

Trust and Security: High trust on federated systems is represented by autonomous decision making particularly in such areas that financial data needs to be mirrored. It is indeed imperative that there are available procedures, which can guarantee that updates of the model are safe and reliable [42]. It may include the application of certain methods including federated anomaly detection or SecAggr and detection of the malicious actions or incorrect model updates that might have a harmful impact on the system integrity.

The additional development of autonomous FL in the financial domain is restricted with the possibility of designing the scalable solutions that would involve the privacy-based mechanisms [44] and real-time decisions. It will help the financial institutions to share the benefits of FL without influence on trusts, security, and fairness.

14.7 CONCLUSION

The application of FL to the financial industry, as has been shown in this chapter, is not only a technical innovation but also an immediate ethical and regulatory necessity. FL offers an influential platform upon which to establish high-performance AI systems that do not violate the privacy of sensitive client information by facilitating decentralized cooperation among the banks, insurers, credit bureaus, and other financial participants. This is not a question of technology preference anymore, in the age defined by the strict data protection laws such as the GDPR, CCPA, and the new AI regulation systems, privacy-by-design is a business and compliance requirement.

However, there is one ethical trilemma that accompanies this promise, and that is balancing privacy, utility, and fairness. DP and SecAgg are techniques that can radically decrease the risk of the exposure of unauthorized data, but they can also add noise or computational requirements that can worsen model performance and make these techniques less useful in reality [1, 17]. Models that are optimized to be accurate but not audited to represent gaps in the model or discrepancies in impact, on the other hand, run a risk of perpetuating or even increasing structural inequalities, disadvantaging marginalized populations who already have access barriers [6, 19]. These tensions are not imaginary, but they are inevitable and cannot be worked out, but they need to be managed in an open way, with open responsibility and constant monitoring.

It is apparent that these challenges cannot be solved individually by a single financial institution which needs collaborative governance for the future of ethical AI in federated financial systems. This demand of a close cooperation among financial institutions, technology suppliers, regulators, and the civil society in designing standards, exchange of best practices as well as effective compliance and oversight. It also implies integrating fairness audit, explainability and privacy protection into the design of FL systems not as optional features, but as fundamental design principles.

In this decentralized era, responsible AI can be implemented by deploying smarter algorithms, securing data pipelines, and aligning technological innovation with wider social, legal, and ethical responsibilities. For federated finance to reach its full transformative potential, stakeholders must work together to protect privacy, maximize model utility, and actively monitor and uphold fairness.

Ultimately, the goal is not to find a perfect balance point in the privacy–utility–fairness trilemma—but to demonstrate, through auditable, explainable, and well-governed systems, that these trade-offs are made conscientiously and in the public interest. By embracing this collaborative and principled approach, the financial sector can harness the immense power of AI while safeguarding the trust, rights, and dignity of the individuals and communities it serves.

REFERENCES

1. Abadi, M., Chu, A., Goodfellow, I., McMahan, H.B., Mironov, I., Talwar, K. and Zhang, L. (2016) 'Deep learning with differential privacy', in *Proceedings of the 2016 ACM SIGSAC Conference on Computer and Communications Security*, pp. 308–318. doi:10.1145/2976749.2978318.
2. Alshkeili, H.M.H.A., Almheiri, S.J. and Khan, M.A. (2025) 'Privacy-preserving interpretability: An explainable federated learning model for predictive maintenance in sustainable manufacturing and industry 4.0', *AI*, 6(6), p. 117. https://doi.org/10.3390/ai6060117.
3. Amirkhanova, D.S., Iavich, M. and Mamyrbayev, O. (2024) 'Lattice-based post-quantum public key encryption scheme using ElGamal's principles', *Cryptography*, 8(3), p. 31. https://doi.org/10.3390/cryptography8030031.
4. Arner, D.W., Zetzsche, D.A. and Buckley, R. P. (2020) 'FinTech and RegTech: Enabling innovation while preserving financial stability', *Georgetown Journal of International Law*, 49(4), pp. 1189–1220.
5. Azimi, V. and Zaydman, M.A. (2023) 'Optimizing equity: Working towards fair machine learning algorithms in laboratory medicine', *The Journal of Applied Laboratory Medicine*, 8(1), pp. 113–128. https://academic.oup.com/jalm/article/8/1/113/6845827.
6. Bagdasaryan, E., Veit, A., Hua, Y., Estrin, D. and Shmatikov, V. (2019) 'Differential privacy has disparate impact on model accuracy', *Advances in Neural Information Processing Systems*, 32. https://arxiv.org/abs/1905.12101.
7. Basel Committee on Banking Supervision (2011) 'Basel III: A global regulatory framework for more resilient banks and banking systems', *Bank for International Settlements*. www.bis.org/publ/bcbs189.pdf (Accessed: https://www.bis.org/publ/bcbs189.pdf4 July 2025).
8. Bellamy, R.K.E., Dey, K., Hind, M., Hoffman, S.C., Houde, S., Kannan, K., Lohia, P., Martino, J., et al. (2018) *AI Fairness 360: An extensible toolkit for detecting, understanding, and mitigating unwanted algorithmic bias*. arXiv:1810.01943 [cs.AI]. Available at: https://arxiv.org/abs/1810.01943 (Accessed: 5 July, 2025).
9. Bogdanova, A., Imakura, A. and Sakurai, T. (2023) 'DC-SHAP method for consistent explainability in privacy-preserving distributed machine learning', *Human-Centric Intelligent Systems*, 3(3), pp. 197–210. https://doi.org/10.1007/s44230-023-00032-4.

10. Bonawitz, K., Ivanov, V., Kreuter, B., et al. (2017) 'Practical secure aggregation for privacy-preserving machine learning'. https://eprint.iacr.org/2017/281.
11. Bonawitz, K. et al. (2017) 'Practical secure aggregation for federated learning', *ACM CCS*.
12. Caldas, S. et al. (2018) 'LEAF: A benchmark for federated settings', *arXiv:1812.01097*. https://arxiv.org/abs/1812.01097.
13. Candrian, C. and Scherer, A. (2022) 'Rise of the machines: Delegating decisions to autonomous AI', *Computers in Human Behavior*, 134, p. 107308. https://doi.org/10.1016/j.chb.2022.107308.
14. Cooper, Y. (2018) 'Amazon ditched AI recruiting tool that favored men for technical jobs', *The Guardian*.
15. Fallah, A., Mokhtari, A. and Ozdaglar, A. (2020) 'Personalized federated learning: A meta-learning approach', *arXiv:2002.07948*. https://arxiv.org/abs/2002.07948.
16. Ganin, Y. and Lempitsky, V. (2015) 'Unsupervised domain adaptation by backpropagation', in *International Conference on Machine Learning*, pp. 1180–1189. https://proceedings.mlr.press/v37/ganin15.
17. Gentry, C. (2009) 'Fully homomorphic encryption using ideal lattices', in *Proceedings of the 41st Annual ACM Symposium on Theory of Computing*, pp. 169–178. doi:10.1145/1536414.1536440.
18. Goodman, B. and Flaxman, S. (2017) 'European Union regulations on algorithmic decision-making and a "right to explanation"', *AI Magazine*, 38(3), pp. 50–57. doi:10.1609/aimag.v38i3.2741.
19. Hardt, M., Price, E. and Srebro, N. (2016) 'Equality of opportunity in supervised learning', *Advances in Neural Information Processing Systems*, 29. https://arxiv.org/abs/1610.02413.
20. Hong, J., Kaye, J., Dodge, H.H., Zhou, J. and ORCATECH (2020) 'Detecting MCI using real-time, ecologically valid data capture methodology', *Alzheimer's & Dementia*, 16, p. e044371. https://alz-journals.onlinelibrary.wiley.com/doi/full/10.1002/alz.044371.
21. Hong, J., Zhu, Z., Yu, S., Wang, Z., Dodge, H.H. and Zhou, J. (2021) 'Federated adversarial debiasing for fair and transferable representations', in *Proceedings of the 27th ACM SIGKDD Conference on Knowledge Discovery & Data Mining*, pp. 617–627. doi:10.1145/3447548.3467281.
22. Kairouz, P. et al. (2021) 'Advances and open problems in federated learning', *Foundations and Trends® in Machine Learning*, 14(1–2), pp. 1–210. doi:10.1561/2200000073.
23. Kalakoti, R., Nõmm, S. and Bahsi, H. (2025) 'Federated learning of explainable AI (FEDXAI) for deep learning-based intrusion detection in IoT networks', *Computer Networks*, p. 111479. https://doi.org/10.1016/j.comnet.2025.111479.
24. Karimireddy, S.P. et al. (2020) 'SCAFFOLD: Stochastic controlled averaging for federated learning', in *Proceedings of the 37th International Conference on Machine Learning (ICML)*. https://arxiv.org/abs/1910.06378.
25. Li, Q., He, B. and Song, D. (2021) 'Model-contrastive federated learning', in *Proceedings of the IEEE/CVF Conference on Computer Vision and Pattern Recognition (CVPR)*, pp. 10713–10722. https://arxiv.org/abs/2102.10056.
26. Li, T. et al. (2020) 'Federated optimization in heterogeneous networks', in *Machine Learning Systems (MLSys)*. https://arxiv.org/abs/1812.06127.
27. Lindell, Y. and Pinkas, B. (2008) 'Secure multiparty computation for privacy-preserving data mining'. https://eprint.iacr.org/2008/197.
28. Lopez-Rojas, E. et al. (2016) 'PaySim: A financial mobile money simulator for fraud detection', *IEEE TrustCom*.
29. Lundberg, S.M. and Lee, S.I. (2017) 'A unified approach to interpreting model predictions', *Advances in Neural Information Processing Systems*, pp. 4768 – 4777. https://dl.acm.org/doi/10.5555/3295222.3295230
30. Malygina, E.S. et al. (2023) 'Post-quantum cryptosystems: Open problems and solutions. Lattice-based cryptosystems', *Journal of Applied and Industrial Mathematics*, 17(4), pp. 767–790. https://doi.org/10.1134/s1990478923040087.

31. Maroto-Gómez, M. et al. (2023) 'A systematic literature review of decision-making and control systems for autonomous and social robots', *International Journal of Social Robotics*, 15(5), pp. 745–789. https://doi.org/10.1007/s12369-023-00977-3.
32. Mayer, R.C., Davis, J.H. and Schoorman, F.D. (1995) 'An integrative model of organizational trust', *Academy of Management Review*, 20(3), pp. 709–734. https://doi.org/10.5465/AMR.1995.9508080335.
33. McMahan, H.B. et al. (2017) 'Communication-efficient learning of deep networks from decentralized data', in *Proceedings of the 20th International Conference on Artificial Intelligence and Statistics (AISTATS). PMLR*, 54, pp. 1273–1282.
34. Medrano-Berumen, C. and Akbaş, M.İ. (2020) 'Validation of decision-making in artificial intelligence-based autonomous vehicles', *Journal of Information and Telecommunication*, 5(1), pp. 83–103. https://doi.org/10.1080/24751839.2020.1824154.
35. Nejatollahi, H. et al. (2019) 'Post-quantum lattice-based cryptography implementations', *ACM Computing Surveys*, 51(6), pp. 1–41. https://doi.org/10.1145/3292548.
36. Nguyen, H.P. and Chen, Y. (2024) 'Lightweight, post-quantum secure cryptography based on ASCON', *Electronics*, 13(22), pp. 4550. https://doi.org/10.3390/electronics13224550.
37. OECD (2021) *OECD AI Principles: Recommendation of the Council on Artificial Intelligence*. Paris: OECD Publishing. https://legalinstruments.oecd.org/en/instruments/OECD-LEGAL-0449 (Accessed: 4 July 2025).
38. Pessach, D. and Shmueli, E. (2023), Rokach, L., Maimon, O., Shmueli, E. (eds), 'Algorithmic fairness', in *Machine Learning for Data Science Handbook*, Cham: Springer International Publishing, pp. 867–886. https://link.springer.com/chapter/10.1007/978-3-031-24628-9_37.
39. Reddi, S. et al. (2020) 'Adaptive federated optimization'. https://arxiv.org/abs/2003.00295.
40. Richards, L.E., Raff, E. and Matuszek, C. (2023) 'Measuring equality in machine learning security defenses: A case study in speech recognition', in *Proceedings of the 16th ACM Workshop on Artificial Intelligence and Security*, pp. 161–171. https://dl.acm.org/doi/abs/10.1145/3605764.3623911.
41. Ridzuan, N.N. et al. (2024) 'AI in the financial sector: The line between innovation, regulation and ethical responsibility', *Information*, 15(8), p. 432. https://doi.org/10.3390/info15080432.
42. Salvini, P. et al. (2023) 'Human involvement in autonomous decision-making systems', *Frontiers in Political Science*, 5. https://doi.org/10.3389/fpos.2023.1238461.
43. Seo, H. et al. (2020) 'Federated knowledge distillation', *arXiv:2011.02367*. https://arxiv.org/abs/2011.02367.
44. Teixeira, R. et al. (2023) 'Balancing privacy and explainability in federated learning', *Research Square* [Preprint]. https://doi.org/10.21203/rs.3.rs-3714454/v1.
45. Tien, J.M. (2019) 'Convergence to real-time decision making', *Frontiers of Engineering Management*, 7(2), pp. 204–222. https://doi.org/10.1007/s42524-019-0040-5.
46. Toreini, E. et al. (2020) 'The relationship between trust in AI and trustworthy machine learning technologies', in *Proceedings of the 2020 Conference on Fairness, Accountability, and Transparency*, pp. 272–283. https://dl.acm.org/doi/abs/10.1145/3351095.3372834.
47. Toreini, E., Mehrnezhad, M. and van Moorsel, A. (2024) 'Fairness as a service (FaaS)', *International Journal of Information Security*, 23(2), pp. 981–997. https://link.springer.com/article/10.1007/s10207-023-00774-z.
48. Tzeng, E. et al. (2017) 'Adversarial discriminative domain adaptation', in *Proceedings of the IEEE Conference on Computer Vision and Pattern Recognition*, pp. 7167–7176. https://openaccess.thecvf.com/content_cvpr_2017/html/Tzeng_Adversarial_Discriminative_Domain_CVPR_2017_paper.html.
49. Veale, M. & Quintais, J. (2025) *The Obligations of Providers of General-Purpose AI Models*, in Zanfir Fortuna, Malgieri, González Fuster & Mantelero (eds.) *The Artificial Intelligence Act — A Thematic Commentary*. November 2025 version. Available at: https://files.michae.lv/papers/VealeQuintaisObligationsofGPAIProvidersNov2025.pdf?ref=michae.lv (Accessed: 15 June 2025).

50. Vellas, B. et al. (2015) 'Endpoints for pre-dementia AD trials', *The Journal of Prevention of Alzheimer's Disease*, 2(2), pp. 128. www.ncbi.nlm.nih.gov/pmc/articles/PMC4523051.
51. Wang, J. et al. (2020) 'Tackling the objective inconsistency problem in heterogeneous federated optimization (FedNova)', *arXiv:2007.07481*. https://arxiv.org/pdf/2007.07481.
52. Xu, J., Yang, Q. and Li, B. (2021) 'Federated learning with differential privacy', *IEEE Transactions on Information Forensics and Security*, 15, pp. 3454–3469. doi:10.1109/TIFS.2020.2988575.
53. Moldovan, D. (2023) 'Algorithmic decision making methods for fair credit scoring', *IEEE Access*, PP(99), pp. 1–1. doi:10.1109/ACCESS.2023.3286018.
54. Yang, Q., Liu, Y., Chen, T. and Tong, Y. (2019) 'Federated machine learning: Concept and applications', *ACM Transactions on Intelligent Systems and Technology*, 10(2), pp. 1–19. doi:10.1145/3298981.
55. Zuboff, S. (2019) *The Age of Surveillance Capitalism: The Fight for a Human Future at the New Frontier of Power*. London: Profile Books.

For Product Safety Concerns and Information please contact our EU
representative GPSR@taylorandfrancis.com
Taylor & Francis Verlag GmbH, Kaufingerstraße 24, 80331 München, Germany

www.ingramcontent.com/pod-product-compliance
Ingram Content Group UK Ltd.
Pitfield, Milton Keynes, MK11 3LW, UK
UKHW022318250926
475702UK00046B/930
9781041115106